LITIGATION IN THE TECHNOLOGY AND CONSTRUCTION COURT

CONSTRUCTION PRACTICE SERIES
Series editors: Philip Britton and Phillip Capper

CONSTRUCTION PRACTICE SERIES

FIDIC Contracts
Law and Practice
Ellis Baker, Ben Mellors, Scott Chalmers
and Anthony Lavers

Construction Contract Variations
Michael Sergeant and Max Wieliczko
Holman Fenwick Willan LLP

Chern on Dispute Boards
Practice and Procedure
Third Edition
Cyril Chern

Adjudication in Construction Law
Darryl Royce

Delay and Disruption in Construction Contracts
Fifth Edition
Andrew Burr

The Law of Construction Disputes
Second Edition
Cyril Chern

Construction Insurance and UK Construction Contracts
Third Edition
Roger ter Haar QC, Marshall Levine and Anna Laney

Construction Law
Second Edition
Julian Bailey

International Contractual and Statutory Adjudication
Andrew Burr

Remedies in Construction Law
Second Edition
Roger ter Haar QC

Professional Negligence in Construction
Second Edition
Ben Patten and Hugh Saunders

Litigation in the Technology and Construction Court
Adam Constable QC, Lucy Garrett QC and
Calum Lamont

For more information about this series, please visit:
www.routledge.com/Construction-Practice-Series/book-series/CPS

LITIGATION IN THE TECHNOLOGY AND CONSTRUCTION COURT

ADAM CONSTABLE QC
LUCY GARRETT QC
CALUM LAMONT

informa law
from Routledge

First published 2019
by Informa Law from Routledge
2 Park Square, Milton Park, Abingdon, Oxon OX14 4RN

and by Informa Law from Routledge
711 Third Avenue, New York, NY 10017

Informa Law from Routledge is an imprint of the Taylor & Francis Group, an informa business

© 2019 Adam Constable QC, Lucy Garrett QC and Calum Lamont

The right of Adam Constable QC, Lucy Garrett QC and Calum Lamont to be identified as authors of this work has been asserted by them in accordance with sections 77 and 78 of the Copyright, Designs and Patents Act 1988.

All rights reserved. No part of this book may be reprinted or reproduced or utilised in any form or by any electronic, mechanical, or other means, now known or hereafter invented, including photocopying and recording, or in any information storage or retrieval system, without permission in writing from the publishers.

Whilst every effort has been made to ensure that the information contained in this book is correct, neither the author nor Informa Law can accept any responsibility for any errors or omissions or for any consequences arising therefrom.

Trademark notice: Product or corporate names may be trademarks or registered trademarks, and are used only for identification and explanation without intent to infringe.

British Library Cataloguing-in-Publication Data
A catalogue record for this book is available from the British Library

Library of Congress Cataloging-in-Publication Data
Names: Constable, Adam, author. | Garrett, Lucy (Lawyer), author. | Lamont, Calum, author.
Title: Litigation in the technology and construction court/By Adam Constable QC, Lucy Garrett QC and Calum Lamont.
Description: New York: Routledge, 2018. | Series: Construction practice series
Identifiers: LCCN 2018016632| ISBN 9781138643284 (hbk) | ISBN 9781315629421 (ebk)
Subjects: LCSH: Great Britain. Technology and Construction Court. | Arbitration (Administrative law)—England.
Classification: LCC KD7179. C66 2018 | DDC 343.4207/8624026—dc23
LC record available at https://lccn.loc.gov/2018016632

ISBN: 978-1-138-64328-4 (hbk)
ISBN: 978-1-315-62942-1 (ebk)

Typeset in Times New Roman
by Apex CoVantage, LLC

Printed and bound by CPI Group (UK) Ltd, Croydon, CR0 4YY

CONTENTS

Forewords	ix
Preface	xiii
Table of cases	xv
Table of legislation	xix

CHAPTER 1 INTRODUCTION TO LITIGATION IN THE TCC	1
What is the TCC?	1
Dispute resolution	2
Arbitration v litigation	2
The TCC Guide	5
CHAPTER 2 AN OVERVIEW OF A CLAIM IN THE TCC	7
Pre-action phase	7
Commencement of the proceedings	9
Pleadings	10
The first Case Management Conference	12
Disclosure	15
Witness statements	17
Expert evidence	18
The Pre-Trial Review	21
The trial	21
Judgment	23
Appeal	24
CHAPTER 3 EVIDENCE	25
Introduction	25
Witness statements	25
Number of witnesses	25
'Expert' factual witnesses	26
Taking and structuring witness statements	27
Sequence of calling witnesses	30
Expert reports and joint statements	30
Do you need an independent expert?	30
Choosing an expert	32

Preparing your expert	32
Reports	33
Joint statements and expert meetings	34
Evidence at trial	35
Documentary evidence	36
Case Management Conference	36
Applications	36
Trial	37
Electronic trial bundles	38
Appeal bundles	40
Administrative matters	40
CHAPTER 4 DELAY CLAIMS	**43**
Introduction	43
Legal requirements in relation to claiming delay	43
Extension of time clauses	43
Prevention principle	45
Float	46
Pleading requirements – delay	47
Civil Procedure Rules	47
Authorities as to pleading requirements	47
Burden of proof	48
Making or defending a delay claim in practice	49
Introduction	49
Step 1: Prospective or retrospective	51
Step 2: Identifying the total period of delay on the project and when the delay occurred	54
Step 3: Identifying the delay events	57
Step 4: Identify the critical path	58
Step 5: Identify how the delay event caused delay to the completion date	60
Step 6: Conclusion	65
Difficulties and complexities	66
Complex/multiple critical paths	66
Relevance of as-planned critical path or near-critical paths at particular points during the project	66
Frequent mistakes in practice	67
Introduction	67
Focus on liability only	67
Focus on delay caused to immediately affected activity only	67
Focus on the last event which delayed completion	67
Ignoring contractual notice provisions	68
Evidence at trial	69
Factual witness evidence	69
Expert evidence	71
Electronic programme-based analysis	71

CHAPTER 5 DELAY AND DISRUPTION MONEY CLAIMS	75
Introduction	75
Contractor's delay-related money claims under the contract	75
Introduction	75
Different tests for time and money	75
Relevance of contractual provisions to valuation	76
Relevance of tender pricing	76
Notice	76
Contractor's critical delay-related claims	77
Introduction	77
Preliminaries/prolongation cost claims	77
Overheads claims	79
Loss of profit claims	80
Increased costs resulting from inflation	80
Disruption claims	80
Introduction	80
Authorities	81
Practicalities	83
'Thickening' costs	84
Subcontractor claims	84
Acceleration claims	84
Employer's claims for delay	87
CHAPTER 6 DEFECTS CLAIMS	89
General nature of a defects claim	89
Prosecuting a defects claim	90
Structure of the statement of case	90
Defending the case	93
Liability defences	93
Quantum defences	93
Limitation	94
Controlling, policing and challenging the presentation of defects claims	95
Instructing appropriate expertise	96
Appointment of experts	96
Investigations	97
Independence of experts and quality of expert evidence	98
CHAPTER 7 PUBLIC PROCUREMENT LITIGATION IN THE TCC	99
Introduction	99
Applications to lift the automatic suspension	100
Disclosure	104
Introductory matters	104
The approach of the TCC to early disclosure in procurement litigation	105
Tactical considerations	107
Handling confidential information	108

CHAPTER 8	COSTS BUDGETING IN THE TCC	113
Introduction		113
Presentation of costs budgets		114
Timing of costs budgets		117
The TCC's approach to consideration of costs budgets		117
Costs budgets and interim payments		119
Practical considerations		119
CHAPTER 9	THE TCC AND ADJUDICATION	121
Introduction		121
Before the adjudication		121
During the adjudication		122
After the adjudication		124
Stays of execution		128
CHAPTER 10	THE TCC AND ADR	131
Introduction		131
What is ADR?		131
Enforcement of contractual ADR schemes		132
Jurisdiction, adjournment or stay?		134
ADR and the Pre-Action Protocol		136
ADR and general case management		137
Cost sanctions		138
The TCC and early neutral evaluation		140
The TCC and mediation		140
CHAPTER 11	THE TCC AND ARBITRATION	141
Stay of proceedings		141
Jurisdiction of the arbitrator		143
Extension of time limits for the referral of disputes		143
Powers of the TCC in relation to procedural aspects of arbitration		144
Appeal		146

Appendix 1	*The Technology and Construction Court Guide*	149
Appendix 2	*Pre-Action Protocol for Construction and Engineering Disputes, 2nd edition*	235
Appendix 3	*TCC Guidance Note on Procedures for Public Procurement Cases*	241
Index		257

FOREWORDS

I

In writing this foreword, I will not duplicate the contents of Chapter 1 in describing the history of the Technology and Construction Court, or the TCC as it is now almost universally known. The court had its origins in the fact that in the second half of the 19th century, another period of extraordinary technological innovation, it was recognised that some cases were just too complicated for juries. It was also the case then, and remains the case now, that the industry sectors that give rise to the business of the TCC are very important to the economy of the nation. Concentrating upon the relevant figures for more recent times, in 2014 for example, the construction industry alone contributed £103 billion in economic output to the UK economy, or 6.5% of the total. Employment figures were similarly impressive. 2.1 million jobs (or 6.2%) of the UK total were in the construction industry in 2015.

The evolution of dispute resolution has continued since 1873. In 1998 what had been called Official Referees' Business became the TCC, but the most important step change in recent years was in 2004. This was when the increasingly important status of the TCC was recognised by the decision by the Lord Chancellor and Lord Chief Justice that all TCC cases in London would be heard by full High Court Judges, rather than the Senior Circuit Judges who had heard such cases before then. This was the birth of the modern TCC. I am very proud, and not a little daunted, to follow in the footsteps of the Judges in Charge since then, the list of whom reads like a Who's Who in this field. Lord Dyson, Sir Rupert Jackson, Sir Vivian Ramsey, Sir Robert Akenhead, Sir Antony Edwards-Stuart and Sir Peter Coulson. The fact that Lord Dyson became the Master of the Rolls, and both Sir Rupert Jackson and Sir Peter Coulson became Lords Justices of Appeal, is further evidence that the importance and legal complexity of the work simply continues to increase. Now one of the two Queen's Bench Division Specialist lists located in the Rolls Building (under the umbrella of the Business and Property Courts) – the other being the Commercial Court, with whom the subject matter of the court overlaps in arbitration claims and oil and gas cases – the TCC continues to enjoy a high reputation as shown by the great number of international disputes that are tried here.

The TCC has always prided itself in being at the forefront of technical innovation. It used written witness statements to stand as evidence-in-chief some years before the Civil Procedure Rules came into force; it has promoted active case management by the Judges themselves; and adopted time limited trials, with guillotines on cross-examination. These are all now seen as standard across the whole civil jurisdiction. In recent times it has adopted the

FOREWORDS

Jackson Reforms on costs management with an unmatched degree of enthusiasm. Recent advances such as the use of electronic bundles continue that trend, and it was the first court to hand down a judgment hyper-linked to the electronic bundle itself in 2016. On the same subject, it also issued a protocol for the preparation and use of electronic bundles, the first court in the world to do so.

But it remains a highly specialised field. This book provides a most useful guide to efficient and effective practice in this highly specialised court. As with all fields of human endeavour, experience matters, and few would wish to strike new ground themselves, rather than draw on the accumulated experience of those who have direct relevant exposure. These authors, who between them have in excess of 50 years' at the specialist Bar, fall into that category. Keating Chambers is one of those that specialise in TCC work. As a practitioners' guide, this book should help to spread to their readers their collective understanding built up over many years and hundreds of different cases.

I was particularly interested to read the authors' collective view on time. "The overarching criterion is almost always time. It is difficult to think of a case where as litigation lawyers one does not feel up against it at one – or more – point in the process through to settlement or judgment". There is no doubt that in order to litigate effectively, and efficiently, one has to observe deadlines and time limits. Some time pressure may be imposed from external sources, but in my experience a great deal of such pressure can often be self-inflicted. This has parallels with construction projects themselves. These are all performed under time pressure, whether construction, infrastructure or IT projects. The Great Pyramid of Khufu at Giza in Egypt (or Great Pyramid of Cheops for classical Greek scholars) was built over about a 20 year period. It is not known if acceleration measures were required in the ancient world if the Pharaoh felt an illness coming on, but if they were, acceleration agreements were perhaps unnecessary. Few modern projects, however, have those luxuries. Construction of HS2 or Crossrail does not just happen, the work needs to be programmed in extraordinary detail. The same applies to complex litigation.

I commend this book to those who litigate in the TCC, and look forward to experiencing its beneficial effects upon the already high standards of practitioners.

Sir Peter Fraser
Judge in Charge of the Technology and Construction Court
The Rolls Building
26 July 2018

II

We live in a legal world where there is ever-greater specialisation. Thirty years ago it was enough to say that you were a construction lawyer (at least to the extent that you ever admitted that in public). Now it is common to say that you specialise in a particular part of the construction field, such as oil and gas work, or public procurement. In those circumstances, a lawyer, however experienced, who is called upon to advise on an area adjacent to, but still outside of, his or her comfort zone will often find themselves baffled by procedures and practices which are entirely new to them.

The principal purpose of this book is to educate everyone (no matter how experienced they are) in the common issues and pitfalls that arise in all kinds of TCC litigation. It does so in a clear and, for a relatively short book, surprisingly comprehensive way. It is practical and user-friendly. It is written by three specialist barristers, with enormous experience of all aspects of the TCC's work. I expect it to become an indispensable part of every construction lawyer's bookshelf or electronic library.

Lord Justice Peter Coulson
Deputy Head of Civil Justice
20 July 2018

PREFACE

The book has been somewhat long awaited, at least amongst ourselves and our extremely patient publishers. Since its inception there have been four presiding Judges in charge, the TCC has even changed its name, and Lucy has taken silk. The genesis of this book came from various late night discussions between the three of us over the past 15-20 years, often whilst working on cases together, and, as always, attempting to pull the evidence into shape against tight deadlines. Whilst the specifics differed, the themes were often the same. Why are we calling so many witnesses? Could or should this report have been prepared differently? Can the true issues be flushed out in the experts' joint statement or will we have to amend?

We came to realise that between the three of us, we had strong views on how cases could be better shaped, resourced, and presented, and whilst those views did not always align, they were sufficiently close to encourage us to develop some kind of practitioner text, and we are hugely grateful to our publishers for buying into the enterprise.

In short, this is not intended to be a law book. Rather, it is a book of ideas, focussing on areas of work which in our experience have tended to require most attention in terms of case analysis and preparation.

In this book we have attempted to cover as broad spectrum of TCC work, but have obviously focussed on the types of case the TCC sees most regularly. As will be obvious from the text, we do consider that there are right ways and wrong ways to fight TCC cases. But we do not suggest that there is a one size fits all solution for each case in any particular practice area. Every case will have its peculiar limitations. Cost is one obvious controlling factor. The overarching criterion is almost always time. It is difficult to think of a case where as litigation lawyers one does not feel up against it at one – or more – point in the process through to settlement or judgment. However, limitations aside, we all strongly believe that there is always scope for a good lawyer to improve, finesse, or salvage any case, even in the most extreme circumstances. What is the best approach from a practical perspective will naturally vary from case to case, but we hope that the disussionin this book will provide useful guidance and food for thought for those charged with prosecuting or defending a TCC case.

As explained above, the purpose of the text is to be both tactical and practical. To some extent at least these concepts are both timeless, and transferrable to other types of litigation – particularly in the civil courts; however, we have endeavoured to illustrate our thinking by

PREFACE

reference to authority where possible. To this end, we have been assisted with updating the text by Christopher Eames at Keating Chambers, to whom we pass on our gratitude.

Where legal principle is referred to, the law is as stated at April 2018. As ever, all errors remain our own.

We very much hope you will enjoy this book.

AC
LG
CL
Keating Chambers
July 2018

TABLE OF CASES

A Lloyd's Syndicate v X [2011] EWHC 2487 (Comm.) 3.27
Absolute Rentals v Glencor Enterprises Ltd [2000] CILL1639 .... 9.23
Adyard Abu Dhabi v SD Marine Services [2011] BLR 384 (Comm.) 4.11, 15, 124
Alfred McAlpine Homes North Ltd v Property & Land Contractors Ltd [1996]
  76 BLR 59 (TCC) 5.22
Alstom v Eurostar [2010] EWHC B32 (Ch) 7.22
Amaryllis No 2 [2009] EWHC 1666 (TCC) 7.44
American Cyanamid Co Ltd v Ethicon Ltd [1975]AC396 .... 7, 14, 7.8, 12–7.14, 7.16
Ascon Contracting Ltd v Alfred McAlpine Isle of Man Ltd (2000) 66 Con LR119 ...... 5.46
Astor Management AG v Atalaya Mining Plc [2017] EWHC 425 (Comm.) 10.7
Balfour Beatty v Chestermount Properties (1993) 62 BLR1 .... 4.7, 4.9–4.12
Banco de Portugal v Waterlow & Sons [1932] AC452 .... 6.20
Bari and others v Alternative Finance Ltd 8.18
Bernard Sport Surfaces Ltd v Astrosoccer4ULtd [2017] EWHC 2425 (TCC) 9.26
Bloomberg LP v Sandberg [2016] EWHC 488 (TCC) 8.20
Bluewater Energy Services BV v Mercon Steel Structures [2014]
  EWHC 2132 (TCC) 4.92–4.95, 4.125
BMG (Mansfield) Ltd v Galford Try Construction Ltd [2013] EWHC 3183 (TCC) 2.38
Bombardier Transportation Ltd v Merseytravel [2017] EWHC 575 (TCC) 7.44
Bouyues v Dahl Jensen [2000] BLR552 .... 9.22–9.23
Bristol Missing Link Ltd v Bristol City Council [2015] EWHC876 (TCC) 7.17
Cable & Wireless Plc v IBM United Kingdom [2002] EWHC2059 .... 10.6, 10.11
Caledonian Modular Ltd v Mar City Developments Ltd [2015] EWHC 1855 (TCC) .. 9.13–9.14
Castle Trustee Ltd v Bombay Palace [2018] EWHC1602 .... 3.31
CIP Properties (AIPT) Ltd v Galliford Try Infrastructure Ltd [2014]
  EWHC 3546 (TCC) 8.1, 8.20, 10.15, 10.23
Cofely Ltd v Bingham & Knowles [2016] BLR187 .... 11.16
Cooperative Group v Birse Developments Ltd [2013] EWHC 3145 (TCC) 6.8, 6.18, 6.22
Cooperative Group v John Allen Associates Ltd [2010] EWHC2300 (TCC) 6.16
Costain v Charles Haswell [2009] EWHC 3140 (TCC) 4.89, 5.16–5.17
Counted4 Community Interest Co v Sunderland City Council [2015] EWHC3898 (TCC) 7.17
Covanta Energy Ltd v Merseyside Waste Disposal Authority [2013] EWHC2964 (TCC) 7.25
Coyne v Morgan [2016] 166 Con LR114 .... 2.38
Croft House Care Ltd v Durham County Council [2010] EWHC 909 (TCC) 7.45
Denton v T H White Ltd [2014] EWCA Civ906 .... 8.5
DN v LB Greenwich [2004] EWCA Civ1569 .... 3.9
DWF LLP v Secretary of State for Business, Innovation and Skills [2014] EWCA Civ900 .... 7.17

TABLE OF CASES

Edwards-Tubb v JD Wetherspoon Plc [2011] 1 WLR1373 ....2.38
Elvanite Full Circle Ltd v AMEC Earth & Environmental (UK) Ltd [2013] EWHC 1643(TCC) .8.25
Emirates Trading Agency LLC v Prime Mineral Exports Private Ltd [2014]
    EWHC 2014 (Comm.)...10.10–10.11
EnergySolutions EU Ltd v Nuclear Decommissioning Agency [2016] EWHC 1988 (TCC)...........7.47
ES v Chesterfield and North Derbyshire Royal Hospital NHS Trust [2003] EWCA Civ1284.........3.9
Eurocom Ltd v Siemens Plc [2014] EWHC 3710 (TCC)..11.16
Exel Europe v University Hospitals Coventry & Warwickshire NHS Trust [2010]
    EWHC 3332 (TCC)..7.14
Ferson Contractors v Levolux AT Ltd [2003] BLR118 ....9.22
Field v Leeds City Council...3.27
Findcharm Ltd v Churchill Group Ltd [2017] EWHC 1108 (TCC) 8.6
Gallaher International Ltd v Tlais Enterprises Ltd [2017] EWHC 2979 (TCC) 3.27
Gem Environmental Building Services Ltd v London Borough of Tower Hamlets
    [2016] EWHC 3045 (TCC) 7.24–7.25
Geodesign Barriers Ltd v The Environment Agency [2015] EWHC
    1121 (TCC)...7.26, 7.29, 7.47, 7.50
Group M UK Ltd v Cabinet Office [2014] EWHC 3401 (TCC)..7.24, 7.47
Group Seven Ltd v Nasir [2016] EWHC 620 (Ch) 8.20
GSK Project Management Ltd v QPR Holdings Ltd [2015] EWHC 2274 (TCC)..........................8.20
Halsey v Milton Keynes General NHS Trust [2004] EWCA Civ576...................................10.25, 10.27
Harbour & General v Environment Agency [2000] 1 Lloyd's Rep65 ....11.11
Harrison v University Hospitals Coventry and Warwickshire NHS Trust [2017] EWCA Civ792.8.22
Henry Boot Construction (UK) Ltd v Malmaison Hotel (Manchester) Ltd (1999) 70 Con LR33....4.2
Henry v News Group Newspapers Ltd [2013] EWCA Civ19..8.22
Herschell Engineering v Breen Property Ltd [2000] BLR272 ....9.7, 9.23
Higginson Securities (Developments) Ltd and another v Hodson [2012] EWHC 1052 (TCC)...10.19
Holloway v Chancery Mead Ltd [2007] EWHC 2495 (TCC) 10.8, 10.10
Hospitals for Sick Children v McLaughlin & Harvey (1990) 19 Con LR25 ....6.20
HSM Offshore BV v Aker Offshore Partner Ltd [2017] EWHC 2979 (TCC)....................3.16, 6.37
Hutton Construction Ltd v Wilson Properties (London) Ltd [2017]
    EWHC 517 (TCC)..9.14–9.15, 9.18
ICI v Merit [2018] EWHC 1577 (TCC)..3.38
Integrated Building Services v PIHL UK Ltd [2010] CSOH80...9.22
Jacobs UK Ltd v Skanska Construction UK [2017] EWHC 2395 (TCC) 9.8
Jamadar v Bradford Teaching Hospitals NHS Foundations Trust [2016] EWCA Civ 8.28
Jerram Falkus v Fenice [2011] EWHC 1935 (TCC)..4.16
John Doyle Construction Ltd v Laing Management (Scotland) Ltd [2002] BLR393....................5.34
John Sisk & Son Holdings Ltd v Wester Health and Social Care Trust [2014] NIQB56 ....7.18
Joseph Gleave v Secretary of State for Defence [2017] EWHC 238 (TCC) 7.17
JSC Mezhdunarodniy Promyshlenniy Bank v Pugachev [2013] EWHC 1983 (Ch).......................8.21
Korbetis v Transgrain [2005] EWHC 1345 (QB)..11.11
Linklaters v Sir Robert McAlpine Ltd [2010] EWHC 1145 (TCC) 6.20
London Borough of Camden v Makers [2009] EWHC 605 (TCC) 9.7
London Underground v Citylink [2007] BLR391 ....5.33–5.34
Lusty v Finsbury Securities Ltd (1991) 58 BLR66 ....3.9
Manorshow Ltd v Boots Opticians [2017] EWHC 2751 (TCC)...6.3
Mears v Leeds [2011] EWHC 40 (QB)...7.44
Meat Corp of Namibia Ltd v Dawn Meats (UK) Ltd [2007] EWHC 464 (Comm.) 3.27

TABLE OF CASES

Melville Dundas Ltd v George Wimpey UK Ltd [2007] BLR257 .... 9.22
Merrix v Heart of England NHS Foundation Trust [2017] EWHC 346 (QB) 8.22
Mirant Asia-Pacific Construction (Hong Kong) Ltd v Ove Arup & Partners International Ltd [2007]
    EWHC 918 (TCC) 4.156
Mitchell v News Group Newspapers Ltd [2013] EWCA Civ1537 .... 8.5, 8.15, 8.28
MT Hojgaard AS v E.ON Climate and Renewables UK Robin Rigg East Ltd
    [2017] UKSC59 .... 6.8, 6.10
Multiplex Constructions (UK) Ltd v Cleveland Bridge UK Ltd [2008] EWHC 2220 (TCC) 3.10
NATS (Services) Ltd v Gatwick Airport Ltd [2014] EWHC 3133 (TCC) 7.17
Northrop Grumman Mission Systems Europe Ltd v BAE Systems [2014] 156 Con LR141 .... 10.29
O'Donnell Developments Ltd v Build Ability Ltd [2009] EWHC 3388 (TCC) 9.25
125 OBS (Nominees1) Ltd v Lend Lease Construction (Europe)
    Ltd [2017] EWHC 25 (TCC) 6.8, 6.43
Openview Security Solutions v Merton LBC [2015] EWHC 2694 (TCC) 7.15
Pearson Driving Assessments Ltd v The Minister for the Cabinet and The Secretary of State for
    Transport [2013] EWHC 2082 (TCC) 7.18
Pegram Shopfitters Ltd v Tally Weijl (UK) Ltd [2003] EWCA Civ1750 .... 9.3
PGF II SA v PMFS Co 1 Ltd [2014] 152 Con LR72 .... 10.26
Rainford House Ltd v Cadogan Ltd [2001] BLR416 .... 9.23
Roche Diagnostics Ltd v The Mid Yorkshire Hospitals NHS Trust [2013]
    EWHC 933 (TCC) 7.23, 7.25, 7.46
Roundstone Nurseries Ltd v Stephenson Holdings Ltd [2009] EWHC 1431 (TCC) 10.15
Sharp v Blank [2015] EWHC 2685 (Ch) 8.28
Straw Realisations (No 1) Ltd v Shaftsbury House (Developments) Ltd
    [2010] EWHC 2597 (TCC) 9.22
Sul America v Enesa Engenharis [2012] 1 Ll R 671 (CA) 10.10
The Ikarian Reefer [2000] 1 WLR603 .... 3.38
Thomas Pink v Victoria's Secret [2015] 3 Costs LR463 .... 8.25
Trollope & Colls v North West Metropolitan Regional Hospital Board [1973] 1 WLR601..4.14–4.15
Twintec Ltd v Volkerfitzpatrick Ltd [2014] EWHC 10 (TCC) 9.5–9.6
Van Oord UK Ltd v Allseas UK Ltd [2015] EWHC 3074 (TCC) 6.35, 6.41
Vasiliou v Hajigeorgiou [2005] 1 WLR2195 .... 2.38
Vector Investments v Williams [2009] EWHC 3601 (TCC) 2.23
Veolia ES Nottinghamshire Ltd v Nottinghamshire County Council [2010] EWCA Civ1214 ...... 7, 44
Walter Lilly v Mackay [2012] BLR 503 (TCC) 4.23, 4.36, 4.73, 4.124, 5.26, 5.28, 5.30,
                                                                                                        5.33–5.34, 5.36, 5.39
Webb Resolutions Ltd v Countrywide Solicitors Ltd [2016] Ch Div 2.6
West African Gas Pipeline Ltd v Willbros Global Holdings Inc [2012] EWHC 396 (TCC) 2.24
Wharf Properties v Eric Cummin [1991] 52 BLR 1 4.21, 4.88
William McIlroy Swindon Ltd v Quinn Insurance Ltd [2010] EWHC 2448 (TCC) 11.12
William Verry Ltd v The London Borough of Camden [2006] EWHC 761 (TCC) 9.22
Wimbledon Construction Co 2000 Ltd v Derek Vago [2005] EWHC 1086 (TCC) 9.23, 9.25
Workplace Technologies Plc v E Squared Ltd [2000] CILL1607 .... 9.5

TABLE OF LEGISLATION

Arbitration Act 1996 ....
    2.10, 11.2–11.3, 11.8–11.9,
    11.11–11.15, 11.17–11.19
COM(2006)195 .... 7.9
Consumer Contracts Regulations 1999 11.6
Defence and Security Public
    Contracts Regulations 2011 .... 7.12
FIA *see* Freedom of Information Act 2000
Freedom of Information Act 2000 ... 7.41–7.42
Housing Grants, Construction and
    Regeneration Act 1996 ....
    1.2, 9.1–9.3, 9.5, 9.7, 9.19

Public Contracts (Amendments)
    Regulations 2009 .... 7.7, 7.10
Public Contracts Regulations 2006
    .... 1.3, 7.8, 7.10
Public Contracts Regulations 2009 .... 7.4
Public Contracts Regulations 2015.
    7.4, 7.10, 7.17–7.18, 7.27–7.28
Remedies Directive (2007/66) ....
    7.7, 7.9, 7.12, 7.14
Remedies Directive (COM(2006)
    final/2) 7.9
Supreme Court Act 1981 .... 2.5

CHAPTER 1

Introduction to litigation in the TCC

What is the TCC?

1.1 The Technology and Construction Court, or TCC as it is regularly referred to, took over the work previously known as 'Official Referees' Business on 9 October 1998. The TCC now forms part of the Business and Property Courts, which were launched in July 2017 and became operational on 2 October 2017. They have been created as a single umbrella for specialist civil jurisdictions across England and Wales.

1.2 The Official Referees were created in 1873 in order to try cases involving technical or detailed issues which it was deemed should no longer be left to judge and jury. By the early part of the twentieth century, much of the workload of the Official Referees related to construction and engineering matters, and this is also the case with the TCC. However, although the core of the work relates to the construction industry, the TCC deals with a broad spectrum of work, including: professional negligence disputes relating to surveyors, engineers, project managers, architects, accountants and other specialist advisers in the construction, engineering and technology fields, as well as allegations of lawyers' negligence arising in connection with planning, property, construction and other technical disputes; claims relating to the supply and provision of materials, goods, plant and other services; claims relating to the design, supply and installation of computers, software and related network systems; dilapidation claims as between landlord and tenant; environmental issues, including pollution and reclamation; nuisance claims relating to land use; claims arising out of fires and explosions, often including issues of insurance coverage; the enforcement of or challenges to adjudicators' decisions arising out of the Housing Grants, Construction and Regeneration Act 1996; challenges to decisions of arbitrators in the construction, engineering and technology fields; disputes involving oil and gas installations, onshore and offshore, and shipbuilding.

1.3 Recently, the variety of work in the TCC has become broader. The types of factually or technically complex cases which have been heard in the TCC have included group actions for personal injury and public nuisance, and procurement disputes arising in connection with the Public Contracts Regulations 2006, quite irrespective of whether the underlying contract is related to the construction industry. However, with the exception of claims to enforce adjudicators' decisions or other claims with special features that justify a hearing before a High Court Judge, the TCC in London will not usually accept cases with a value of less than £250,000 unless there is good reason for it to do so. The TCC Guide sets out a non-exhaustive list of special features which will usually justify listing the case in the High Court.[1] These include: international cases whatever their value (international cases will generally involve one or more parties resident outside the UK and/or involve an overseas project or development); cases involving new or difficult points of law; any test case or case which will be joined with others which will be treated as test cases; complex nuisance claims brought by a number of parties, even where the sums claimed are small; and claims for injunctive relief.

1.4 There are ten regional centres around the country at which the TCC operates: Birmingham, Bristol, Cardiff, Chester, Exeter, Leeds, Liverpool, Newcastle, Nottingham and Manchester. There are full-time TCC Judges at Birmingham, Manchester and Leeds. At the regional centres, both High Court Judges and County Court Judges hear claims. Since 2004, the Judges of the TCC in London have been exclusively High Court Judges. The TCC in London is situated in the Rolls Building on Fetter Lane, which as part of the Business and Property Courts now forms the largest specialist centre for financial, business and property litigation in the world.

Dispute resolution

1.5 In virtually all construction projects, the question is not whether a dispute will arise, but how the dispute will be resolved. The three key variables are time, cost and quality, and it is the relationship between these variables that drives every disagreement. There is a wide range of tools available to resolve disputes in the modern world. Some of these tools – such as dispute review boards – are designed to resolve disputes as they arise during the course of the project. Adjudication, a statutorily mandated process in which disputes are to be heard and temporarily determined within 28 days, was also intended to be used primarily during the course of a project to maintain cash flow and while it is commonly utilised in this way, it has also become a vehicle for large final account disputes after the project has been completed. Adjudication has rendered 'expert determination' a rarity nowadays, but it is still contractually available or required in some types of standard form, particularly in the shipbuilding context, for particular types of technical dispute. Arbitration is a private and binding alternative to litigation for finally determining disputes. Alongside each of these methods, there sit numerous creative alternatives aimed more at achieving consensual resolution: mediation, conciliation and early neutral evaluation.

Arbitration v litigation

1.6 Arbitration has had a long history as the most common method of determining disputes in the construction industry, and was the default contractual mechanism within the

---

1 See also *West Country Renovations Ltd v McDowell* [2012] EWHC 307, in which Akenhead J transferred a case from the TCC to the Central London County Court, notwithstanding the parties' representations that the matter should be dealt with in the TCC, saying: 'The case under consideration is a very standard construction case, namely a disputed final account with issues about proof of cost, recoverability of certain types of work, the reasonableness of various rates and the applicability and impact of a possible cap. Without in any way belittling the importance of the case to the parties themselves, there is nothing of general public importance, such as some novel point of law or construction of a standard building contract. There is no good reason to think that the Central London County Court TCC designated Judges will not effectively case manage and then try this case within a reasonable time.'

most commonly used standard forms for construction projects (the 'JCT' form) and engineering projects (the 'ICE' form). However, over the past decade or so, there has been a move away from what is called 'domestic' (i.e. non-international) arbitration, as the TCC has grown in popularity. Arbitration's success grew from the perception of having significant advantages over litigation. However, over time, nearly every advantage has been worn away. The first perceived benefit was the experience of the individual who was to decide the case. Arbitrators, often non-lawyers, would be drawn from the industry and were familiar with first-hand experience of the disputes which they were required to decide. However, the TCC Judges are generally drawn from a pool of solicitors or barristers who have worked principally or largely in the field of work in which the TCC specialises, with many years' technical and legal experience. Moreover, the pool of Judges is small and the quality high and therefore litigation presents a considerably less variable alternative than relying upon an institution to nominate an arbitrator from a range of individuals whose abilities may vary significantly. This becomes less of an issue where the parties agree on the identity of their chosen arbitrator, but this leads to the second perceived advantage: speed.

1.7 Litigation was traditionally perceived (and perhaps rightly so) as being slow compared with arbitration. However, the case management techniques introduced by the TCC (and now largely adopted across the Court system) have meant that litigation is extremely efficient, with even the most complex cases concluded to judgment within a year to 18 months from service of a Claim Form. While many arbitrations will be similarly processed, arbitrators are usually less forthright than Judges in demanding a swift timescale in the face of opposition from one or more of the parties. Access is readily available to the Courts, which can usually hear urgent applications quickly in front of one of the team of Judges; by contrast, the ability of an arbitrator to determine an urgent application will depend on his or her availability, and there is no option for another arbitrator to step in at short notice. Furthermore, the timing of a final hearing is likely to be as dependent upon the availability of the individual arbitrator as it is on the needs or wishes of the parties; by contrast, while the final hearing in Court will be set by reference to the availability of the Court, it is rare for the Court not to be able to accommodate a swift overall procedure as the availability of a particular Judge (as opposed to one of the pool) is not a necessary consideration. While it will of course vary from case to case, in general terms the TCC will expect to hold the final hearing within about a year of the matter first coming before the Court, which is usually shortly after the defence has been served. Sometimes it can be considerably quicker. The overall time period in which a dispute can be resolved is then, obviously, linked to the third consideration: cost.

1.8 While historically it was generally the case that arbitration was more efficient and less expensive, this too is no longer the case. At best, the arbitration and litigation are likely to be comparable, once the cost of the arbitrator is removed. However, this of itself can be a significant cost when compared with Court fees (even given the recent increases). Traditionally, one area in which parties have considered that arbitration offers potential cost savings relates to disclosure. 'Standard' disclosure, in which in broad terms a party has to make efforts to search for all relevant documents whether helpful or unhelpful to its case, is the default position in litigation, but in arbitration it is more common that parties are in the first instance only required to provide those documents which they rely upon, and thereafter to provide categories of documents requested (and if disputed, ordered by the arbitrator). This is often considered less burdensome than standard disclosure. However, while it is now common for the Court to be more sensitive to the burden of disclosure and will in the appropriate case (and particularly where the parties agreed) order disclosure by reference to time periods, and issues, and so this perceived benefit is also being eroded.

1.9 The final advantage is considered to be the confidentiality associated with arbitration, which is private. Litigation is public. However, there are limits on the confidential nature of arbitration: for example, if there is an appeal, then the appeal will be in Court and the arbitration will no longer be private. Moreover, the fact that litigation is public, and any judgment openly available, itself can have advantages and in the right case itself may present leverage in reaching a negotiated settlement. It is therefore a matter of legitimate debate as to whether confidentiality presents any real benefit at all.

1.10 In the context of the types of case with which the TCC is concerned, there is particular benefit to litigation: the ability to have multi-party disputes. Many of the disputes in the construction industry involve a number of parties: while the kernel of the dispute may lay between the employer and the contractor, the real dispute may relate to the activities of a sub-contractor, or a designer or engineer. In Court proceedings, it is generally straightforward to involve all the relevant parties – a contractor bringing its sub-contractor into the litigation via its contract, or a party responsible for design issues by contribution proceedings, for example. However, absent the consent of all the parties, this is rarely possible in arbitration. A contractor may therefore find itself facing a claim in arbitration and then having to bring separate proceedings in front of a different Tribunal (for example, a different arbitrator, or in Court in front of a Judge). This brings with it the additional time and cost and, of most concern, an inherent risk of different or inconsistent findings. It is obvious to see that the ability to bring others into the proceedings is advantageous to a party facing a claim and wishing to divert the allegations in a different direction. Primarily, therefore, it is advantageous to contractors who are most likely to want to pass a claim on; it is less obviously advantageous to an employer who may prefer the simplicity of a single claim against a 'one stop' contractor rather than the inevitable increase in time and cost of multi-party proceedings. It may be, therefore, that the limited bilateral nature of arbitration is a sufficient perceived advantage to employers, and this is the reason that arbitration clauses still exist in domestic construction contracts. However, the practical reality of dispute resolution is that an employer is most likely to be advantaged by a mechanism that increases the prospect of reaching a commercial resolution to the matter. In practical terms, the inability for a contractor or engineer to bring other parties into an arbitration may well make the overall dispute more difficult to settle, and therefore even this advantage is questionable.

1.11 It is therefore fairly easy to see why domestic arbitration in the domestic construction industry has significantly fallen away, replaced by a combination of adjudication and litigation in the TCC. This has been reflected in the JCT's removal of arbitration as the default dispute resolution mechanism, although it remains so in the ICE and NEC contracts, and in most shipbuilding contracts. While arbitration still has an important role in international dispute resolution, it is difficult to see why a party to a domestic project would choose to arbitrate rather than litigate in the TCC.

The TCC Guide

1.12 HM Courts and Tribunals Service publishes a guide to litigation in the TCC. The second edition of the guide, now in its third revision, was published in 2015. The purpose of the document is to provide 'straightforward, practical guidance on the conduct of litigation in the TCC'. It describes the main elements of the practice that is likely to be followed in most TCC cases, and indeed which forms the subject matter of this book. The document is useful and those intending to commence litigation in the TCC should become familiar with its guidance.[2]

---

2 See Appendix 1.

CHAPTER 2

An overview of a claim in the TCC

2.1 While there are countless variations on a theme, the general shape of litigation in the TCC forms a well-trodden path. This is as follows:

- The pre-action phase
- Commencement of proceedings
- Pleadings
- The first Case Management Conference
- Disclosure
- Witness statements
- Expert reports (joint and individual)
- Pre-Trial Review
- Trial
- Judgment
- Appeal

Pre-action phase

2.2 There is a published Pre-Action Protocol[1] for Construction and Engineering Disputes. This is the most obviously relevant Pre-Action Protocol applicable to work in the TCC, and while there is also a Professional Negligence Pre-Action Protocol, it is prevailed over by the Construction and Engineering Disputes one if the claim is one against architects, engineers or quantity surveyors. The purpose of the Pre-Action Protocol is to encourage the exchange of early and full information about the prospective claim, to enable parties to avoid litigation by settling prior to the commencement of proceedings and to support the efficient management of proceedings if they cannot be avoided. The pre-action process must be complied with in relation to any prospective litigation which falls within the ambit of the protocol, save in limited circumstances (which include where the same issues have just been adjudicated). The basic structure of the pre-action phase is the provision of a letter of claim, a letter of response and a meeting.

2.3 As explained in the TCC Guide, the protocol does not contemplate an extended process and it should not be drawn out. The letter of claim should explain the proposed claim in sufficient detail to enable the potential defendant to understand and investigate the allegations. While the guide states that only essential documents need be supplied, in practice defending parties often make relatively broad requests for documentation at the pre-action stage. It is clear that the claimant will usually be well justified in refusing broad requests; the claimant will need to balance the proportionality of agreeing to such requests with the

---

1 See Appendix 2.

fact that, unless satisfied, the defendant may be unwilling to enter meaningful commercial negotiations. It is not necessary as part of the letter of claim to provide an expert report, although it must identify the name of any experts who have already been instructed. In relation to certain types of claim, however, there will potentially be a strategic advantage to the provision of a report. For example, in professional negligence actions, it is improbable that a claim will settle until the defendant has seen a report supporting the allegations of negligence. The disclosure of such a report at an early stage in a strong case is likely therefore to be beneficial to the claimant's prospects of swift settlement.

2.4 The defendant has two weeks to acknowledge the letter of claim and then a further two weeks (i.e. 28 days from the date of the letter of claim) to provide a response. As recognised by the TCC Guide, it is usual in complex cases for an extension of time to be agreed between the parties, and the protocol sanctions this up to a period of three months. The meeting is to be a without prejudice meeting. Often, parties will agree to hold a mediation in lieu of the pre-action meeting.

2.5 Ordinarily, costs incurred during the pre-action phase are not recoverable if the matter is resolved without the need for litigation. Section 51 of the Supreme Court Act 1981 provides that 'the costs of and incidental to the proceedings . . . shall be in the discretion of the Court'. While pre-action costs can be costs 'incidental to' any subsequent proceedings,[2] if there is no litigation, there are no costs of litigation.[3] The requirement that the parties engage in pre-action correspondence was deliberately imposed, at least in part, with a view to extending the period during which each party would conduct its case on the basis that it was not incurring a liability to pay the other party's costs if no action was commenced. The Courts have observed that cost shifting tends to increase costs, because parties feel able to incur costs in the expectation that the other party will pay them.[4] Therefore, should the claiming party decide that it will not proceed having seen the content of the defendant's response, the erstwhile prospective defendant will not be able to obtain any order from the Court requiring its costs to be paid. Similarly, where proceedings are started, but in doing so, the claimant abandons some of those claims, it will only be in exceptional circumstances that the claimant would be required to pay the costs of the defendant in relation to those abandoned claims.[5]

2.6 Where the Claim Form has been served, the costs incurred pre-action in relation to claims which ultimately form part of the litigation are costs incidental to that litigation and are likely to form part of the pot of costs recoverable in principle. In *Webb Resolutions Ltd v Countrywide Solicitors Ltd*,[6] once the Claim Form had been issued, the jurisdiction of the Court over the costs, which could include pre-action costs, was triggered. In *Webb*, the Court considered that it would be wrong to ignore the considerable expense that the defendant had incurred in dealing with the claim, and the disproportionate nature of the costs incurred by both parties.

2.7 Once proceedings have been issued, a party who has failed to comply with the Pre-Action Protocol can be penalised by the Court. This might take the form of particular case management directions, or in costs, or in terms of the interest rate payable on any sum of money payable. The Court will be concerned with substantive rather than technical

---

2 See *McGlinn v Waltham Contractors Ltd* [2005] EWHC 1419 (TCC).
3 See *In re Gibson's Settlement Trusts* [1981] Ch 179 and the discussion in *McGlinn* (n 1).
4 See the discussion in *Citation Plc v Ellis Whittam Ltd* [2012] EWHC 764 (QB).
5 See *McGlinn* (n 1).
6 [2016] Ch Div.

breach. It is to be remembered that the need to comply with the Pre-Action Protocol does not affect statutory limitation periods, so if a party finds itself against time limits it should issue and if necessary serve the Claim Form to preserve its rights and seek (by consent or otherwise) a stay of proceedings to then allow the Pre-Action Protocol to be complied with. As noted above, in these circumstances, however, the Court will have a discretion to award costs to the defendant if the matter is resolved during the protocol process.

Commencement of the proceedings

2.8 All proceedings must be started using a Claim Form under the relevant part of the Civil Procedure Rules (CPR). Part 7 claims are for most claims; Part 8 (considered further in the context of adjudication enforcement in Chapter 9 below) is intended for disputes which are unlikely to involve a substantial dispute of fact;[7] Part 62 (considered in Chapter 11) relates to an 'arbitration' Claim Form, used in circumstances where orders ancillary to arbitrations are sought. The Claim Form should be marked 'Technology and Construction Court' in the appropriate place.

2.9 In the most straightforward of claims (for example, perhaps a claim for moneys unpaid pursuant to an invoice), Particulars of Claim can be provided with the Claim Form, but if they are not they must be served within 14 days after the service of the Claim Form. The Claim Form, as with all statements of case, must be served with a statement of truth. If the Claim Form has been issued by the TCC in the Rolls Building in London, it is then generally to be served on the defendant by the claimant. This contrasts with the procedure in some other Court Centres where the Court Centre itself effects service of the document. A Claim Form must generally be served within four months of its issue. If the Claim Form has not been served within that time, it expires and a further Claim Form has to be issued. This is not of itself a problem unless the claimant's case is on the cusp of the limitation period. In such circumstances, it is obviously inadvisable for the claimant to leave service to the last minute.

2.10 The defendant, when receiving the Claim Form, will be provided with a form for the Acknowledgement of Service. This has to be done within 14 days. If the defendant is going to dispute the jurisdiction of the Court, it must comply with Part 11 of the CPR. However, claims that the dispute in question should be decided by some other contractually required form of dispute resolution (such as arbitration) is not generally regarded as a matter which ousts the jurisdiction of the Court in the sense intended by Part 11:[8] instead, it is for the receiving party to apply to the Court for a stay of proceedings. The stay is mandatory if there is a valid arbitration agreement in place, pursuant to section 9 of the Arbitration Act 1996. If there is some other sufficiently clear dispute escalation clause (for example, a requirement that the parties attempt to settle the matter by a defined process prior to the commencement of proceedings), the Court will generally give effect to such clauses and, again, stay the proceedings pending compliance.[9] However, the stay is, in these circumstances, discretionary rather than mandatory.

---

7 See, for example, *Victory House General Partner Ltd v RGB P&C Ltd* [2018] EWHC 102 (TCC) at [6].
8 See, for example, *Yorkshire Water v Taylor Woodrow* (2002) 90 Con LR 84.
9 See, for example, *Hollowat v Chancery Mead Ltd* [2007] EWHC 2495.

Pleadings

2.11 Pleadings in TCC litigation can be voluminous. Noticeably, the TCC does not adopt the same position as the Commercial Court, where the guidance requires that pleadings be limited to 25 pages unless there are good reasons. However, the fact that the Judges are experienced in understanding and assimilating large and complex pleadings should not be a licence for unnecessary complexity and verbiage.

2.12 A good Particulars of Claim should be well structured. It is likely that, particularly in the case of a lengthy document, there will be an introduction or overview that sets out at a high level the nature of the claim. Ordinarily, a pleading in a TCC case will then deal with the following:

(1) *The contractual (or other) relationship between the parties, and key relevant clauses of the contract or other obligations (for example, statutory) on which the claim will rely.* In defects cases, there are often a number of relevant sections from the main body of the agreement, the conditions and the specifications. It is often convenient that these are relegated to an appendix to the pleading.

(2) *In delay claims, the identification of the main programme obligations* and those activities which the claiming party alleges are critical to completion of the project will usually be essential, and if not included within the claim can be the subject of legitimate requests for further information.

(3) *A narrative or chronological statement of the key events giving rise to the claims.* Again, in a delay claim, this might be lengthy and is likely to draw on the content and structure of expert evidence which has been prepared for the purposes of pleading the claim. For example, it might be that the pleading itself breaks up the overall chronology into mini-periods or 'windows', which is commonplace in delay analysis (see generally Chapter 4), at the end of each of which will be the additional and aggregate delay caused. By contrast, in a defects claim, it is likely that the key information will be a description of what has gone wrong, the investigations undertaken and the findings. Again, this would involve pleading the key elements of expert evidence which will in due course be relied upon (for example, the surveys of water ingress, the concrete test results, the measured movement and cracks in a building).

(4) *A section on breach which interrelates the content of the two preceding sections* (i.e. it explains how the facts set out in the statement of key events constitute a breach of obligation, whether contractual, tortious or statutory). This is a critical element of the pleading and will often constitute the heart of any agenda for an ultimate trial. While it is sometimes tempting to elongate the list of failings by characterising the same underlying issue in numerous different ways, this is not likely to assist either clarity or simplicity and will almost certainly not improve the claim; it is a temptation that should be resisted.

(5) *Causation.* It is necessary to include a statement of what loss or damage has been caused by the breach. In many cases, causation is straightforward to articulate; in other cases, the linkage between cause and effect may be more opaque. In an ideal world, a breach leads to a discrete and identifiable consequence which can then be quantified. In the real world, breaches often interrelate and interact, so

that an aggregated effect cannot sensibly be pinned to a single cause. This can be particularly true for the main types of cases grappled with in the TCC: arguments about causation are very often at the heart of TCC litigation. Where there are a number of defects, potentially the responsibility of different parties (or to different degrees), questions will inevitably arise about their relationship with the loss. Do they interact sequentially, consecutively or concurrently? Would the loss said to be caused by Defect B have been caused by Defect A in any event? Similarly, in cases for extensions of time or loss and expense, the competing causes of delays will usually be central. The pleading needs to get the balance right in terms of the amount of information provided: it is today generally regarded that causation is a matter of evidence and for the Court to decide having heard that evidence, so that a skirmish on the pleadings is unlikely to get traction unless the claimant has failed to articulate, in the most basic way, the case the defendant has to answer.[10] However, the basics would generally include, as suggested above, the identification of the contended critical path and how periods of claimed delay arise through the project. Similarly, in a defects claim, the pleader should ideally identify which claimed sums relate to which breaches, and if the case is ultimately one where an aggregation of defects causes an aggregated loss, this should be stated.

(6) *Quantification of loss*. The pleading must then quantify the losses which have been caused. Actual losses incurred should be capable of precise identification; future losses will by definition be estimates. However, it is usually only in circumstances where a future loss is dependent upon a third-party action that the Court would consider granting an indemnity in respect of future losses: generally, the Court will estimate the future loss and award damages (discounted for early receipt).

2.13 The stereotypical TCC claim is that in which a Scott Schedule features in the pleadings. This is a document in which elements of the claim or counterclaim are set out by way of a table, often in landscape format, in which the case on breach, causation and loss is set out item by item, and to which the responding party sets out its case in the adjacent columns. The last column is commonly for the Judge to set out its decision. As explained in the TCC Guide, the secret of an effective Scott Schedule lies in the information that is to be provided and its brevity. Thus, the parties should agree the column headings (and if there is a dispute about this, the Court can give guidance). Brevity, however, must be tempered to some degree by the need for detail. It is often useful for the parties to sub-number points within the columns and in terms of formatting, align related points across the page.

2.14 It is open to a party to serve on the other a Request for Further Information, pursuant to Part 18 of the CPR. This often, but not always, arises in relation to pleadings. Pre-CPR, it was almost a matter of course for a party to serve very lengthy requests for 'further and better particulars' (as they were then called). These could run to hundreds of pages and many hundreds of questions were said to arise, somewhat formulaically, out of a lack of clarity in the pleaded case. Happily, it is rare for such documents to form part of case strategy nowadays, and it is unlikely that the Court would look too kindly upon such an approach.

---

10 See, for example, in the context of delay claims, the judgment of Ramsey J in *London Underground Ltd v Citylink Telecommunications Ltd* [2007] BLR 391, and Chapter 4 of this book.

The Court, instead, will consider whether the information really is necessary to permit one party to understand the case being advanced; and it will also be conscious of the distinction between the summary of facts which the pleading requires, and more detailed evidence. Similarly, requests for documentation prior to disclosure might well be considered inappropriate. However, where a party raises a limited number of pertinent questions genuinely arising, and which should be relatively straightforward to answer, modern Judges are likely to be unimpressed with a failure to provide a constructive response. Often, the Judges in the TCC may adopt a practical approach to the provision of such information through expert discussions, rather than strictly through pleadings, and will expect of the parties a similarly constructive approach to sensible case management.

The first Case Management Conference

2.15 The parties are expected to complete the case management information sheet. In this, the parties set out various details relating to the claim and the draft directions sought. Ideally, the parties should cooperate in advance of the service of these forms so that agreed directions (or areas of disagreement) can be identified. The parties are also required to serve a disclosure report not less than 14 days before the first Case Management Conference (CMC), and no fewer than seven days before, the parties should discuss and seek to agree proposals for disclosure and to file cost budgets. (In relation to cost budgeting, see generally Chapter 8 below.) It is usual in larger cases that advocates will prepare notes for the hearing which set out the remaining issues and briefly summarise the arguments being advanced to support the parties' positions.

2.16 The standard matters which are discussed, agreed or directed at the first CMC are as follows:

(1) *The addition of other parties.* If the first CMC takes place before the service of the defence, which is sometimes necessary but not usually ideal, the defendants ought to be candid about whether they plan to serve any additional claims as part of their defence. This is likely to affect the remaining timetable; it may well be that the Court would simply wish to adjourn the CMC until the relevant additional claims have been served and, potentially, defences in those matters completed.

(2) *The completion of pleadings.* A CMC is often heard after the service of defences, but before the 'close' of pleadings. If this is so, dates for the service of a Reply, or a Defence to Counterclaim, and sometimes further pleadings (such as a Rejoinder), are set down. It may be, in addition, that if a party has served a Part 18 Request for Further Information, any disputes relating to whether or to what extent such a document requires a response will be dealt with.

(3) *Preliminary issues or split trial.* Whether there should be any preliminary issues, or whether the trial should be split (for example, between liability and causation, followed by quantum). Preliminary issues are where the Court considers and delivers a binding judgment on particular issues in advance of the main trial. As pointed out in the TCC Guide (Section 8), preliminary issues can be an extremely cost-effective and efficient way of narrowing the issues between the parties and, in certain cases, of resolving disputes altogether. Generally, an issue would only be considered suitable for a preliminary issue if: (1) it was capable of resolving

the whole of the proceedings or a significant element of it; an example of this might be a limitation point, where, if correct, the claim fails (although note the warning at 8.4.1 of the TCC Guide that limitation points can often require considerable evidence); (2) it was capable of significantly reducing the scope and therefore the costs of the main trial; an example of this is where it is alleged that there was an oral agreement resolving the final account dispute, such that if correct, substantial factual and quantum evidence would be unnecessary; or (3) it was capable of significantly improving the possibility of a settlement of the whole proceedings; an example of this is the construction and application of a limitation of liability clause, the resolution of which would substantially alter the financial dynamic of the litigation. A preliminary issue is normally only ordered if there would be limited oral evidence; and the TCC guidance suggests that it is generally considered that a preliminary issue hearing would not take more than four days even in a larger and more complex matter. While, obviously, a preliminary issue in the correct case can unlock a dispute, it is suggested that some caution ought to be exercised in determining whether a preliminary issue is sensible. For example, strategically it might be that *not* deciding a discrete point will make the overall case more, rather than less, likely to settle. Also, it may be that deciding a particular issue which is not determinative of the whole matter at an early stage allows the party which has lost the point to recast its case, or at least change the emphasis, whereas allowing the point to run to trial deprives the party of the opportunity to regroup in this way.

A split trial is another, related form of trial management. The most common type of split is where liability and causation are determined in the first hearing, and detailed quantum evidence is considered in a further hearing. It is the experience of the authors that split trials are far less common than they used to be, and this probably stems from a combination of factors. First, quantum experts are far more involved and encouraged to reach agreement on a 'figures as figures' basis than previously. This means that the 'quantum' part of a trial is often straightforward, even if there are potentially a number of variables by way of alternative remedial schemes, for example. The second is an awareness that splitting out quantum may, at least in the short term, affect the overall ability to settle the case and increases the prospect of the liability part of the trial going ahead. This is because the quantum part of the case often focusses the parties' attention on the sums at stake in a way that considering liability in vacuum from this evidence does not. Even if parties are considering a split trial, they will often want to obtain disclosure of quantum material at the normal time (in order to advance the commercial understanding of the financial claims) and therefore splitting the trial may achieve little cost saving: indeed, overall, it is more likely than not to be a more expensive way to conduct the case. Finally, parties rightly consider that there may be relevant material in the quantum part of a dispute which sheds light on other aspects of the case. For example, it is often the quantum part of a variation claim which is capable of the most effective attack, and an employer would be best served having those lines of cross-examination available so as to, potentially, affect the credibility of the contractor rather than have a hearing only on liability aspects alone.

(4) *Disclosure*. In large and complex TCC litigation, disclosure can be an enormous task. This is briefly discussed further below. Disputes as to the structure or format of disclosure, the identity of custodians or relevant date ranges, and the timing of disclosure are all matters frequently canvassed at the first CMC unless there is agreement between the parties.

(5) *Witness statements*. The main issue arising at the CMC is usually when these will be served, and sometimes whether there should be a direction for responsive statements.

(6) *Expert reports*. Apart from timing, the most common issues discussed at the first CMC in the TCC will be the discipline of the experts. Again, expert evidence is discussed further below.

(7) *The date and length of the trial*. The TCC generally sits for four days each week hearing trials, and reserves Fridays for interlocutory matters and applications. Thus, a 'two-week' case in the TCC would generally be considered to be eight days. Ordinarily, one might allow a short period for the Court to read into the case, and oral openings. Thereafter, the estimate will be based upon the time it is anticipated is necessary to hear factual and expert evidence. Closings might be oral immediately following the evidence (in a short or simple case), or be followed by written, and sometimes written and oral, closings. Aside from setting a conservative period in which to hear the evidence, it is unlikely that the Court will be interested in discussing the shape of these matters at the first CMC. They are often not decided until the trial itself. The complexity of the matter will obviously influence how soon the trial will be set. As a rule of thumb, it is likely that the Court will consider that all but the most complex and lengthy matters are likely to be capable of being prepared for trial in about a year from the date of the first CMC.

(8) *Cost budgets*. Since the introduction of cost budgeting, it is usual that some part of the first CMC is spent arguing over cost budgets. See generally Chapter 8 below.

(9) *Alternative dispute resolution (ADR)*. As part of the Case Management Information Sheet, the parties are requested to indicate whether they wish there to be a one-month stay to attempt to settle the claim, either by informal discussion or by ADR. If all the parties are agreed that a certain window for mediation or other commercial discussions should be built into the timetable, it is quite likely (but not certain) that the Court will give effect to that agreement; but otherwise the present approach of the TCC is generally to set directions for trial and will not involve itself in resolving disputes as to when the best time to attempt settlement might be.[11]

2.17 At the conclusion of the first CMC, the Court will set a date for a further CMC if the matter is complex, and the date for the Pre-Trial Review (PTR), usually just after the final procedural direction (likely to be the exchange of reply expert reports or a further joint statement) and a few weeks before the trial itself.

---

11 See *CIP Properties v Galliford Try & Ors* [2014] EWHC 3546 (TCC), considered further in the context of ADR in Chapter 8.

Disclosure

2.18 A common feature of litigation in the TCC is the seemingly (and, sometimes actually) overwhelming amount of documentation which is potentially relevant to the dispute if the usual CPR test of 'standard disclosure' is applied. However, it is also very often the case that by the time of a trial, the number of documents that are in fact key is very small. Notwithstanding a pool of documents running into the hundreds of thousands, or millions, most cases turn on a relative handful, and rarely more than a few hundred in even the most complex delay cases.

2.19 Knowing this does not, however, make the task of identification and management of documentation in TCC litigation any easier. As the TCC Guide points out (at 11.1.1), the CPR now provides a menu of different disclosure options, of which standard disclosure is now only one. The Court will be proactive in considering the most sensible and proportionate disclosure order. The options available include:

- an order dispensing with disclosure;
- an order that a party disclose the documents on which it relies, and at the same time request any specific disclosure it requires from any other party;
- an order that directs, where practicable, the disclosure to be given by each party on an issue-by-issue basis;
- an order that each party disclose any documents which it is reasonable to suppose may contain information which enables that party to advance its own case or to damage that of any other party, or which leads to an enquiry which has either of those consequences; or
- any other order in relation to disclosure that the Court considers appropriate.

2.20 Standard disclosure is often not appropriate in TCC litigation, on account of the amount of documentation and the potential disproportionate cost. The Court might also take account of the fact that many of the documents are common to the parties, or the extent of voluntary disclosure during the pre-action stage.

2.21 In many cases where a relatively large sum is at stake, the parties engage 'platform providers', which is effectively a sophisticated software package that assists with document management and the task of disclosure. The TCC will expect the parties to engage and cooperate on the management of e-disclosure; specific guidance can be found in Practice Direction 31B (Disclosure of Electronic Documents), and in the protocol for e-disclosure prepared by TeCSA and TECBAR and the Society for Computers and Law. The TCC Guide points out that the latter protocol was developed in consultation with the TCC Judges and is likely to be ordered by the Court if the parties have not agreed on any alternative by the time of the first CMC.

2.22 The basic process of modern e-disclosure will be along the following lines:

(1) To identify the pool of documents which could potentially be relevant.
(2) This encompasses both hard copy and electronic documents.
(3) In terms of electronic documents, many construction projects have live platforms during the currency of the project on which documents, drawings and the like are loaded and exchanged; this is obviously a key place to start if it exists.

(4) For other electronic disclosure, the main sources of documentation will be the companies' or personnel's electronic filing system (which might be central, personal or a combination of the two) and email exchanges. For both, it is key to identify relevant date ranges and 'custodians' (i.e. people whose emails are likely to be relevant). Hard-copy documents which only exist in hard copy can also be added to the electronic pool of information by turning the documents into (ideally, searchable) PDF form.

(5) The pool of documents is then usually uploaded to a single, searchable platform, is 'de-duplicated' and reduced by reference to 'keywords', which again the parties ought to agree. It may be that different key words apply to each side's pool, although obviously there will be overlap.

(6) Many systems employ intelligent learning techniques to carry out a second pass of the reduced pool, whereby lawyers will review relatively small selections of documents (for example, 1,000 at a time), marking for relevance or lack of relevance. The system 'learns' relevance in the context of the case through this process, which can be repeated a number of times, whereupon the pool is then reduced further by this intelligent filtering.

(7) At some point, the much reduced (but often still large) pool of documents must then be reviewed in the 'traditional' way by a team for both relevance and privilege.

2.23 This is, undoubtedly, a time-consuming and expensive exercise. There remains the touchstone of reasonableness and proportionality, and careful thought needs to be given to ways in which parties will be subject to criticism not only if the process fails to identify relevant documents (which leads to applications for specific disclosure); but also if the process does not weed out duplicates and irrelevant material so that excessive documentation is provided. Two decisions in the TCC demonstrate the Court's willingness to scrutinise carefully the adequacy of a party's approach to disclosure and impose cost sanctions where criticism is justified. In *Vector Investments v Williams*,[12] Ramsey J found that there were unsatisfactory aspects of the disclosure in terms of irrelevant and duplicated documents and the way in which they were organised; and concluded that the approach taken by the claimant was to disclose whole files which contained duplicate and unnecessary documents and that this led to unnecessary costs being incurred by the defendant in carrying out the inspection. Ramsey J considered that a comparison of the trial bundle, which contained 70 bundles, to over 800 bundles produced by the claimant for inspection, indicated to some extent that irrelevant documents or documents not necessary for standard disclosure were included. On the basis of the information, the Judge concluded that the claimant should pay £20,000 in respect of the wasted costs.

2.24 Similarly, in *West African Gas Pipeline Ltd v Willbros Global Holdings Inc*,[13] Ramsey J considered a raft of criticisms and found that there were mistakes or errors in disclosure, ordering one of the parties should pay significant wasted costs (£134,000 as an interim payment on account). The first problem was the failure properly to de-duplicate documents, which inevitably led to wasted time and costs in reviewing a number of copies

---

12 [2009] EWHC 3601 (TCC).
13 [2012] EWHC 396 (TCC).

of the same document. The Court accepted that de-duplication of electronic documents has a number of technically complex facets, but noted that there was a serious failure in the de-duplication process (in particular, that there were 24,341 duplicates in disclosure in one tranche, 2,604 duplicates in another and 13,328 duplicates in a third tranche, with smaller numbers of duplicates in other tranches of disclosure). The second main area of difficulty was the failure to gather together or 'harvest' a consistent and complete set of electronic data for the purpose of electronic disclosure. There were a number of errors: for example, the provision of incomplete e-room documents, the failure to obtain a copy of the relevant folders and sub-folders on the disclosure platform and the failure, in consultation with the relevant custodians, properly to gather those custodians' documents. The Court found that a considerable amount of disclosable documentation latterly disclosed should have been gathered together initially. The mistakes resulted from an inadequate initial review and gathering together of a complete set of electronic documentation. The third and significant difficulty arose because of a failure properly to review documents which were located in the searches of the electronic database. The review process had been outsourced to a third party, although the process was said to have been subject to supervision by lawyers. However, the number of documents which were reviewed and initially marked wrongly as non-disclosable clearly drew attention to the inadequacy of the review process. On the basis of these failings, the Court ordered that the claimant pay significant costs of dealing with the review of disclosure by the defendant.

Witness statements

2.25 The purpose of witness statements is to provide the factual evidence upon which each party relies.

2.26 It is not uncommon for TCC Judges to remark in the course of a trial that the length and content of factual witness statements is unnecessary and unhelpful. The TCC Guide reflects these views, in reminding practitioners that witness statements should not reproduce or paraphrase at length passages from other documents, save where it is necessary in order to make the statement reasonably intelligible. The Court has the power to make a witness re-serve its statement excluding irrelevant material or make a costs order by way of sanction.

2.27 Parties, therefore, should be acute to limiting the content of witness statements to the facts necessary to prove a claim. It is rarely necessary for witnesses to give their understanding of the contractual obligations or opinion evidence. In TCC litigation, where technical matters are in dispute, it is often the case that factual witness statements are to some extent a hybrid of technical expert and factual witness evidence: however, most of the time it must be remembered that the witness is being called to give evidence of fact. It may in some circumstances be relevant to provide factual evidence of a particular opinion held at the relevant time. For example, in a technical professional negligence case, it may very well be appropriate for a professional to explain why they acted in a certain way at the time, which will include evidence of their opinion on certain matters. On the other hand, a factual witness who was not directly involved in matters at the time, giving opinion evidence as to correctness or otherwise of a particular course of action should ordinarily be inadmissible.

2.28 It will be a matter of strategy as to whether, at an interlocutory phase, a formal application is made to exclude parts of the evidence, or simply to save such submissions for trial.

2.29 Another issue frequently arising at interlocutory hearings is the interrelationship between disclosure and witness statements. Statements ordinarily follow disclosure, and it is of course wise to ensure witnesses are aware of relevant contemporaneous documentation which they may be cross-examined upon in due course, even if they do not refer to it in their statement. However, the TCC Judges are generally sympathetic to the submission that it is not necessary that extensive review of the other parties' disclosure has taken place prior to the service of witness evidence. This is because their factual evidence should not be a commentary on the other side's internal documents which, by definition, they did not see at the time and cannot give factual evidence about. Such documentation should be deployed in cross-examination, rather than discussed by factual witnesses in what would effectively be opinion, speculation or submission.

2.30 In relation to supplemental witness evidence, the general approach by the TCC is that a witness should set out in their witness statement their complete evidence relevant to the issues in the case and should not include evidence on the basis that it might be needed depending on what the other party's witnesses might say. The purpose of a supplemental witness statement is not to provide general commentary on the other side's evidence, but to identify particular matters contained in the other party's witness statement which require the provision of specific further factual evidence. It is often the approach of the TCC Judges, therefore, not to include an order for responsive or supplemental witness evidence in the first set of directions, but to allow the parties liberty to apply for supplemental evidence should the need arise.

Expert evidence

2.31 A feature of litigation in the TCC is that most cases involve some form of expert evidence. The TCC usually thinks in terms of three broad categories of expert: technical or scientific experts, such as engineers (civil, structural, chemical, process, marine, IT, etc.) and architects or designers; 'planning' or 'programming' experts, in the context of delay cases, and experts relating to quantum (usually quantity surveying, but sometimes valuation or forensic accounting, evidence). Clearly, in some cases, there will be an overlap in expertise: in a valuer's negligence case, for example, the liability and quantum expert might well be combined; similarly, it is sometimes the case that experts in project management cases may be able to give evidence relating to planning or programming.

2.32 In lower value cases, the Court will give active consideration to whether experts ought to be appointed jointly by the parties; and it may be that this is considered for some but not all of the expert evidence (for example, parties can instruct individual technical experts on the question of liability, but a single joint expert for quantum; or it may be that the defendants jointly instruct a quantum expert). There is no right answer: the Court will take a view balancing proportionality with the 'right' of a party to call such evidence as it considers appropriate. As noted in the TCC Guide, there is an inevitable tension arising from the need for parties to instruct and rely on expert opinions from an early pre-action stage and the need for the Court to seek, wherever possible, to reduce the cost of expert evidence by dispensing with it altogether or by encouraging the appointment of jointly instructed experts. This is because the Court can only consider directing joint appointments or limiting expert evidence long after a party may have incurred the cost of obtaining expert evidence and has already relied on it. The Court, therefore, understands that the introduction of a single joint expert following a pre-action stage may, in fact, increase rather than decrease costs; however, it will have expected the parties to consider constructively what approach may be best.

2.33 The usual procedure for a single joint expert will involve the preparation of the expert's instructions. These instructions should clearly identify those issues or matters where the parties are in conflict, whether on the facts or on matters of opinion. If the parties can agree joint instructions, then a single set of instructions should be delivered to the expert. However, rule 35.8 expressly permits separate instructions and these are necessary where joint instructions cannot be agreed. The parties should also agree a bundle of the relevant material to be provided. After the expert has prepared a written report, there should be a procedure by which the parties can provide any written questions, which must be answered in writing. It will often be the case that the single joint expert's report, supplemented by any written answers to questions from the parties, will be sufficient for the purposes of the trial. However, parties will be entitled (subject to the view of the Court) to require an expert to attend to give oral evidence and be cross-examined. The TCC Guide notes that cross-examination 'should be conducted with appropriate restraint', since the witness has been instructed by the parties. While it is unlikely that allegations of absence of independence are unlikely to get an advocate very far where an expert has been jointly instructed, it may obviously still be the case that views have been unsatisfactorily arrived at or substantiated, and the Court will allow such views to be tested robustly in the usual way.

2.34 It is usual that, where each party is entitled to an expert of a particular discipline, those experts will be required to undertake discussions and produce a statement of matters agreed and not agreed. The standard (but not obligatory) approach of the TCC is that joint statements should be served in advance of the experts' unilateral reports.[14] This is generally regarded (at least by those practising regularly in the TCC) as helping to define issues sooner and to avoid unnecessarily lengthy reports in which both experts in fact then cover much of the same common ground. By contrast, the standard approach in the Commercial Court is the opposite: for experts to produce their own reports first and then meet to narrow the differences. It may be that, in fact, there are advantages and disadvantages for different disciplines to adopt different approaches, although this leads to a more complex set of directions. For instance, there is usually a considerable advantage gained from early meetings of the programming experts, who can identify, for example, the appropriate (or at least competing) baseline programmes, and often an as-built programme and critical path. They can discuss and agree methodology. This makes it much less likely that the reports will end up being ships passing in the night. By contrast, technical experts dealing with a specific defect may have little to agree upon and the exercise of trying to accommodate agreement at an early stage, prior to report writing, can increase costs unnecessarily without bringing a particular advantage to the litigation. The parties should also give consideration, if the overall timetable allows, to whether some disciplines ought to serve their evidence after seeing the reports of others. Most obviously, for example, there might be sense in quantum

---

14 See the brief comment of Coulson J (as he then was) in *CIP Properties* (n 10) at [5].

experts serving their evidence after having seen the technical experts' evidence dealing with competing remedial schemes.

2.35 Particular cooperation will be expected from the parties' experts where tests, surveys, investigations, sample gathering or other technical methods of obtaining primary factual evidence are needed. Parties' experts will be expected to ensure that any laboratory testing or experiments are carried out jointly, pursuant to an agreed procedure, or by an independent laboratory on behalf of all parties.

2.36 The experts will ordinarily meet and conduct their discussions for the purposes of a joint report in the absence of the parties or their legal advisers. While it is appropriate for the legal team to give guidance in terms of the 'agenda' for the experts (i.e. to help identify what is or is not an expert issue for consideration), it is inappropriate for lawyers to be involved in the drafting of the joint expert report or to dictate what the experts can or cannot say. The TCC notes that legal advisers should only invite the experts to consider amending any draft joint statement in exceptional circumstances where there are serious concerns that the Court may misunderstand or be misled by the terms of the joint statement. The difficulty which can arise in practice is, in light of the without-prejudice nature of discussions and the effect of privilege, it is difficult to police, but egregious interference by legal advisers will be taken seriously by the Court should it be necessary to raise concerns.

2.37 It is routine for parties to disclose initial or preliminary reports at the pre-action stage. In a professional negligence action, it is essential for the credibility of a claiming party that a report supporting the allegation of negligence exists prior to commencing proceedings. Indeed, in the majority of cases (although not every case), it would be regarded as inappropriate for a party to launch professional negligence proceedings without the support of an expert prepared to explain why the defendant's conduct had fallen below the relevant standard.

2.38 Recent cases in the TCC have also sought to prevent or discourage what is known as 'expert shopping'. The expression describes the situation in which a party obtains the opinion from one expert which it regards as unfavourable and thus does not wish to put such opinion in evidence, and then obtains the opinion from a second expert, which is favourable, and which it therefore does wish to put in evidence. In *Coyne v Morgan*,[15] the TCC Judge considered the relevant authorities and set out the following principles:

- The Court has a wide and general power to exercise its discretion whether to impose terms when granting permission to a party to adduce expert opinion evidence.
- In exercising that power or discretion, the Court may give permission for a party to rely on a second replacement expert, but such power or discretion is usually exercised on condition that the report of the first expert is disclosed: see Dyson LJ at paragraphs 27 and 29 of his judgment in *Vasiliou v Hajigeorgiou*.[16]
- Once the parties have engaged in a relevant Pre-Action Protocol process, and an expert has prepared a report in the context of such process, that expert then owes

---

15 [2016] 166 Con LR 114.
16 [2005] 1 WLR 2195. Cf. *Vilca v Xstrata Ltd* [2017] BLR 460, where Stuart-Smith J held that there was no need to order that the first report be disclosed in circumstances where the first expert had to be replaced because she had fallen ill and withdrawn from the case.

a duty to the Court irrespective of his or her instruction by one of the parties, and accordingly there is no justification for not disclosing such a report: see Hughes LJ at paragraph 30 of his judgment in *Edwards-Tubb v JD Weatherspoon Plc*.[17]

- While the Court discourages the practice of 'expert shopping', the Court's power to exercise its discretion whether to impose terms when giving permission to a party to adduce expert opinion evidence arises irrespective of the occurrence of any 'expert shopping'. It is a power to be exercised reasonably on a case-by-case basis, in each case having regard to all the circumstances of that particular case. The fact that an expert had produced a report in the course or context of a relevant Pre-Action Protocol process was likely to be a critical or decisive factor, rather than there having been any instance of 'expert shopping'.
- The Court will require strong evidence of 'expert shopping' before imposing a term that a party discloses other forms of document than the report of the first expert (such as attendance notes and memoranda made by a party's solicitor of his or her discussions with the first expert) as a condition of giving permission to rely on the second expert: see paragraphs 29 to 32 of the judgment of Edwards-Stuart J in *BMG (Mansfield) Ltd v Galford Try Construction Ltd*.[18]

2.39 It therefore follows that it will normally be the case that permission to rely upon a second appointed expert will only be given on the basis that any report provided by the first is disclosed, irrespective of the circumstances in which the second expert comes to be instructed. Only where there is 'expert shopping' will wider disclosure of other material, which otherwise would be privileged, be required to be disclosed.

The Pre-Trial Review

2.40 The PTR is usually held after the last procedural direction and four to six weeks before the trial itself. The TCC will expect it to be attended by trial advocates. The purpose of the PTR is to consider any outstanding directions needed for trial, identify the issues that will be decided at trial and consider any matters relevant to the efficient management of the hearing. If not agreed or already directed, this will include matters relating to the bundle, any reading time and a pre-trial reading list for the Court, the length and timing of any written and/or oral opening submissions, the need for a site visit, the order of witnesses and a draft timetable for the trial, any issues relating to the allocation of time between the parties and any particular requirements for the giving of evidence (for example, video conferencing or translators).

The trial

2.41 In the standard TCC case, the Court will expect written opening submissions in advance of the hearing, referenced into the agreed bundle.

2.42 The bundle will ordinarily consist of the pleadings, contract documents, witness statements, expert reports and usually a chronological bundle of relevant project

---
17 [2011] 1 WLR 1373.
18 [2013] EWHC 3183 (TCC).

correspondence, other minutes or reports, relevant drawings or technical documents or specifications, and quantum documents. The extent to which all of the documentation is necessary to be available in hard copy will depend on the amount of documentation and the issues in the case, but it is increasingly common for the trial bundle to be a hybrid of hard copy and electronic files. To the extent that parts of the electronic bundle are to be referred to, either hard-copy extracts can be provided or documents viewed on a document management system. The bundle should be sensibly paginated: usually each category of documents is given a separate file name (for example, A, B1, B2, C, etc) and pagination runs numerically within each category.

2.43 The opening should provide a pre-reading list for the Court, and then summarise the parties' positions in relation to the key issues (ideally, by reference to an agreed list of issues). The TCC Guide indicates that the openings should be of modest length and proportionate to the size and complexity of the case.

2.44 Many trials in the TCC, and almost all longer trials, are conducted with simultaneous transcripts of the evidence being provided: this involves 'live' transcription onto screens situated in Court and a cleaned transcript provided shortly after the end of each day of the hearing. While an added expense to the parties, the TCC regards simultaneous transcription as helpful in long trials or those which involve any significant amount of detailed or technical evidence. A principal advantage noted by the TCC Guide is that these services enable all but the shortest trials to be conducted so as to reduce the overall length of the trial appreciably, since the Judge does not have to note the evidence or submissions in longhand as the trial proceeds. This ultimately, therefore, produces a cost saving to the parties. The existence of transcripts is also likely to reduce the judgment writing time and the risk of errors in the judgment.

2.45 Given the existence of written opening documents, the Court will anticipate relatively short oral openings, even in the most lengthy and complex cases (for example, half a day or at most a day for each party), prior to the evidence. The standard procedure is for all factual evidence to be called first: the claimant's witnesses and then the defendants, and then the expert evidence by discipline (for example, the claimant's engineer and then the defendant's engineer; followed by other disciplines in the same way).

2.46 The time available to the parties during a hearing is allocated fairly between the parties: however, this does not necessarily mean a precisely equal allocation of time. The TCC is flexible in its approach and there may be numerous reasons to depart from an even split of time. One party may have many more issues or rely on witnesses giving evidence through translation (which inevitably slows cross-examination down). Indeed, the TCC Guide notes that 'usually' the allocation of time to account for the particular circumstances of a given case will not result in an equal split. The Court will rarely impose strict guillotines by way of time for particular witnesses, but will have in mind the need for fairness in requiring all parties to keep to their allocated time. Sometimes, by agreement, the parties adopt a strict 'chess-clock' arrangement, based upon an equal split of time which the parties can use for submissions, examination, cross-examination or re-examination as they see fit.

2.47 In the TCC, witnesses' statements (or, in the case of expert witnesses, their reports) stand as their evidence in chief. While it may be that few additional questions might be asked in chief, this requires the permission of the Judge. This is usually permissible if the questions relate to matters relevant to the witnesses' evidence which have come up during the course of the trial. Generally, however, after attesting to the truth of the facts (or opinions), the witness is subject to cross-examination. In English Courts, the coaching of witnesses or the suggestion of answers that may be given, either in the preparation of witness statements or before a witness starts to give evidence, is not permitted. 'Witness familiarisation' is permissible, but coaching is not. Familiarisation is the process of helping witnesses understand in advance what will be expected of them, for example with the layout of the Court, the likely sequence of events when the witness is giving evidence and a balanced appraisal of the different responsibilities of the various participants.[19] The Professional Standards Committee of the Bar Council has provided guidance which makes clear that it is also appropriate, as part of a witness familiarisation process, for advocates to advise witnesses as to the basic requirements for giving evidence (for example, the need to listen to and answer the question put, to speak clearly and slowly in order to ensure that the Court hears what the witness is saying, and to avoid irrelevant comments). This is consistent with a duty to the Court to ensure that the client's case is presented clearly and without undue waste of the Court's time. Of particular relevance to litigation in the TCC is that expert witnesses, and witnesses who are to give evidence of a technical nature, can be given guidance about the need to give comprehensive and comprehensible evidence of a specialist kind to a Judge, and to resist the pressure to go further in evidence than matters covered by the witnesses' specific expertise. However, great care must be taken not to do or say anything which could be interpreted as manufacturing or in any way influencing the content of the evidence that the expert is to give in the witness box. It is also key that in any witness familiarisation process (which may give witnesses a taste of giving evidence in a mock trial), none of the material should bear any similarity whatsoever to the issues in the proceedings to be attended by the witnesses.

2.48 It is increasingly common for experts to give evidence concurrently. This is called 'hot-tubbing'. It is particularly effective for quantum evidence if there are a relatively small number of remaining issues of principle, which can be explored by the parties and the Court on an issue-by-issue basis. There is no set rule as to how concurrent evidence should proceed, but it is usually essential for an efficient session that the parties, or maybe the experts themselves, produce an agenda. The experts can briefly explain their competing positions on the particular point, counsel can ask questions and the Judge can ask questions, to either or both of the experts.

2.49 The timing and form of closing submissions is generally discussed and agreed during the trial. It may take the form of written closings, oral closings or a combination of the two, with oral submissions supplementing and following written submission. Again, the Court will generally find it of use if the parties prepare closings by reference to an agreed list of issues. The TCC Judges are active in managing the process, sometimes identifying a draft structure of the prospective judgment, discussing with counsel and seeking closing submissions in a form which follows the anticipated judgment structure.

Judgment

2.50 Judgments in very short or straightforward matters might be given orally following the close of the case. It is, however, much more usual for the TCC Judges to provide written

---

19 See the discussion of the boundary between these in *R v Momodou* [2005] EWCA Crim 177 at [61]-[62].

judgments some time after the hearing and closing submissions. If judgment is reserved in this way, it is ordinarily provided first in draft form, and the parties are invited to provide corrections of a typographical rather than substantive nature. Save in exceptional circumstances, the TCC Guide indicates that reserved judgments will be handed down within three months of the trial's conclusion.

Appeal

2.51 A party requires permission to appeal a decision of a TCC Judge to the Court of Appeal. That permission may be granted by the Judge themselves following an application, usually on handing down of judgment. If the Judge thinks that the arguments are relatively finely balanced and the question is one of particular importance in the industry, he or she may recognise that permission should be granted. However, more often than not, the Judge at first instance will refuse the application for permission to appeal and leave it to the party or parties to seek permission from the Court of Appeal.

2.52 The Court of Appeal has held that decisions of the TCC have special characteristics which affect the readiness of the Court of Appeal to reconsider them on appeal. Firstly, the findings of fact often fall within an area of specialist expertise, where the evidence is technical in nature and given by experienced experts. This is the sort of evidence which TCC Judges are familiar with and well placed to assess; secondly, the conclusions of fact will involve weighing a number of different factors and which are often a matter of degree; and, thirdly, decisions may deal with factual minutiae not easily susceptible to reconsideration on appeal. The burden, therefore, on a party applying to the Court of Appeal for permission to appeal from a TCC decision on questions of fact will be hard to discharge. The more complicated and technical the case, the harder that burden is.[20]

---

20 See *Skanska Construction UK Ltd v Egger (Barony) Ltd* [2002] EWCA Civ 1914; *Yorkshire Water Services Ltd v Taylor Woodrow Construction Northern Ltd* [2005] EWCA 894.

CHAPTER 3

Evidence

Introduction

3.1 This chapter deals with general guidance as to the deployment of evidence in TCC litigation. It should be read in conjunction with the more specific advice given in the chapters dedicated to a certain type of claim, such as defects or delay, and, of course, to the requirements of the CPR and the TCC Guide.

3.2 The principle which underlies all this advice is that all evidence in the case should be deployed in the way which makes the task of understanding the issues and deciding the case as easy as possible for the Judge. This is because evidence which is readily comprehensible and sensibly structured is more persuasive.

3.3 Advice on dealing with disclosure is outside the scope of this book. Practitioners should refer to the White Book and to the outcome of the pilot scheme trialling (at the time of writing) the draft Practice Direction for disclosure for the Business and Property Courts.[1]

Witness statements

Number of witnesses

3.4 The first issue to consider in relation to witnesses is how many are needed, and who should you choose from the client's team.

3.5 The first task is always to analyse what the issues in the case are and, in relation to each issue, whether it is a matter of factual dispute or opinion evidence. It is necessary to go through the pleadings carefully to identify the factual disputes which will require a factual witness to speak to them. In principle, factual evidence from a witness should not be adduced in relation to issues which turn solely on expert evidence.[2] Ideally, the person at the client who has the most direct knowledge of the particular issue will be the person who gives evidence on it.

3.6 Often, several individuals at the client have personal knowledge both generally as to what happened on the project and as to specific issues. Whether only one person gives evidence on a particular issue or more than one will depend on the following factors:

– What is the nature of the issue? If it is a case of telling an overall story of the project, it is likely that one person (ideally in a project management role in which it would have been their job to have an overall view) should give that evidence. If the issue relates to a disputed oral agreement at a meeting attended by more

---
1 See https://www.judiciary.gov.uk/wp-content/uploads/2017/11/draft-practice-direction-2-nov-2017.pdf.
2 See further discussion below.

than one individual, it may be important for everyone who was there to give their evidence as to what happened.
- The number of persons giving evidence about an issue will also be affected by the importance of the issue. It is frequently the case that there are multitudes of minor disagreements as to what happened; it is rare that these are determinative of the case. The focus of the evidence should be directed at issues which will be key to the Judge's decision.
- The Judge will not decide the case on the basis that one side had four witnesses giving evidence on a particular issue and the other side had two. More is not necessarily better; clarity and consistency is more persuasive than mere repetition. Further, multiple witnesses giving the same evidence can give the impression of a party line.
- If more than one witness gives evidence on the same issue, there is an advantage in that the issue is not dependent on the evidence of one person who might be seriously undermined in cross-examination. Further witnesses may provide a second chance. There is also a disadvantage in that the more witnesses called, the greater the chance of duplication (tiresome and unpersuasive for the Judge) and inconsistencies (damaging for the credibility of all relevant witnesses and damaging to the claim), particularly during cross-examination.

3.7 The experience of the editors is that as a very general rule it is better to call the minimum necessary number of factual witnesses required to prove the claim.

'Expert' factual witnesses

3.8 In some cases, the distinction between a factual and expert issue will not be wholly clear. In TCC litigation, it is often the case that a technical issue is in dispute, about which members of the project team took decisions during the course of the works, based on their own expertise as engineer or other qualification. In a professional negligence case, the professional in question will have evidence to give as to why and on what basis he or she took the decisions they did at the time.

3.9 The Court of Appeal held in *Lusty v Finsbury Securites Ltd*[3] that an architect suing for fees could give opinion evidence as to the value of his work. In *DN v LB Greenwich*[4], the Court of Appeal considered the position of the defendant professional in a professional negligence action giving evidence as to his own actions. Brooke LJ said:

> 25. It very often happens in professional negligence cases that a defendant will give evidence to a judge which constitutes the reason why he considers that his conduct did not fall below the standard of care reasonably to be expected of him. He may do this by reference to the professional literature that was reasonably available to him as a busy practitioner or be reference to reasonable limits of his professional experience; or he may seek to rebut, as one professional man against another, the criticisms made of him by the claimant's expert(s). Such evidence is common, and it is certainly admissible. Mr Phillips, who appeared for the claimant at the trial, did not believe he had told the judge that Mr Moreland's evidence on matters of this kind was

---
3 (1991) 58 BLR 66.
4 [2004] EWCA Civ 1569.

inadmissible, and neither of the very experienced leading counsel who appeared in this counsel who appeared in this Court was willing to support the judge's view of the matter.

26. Of course a defendant's evidence on matters of this kind may lack the objectivity to be accorded to the evidence of an independent expert, but this consideration goes to the cogency of the evidence, not to its admissibility. That such evidence was in principle admissible should have been reasonably apparent from the judgments in this Court in *ES v Chesterfield and North Derbyshire Royal Hospital NHS Trust* [2003] EWCA Civ 1284 at [24], [31]–[32] and [41], [2004] Lloyd's Rep Med 90.

3.10 The issue arose again in *Multiplex Constructions (UK) Ltd v Cleveland Bridge UK Ltd*,[5] in which the admissibility of the factual witness statement of an engineer (who had been part of CBUK's design subcontractor's project team) was challenged. The statement dealt in detail with allegations of negligence in relation to the design of the Wembley roof, with which the engineer had personal involvement. As Mr Justice Jackson held at [666], the engineer was 'a factual witness who (a) is possessed of considerable engineering expertise and (b) has personal knowledge of the roof design and erection engineering decisions which were made in [the relevant period]'.

3.11 The Judge reviewed the authorities and concluded that:

> 671. As a matter of practice in the TCC, technical and expert opinions are frequently expressed by factual witnesses in the course of their narrative evidence without objection being taken. Such opinion evidence does not have the same standing as the evidence of independent experts who are called pursuant to CPR rule 35. However, such evidence is usually valuable and it often leads to considerable saving of costs.
>
> 672. Having regard to the guidance of the Court of Appeal and the established practice in TCC cases, I conclude that in construction litigation an engineer who is giving factual evidence may also proffer (a) statements of opinion which are reasonably related to the facts within his knowledge and (b) relevant comments based upon his own experience. For example, an engineer after describing the foundation system which he designed may (and in practice frequently does) go on to explain why he believes that this was appropriate to the known ground conditions. Or an engineer brought in by a claimant to design remedial works (which are subsequently challenged as excessive) may refer to his experience of rectifying comparable building failures in the past. For example, such evidence may be given in cases about concrete failure through ASR (a world wide problem).

3.12 It follows that factual witnesses in the TCC will often give opinion evidence. It is important that such witnesses confine themselves to the points on which their opinion is relevant within the guidance given in the authorities and do not seek to argue the case (see further below).

Taking and structuring witness statements

3.13 The first steps in taking a witness statement should be done before speaking to the relevant witness. It is necessary clearly to identify the issues which the relevant witness will be speaking to and the nature of the dispute relevant to that issue. The lawyer should then obtain and familiarise themselves with all the relevant contemporaneous documents. Any points arising out of the contemporaneous documents which are either consistent with

---

5 [2008] EWHC 2220 (TCC) at [657]-[676], not challenged on appeal.

or, in particular, inconsistent with those parts of the client's case which the particular witness is speaking to should be identified.

3.14 At the meeting with the witness, each issue should be dealt with in turn, and the witness should have the opportunity to review all the documents either during the interview or beforehand. It often makes sense to deal with the issues either in value order of the relevant claim, or (in particular if taking a delay/disruption statement[6]) in chronological order of events on the project, although naturally the focus should be on the bigger claims here too.

3.15 The statement itself should be structured in the same way, with clear headings and introductions to the issue to which the witness will speak. This can and should be done by way of references back to the pleadings by saying, for example, 'I have been shown paragraphs x to y of the Defence . . .'.

3.16 In many cases, the dispute will have a contractual element as well as a factual one. It is, of course, not the function of the witnesses to discuss the contract. However, it is often the case in final account claims that entitlement to particular monies claimed (requiring factual proof of the claim) arises under a particular provision of the contract. Where there is a dispute as to this, this should be briefly acknowledged by the witness in the statement, but the witness should still identify the contractual head of claim (even if this is on the basis of a statement 'I am advised by my solicitors that the relevant clause of the contract here is . . .'). This is because it is necessary to link the factual evidence back to both the pleadings and the contract, so as to enable easy understanding of the issue to which the factual evidence goes. The need for this type of link was discussed by Coulson J (as he then was) in *HSM Offshore BV v Aker Offshore Partner Ltd*[7] at [167] to [170].

3.17 If the statement is lengthy, the editors' experience is that it is useful to have a table of contents. Once again, this is because it is essential to make the statement as easy as possible for the Judge to understand and navigate; comprehensible documents are more persuasive.

3.18 As much as possible of what the witness says should be tied back to the relevant contemporaneous documents. This is because:

– Generally speaking, contemporaneous documents are likely to be treated by the Judge as a more reliable record of what the parties thought and said at the time than the witnesses' recollection of events (that often took place years before). There might, of course, be particular circumstances where this is not the case, but it would be necessary to explain why there is a problem with a particular contemporaneous document. Ignoring the issue will not help.
– Where a witness has referred to a document in his or her statement, it is more difficult for the person carrying out the cross-examination not to refer to that document during the cross-examination. In this way, the witness is provided with a reminder of what was actually happening at the time and a reminder of the reason for his or her comments in the statement.

---

6 See further Chapter 4
7 [2017] EWHC 2979 (TCC); 175 Con LR 155.

3.19 It is important not to misrepresent documents in a witness statement. Common mistakes, which make for easy cross-examination and at the very least may help undermine the credibility of the witness, are to refer to only part of a document or to refer to only one letter or email in a series, in circumstances where the picture given by the whole is different from that created by only a part. The lawyer taking the statement should have checked the whole chain/context, because sometimes witnesses who are telling the truth as they believe it to be have convinced themselves that the partial picture is the accurate one.

3.20 It is, however, key that the statement is not simply a recital of the correspondence; in particular, it should not consist of quotations from the letters except where this is absolutely necessary to a particular point being made. A series of quotations from the documents do not amount to a witness statement and will not be persuasive to the Judge.

3.21 If there is a difficult point (such as a mistake in the pleadings, especially where the pleadings have been drafted with the assistance of that witness, or where the documents are inconsistent with what the witness is saying), this should usually be dealt with head on in the witness statement. It should be assumed that the other side will, by the time of the trial, have spotted the problem even if they have not yet. Often, a witness statement is silent on quite obvious difficulties, which again provides the cross-examiner with an easy way in to undermine the witness's credibility and sometimes their honesty. Where a witness frankly acknowledges the mistake or difficulty, and states his or her position on it, it is much harder for the cross-examiner to show that the witness is unreliable, and much harder to place damaging emphasis on the problem.

3.22 If two (or more) people are giving evidence about what was said at an important meeting, their evidence should be taken separately. The lawyers should not allow them to discuss what happened at the meeting with each other before their statements are signed. If there are inconsistencies between their accounts, these will either be minor and indicate to the Judge that the statements were not produced jointly (and therefore are overall more reliable) or they will be material, in which case it is better for the client that the problem is identified at witness statement stage rather than during cross-examination, and the appropriate advice can be given. Beware of taking a 'tactical' decision to remain silent in a statement on a difficult area with a view to settlement before trial. Absence of evidence on a particular issue is often as telling to the other side as an admission would have been, and in the worst case scenario settlement cannot be achieved and the case ends up at trial with a damagingly partial statement.

3.23 The statement should not include submissions/arguments on the case, or criticisms of the other side's case/behaviour save insofar as absolutely necessary in relation to a disputed factual issue. Witnesses often feel angry and resentful. It is difficult not to take disputes personally. It is, however, necessary to make the statement as calm and as neutral as possible, because emotion is not persuasive. Witnesses generally understand this when it is explained to them, and in any case if necessary the statement can start or end with a paragraph setting out the witness's shock or disappointment on any particular point. This gets the witness's feeling across without undermining the credibility of everything else they have to say.

EVIDENCE

Sequence of calling witnesses

3.24 It is necessary to decide the order in which the client's factual witnesses will be called at the trial. Again, there is no set rule. The key factors to be weighed in the balance are as follows:

- It is desirable to call someone expected to be a 'good' witness (calm, clear, good memory, good knowledge) first and last, so as to start and end with a good impression on the Judge. Note that first and last can refer to a group of witnesses dealing with particular issues such as liability and is not limited simply to first and last out of all the witnesses.
- Witnesses dealing with major issues in the case should be called first, or in a group relating to that issue. This makes it easier for the Judge to understand the evidence that is being given.
- If seeing the case through a particular lens or understanding a particular issue first would suit your client's case, that may be a reason to prioritise calling one witness dealing with that issue first/earlier than you otherwise might.
- However, there will be a logical legal order of issues (at the simplest level, liability first and quantum last) which will make the case easier to understand for the Judge and this should also be taken into account.

3.25 The aim, of course, is to present your client's case in the most attractive way possible within the bounds of also presenting it as clearly as possible.

Expert reports and joint statements

Do you need an independent expert?

3.26 Whether or not it is essential to instruct an independent expert (as opposed to relying on an employee or the client's consultant used to put together the claim) on an issue requiring opinion evidence depends on the nature of the issue and, in practical terms, the value of the claim. In some cases, it may be that the relevant expertise is very technical indeed with few individuals appropriately qualified to comment on the issue.

3.27 The Court has consistently taken the view that whether this is appropriate depends on the particular facts of the case:

- The Court of Appeal held in *Field v Leeds City Council* that it was not necessarily inappropriate to use an employee of one of the parties as an expert. While acknowledging the potential difficulties, Lord Justice Waller said that the test was 'whether, (i) it can be demonstrated whether that person has relevant expertise in an area in issue in the case; and (ii) that it can be demonstrated that he or she is aware of their primary duty to the court if they give expert evidence' (at [26]). The Commercial Court permitted a defendant to rely on the evidence of an employee in *Gallaher International Ltd v Tlais Enterprises Ltd*,[8] a case which includes a useful discussion of the relevant factors applicable to the decision.

---

8 [2017] EWHC 2979 (TCC); 175 Con LR 155.

- The same result applied to a party's consultant in *Meat Corp of Namibia Ltd v Dawn Meats (UK) Ltd*[9] and in *A Lloyd's Syndicate v X*.[10]
- Where there is a conflict of interest, again the outcome will depend on the particular facts of the case.[11]

3.28 If an expert is used who has a connection with the client, it is essential that full disclosure is given, and as early as possible so that if necessary the issue can be discussed in the course of case management. The connection should also be recorded in the report.[12]

3.29 Any employee or client consultant expert can expect to be cross-examined on whether he or she has been able to approach the issues independently, and consistently with their duty to the Court, given the connection with the client. This inevitably introduces an element of weakness into the case. The closer the connection or relationship, and a fortiori if there is a conflict of interest, the higher the risk that the evidence will be rejected at the trial, or the weight to be given to the evidence will be fatally undermined.

3.30 If the case is high value and/or complex, it is very likely that the client is best advised to retain an independent expert.

3.31 A different question arises in relation to delay experts. Causation of delay is a question of fact, not a question of opinion at all.[13] There have been commentators who suggest that a delay expert report is not only unnecessary, but in fact inadmissible in its common form of a detailed review of factual matters.[14] In the editors' experience:

- The factual delay story can and should be told via the factual witness statements. This is the appropriate place for it given that causation is an issue of fact.
- Delay experts can give useful and properly expert evidence on:
    o The critical path. However, this will be based (in a retrospective critical path) on the facts of what actually happened, and so their conclusions will necessarily be dependent on the facts as established at the trial.
    o The periods of time when project delay occurred (whether on a prospective or retrospective basis).
- The delay expert should also review factual matters, including the contemporaneous documents relevant to his or her conclusions, and this can be a convenient way of introducing the story to the Judge. However, if the factual story of the project is only to be found in the delay expert's report, that party risks having its entire case undermined via the cross-examination of the factual witnesses, before any challenge has to be made to the expert at all.

---

9 [2007] EWHC 464 (Comm).
10 [2011] EWHC 2487 (Comm).
11 *Toth v Jarman* [2006] EWCA Civ 1028.
12 See, for example, *Rowley v Dunlop* [2014] EWHC 2763 (Ch); *Armchair Passenger Transport Ltd v Helical Barr Plc* [2003] EWHC 367 (QB); and *Thefaut v Johnston* [2017] EWHC 497 (QB).
13 See the observations of Jefford J as to the (ir)relevance the programming expertise in straight forward delay case in Castle Trustee Ltd v Bombay Palace [2018] EWHC 1602.
14 See, for example, the comments of Coulson J (as he then was) in *Van Oord UK Ltd v Allseas UK Ltd* [2015] EWHC 3074 (TCC) at [77].

3.32 Delay analysis, including the use of electronic programmes, is discussed in more detail in Chapter 4.

Choosing an expert

3.33 It should go without saying that an expert should have the appropriate technical expertise to comment on the relevant issue. Surprisingly frequently, chemists are instructed to comment on matters of civil engineering, and naval architects on issues of onshore planning.

3.34 It is also often useful if the expert has both practical and academic experience of the particular issue. In construction cases, there are usually questions of what is practical to do in particular circumstances, as well as what is strictly speaking technically possible, and it is advantageous if the expert has project experience. This is particularly important for a delay/planning expert.

3.35 Other factors to look out for are:

- Experience in giving evidence and in particular being cross-examined.
- Whether the expert has sufficient availability for the case. Very well established experts, who are in demand, sometimes do not have time to spend on all matters on which they are retained, and the bulk of the work is done by members of their team. This is not necessarily a fatal problem, but means that the client is not in fact getting the personal experience of the named expert, and it can mean that the expert is not sufficiently familiar with the claim both at report stage and at trial.
- Whether the expert has a proactive, can-do attitude and will take responsibility for asking for missing information as he or she investigates the case. It is obviously unhelpful for the practitioner to receive a draft report a week before the deadline which identifies tracts of missing documentation which were readily available on request.
- Reputation among other lawyers with direct experience of that expert.

Preparing your expert

3.36 To get the best out of your expert, it is necessary for the lawyer to issue clear instructions and provide all relevant background information. This involves a similar process to taking a witness statement, in that the starting point is the pleaded issues and relevant aspects of the contract. Clear instructions should be provided, listing the issues on which the expert is asked to opine (but remembering that the instructions, if not included within the report, may well be disclosable in due course: see CPR Part 35.10(3)[15]). It is obviously necessary for your expert to have a complete picture, but beware the provision to the expert of privileged material, as part of the instructions may mean that privilege in that material is waived.

3.37 The issues should be listed in a logical order: for example, if an engineer is giving an opinion on a series of variations, this can either be done in order of the variation number or in order of value of variation claim, starting with the highest (as long as there is a contents page to the report so that either way a specific variation can easily be found). If the

---

15 'The expert's report must state the substance of all material instructions, whether written or oral, on the basis of which the report was written' (CPR 35.10(3)).

expert is opining on delay, the claims should always be considered in chronological order (failure to do this often indicates that the analysis is not based on the facts).

3.38 The legal team must ensure that the expert has in fact acted independently.[16] The expert needs to have reviewed both sides' relevant factual evidence, and where necessary needs to express a different view depending on which factual position is eventually found by the Judge to be correct. The expert must take into account and give proper weight to all the matters raised by the other side. There are a series of cases in which an expert who acted as a hired gun caused catastrophic damage at the trial to the client's case[17] – it is not an advantage in the long run to have an expert who supports the client's case without testing and questioning it.

3.39 In a larger case, it is sensible to have a meeting with the expert once he or she has had time to absorb the materials and form a preliminary view, so that their views can be discussed and any material facts which have been missed can be drawn to the expert's attention.

3.40 It is also a good idea to give the expert an understanding of where their evidence fits in the case as a whole and where it interrelates to other issues. Sometimes, experts unnecessarily give points away because they are unaware that the issue is significant.

3.41 The editors' experience is that it is necessary to get the experts started as early as possible. Deadlines for draft reports or chapters of reports should be imposed on an early and rolling basis.

Reports

3.42 It goes without saying that an expert's report must comply with CPR Part 35.

3.43 The report should be structured by reference to pleaded issues, with informative headings and introductions to particular issues summarising the dispute before discussing the issue, so that it is possible for the Judge to understand the context of the discussion (exactly as for witness statements). If the instructions have been sufficiently clear, it is likely that the report can follow the structure in the instructions. The report needs to provide a clear agenda or road map for the person reading it: clear and comprehensible documents are persuasive ones.

3.44 As for witness statements, in some cases, relevant terms of the contract may need to be identified either as context for the expert's opinion on a dispute, or in some cases such as valuation disputes the expert may well be giving his or her expert opinion on the practical application of the contractual rule.

3.45 It is essential that technical evidence is comprehensible to a lay person with no understanding of the issues: this is the position that the Judge will be in. Experts, especially if they work in very specialised fields, tend to assume a significant amount of knowledge on the part of their audience. Matters which to them are obvious are often wholly opaque to the lay reader.

---

16 The duties of an independent expert are set out in the well-known passages of the judgment in *The Ikarian Reefer* [2000] 1 WLR 603. In the recent case of *ICI v Merit* [2018] EWHC 1577 (TCC), Fraser J had some stinging criticisms for one party's expert witnesses and suggested that there is an increasing (and problematic) trend for partisan experts in the TCC: "It is a matter of concern that in a TCC case, with the sums at stake exceeding 10 million, there should be such a preponderance of partisan experts, all called by the same party". See also the Jefford J' criticism of the programming evidence in Castle Trustee Ltd v Bombay Palace [2018] EWHC 1602, questioning the need for any such evidence at all.

17 *Van Oord UK Ltd v Allseas UK Ltd* [2015] EWHC 3074 (TCC) at [80]ff; *Great Eastern Hotel Co Ltd v John Laing Construction Ltd* [2005] EWHC 181 at [66], [111], [128], [184]–[185]; *McAlpine v Humberoak* (1992) 58 BLR 1 at 28.

3.46 It is the job of the legal team to ensure that technical matters are fully and clearly explained. The legal team must have the confidence to state when they don't understand: if the lawyers don't understand, the likelihood is that the Judge won't either (or the position being put forward is wrong – equally important to know). An incomprehensible technical report is useless in putting forward the client's case. The editors generally advise their experts to seek to make their reports comprehensible to an intelligent 11-year-old.[18] Usually, the first draft produced even on this basis requires further work to ensure it can be understood.

3.47 A contents page is essential in an expert report.

Joint statements and expert meetings

3.48 The TCC approach is to order joint statements prior to expert reports, with reports limited to matters in dispute in the joint statements. This is the opposite way round to the Commercial Court, which generally orders reports, reply reports and then joint statements. A Judge will, however, be used to the approach of his or her particular Court and will be unlikely to be persuaded to make a different order than the 'usual' in the absence of very specific circumstances. In the editors' experience, each method has advantages and disadvantages and it is not a matter which is of particular importance either way.

3.49 Before the expert attends any meetings with his or her opposite number, it is essential that he or she is well briefed both on the substance of the subject matter of the report and as to the position in the litigation. It assists the expert if the lawyers can advise as to any particular strategy the other side are trying to implement, so that the expert is aware of the reasons behind particular actions and can if necessary hold the line (for example, where the other side are trying to delay matters, it is important that your expert is aware of this and chases up for responses appropriately).

3.50 It is not appropriate, and rarely beneficial, for the lawyers to seek to provide draft joint statements for discussion by the experts. However, it is often useful for the legal team to review a draft provided by the expert (or the other side's expert) to ensure that all relevant points have been covered and/or that there are no basic mistakes in the text.

3.51 There are sometimes disputes as to what can and cannot be said in a joint statement. The essential rule is that either expert can say anything they like. A debate as to whether the other side's expert is 'allowed' to include any particular matter in the joint statement is usually a waste of time; if what the other expert says is wrong, or irrelevant, or too lengthy, or omits some relevant information, then these points can be explored in cross-examination, if necessary. Indeed, sometimes an obviously unhelpful or argumentative approach by the other side's expert in a joint report can show the expert as partisan. All that matters is that your client's expert has clearly expressed his or her opinion on the relevant points.

3.52 This opinion should be expressed as shortly as possible. The purpose of the joint statement is to record where the experts agree, where they disagree and very briefly the reasons for the disagreement. The function is not to repeat all the matters that have been/will be canvassed in the reports, but to narrow the issues where possible and clearly identify them where not possible. It is sensible to advise your expert not to be drawn in to lengthy back-and-forth exchanges recorded in the draft joint statement; it is not necessary for the client's expert to have the last word.

---

18 And acknowledge their debt to Adrian Williamson QC for this useful formula.

3.53 The focus of the lawyers should be on seeking to ensure that the joint statement is a useful document for the Judge, without, of course, interfering in the process of discussion/agreement between the experts.

Evidence at trial

3.54 Expert evidence will be given after the factual evidence has been heard, and usually the approach taken is that the claimant's and defendant's experts give evidence in pairs by discipline. Usually, the general sequence is for technical/liability experts to give evidence first, followed by delay experts, followed lastly by the quantum experts (which reflects the sequence liability, causation, quantum).

3.55 It is often useful for the experts to agree relevant photographs, plans or models which can then be either explained in oral opening submissions by one of the parties, or explained jointly by the experts directly to the Judge at an appropriate point of the trial in a pre-agreed format/script. This type of general introduction to the technical issues can save a significant amount of time at the trial, and is often essential to the advocate in efficiently presenting the client's case. Consideration should be given to the production and agreement of suitable materials in the lead up to the PTR, if not earlier.

3.56 The TCC Guide requires the parties to consider with the Court at the PTR whether any of the experts should give evidence simultaneously, colloquially referred to as 'hot-tubbing'. The Guide states at paragraph 13.8.2:

> When this method is adopted there is generally a need for experts to be cross-examined on general matters and key issues before they are invited to give evidence concurrently on particular issues. Procedures vary but, for instance, a party may ask its expert to explain his or her view on an issue, then ask the other party's expert for his or her view and then return to that party's expert for a comment on that view. Alternatively, or in addition, questions may be asked by the judge or the experts themselves may each ask the other questions. The process is often most useful where there are a large number of items to be dealt with and the procedure allows the Court to have the evidence on each item dealt with on the same occasion rather than having the evidence divided with the inability to have each expert's views expressed clearly. Frequently, it allows the extent of agreement and reason for disagreement to be seen more clearly. The giving of concurrent evidence may be consented to by the parties and the judge will consider whether, in the absence of consent, any modification is required to the procedure for giving concurrent evidence set out in the CPR (at PD 35, paragraph 11).

3.57 In terms of tactical considerations, the editors' experience is as follows:

- Hot-tubbing carries with it some significant risk, because there is much less control by the advocate over the answers given by the expert. This means that the other side's expert may well be able to gloss over difficulties or place emphasis elsewhere in a way that is significantly more difficult in cross-examination.
- Hot-tubbing requires a significant amount of preparation by the Court if it is to be useful, because by its nature there is no or hardly any lead up to the discussion of the particular issue in the way that there is in a cross-examination. This is likely the reason that the TCC Guide prefers that there is some cross-examination on key issues prior to any hot-tubbing.
- It is most useful in relation to quantum evidence where there are a series of variation or other payment claims involving multiple small issues, or similarly where

there are multiple minor defects claims, as the Court can then hear each side's points on each issue at the same time and quickly. However, even in these circumstances, the legal teams should endeavour to identify where the same or similar issues arise across multiple claims, so that where possible they can be dealt with in groups.

Documentary evidence

3.58 The presentation of the documentary evidence is often left to the last minute, badly done and therefore hard to use. This is a mistake: in order for the client's case to be presented persuasively whether in submissions or via cross-examination, it is essential that the hearing bundles are easy to use, well-structured and contain legible documents.

3.59 In the discussion below, it is assumed that practitioners will have turned first to the relevant Court Guides and/or Practice Directions which contain specific requirements for certain Courts and hearings.

3.60 The aim for any bundle is to reduce the number of documents before the Court to the minimum necessary for the relevant hearing.

Case Management Conference

3.61 The convenient sequence of documents in the bundle for a CMC is usually:

– Pleadings (including Requests for Further Information). The Claim Form is usually irrelevant unless the date is important.
– Case Summary if any.
– Orders.
– Court administrative documents, such as allocation questionnaires.
– Any correspondence relevant to a live issue at the CMC.
– Costs budget documents.

3.62 If there are any applications, they should be structured as set out below.

3.63 See below for recommendations regarding the physical bundles themselves.

Applications

3.64 The convenient sequence for the hearing of a specific application is usually:

– Application notice.
– Order sought.
– Witness statement/other documents served in support of the application. It is usually convenient for applications for any documents exhibited to a witness statement to remain as an exhibit.
– Response to application.
– Reply to response to application.

EVIDENCE

3.65 The CMC bundle should also be provided to ensure the pleadings and orders are available, or the pleadings and orders should be included in the application bundle.

3.66 See below for recommendations regarding the physical bundles themselves.

Trial

3.67 The convenient sequence of trial bundles is usually:

- Pleadings (including Requests for Further Information).
- Orders.
- Witness statements (claimant then defendant). Exhibits should be removed from statements and incorporated into the chronological bundle or an issue-specific bundle as appropriate. Cross-references to the new location of the document need to be added to the statements: see paragraph 15.2.3 of the TCC Guide.
- Reply witness statements (claimant then defendant). As above regarding exhibits.
- Expert reports (claimant then defendant, in each case running liability, delay (if any), then quantum). Exhibits consisting of contemporaneous documents should be incorporated into the relevant bundle as with witness statements. Exhibits produced by the expert such as articles, standards, etc. should either remain appended to the relevant report or be collected in some easily identifiable separate bundle.
- Reply expert reports (claimant then defendant). As above regarding exhibits.
- Expert joint statements.
- Chronological bundle (earliest date first, most recent date last).
- Any issue-specific bundles.

3.68 Administrative Court documents, such as disclosure lists and inter-solicitor correspondence, are usually not needed for the trial and can be omitted. It is very rare that inter-solicitor correspondence is relevant to anything other than costs, and even then it is usually only a very small percentage of the total correspondence.

3.69 Issue-specific bundles need careful consideration. They can be convenient, but if there is risk of duplicating documents within the issue bundle and the chronological run, this suggests that they are less likely to be useful.

3.70 The chronological bundle will be key in most TCC cases, because the precise sequence of events is often crucial both to liability (for variations, measured works and delay/disruption) and, of course, to establishing causation in any delay/disruption claim. The chronological bundle should take the longest time to prepare, but without care it can be a chaotic jumble. Points to note are as follows:

- The sensible starting point is all contemporaneous documents referred to in the witness statements and the expert evidence.
- The parties should immediately exempt from this all large documents such as technical guidance documents, method statements, standards, plans/drawings and documents relied on by experts which are not documents created/exchanged by the parties at the time. These can be included in a 'technical documents' bundle or a 'plans' bundle. If documents are being held electronically, it is often possible to identify all documents over a certain number of pages, say 20, and as a starting

point strip all these out of the proposed chronological run to be reviewed separately for relevance.
- The next stage should be including the documents from the client's own disclosure which support the client's case (in practice, almost all of these are likely to have been referred to in witness statements/reports if the approach suggested above has been taken), and documents from the other side's disclosure which are either damaging to their case or support the client's case. Identifying these documents requires there to have been a proper review of the disclosure, with documents sufficiently relevant to justify inclusion in the trial bundle identified at that time. It is very often the case that this task is not done, or not done sufficiently in advance, and what goes into the trial bundle is just most of the disclosure. This makes the task of preparing the case very much more difficult than it should be, and reduces the prospect of the Judge having any time to read a bundle containing mostly irrelevant documents.
- Unless there is an issue about the development of a particular document which makes each draft of it relevant, the drafts of documents can be omitted from the bundle. Sometimes it is only relevant *when* the drafts were exchanged; in that case, the covering email only is sufficient.
- Duplicated emails make a bundle difficult to read and understand and often mean that documents are included out of chronological order. The parties should agree to share the task of de-duplicating a draft chronological bundle. In the editors' experience, this cannot be done effectively using electronic means alone, because slight differences in the metadata of identical emails (such as different time stamps or coding used by different computers) mean that the software wrongly includes practically identical documents. The draft chronological bundle needs to be prepared sufficiently far in advance that each side can go through half of it, removing duplication/ensuring correct chronological order. Note that avoidance of unnecessary duplication of emails is a requirement by paragraph 15.2.3 of the TCC Guide.
- If there are documents or a series of documents which are key to your client's case, pay particular attention to ensuring that those documents are in the bundle, that they are in the exactly correct chronological order and that all relevant attachments are included in a paginated and legible form. Sometimes the time a sequence of documents is sent on a single day is relevant: take care to ensure that the right sequence is maintained. While, therefore, the bundle might be regarded as a somewhat mechanical process, it is important that there is oversight by lawyers who understand the issues in the case and can give, where required, careful instructions to those preparing the files.

3.71 See below for recommendations regarding the physical bundles themselves.

Electronic trial bundles

3.72 Where the volume of documents is high, use of electronic trial bundles using software platforms is becoming more common.

3.73 All of the points above regarding preparation of the bundles are even more important in relation to an electronic bundle. It must be noted that a bundle management platform is often not the same as a document management system – it cannot efficiently be used to search and sort documents. It is primarily a document presentation system. This means that proper organisation and de-duplication of the documents must take place before they are loaded onto the system.

3.74 The software has vastly improved in recent years, but in the editors' experience, it has some material downsides which should be taken into account when deciding what is best in any given case. It is also important that these matters are discussed with the Judge because there will also be subjective preferences that may need to be given consideration when making any decision:

- The key problem remains the same as the key problem on document management platforms. The software identifies the title of the document in question and its date by reading its metadata. If it is an email, the software uses the subject line and the date of the email: this works well. However, for all other documents, such as meeting minutes and letters:
  o If a native version of the document has been uploaded (i.e. a word document or pdf saved on a computer), the software uses the title that the document has been saved as and the date it was created/saved. The title of a document is often a reference number which makes perfect sense within the client's system, but tells the user nothing about the contents of the document. The date the document was created/saved is usually the wrong date for the purposes of the litigation, because the relevant date will be the date of the meeting itself, or the date the letter was sent. This problem is not solved in practice by making the documents Optical Character Recognition (OCR) searchable, because the software does not search the document for the purpose of its indexing/sorting.
  o If a hard-copy document has been scanned into the system, it has a title which is simply a gibberish scan reference number, and no date at all. In an electronic document management system, or in an electronic trial bundle, such a document is the equivalent of a blank piece of paper. It cannot be sorted into chronological order and there is no way of telling without opening it what it is. The solution to this is for the client to pay to have its documents' metadata amended to include the title and date of the document. Platform providers usually offer this service (at a price) and the fields to be filled in and the source of the information can be specified in advance to avoid mistakes. This has to be done before the documents are uploaded to any electronic bundle.
- On most electronic bundle systems, it is possible to annotate/comment on documents and share the annotations with the legal team. However, this functionality is still not as good or convenient as paper and post-it notes. On some systems, for example, notes on documents appear on a different page to the document itself and it is difficult to view them simultaneously. This is very inconvenient.
- The editors' experience (both as advocates and arbitrators) is that the system can be inconvenient for the Judge. The relevant page of a document is brought up on

screen during cross-examination, but there is no time for the Judge to make notes on the document itself, and no way for the Judge to quickly read before and after that page in the bundle. It is difficult for the Judge easily to find that page again. It remains the case that for a sensible subset of the overall bundle, hard copies are the most efficient way to conduct the trial, and a sensible attempt at combining electronic and hard bundle techniques is the optimal solution.
- Most electronic bundles are stored in the cloud and thus documents have to be downloaded in order to be viewed. This can be very slow and this is a problem during a hearing.

3.75 It is therefore still necessary to give very careful consideration to whether the client's and the other side's documents are in an appropriate form to be used in an electronic bundle and as to whether this really will work better/be efficient at trial for the Judge and the parties. The TCC issued guidance in respect of electronic trial bundles and electronic presentation of evidence in July 2016 which should be carefully digested and followed.

Appeal bundles

3.76 Practice Direction 52 has clear rules for appeal bundles. Follow them to the letter.

Administrative matters

3.77 The matters set out below are often overlooked. They make an enormous difference to the efficient conduct of the hearing, and the consequent happiness of the Judge. The happier the Judge, the better for the client.

3.78 Best practice (which makes bundles easy to navigate for the Judge, but which also makes preparation quicker and therefore more effective for the person carrying out the oral advocacy at the hearing) includes:

- Subject only to the third bullet, below, every single page of the bundle should be paginated in the bottom right-hand side. If the bundle includes plans or spreadsheets, these too must be paginated. Lack of pagination causes an enormous waste of time.
- Pagination should run from 1 to x within each bundle. Do not paginate a trial bundle running to 40 lever arch files from 1 to infinity sequentially through all the bundles. It takes a long time to refer to page 17,680.
- If you are putting together an application bundle, and every document in the bundle has its own internal pagination, then as long as each document is behind a numbered tab, it is not necessary to repaginate the whole bundle. The whole point is that it is easy to turn up the correct page in the bundle – this can be done efficiently with tabs and internal pagination. See further paragraph 15.2.3 of the TCC Guide.
- Bundle inserts should be numbered page 1.1, 1.2, etc. (not 1(a) or 1(i)).
- Spine labels:
    o Omit the formal Court heading and include only the parties' names in one line. Everyone already knows which Court the case is in and including the

formal heading just means that the essential information discussed below is squashed into a small, unreadable font.
  - Each bundle should be clearly numbered or have a letter/number combination relevant to the type of document within it appearing on the spine. The numbers/letters should be in large print so they are easy to see.
  - The label should also state what is in the bundle: 'witness statements' or, in the case of a chronological bundle, the dates between which the documents in the bundle run. Avoid detail: the aim is to include key information in a legible font.
- The same information as is on the spine labels should be printed on labels which are stuck to the front top right of the file, and the inside top left of the file. In this way, the Judge (and the parties) can find the right bundle when it is lying open or shut on the desk. Note that this is a requirement of paragraph 15.2.2 of the TCC Guide.
- A standard A4 lever arch file should only contain about 350 pages. Anything else is over-filling the bundle and makes it more likely to break and always more difficult to use. Further, there are bound to be inserts into the bundle during the trial. As soon as the bundle gets even close to being overfilled by inserts, agree with the other side to split the bundle and agree the new numbering. Make sure both parties and the Judge have the same new numbering.
- Don't use four-ring lever arch files. They are maddening.
- Ask the Judge whether they prefer single or double-sided bundles and A4 or A5 files.
- For pleadings, if there are amendments, they should be done with strikethrough and underline. If so, it is only necessary to include the latest version of the amended pleading as that contains all prior versions within it.
- If there are Requests for Further Information (coming within the category of pleadings), then the Replies to the Requests should have been produced by reproducing the Request before inserting the Reply. If this is the case, only include the Replies and not both the Request and the Reply.
- If there are photographs, plans or excel spreadsheets included in the bundle, they must be legible, in colour where necessary and consideration must be given to producing them in A3 or (if a really important plan/drawing) in a larger size, if that is what is necessary to ensure that the document can be read.
- There must be a sensible overall index and an index, in a useful format, in the front of each file: see further paragraph 15.2.2 of the TCC Guide.

CHAPTER 4

Delay claims

Introduction

4.1 One of the most significant problems that can occur on a construction project of any kind is delay to the works. In infrastructure and other civil projects, it is invariably very expensive: for the employer it means that the asset and therefore the revenue stream is not received when planned, and for the contractor it means he must keep his entire site operation active much longer than the period for which he priced. Sufficient delay can lead to termination for default. In shipbuilding and similar projects, the same considerations as to expense apply, and there is usually an express contractual term permitting the owner to terminate, and recover any instalments of the price previously paid, if the delay extends longer than a certain period after the delivery date.

4.2 Delay is therefore often the most expensive problem on any project. It is also one of the most common. This chapter does not deal with the substantive law relating to the perennial debate surrounding the recovery of time and money (particularly where there is concurrent delay),[1] but focusses on the practical requirements of successfully pursuing and defending a delay claim. It assumes that the correct legal position under most contracts will be that:

- the *Malmaison* approach to recovery of time and money under the contract is correct; and
- in a claim for damages, the contractor has to satisfy the 'but for' test.

Legal requirements in relation to claiming delay

4.3 The starting point for any consideration of what is, practically, required to prove a delay claim must be the extension of time clause in the contract itself.

Extension of time clauses

4.4 The extension of time clause will almost always require that the event relied on *in fact* caused delay, not just to a specific activity, but to the project as a whole. A need to prove causation in fact has been held to arise under the JCT Standard Form of Contract and under the Shipbuilder's Association of Japan standard form. Delay to the progress of the

---

1 For a full discussion of these issues, see ch 9 of *Keating on Construction Contracts* (10th edn, 2016) and ch 7 of *Keating on Offshore Construction and Marine Engineering* (1st edn, 2015).

works overall and thus to the completion date (as opposed to delay merely to an activity) is usually referred to as 'critical delay'.[2] This is a key concept in delay claims.

4.5 It is thought that any clause which includes wording expressly referring to the need for a delay event to have caused or contributed to the delay to the relevant completion date will include this requirement, since (1) this is the natural meaning of such wording and (2) it would be commercially surprising if the parties had agreed in their contract to relieve the contractor of its obligation to pay liquidated damages for failure to meet the completion date in relation to delays which did not as a matter of fact affect the completion date.

4.6 This is the case whether the clause in question refers to a prospective or a retrospective delay analysis or is on the face of it silent on this issue.[3]

4.7 Any consideration of what this means in practice must start with the decision in *Balfour Beatty v Chestermount Properties*.[4] Colman J described the purpose of the extension of time regime as follows (at 27 and 34):[5]

> The underlying objective [of the extension of time regime] is to arrive at the aggregate period of time within which the contract works as ultimately defined ought to have been completed having regard to the incidence of non-contractor's risk events and to calculate the excess time if any, over that period, which the contractor took to complete the works. In essence, the architect is concerned to arrive at an aggregate period for completion of the contractual works, having regard to the occurrence of non-contractor's risk events and to calculate the extent to which the completion of the works has exceeded that period . . .
>
> Fundamental to this exercise is an assessment of whether the relevant event occurring during a period of culpable delay has caused delay to the completion of the works and, if so, how much delay . . .

4.8 In practical terms, the significance of this guidance is, as the editors of the BLRs commented in their report of the case (at 10):[6]

> The practical value of the judgment of Colman J is that it should put an end to hypothetical questions about the potential as opposed to the actual effect of causes of delay which entitle a contractor to an extension of time. In many cases it will be a simple exercise to determine whether, for example, a variation did in fact further delay completion in a period of culpable delay. It may be found that no such delay can be established. If it can, then a fair period is added to the then applicable date to produce the requisite extension of time . . .

4.9 These comments were made in 1993. Sadly, such hypothetical questions remain common in both litigation and arbitration. This is, however, because the approach in *Balfour Beatty* is honoured more in the breach than the observance.

4.10 The key aspect of these passages from *Balfour Beatty* is the emphasis on (1) actual delay, which must (2) be to the completion date.

---

2 See below for discussion of the critical path, etc.
3 See paragraphs 4.34ff, below.
4 (1993) 62 BLR 1.
5 Colman J was discussing the extension of time mechanism under the JCT construction contract, pursuant to which the parties appoint an architect to carry out the function of assessing extensions of time during the course of the project and the contractual consequences of delay are limited to liquidated damages rather than a termination right. However, the regime and its purpose are materially identical under all the standard forms of contract typically featuring in TCC litigation (including FIDIC and shipbuilding standard forms).
6 (1993) 62 BLR 1.

4.11 These passages have been applied in many subsequent cases.[7] There is a particularly helpful discussion in the judgment of Hamblen J in *Adyard*. Although this is also a prevention principle case, claims under the contract were discussed in detail as a result of the claimant yard's alternative case, which was that the yard was entitled to an extension of time for any varied work which took place past the completion date, irrespective of any prior culpable delay which had occurred and irrespective of whether the varied work in fact affected any follow-on work. Hamblen J said:

> 262. Mr Breeze gave a helpful example of the extreme consequences in practical terms of this approach:
>
> '1.1.1 Assuming (as is in fact appropriate in the present case) that the contractor is many months in delay by reason of its own default. The employer decides a week before the (original unextended) contract completion date that he wishes a wall to be painted blue instead of the contractually specified red. At the time of the instruction, because of the contractor's delays, the wall is not even built yet. The paint will take five weeks to procure, but will still arrive before the completion of the wall and the date upon which the contractor would require the paint in line with his delayed progress. Mr Swan's analysis would appear to entitle the contractor to four weeks' extension of time (by adding five weeks to the date of impact, and comparing with the original contract completion date). However, I would suggest that common sense tells the observer that such an extension was neither fair nor reasonable, where the employer's actions have not actually delayed the progress of the contractor by a single day.'
>
> 263. In my judgment Adyard's approach is wrong as a matter of both principle and authority. It is also contrary to common sense, as the above example illustrates.
>
> 264. It is wrong in principle because in essence Adyard's case is that there is no need to prove causation in fact. On its case there is no need to prove the event or act causes any actual delay to the progress of the works. Notional or theoretical delay suffices . . . In relation to the extension of time claim it is also contrary to the express causal requirements set out in the contracts in this case . . .
>
> 266. In relation to extensions of time, Adyard's argument is essentially a variation of the gross entitlement approach rejected by Colman J in the Balfour Beatty case . . .

4.12 Hamblen J went on to review the relevant authorities with specific reference to the need to prove delay as a matter of fact in all the authorities following *Balfour Beatty* up to 2011 (at [267]–[280] and [283]–[288]). The reader is referred to this review for a useful summary of the relevant law as to the requirement to prove causation of delay to the progress of the works overall and therefore to the completion date. This analysis has been accepted in all subsequent cases.[8]

Prevention principle

4.13 It is worth emphasising that the same requirement to prove actual delay to the completion or delivery date applies if the claim is being brought pursuant to the prevention principle rather than as a claim under the contract pursuant to an extension of time clause.

---

7 Including *Henry Boot Construction (UK) Ltd v Malmaison Hotel (Manchester) Ltd* (1999) 70 Con LR 33; *Royal Brompton Hospital NHS Trust v Hammon (No 7)* [2001] EWCA Civ 206; (2001) 76 Con LR 148; *De Beers UK Ltd v Atos Origin IT Services UK Ltd* [2011] BLR 274 (TCC); *Adyard Abu Dhabi v SD Marine Services* [2011] BLR 384 (Comm); *Walter Lilly v Mackay* [2012] BLR 503 (TCC) at [364]–[365]; *Saga Cruises BDF Ltd v Fincantieri SPA* [2016] EWHC 1875 (Comm) at [250].

8 See *Zhoushan Jinhaiwan Shipyard Co Ltd v Golden Exquisite Inc* [2014] EWHC 4050 (Comm); [2015] 1 Lloyd's Rep. 283, *Saga Cruises BDF Ltd v Fincantieri SpA* [2016] EWHC 1875 (Comm); 167 Con. LR 29, *North Midland Building Ltd v Cyden Homes Ltd* [2017] EWHC 2414 (TCC); [2017] BLR 605 and *Carillion Construction Ltd v Woods Bagot Europe Ltd* [2017] EWCA Civ 65; [2017] BLR 203.

4.14 In *Trollope & Colls v North West Metropolitan Regional Hospital Board*,[9] Lord Denning said at page 607:

> It is well settled that in building contracts – and in other contracts too – when there is a stipulation for work to be done in a limited time, if the other party by his conduct – it may be quite legitimate conduct, such as ordering extra work – *renders it impossible or impracticable for the other party to do his work within the stipulated time*, then the one whose conduct caused the trouble can no longer insist upon strict adherence to the time stated. He cannot claim any penalties or liquidated damages for non-completion in that time.[10]

4.15 In *Adyard*, Hamblen J cited *Trollope* and continued:[11]

> 282. . . . The conduct therefore has to render it 'impossible or impracticable for the other party to do the work within the stipulated time.' The act relied on must actually prevent the contractor from carrying out the works within the contract period, or, in other words, must cause some *actual* delay.[12]

4.16 This was again upheld in *Jerram Falkus v Fenice*.[13] The requirement to prove 'but for' causation of actual delay in a claim under the prevention principle has been held to mean that a prevention principle claim cannot be established where there is concurrent delay.[14]

Float

4.17 The analysis in the above authorities shows that the question of who owns the float has a straightforward answer in most contracts (absent any specific contractual provisions to the contrary[15]). Since the contractor must establish delay to the progress of the works which causes delay *to the completion date*, in the event that an employer-risk delay event does not cause delay to the completion date because some float is built in to the programme, then the contractor is not entitled to an extension of time. It follows that the float is 'owned' by the project, or in other words by whichever party 'gets to it first'. This means that if a series of events each separately causing separate periods of delay[16] occurs:

- Events 1 and 2 may have no effect on the completion date because sufficient float remains in the programme to accommodate that delay albeit that those events use up all the float.
- Event 3 may only have an effect on the completion date because by the time at which it occurs, all the float had already been used up by events 1 and 2.

4.18 If events 1 and 2 are employer-risk events and event 3 is a contractor-risk event, this may mean that the contractor is not entitled to an extension of time. However, there

---

9 [1973] 1 WLR 601.
10 This part of Lord Denning's judgment was expressly upheld in the House of Lords at [1973] 1 WLR 601. Emphasis added.
11 See also paragraphs 264ff quoted above.
12 Emphasis in the original.
13 [2011] EWHC 1935 (TCC); 138 Con LR 21.
14 *Jerram Falkus v Fenice* [2011] EWHC 1935 (TCC); 138 ConLR 21; *North Midland v Cyden* [2017] EWHC 2414 (TCC); [2017] All ER (D) 13 (Oct).
15 In some contracts such as the NEC, there are express allocations of risk in relation to float, and different types of float are defined. In such contracts, naturally the contractual allocation of risk prevails so that in some instances the contractor is entitled to 'keep' his float in the event of an employer-risk event.
16 In other words, not concurrent delay.

are certain circumstances in which it remains possible to bring a good claim: for example, if events 1 and 2 had the effect of pushing an activity into a winter period, and event 3 either would not have caused any delay, or would have caused a lesser period of delay, if the activity it affected had been carried out during the summer. As always in a delay claim, there is no general rule and the correct answer depends entirely on the specific facts of the case.

Pleading requirements – delay

Civil Procedure Rules

4.19 A claim in the TCC must comply with the requirements of CPR Part 16.4. This requires that the Particulars of Claim include 'a concise statement of the facts on which the claimant relies'. By CPR Part 16.5, the defendant must state which of the allegations in the Particulars of Claim he admits, denies or requires the claimant to prove, and where he denies an allegation, he 'must state his reasons for doing so' and 'if he intends to put forward a different version of events from that given by the claimant, he must state his own version'.

4.20 It will follow from the above discussion as to principle, that the statement of the facts relied on should include a brief summary of the activities affected by the delay event, including an explanation of the link, or more likely series of links, between subsequent activities[17] which explains how and why the event relied on *in fact* caused delay to the completion date. In the event that a defendant disagrees with that case, she in his turn has to explain why it is wrong: this will involve a factual assertion either that a particular activity was not affected at all; did not constrain subsequent activities in the manner alleged and/or did not in any event affect the completion date.

Authorities as to pleading requirements

4.21 There are very few authorities which specifically discuss pleading requirements for a delay claim. In *Wharf Properties v Eric Cumin*,[18] the Privy Council had to consider an appeal from the Court of Appeal, which had struck out a claim for delay on the basis that it had no prospects of success as it did not plead a proper causation case. The claim was a professional negligence claim for damages rather than a claim under a contract, but the requirement to plead and prove causation in fact is the same, so the reasoning is applicable to a typical delay construction delay claim. Lord Oliver said (at 18 to 19):

> The Court then went on to consider whether, the action being one in which the real cause of action rested upon the establishment of an essential link between the action or inaction alleged on the part of ECA and the damage which was claimed by way of relief, the statement of claim pleaded all the 'material facts' relied upon by Wharf for their claim as provided by Order 18, rule 7(1) of the Rules of the Supreme Court . . . ECA's contention was that the substantial cause of action, the right to recover for damage sustained, depended upon establishing, first, a breach of contract, secondly (in a case where, as here, the breaches alleged consisted of negligence in the performance of contractual duties) that there had occurred an immediate intervening

---

17 See detailed discussion of constraints below.
18 [1991] 52 BLR 1.

event alleged to have been occasioned by the breach and, thirdly, that the damage claimed was the financial consequence of that intervening event. *In this case the intervening event alleged in each case was 'delay' but (as has already been observed) there was simply no correlation between the delays to be ascribed respectively to the several breaches pleaded and the overall delay pleaded nor (except in the case of the loss of rent claimed) between the overall delay and the financial loss claimed. Thus, the court concluded, the statement of claim, in omitting to plead in relation to each breach alleged, the essential link between the breach and the financial consequences, omitted 'material facts' and ought to be struck out.* Power JA observed that 'in a pleading such as the present one where substantial special damages are sought they must be supported by material facts sufficient when proved to establish the respondents' entitlement thereto . . .'.[19]

4.22 Lord Oliver stated that the Privy Council could not go as far as the Court of Appeal in striking out the pleading for disclosing no cause of action at all, because it was 'at least theoretically possible' albeit 'a very unlikely event' that Wharf might establish an entitlement to some money on the basis of the pleaded case (at 20). However, the Privy Council went on to strike out the pleading as an abuse of the process of the Court. Wharf sought to rely on the cases (usually referred to in the construction industry as global claims cases) dealing with the required particularisation of financial losses.[20] Lord Oliver stated (at 20–21 and 23):

> Those cases establish no more than this, that in cases where the full extent of extra costs incurred through delay depend upon a complex interaction between the consequences of various events, so that it may be difficult to make an accurate apportionment of the total extra costs, it may be proper for an arbitrator to make individual financial awards in respect of claims which can conveniently be dealt with in isolation and a supplementary award in respect of the financial consequences of the remainder as a composite whole. This has, however, *no bearing upon the obligation of a plaintiff to plead his case with such particularity as is sufficient to alert the opposite party to the case which is going to be made against him at the trial*. ECA are concerned at this stage not so much with quantification of the financial consequences the point with which the two cases referred to were concerned but with *the specification of the factual consequences of the breaches pleaded in terms of periods of delay. The failure even to attempt to specify any discernible nexus between the wrong alleged and the consequent delay provides*, to use Mr Thomas' phrase, 'no agenda' for the trial . . .[21]

4.23 These comments were cited and approved in *Walter Lilly* at [474]–[486] (in the context of a discussion of global claims[22]). The 'nexus' referred to by Lord Oliver is the link, or series of links, between the originally delayed critical path activity, subsequent or follow-on activities[23] and the delay to the completion date discussed above. Guidance on identifying, setting out and proving that nexus is laid out below.

Burden of proof

4.24 It is for the contractor to establish that it is entitled to an extension of time. The default position under the contract will be that the employer is entitled to liquidated

---

19 Emphasis added.
20 Discussed further below.
21 Emphasis added.
22 See Chapter 5.
23 See discussion below.

damages in the event that the project is not completed by the completion date. Accordingly, the contractor has the burden of proof in any claim.

4.25 However, this is usually of limited practical consequence. The employer will almost always have a positive case on the facts (the delay to the project was not caused by the matters relied on by the contractor, but by other matters which were at the contractor's risk and/or the contractor is factually wrong as to the extent of the delay caused). The employer has the burden of proving that positive case. In some rare cases, an employer may limit itself to contending that the contractor's claim is wrong, without putting forward an alternative explanation for the delay to the project. This is a risky strategy, since it is difficult effectively to test the credibility of claimed reasons for the delay in the absence of any rival explanation for that delay. Even in those cases, where the contention that the contractor's claim is wrong involves factual disputes, the employer will have the burden of proving its version of the facts.

Making or defending a delay claim in practice

Introduction

4.26 The principles set out in the authorities do not provide the practitioner with a straightforward template for preparing or defending a claim for delay. This section attempts to set out practical guidance as to the steps which should be taken (and which a defendant should check have been taken) in order to produce a robust delay claim likely to withstand testing in the TCC.

4.27 There are three overarching points relating to case strategy to make at the outset:

4.28 First, it is useful to identify the types of problems which have occurred on the project in question. There are essentially two kinds of project in the context of delay:

- A project with a series of identifiable problems (mistake in concrete pour; a subcontractor becomes insolvent; major variations; delay in equipment supply) which push an otherwise successful project off course.
- Death by a thousand cuts: poor project management and inefficiency and/or delays in decision-making (whether on the part of employer or contractor) lead to poor progress overall even in the absence of any specific problems.

4.29 The first type of project is more straightforward to prepare both in terms of claim and defence. This is because what happened and the effect it had is relatively clear-cut (even if there are a number of delaying events and the project extended over several years). In particular, where a specific problem has occurred, such as, for example, a subcontractor becoming insolvent, it is usually fairly clear on the facts which activities are directly affected (those carried out by that subcontractor), and fairly clear which subsequent activities are affected by delays to those activities. In such cases, both sides' focus will be on the specific activities affected and the nature and extent of that effect, and the existence or otherwise of constraints on subsequent activities. The dispute is therefore likely to be more focussed.

4.30 However, where there is no clear reason for the delay, it can for obvious reasons be more difficult to plead and prove a delay claim, especially given the fact that it is the contractor's burden to do so: the default position under the contract will be that there is no extension of time and the employer is entitled to his liquidated damages and/or other rights. Ironically, such claims are also harder to defend, because although it is usually easy to list a series of allegations as to the poor project management performance of the contractor, it is difficult to establish a causative link between that poor project management and the specific delay occurring on site. The best approach in these circumstances is usually to use the contemporaneous progress data to show that the contractor consistently fell behind either in periods for which no delay claim is made, or in relation to activities which are separate from those relied on for the delay claim.

4.31 Secondly, in making or defending a delay claim, it is easy to assume that the delay event which caused the most delay is the most important in the case and therefore requires the most attention. However, it is not invariably the case that the event causing the most delay also caused the most additional cost to be incurred.[24] Prolongation or preliminaries costs must be caused by the relevant period of critical delay (not relate simply to the period after the original completion date by which the project has been extended).[25] Preliminaries costs will usually be very much higher during the middle of the project when multiple activities are ongoing simultaneously than they are either at the beginning or at the end of the project (forming a bell curve). It follows that a shorter period of critical delay occurring in the middle of a project may in fact give rise to a bigger time-related cost claim than a longer period of delay towards the end. It is, of course, essential in any claim or defence to follow the money: often matters of quantum, especially delay and disruption-related quantum, are not examined in any detail until a late stage of the litigation. The better approach is to form a view at an early stage where the real money claim lies.

4.32 Thirdly, it will be apparent from the discussion above and below that the key element of a successful delay claim is the issue of *factual* causation. For this reason, it is necessary to establish what actually happened during the project. The factual witnesses will be key, but the importance of the contemporaneous records cannot be over-emphasised. This is for two main reasons. First, the contemporaneous documents, including meeting minutes and progress reports as well as formal correspondence and emails, will be the best record of what was in fact happening at any given time on the project. They will be essential in proving the case (whether claiming or defending). The trial Judge will place more weight on the contemporaneous records than she will on the recollection (often several years later) of the factual witnesses. Secondly, as a broader credibility point, it is very rare for an event causing critical delay to occur, but of which neither party is aware at the time or very shortly after. When such an event occurs, in the overwhelming majority of cases both parties know about it immediately, and there is usually protracted and often detailed discussion both as to the contractual risk allocation of the event, and as to the practical steps to be taken on site to deal with it in the best way in order to mitigate the problems caused. If a matter said to have caused critical delay was not mentioned in the contemporaneous documents, the practical starting point of the trial Judge in the TCC will be that it is unlikely to have in

---

24 Particularly in circumstances where there is a cap on liquidated damages so that after a claimant acquires a sufficient extension of time to operate as a complete defence to the liquidated damages claim, the only relevance of the extension of time is to the contractor's claim for prolongation costs.

25 See discussion below.

fact had the effect alleged.[26] A party will need to have a good explanation in order to rebut this presumption.

4.33 Therefore, the very first task for any party preparing or defending a delay claim is to obtain and review the contemporaneous documents. This is an essential part of the steps discussed below.

Step 1: Prospective or retrospective

4.34 The first step is to decide whether the contract requires a prospective or a retrospective analysis. The meaning of this jargon is as follows:

- A prospective approach seeks to ascertain the probable future effect of a delay event, as at the time that it occurred (or at intervals, often monthly or every time an updated programme was issued, during the project). If a claim for an extension of time is made during the course of the project, the contract administrator (or whoever is the relevant entity) will of necessity have to carry out a prospective analysis because by definition the project is still ongoing so he cannot possibly know what will happen in the end. The key feature of a prospective analysis is (even if it is carried out post-project) that it takes no account of what actually happened, but relies solely on what would probably have happened from the point of view of a person looking forward at the time of the delay event.
- A retrospective approach ascertains the actual effect of a delay event, based on what in fact happened on the project. It can only be carried out once the project is completed, or if carried out during the project can only deal with the effect of delay events in the past. If the effect of a delay event is or is potentially ongoing as at the date of the analysis, then it is retrospective up to the date of the analysis and after that is necessarily prospective. The key feature of a retrospective analysis is that it is based on the known facts of what actually happened.

4.35 Questions are sometimes asked as to how a prospective analysis can in principle be reconciled with the authorities referred to above which require the claimant to prove that a delay event as a matter of fact caused delay to the completion date. The explanation is that (assuming the contract requires the use of a prospective analysis) such an analysis is capable of ascertaining which delay events affected the completion date or otherwise, within the limits of this being a probability rather than known facts. However, use of a prospective analysis in litigation which invariably reaches trial after the project has completed is problematic, as discussed further below.

Retrospective and prospective analysis give the same results?

4.36 The experts in *Walter Lilly* agreed that 'if each approach was done correctly, they should produce the same result'.[27] As a statement of a general rule, this is not correct, as

---

26 See, for example, the comments of Coulson J (as he then was) in *Van Oord UK Ltd v Allseas UK Ltd* [2015] EWHC 3074 (TCC) at [51]–[52].
27 *Walter Lilly* at [380].

discussed further below. It is suggested that this is best understood as applicable only to the specific facts of the dispute in that case.[28]

Contractual requirements for a prospective approach

4.37 There are two standard forms of contract in use in the United Kingdom which envisage a prospective assessment of delay at least at certain points during the project.

4.38 The JCT Standard Form of Contract (and many of the other contracts in the JCT suite) envisages a two-stage process for the assessment of delay. If a claim for an extension of time is made during the project, the contract administrator is obliged to review it and grant any appropriate extension at the time it is made.[29] An assessment made at this time will necessarily be a prospective one. However, the contract provides for a further assessment of any extension which may be due after the original completion date (if occurring before practical completion) or within 12 weeks after the date of practical completion.[30] This assessment will almost always be carried out after practical completion when the project is finished and the clause requires the contract administrator to review the project and come to an overall assessment of any extension of time due to the contractor (whether or not for a cause notified by the contractor). It is submitted that the intention is that this assessment is a retrospective one.[31]

4.39 The intention of the NEC standard forms of contract is that all claims and/or disputes are dealt with as soon as or shortly after they arise (via adjudications during the course of the project if necessary) and it does not contain any default mechanism if this procedure is not followed. Consistently with this approach, NEC 4 envisages a prospective assessment of the entitlement to an extension of time at the time that the claim is made.[32] However, NEC 4 has no 'review' clause similar to the JCT Standard Form triggered by the end of the project.[33] On the face of the contract, therefore, the only basis on which an extension of time can be claimed is a prospective basis.

4.40 However, for the reasons discussed below as to the problems with prospective analyses, it would be commercially surprising if the parties intended this to apply to disputes being dealt with after the project is complete. A discussion of the legal position is outside the scope of this book,[34] but it is submitted that parties should be very slow to conclude that a prospective analysis is appropriate in TCC litigation.

Problems with prospective analyses

4.41 There are three key problems with using a prospective analysis of delay in litigation in the TCC.

---

28 See also the discussion in SCL Paper D196 dated December 2016, *Delay Analysis: Backwards or Forwards – Does It Make a Difference?* by John Marshall.
29 See clause 2.25.1 of the Standard Form.
30 See clause 2.25.3 of the Standard Form.
31 As held by Mr Justice Akenhead in *Walter Lilly* at [362]. It is suggested that Akenhead J's comments at [363] as to both these subclauses meaning 'the same thing' were a reference to both subclauses requiring proof of delay which in fact affected the completion date (whether assessed prospectively or retrospectively), not that both subclauses require a prospective approach to delay analysis.
32 See clause 60.1.
33 It also has no final account process; the contracts work on the assumption that if the NEC mechanism has been operated correctly, all claims for payment will have been dealt with an ongoing basis during the project.
34 For detailed discussion see ch 9 of *Keating on Construction Contracts* (10th edn, 2016) and ch 7 of *Keating on Offshore Construction and Marine Engineering* (1st edn, 2015).

4.42 The first is the problem inherent in a prospective analysis: its prediction might be (and often is) wrong. One example will suffice to demonstrate a typical problem. A project involves earthworks which must be carried out during the summer weather window between April and September. The earthworks have to be finished before the contractor can start building the required structure. Both earthworks and structure are on the critical path.[35] The contractor's programme correctly shows the earthworks being carried out between July and September (thus taking three months). The activity for the structure follows immediately thereafter. Assume a delay event occurs at the end of August and causes one month of delay to the progress of the earthworks activity.

4.43 A person assessing the probable effect of that delay event on the project as at the end of August would conclude that the earthworks activity will now hit the winter weather window, meaning that it has to stop when only part-completed and await the better weather the following year to resume. Given that the structure can only commence when the earthworks are completed, this means that the delay to the earthworks activity causes delay to the start of the structural works of about seven months (a six-month delay between October and March in which no progress can be made on earthworks + one month remaining time to complete the earthworks activity in April). On a prospective analysis, the actual delay to the completion date caused by the original delay event is therefore seven months. However, what in fact happens is that the weather in October is unseasonably fine. Although the earthworks activity has to stop and start again due to the delay event, in the event it is possible to complete it during October. The structure can then be started in November. Further, the contractor makes excellent progress on the structure and completes it in a duration which is one month shorter than the original plan. Accordingly, as a matter of fact, there was no delay to the completion date (a one-month delay to the earthworks activity caused the structure to start one month late, but it was finished one month early, meaning no overall net delay).

4.44 There are, therefore, two aspects to the first problem with a prospective analysis: (1) the assessment of delay may be wrong when judged against what actually happened;[36] and (2) in some cases, it can produce an assessment of delay (and thus an extension of time entitlement) which is longer than the actual delay which occurred on the project, as in the above example.[37]

4.45 It is in the main for this reason[38] that in contracts where it is envisaged that the contract administrator will grant extensions of time during the project and approximately contemporaneously with the contractor's application (which are therefore prospectively assessed), it is usual for a contract administrator initially to grant only very short extensions of time even for major delays to critical activities which occur early in the project. The delay that *in fact* occurs to the completion date due to the original event may be less than

---

35 See discussion below.

36 This can obviously go either way: the error might be in favour of either the contractor or the employer. The drafters of the NEC have stated that the intention of that contract is to prefer certainty over accuracy. In practice, a prospective analysis tends to favour the contractor. This is probably the reason that such analyses are often used in adjudication claims. It is perhaps hoped that the short duration of the procedure will mean that the claim is not analysed as robustly. In the experience of the editors, this hope is usually misplaced.

37 For this reason, the 2nd edition of the SCL Protocol no longer recommends a prospective method as the 'best' form of delay analysis.

38 The other reasons are (1) that such contracts usually also provide that an extension of time cannot later be reduced and (2) the natural reluctance of the employer to allow additional time.

the amount of delay to the original activity, even on the assumption that that activity was critical. The contract administrator prefers to wait and see what actually transpires before awarding an extension of time.

4.46 It should be noted that the converse may also be true. Events occurring after the original activity delay may have the effect of increasing, rather than reducing, the delay to the completion date caused by the original event. An obvious example is where the delay to the original activity on the critical path has the effect of pushing subsequent weather-sensitive critical path works into winter, thus as a matter of fact prolonging those works beyond their planned period.[39]

4.47 The second key problem with a prospective analysis is that a prospective analysis of delay is unlikely to suffice as the basis for a claim for prolongation costs, in relation to which the orthodox view is that the contractor is entitled only to his actual costs in fact caused by the delay. A prospective analysis does not identify the actual delay which in fact occurred on the project.

4.48 These issues lead on to the third and final key problem with a prospective analysis when used in TCC litigation. Such litigation almost invariably reaches trial after the project has completed and therefore the facts of what happened are known. Because a prospective analysis has no necessary connection with these facts, a TCC Judge will be very reluctant to accept the results of such a delay analysis at trial. Parties should be aware that the inherent lack of credibility in a prospective analysis may well be fatal to their claim.

4.49 For these reasons, the discussion below assumes that a retrospective analysis will be used (although much of this guidance is applicable to either type of claim).

Step 2: Identifying the total period of delay on the project and when the delay occurred

4.50 The next step is to work out when the delay on the project occurred and, of course, how much total delay was incurred to the original completion date. Delay on a project very rarely occurs once and due to one event. The more usual scenario is that there are periods where the contractor was able to progress as planned, interspersed with the occurrence of delay events (whether contractor or employer risk). Identifying the periods in which the project slowed down or even stopped provides a sensible focus for a more detailed analysis of what happened, in order to establish the causative link between the delay event and delay to the completion date.

4.51 The easiest and most straightforward way to do this in the first instance is to carry out a comparison between the as-planned[40] and the as-built[41] programmes or, in an even simpler method, to compare the originally planned dates for the achievement of key milestones on the project with the dates on which they were actually achieved.[42]

4.52 The difference (if any) between the as-planned and the as-built dates for any particular activity or key milestone is, as a matter of fact, the actual delay that was incurred

---

39 It obviously could not be known at the time of the delay to the original critical path activity whether the subsequent weather-sensitive works would *in fact* be affected by weather (even if it was known that they would in principle be taking place in the winter season).
40 See definition below.
41 See definition below.
42 Some contracts require the production of a schedule of key milestones, but even if not, the client will be able to identify appropriate points in the project.

to that activity or milestone.[43] It is not the same as the delay to the completion date. For example, the actual delay in achieving milestone 1 might be six months, and the actual delay in achieving milestone 2 might be three months. This tells you that, on the face of it, the contractor managed to recover three months of delay between milestones 1 and 2 (and that by the time milestone 2 was reached, the maximum actual delay to the project overall/the completion date was only three months and not six). It follows that it would be sensible to focus investigation on what happened to delay milestone 1, since it would appear that progress was faster than planned between milestones 1 and 2.

4.53 The comparison between the original completion date and the actual date of practical completion of course provides the period of the actual delay which occurred on the project and represents the maximum extension of time claim.

4.54 Assuming the claim is for 100 per cent of the delay on the project, the specific delays caused by individual delaying events must add up to the same number of days as the difference between the as-planned and actual completion dates. If the claim is not for 100 per cent of the delay on the project, obviously the number of days claimed can be lower, but the total number of days' delay cannot be ignored. A key basic credibility test for any delay claim is whether the number of days claimed makes sense in the context of the overall delay to the project. For example, if a contractor was delayed by three months in a one-year project because a key subcontractor became insolvent, but claims to have been delayed by employer-risk events for four months out of a total five-month delay to the project, this should raise questions as to the correctness of its claim. It may be, of course, that the contractor can show that the subcontractor's works were not critical, or that it was otherwise able to deal with the problems caused, or that there was concurrent delay, but as a common sense starting point, the claim lacks credibility.

As-planned or baseline programme

4.55 This refers to the contractor's original planned programme for the works, which may have been produced pursuant to a contractual obligation and subject to review by the employer, or may have been produced for the contractor's own planning and project management purposes. The important point is to identify the programme which most accurately represents the contractor's planned intent at the beginning of the project.

4.56 The programme will include the sequence in which the contractor plans to carry out the necessary activities, and a planned duration for each activity. There will therefore be a start and end date for each activity. Some programmes will also include the planned resource to be allocated.

4.57 In modern projects, the programme is usually but not always produced using software such as Primavera or Microsoft Project. In this book, a programme produced using such software is referred to as an 'electronic programme'. There are differences between the level of sophistication of the differing types of software, but these differences are usually much more relevant to the utility of the software for project management during the course of the works than to its utility in delay analysis. For the purposes of an as-planned versus as-built comparison, the programme does not have to be electronic.

---

43 See Step 4: Identify the critical path.

Realism of baseline programme and relevance to delay analysis

4.58 In order to provide a sensible basis of comparison with the actual events, the baseline programme must, of course, be a realistic plan for carrying out the works by the completion date. If it is unrealistic – for example, because the contractor has planned to carry out a particular activity which would reasonably, with reasonable resource, take three months in only one month, then effectively delay is built in to the programme: the activity would always have taken three months, so that when that activity is delayed by two months, such delay is not due to an event occurring on site affecting that activity, but to the inherent inadequacies of the programme (and therefore is the contractor's risk).

4.59 It follows that it is important to check that the baseline programme is reasonable or realistic in this sense. In practice, a baseline programme is often produced pursuant to a contractual obligation and has frequently been reviewed and approved (or not disapproved) by the employer at the time it was produced. It will be more difficult in these circumstances to establish that the programme was unrealistic.

4.60 Some projects are 'fast track' projects. This is sometimes explicitly set out in the contract documents, but other hallmarks are contractually fixed dates for a design freeze and short time periods for the employer's team to review and approve drawings, etc. In these projects, the contractor may have planned to have greater than usual resource allocated to the works, so that a shorter programme than 'normal' for such works may in fact be realistic.

4.61 The critical path for the works shown on the baseline or as-planned programme is usually irrelevant for the reasons explained at paragraph 4.115, subject to the point made at paragraph 4.116.

4.62 If the baseline programme has been produced using software, it will be an electronic programme and include logic links. The use of an electronic programme for delay analysis is discussed in detail at paragraph 4.144 and following, below. If an electronic programme-based method of delay analysis is not used, the primary relevance of the logic links in a baseline programme is in producing the as-planned critical path (as shown by the software): as stated below, this is unlikely to be of practical use.

Changing baseline

4.63 It will almost always be the case that the contractor's baseline programme changes during the course of the works to take account of actual progress on the project. If this happens, and the change to the baseline is material, then it is necessary to use the updated/revised programme as the new baseline against which to measure delay, *from the time that the change was implemented.*

4.64 This is because if an outdated baseline programme is used in the as-planned versus as-built comparison, an inaccurate picture of actual progress on the project will result.

As-built programme

4.65 The as-built programme can refer to two sources of data:

– The contractor's baseline programme, which has been updated throughout the course of the works with actual or as-built progress information for each activity on the programme. By the time the works reach practical completion, in theory such a programme is a complete record of when each activity in fact started and finished.

- A spreadsheet or other source of data containing the same information as an updated programme. In other words, the as-built programme does not have to be a programme. Any document which contains reliable information as to the actual start and finish dates of activities on the project can be used to carry out the comparison suggested above.

4.66 The as-built data included in a programme/other source of data is not always correct. It must be checked against information in the contemporaneous documents. Sometimes, a programme is updated with a finish date for an activity in advance of the actual finish date, and a progress report, meeting minute or contemporaneous email will record the correct date. In other cases, it is necessary to check the method of progress reporting. On some projects, the contractor may estimate how long a particular activity is planned to take not by time, but by resource, such as an estimated number of man-hours. If the estimate is accurate, then approximately the same man-hours are actually spent as were planned, and progress reporting by number of man-hours incurred will reflect the physical progress of the activity on site. However, if the activity takes longer than planned, it will very frequently use more man-hours than planned, leading to a situation where progress is reported as 90 per cent complete because 90 per cent of the planned man-hours have been expended, but in fact the activity is physically only 50 per cent complete.

Step 3: Identifying the delay events

4.67 The best source to identify the events that caused delay is a factual witness with an overall supervisory role on the project who was on site either permanently or regularly. For the contractor, this will usually be the project manager and, for the employer, it may be the employer's agent/contract administrator if there is one, or possibly a direct employee if that person had a significant site presence. A useful way to approach the identification of the delay events is to ask the witness what was keeping him up at night at any particular time during the project, and why. To assist the witness and in order to obtain the most accurate and useful information, it is sensible to discuss the project chronologically: what went wrong in month 1, what went wrong in month 2, etc.

4.68 The contractor will usually have formally notified the employer of events which it considered did or were likely to cause delay during the project. These notices are also a helpful starting point. However, caution is required: either because the notification consists simply of an event which is said to have caused delay without any description of *how* it caused delay (the causal nexus), and/or because the contractor gave very numerous notifications of delay events ranging from major changes to matters which are questionable both in terms of liability and actual delay impact, and/or because the party believes that a major cause of delay on a project was not formally notified at all.[44]

4.69 Any delay event identified in this way must then be cross-checked against the other contemporaneous project documentation of which the most important categories for these purposes are progress reports and progress meeting minutes. In the event that a matter said

---

44 See discussion at paragraphs 4.126ff as to contractually required notice.

to have caused delay was not discussed contemporaneously, this seriously and possibly fatally undermines its credibility at trial: see paragraph 4.32, above.

4.70 The delay events identified must, of course, fall within those matters which the contract allocates as employer-risk matters in order to be capable of forming the basis of an extension of time claim.

Step 4: Identify the critical path

Critical path

4.71 The critical path is usually defined as the longest sequence of activities in a project plan which must be completed on time for the project to complete on due date. It always exists whether or not it is identifiable on a programme because, as a matter of fact, there *is* a particular longest sequence of activities which it is necessary to complete on time in order to achieve the completion date.

4.72 The critical path may, however, change during the project if the planned sequencing or duration of a particular activity or activities is changed. Since this almost always occurs (whether or not in response to a delay event), the as-built critical path is likely to be different from the as-planned critical path. This is of key importance when considering which events in fact caused delay to the completion date on a retrospective basis and usually means that the as-planned critical path is not of practical interest in claim terms.[45]

Importance of the critical path for delay claims

4.73 Since the activities on the critical path represent the longest sequence of activities which must be completed on time to allow the project to complete on the completion date, it is only delay to a critical path activity which is, in principle,[46] capable of delaying the works as a whole so as to delay the completion date.[47] It follows that the critical path is of paramount importance in a delay claim. This is now the accepted position in the TCC: in *Walter Lilly*, Akenhead J said at [98]: '[The expert] broadly, logically and conventionally, adopted the approach of establishing critical delay by reference to the longest sequence(s) of events which marked the longest path through the project.'

4.74 Since the critical path consists of the chain of the longest sequence of activities which must be completed on time to allow the project to complete on the completion date, it follows that not all activities forming part of the works are on the critical path. In principle, activities not on the critical path can be delayed, sometimes very significantly delayed, without causing any delay to the overall completion date. This is easiest to demonstrate via a simple example.

4.75 Assume the project is to build a house with a landscaped garden and demolish an existing wall surrounding the garden. The construction of the house involves digging foundations, pouring the concrete for the foundations, building the house itself (walls and internal floors) and building the roof. The contractor must also landscape the garden and demolish the external wall.

---

45 Subject to the point about decision-making during the project: see paragraph 4.116, below.
46 See also paragraphs 4.121ff below.
47 This is the meaning of 'critical delay'.

4.76 Absent any other information, the common-sense starting point is that the longest sequence of activities which must be completed on time in order to allow the project to finish by the completion date runs through the activities directly relating to the house itself: earthworks for the foundations, pouring concrete, walls and finally roof. The activities have to be done in that order, due to the physical constraints between each relevant activity: digging foundations must come before pouring concrete; foundations must be complete before walls can start, etc.

4.77 This sequence of activities, in that order, is the critical path for this project. The activities of carrying out the landscaping and demolishing the external wall can be carried out any time over that entire period without affecting the progress of the critical activities at all. It follows that if a delay event causes delay to the progress of landscaping, but does not affect the critical activities, it will not affect the completion date and so will not entitle the contractor to any extension of time.

4.78 If the actual relationship between activities on site is different from the above, the critical path might run through a different sequence. Assume, for example, that in order to dig the foundations, the contractor needs to get large excavating equipment on site, and can only do this by first demolishing the external wall for access. In that scenario, the critical path for the same works would run through demolishing the external wall, digging the foundations, pouring concrete, etc. The landscaping can be done at any convenient point after the excavating equipment has left (assuming, of course, that the access needed for the equipment affected all of the area to be landscaped; it may be that some or even most of the landscaping could be done while the excavating equipment is working).

4.79 The more constrained the site, the more it is likely that issues of access will mean that the activities have to be carried out in a specific sequence which will affect the critical path. For example, tunnelling works are very constrained because equipment must both enter and leave the site by the same route. The need to allow for this may mean follow-on works cannot start even though the physical predecessor[48] work has been completed.

4.80 In other words, the critical path of any given project turns on the specific physical constraints which exist on that project between the major activities which have to be completed on time in order to meet the completion date.

Identifying the critical path in practice

4.81 As discussed above, it is assumed in this section that a retrospective analysis of delay is being undertaken. This means it is necessary to use the as-built not the as-planned critical path: activities which were not critical in the planned programme for the works can become critical either due to being delayed so extensively themselves or due to delays in other parts of the works.

4.82 There is no formula for identifying the critical path. It is a matter of common sense since it arises from the physical and technical reality of the project under discussion, as can be seen from the discussion of the very simple house-building project above.

4.83 In modern projects, there will usually be an updated as-built electronic programme. This is often used to show the as-built critical path: the software is programmed to show the longest path through the works, usually by turning the relevant activities red. This can

---

48 See discussion at paragraphs 4.96ff, below.

be a useful starting point. However, the critical path shown on an electronic programme (whether as-planned or as-built) is only as accurate as the information available to the software. Its accuracy depends on whether the sequencing and durations of the activities and the logic links used accurately reflect the physical reality on the ground and the actual constraints between activities.[49]

4.84 A useful practical way of testing whether a particular proposed critical path is correct is to ask for a factual explanation of why each activity was critical. As in the example given above relating to construction of a house and landscaped garden, it should be possible to give logical reasons why the activity of digging the foundations was more important to overall progress of the works than carrying out the landscaping, or as to why it was essential to demolish the external wall first.

4.85 Use common sense: if in an ordinary house-building project the electronic programme is saying that the critical path ran through the fitting out of the downstairs toilet, it is likely that this is the result of a mistake in the electronic programme, not that it is really the case that delay to that activity was driving the progress of the works overall.

4.86 It is not necessary to have an electronic programme in order to identify the critical path. As discussed above, the activities that are on the critical path are factual/technical issues determined by which important activities are constrained by previous activities and are a matter of common sense. Even if a contractor did not have a monthly updated critical path analysis, this does not mean that the contractor would not have had a good understanding of what was in fact critical or that it cannot be determined in retrospect. Of course, the more complicated the project, the more difficult this might be without a good contemporaneous understanding and record of what was happening in fact.

4.87 Indeed, it is sometimes suggested that it is necessary to have carried out a 'critical path analysis' using an electronic programme in order to establish delay to the completion date. A 'critical path analysis' usually refers to an identification of where the critical path lies using an electronic programme. Insofar as it is suggested an electronic programme-based analysis is required, this is not the case. As discussed above, the programme is only as good as the information input into it. An electronic programme-based result should never be accepted as superior to an analysis based on the facts and common sense. A critical path analysis, insofar as this refers simply to the process of identifying the as-built critical path, is, however, essential.

Step 5: Identify how the delay event caused delay to the completion date

Introduction

4.88 In order to succeed in a delay claim, it is necessary to show not just that one initial activity on the critical path was delayed by the relevant delay event, but that this activity delay had a knock-on effect, via the chain of critical path activities, on the completion date: the nexus between activities referred to by Lord Oliver in *Wharf Properties*.[50]

4.89 A particularly clear statement of the need to prove not just that a specific activity has been delayed by the particular problem relied on, but that the problem caused delay to the overall progress of the works and thus the completion date, can be found in

---

49 See paragraphs 4.144ff as to discussion of the use of electronic programmes in delay analysis.
50 See paragraphs 4.19ff, above.

Costain v Charles Haswell.[51] In that case, Richard Fernyhough QC (sitting as a Deputy High Court Judge) considered a claim by Costain for time-related costs in relation to delays to foundations which occurred in a four-month period from October 2002 to January 2003. It was common ground that the foundation works were delayed and common ground that at that time those works were on the critical path of the project, so that, 'all other things being equal, and if no later mitigation measures were taken, those delays would ultimately delay the completion of the project as a whole' (at [181]). However, even in those circumstances:

> 182. Costain has assessed the prolongation costs of the delay claim on the basis of the weekly general site overheads of the whole project over the period October 2002–January 2003. The claim is put this way on the basis that, *since the foundation works were on the critical path of the project, any delays to them would inevitably cause delayed completion of the whole project therefore it is right to claim the weekly prolongation costs of the whole project being delayed for a like period* . . .
>
> 183. When an extension of time of the project completion date is claimed, *the contractor needs to establish that a delay to an activity on the critical path has occurred of a certain number of days or weeks <u>and</u> that that delay has in fact pushed out the completion date at the end of the project by a given number of days or weeks*, after taking account of any mitigation or acceleration measures. If the contractor establishes those facts, he is entitled to an extension of time for completion of the whole project including, of course all those activities which were not in fact delayed by the delaying events at all, i.e. they were not on the critical path . . .[52]

4.90 There is an important distinction here between delay to an activity which is on the critical path, and demonstrating that this activity delay did in fact translate into delay to the completion date. As the learned Judge commented, if an activity which is on the critical path is delayed, 'all other things being equal', this will cause a delay to the completion date.[53] However, the claimant contractor has the burden of proving this. There are many things which can happen on a project, after the occurrence of an event which affects an activity on the critical path, which can have the effect of reducing or even eliminating the delay to the completion date, without the contractor taking any additional or special acceleration measures. For example, a subsequent activity may take less time than planned or there may be a variation which reduces the contract scope and thus reduces the time taken for the remaining work (remaining after the delayed activity). Further, the contractor may, without any increase in cost to him, be able to re-sequence the works in such a way as to save time. This type of step is often taken 'for the good of the project' irrespective of contractual responsibility for the event.

4.91 In many delay claims, it is the link, or more usually the series of links, between the originally affected critical path activity and the actual delay to the completion date which is entirely missing from the analysis. Establishing this causation link or nexus is essential for success in the claim.

4.92 The decision in *Bluewater Energy Services BV v Mercon Steel Structures*[54] is a good example of a delay claim where the *factual* causative link between the originally delayed critical path activity and the delay to the completion date could not be established.[55]

---

51 [2009] EWHC 3140 (TCC).
52 Emphasis added.
53 See definition of critical path at paragraphs 4.71ff, above.
54 [2014] EWHC 2132 (TCC); 155 ConLR 85.
55 For further discussion of the substantive law issues arising out of this case, see paragraphs 7–043–7–048 of *Keating on Offshore Construction and Marine Engineering* (1st edn, 2015).

4.93 The facts were as follows. Mercon (as subcontractor) was obliged to fabricate part of a soft yoke mooring system (SYMS) for installation as part of the development of an offshore oil field in the Caspian Sea. The contract contained milestone dates, which included a milestone for completion of the SYMS structure (Milestone C6) and a subsequent milestone for load-out of the completed structure (Milestone C9 in September 2008), for which Bluewater had to provide the vessel. Obviously, the SYMS structure had to be completed before it could be loaded out. Completion of the structure and provision of a vessel were both, therefore, in principle on the critical path to load-out.

4.94 In January 2008, Bluewater stated that it did not intend to provide a vessel for load-out until June 2009 (so that the SYMS would have to be stored between the date on which it was completed and June 2009). Bluewater lawfully terminated the contract in February 2009, at which point the SYMS structure was still not complete and Milestone C6 had therefore not been achieved. Mercon argued that it was entitled to an extension of time to Milestone C9 to June 2009 (because that milestone could not be achieved without a vessel) and therefore any delay to Milestone C6 would not have any causative effect and/or was concurrent with the load-out delay. Mercon's case was that the project was *already* delayed by the load-out delay, which it will be appreciated occurred first in time. Mr Justice Ramsey held:

> 308. Bluewater submits that the correct analysis is that a storage activity was inserted between the completion of Milestone C6 and the start of Milestone C9. On this basis Bluewater says that the critical path runs through completion of the structure (C6) into storage and then to load out (C9) and that the delays to completion of C6 were the actual cause of delay to the critical path of the project. It submits that this causes delay to progress of the works towards achieving C9 but there is then further delay caused by the requirement to store the structure. On this basis the delay to the completion of Milestone C6 and the delay to the Milestone C9 run consecutively.
>
> 309. Bluewater submits that on this project the Milestones are broadly linear so that delays to a preceding Milestone cause delay to a following Milestone. On this basis Bluewater says that the approach of the planning experts has therefore been to assess delay to a later Milestone by taking the accrued delay to the preceding Milestone and adding the additional delay to the succeeding Milestone. It says that this approach was applied consistently by the planning experts up to Milestone C6 but that Mr Cookson then changed his approach and ignores the accrued delays to C6 when assessing the cause of delay to C9.
>
> 310. In relation to delay to load out caused by the instruction to carry out storage after the completion of Milestone C6 because Milestone C9 could not commence until 1 June 2009, I do not see that this affects the position in respect of delay to Milestone C6 which had not been completed before termination. Milestone C9 was dependent on the completion of Milestone C6. In order to load out the integrated SYMS under Milestone C9 it was necessary for the integrated SYMS to be 'ready for Load-Out' under Milestone C6. Once there was an integrated SYMS ready for load out *then it would only be at that stage that an instruction to store the integrated SYMS would cause a delay to the load out of the integrated SYMS under Milestone C9.*
>
> 311. Equally in the absence of a vessel to load out there would then be a delay to load out. However, *unless and until there was an integrated SYMS ready for load out there would be no delay to the subsequent Milestone C9 caused by the absence of a load out vessel or the need for storage in the meantime. Until the time had come for load out by having an integrated SYMS, any operations which might then affect load out for Milestone C9 would not be an operative cause of delay.* They would not delay the completion of Milestone C6 and until Milestone C6 was complete whilst they may be predicted to cause delay to Milestone C9 they would not actually do so until the time when it was possible to commence Milestone C9 had arrived. For instance, it may be that Lukoil would change its mind and make a vessel available and *it was only when the need for storage or the absence of a vessel impacted can it be said that delay is caused.*

312. On that basis, because the instruction to carry out storage and/or the absence of a load out vessel until 1 June 2009 had not impacted on the work necessary to complete Milestone C6 by February 2009 so as to be causative of delay by the date of termination, I do not consider that Mercon can rely on a cause of delay which would only impact on Milestone C9, after completion of Milestone C6.[56]

4.95 It will be appreciated that, had the contract not been terminated in February 2009, what might have happened was that the SYMS structure was completed, and there was a storage period between that completion and load-out due to the absence of a vessel. However, as a matter of fact, events did not progress that far. As a matter of fact, in February 2009, all that had happened was that the SYMS structure was in delay. The failure to provide a vessel could not *in fact* cause any delay to the project until the structure was complete and ready to be loaded out.[57] Therefore, what happened in this case was that events in February 2009 meant that what looked in 2008 like inevitable critical delay caused by Bluewater's decision to postpone provision of the vessel *in fact* caused no delay at all.

Identify the constraints between follow-on activities leading up to the completion date

4.96 In order to establish the causative nexus between activities, it is necessary to understand how – by what mechanism – one activity on the project affects the progress of the next, and so on up to the completion date. The mechanism is often referred to as the relevant constraint. Two activities which are linked together by a constraint are often called (using jargon from electronic programmes) 'predecessor' and 'successor' activities. The intention is to indicate that the predecessor activity *must* come before the successor activity due to the nature of the constraint on the successor activity imposed by the predecessor activity.

4.97 There are only three types of constraint (discussed in more detail below) which can affect the sequence in which the activities making up the works can be carried out on site and/or the duration of each activity:

– Physical constraints: it is impossible to fill a hole with concrete until the hole has been dug.
– Resource constraints: it will take one man longer to paint a room than four men.
– Contractor's preference: the contractor may prefer to carry out work in a particular order because it suits his workforce or arrangements with his subcontractors, etc. Often the contractor's preference is based on the most economical way of carrying out the relevant work.

4.98 When analysing the delay which has occurred on a project, it is essential to understand *why* (or why not) delay to one activity caused delay to the next activity in the sequence. If the activity is capable of affecting a subsequent activity, the reason will always be one of the three types of constraint set out above. In a credible and persuasive delay

---

56 Emphasis added.
57 It is relevant to note that it was not contended by Mercon that it was pacing the fabrication of the structure as a result of Bluewater's change in the load-out date, in which case on the facts it may well have been the case that the load-out delay was the cause of the delay in completing the structure.

claim, the specific nature of the constraint between each of the activities in the chain of activities causing delay to the completion date will clearly be explained.

4.99 It is often the case that there are hidden dependencies or relationships which are not shown in either an electronic or hard-copy programme. For example, it may be that certain items of equipment are to be fabricated off site. The series of activities and the duration required for the fabrication of this equipment may not be shown on the programme. However, the availability of this equipment is just as much a constraint on progress as anything shown on the programme.

Physical constraints

4.100 A physical constraint can take many forms. It may be a simple physical impossibility to start the follow-on activity before the first activity is completed (as in the example given above). The physical impossibility may, of course, be much more technically complex and therefore require more explanation, ranging from the need to allow concrete to cure in order that it reaches a certain strength before the next stage of the works can commence, up to matters such as chemical reactions or other complex interactions. The physical constraint may also be an issue, such as site congestion and/or restrictions on access: a large crane needed for one activity can block access to a different part of the site needed for another activity, or there may be a restriction on the hours during which a particular access can be used, or it may be that there is an existing structure on an area where a new structure is to be built, which has to be removed before work can start. In addition, the work in question (such as earthworks or particular coating systems) may be subject to a weather constraint.

Resource constraints

4.101 A resource constraint can affect both the sequence and the duration of activities. It affects duration most obviously, since it is very often possible to carry out an activity quicker if more resource is applied. However, this is not always the case: five men cannot paint the inside of a telephone box quicker than one man and, similarly, a very congested site can slow down progress overall. The effect of a change in resource on the duration of an activity must always be considered in the specific factual context of that activity itself and the works overall. Resource can also affect sequencing. For example, the resource constraint might be the availability of cranes being used elsewhere on site or only available for hire from a certain point. A contractor may therefore plan the sequence of works so as to start a particular piece of work later than might appear to be required, to allow for the movement of the cranes. A further typical type of resource constraint is the availability of skilled labour. Obviously it is up to the contractor to provide for sufficient skilled labour to carry out the original scope works, but there can be cases where the contractor has a gang with a particular skill which only does a particular task in different areas on site, and the sequence in which follow-on work from that task can be completed is dependent on the progress of that gang.

Contractor's preference

4.102 Where the constraint is the contractor's preference, this can often cause the contractor problems in establishing its claim for additional time, although it may not affect a claim for additional money if a changed sequence can be demonstrated to be more expensive than planned at tender stage. This is because, firstly, most contracts include an obligation on the contractor to make reasonable efforts to mitigate all delay, irrespective of whether that delay was caused by the employer or the contractor; and, secondly, it is very often the case that the sequence or even duration of activities can be changed with little difficulty. Contractors are often able to absorb a certain amount of delay by these means.

Effect of constraint on successor activities

4.103 Once the constraint between two activities in a sequence has been identified, the next step is to identify the specific effect that the problem with the first activity had on the successor activity.

4.104 There are only three possible effects:

– the successor activity can start later than planned (but take about the same time as originally planned to undertake);
– the successor activity can take longer than planned to carry out (but might in this case start approximately on time); or
– the successor activity can both start later than planned and take longer to carry out.

4.105 It is necessary to identify the relevant effect for each activity in the chain of activities on the critical path leading up to the completion date.

Step 6: Conclusion

4.106 Once it is established how the original activity subject to the delay event was affected, and how the delay to that activity affected the follow-on or successor activity, and the next activity, etc., right up to the completion date, the claim for delay will be established. If this process is followed, the precise amount of the delay caused by the individual delay event will also be established.

4.107 In summary, following the process above will enable a party to establish the story of the project so far as relevant to the delay claim:

– What was the *specific* event which caused delay?
– What immediate problem did it cause? What immediate *specific* work activity was stopped/prolonged/started later than planned?
– What *specific* follow-on or successor work activity was stopped/prolonged/started later than planned as a result of the issue with the immediately affected work? Why and how? What was the constraint between those activities which meant this was the case?
– How and why (via what chain of activities) did that affect the completion date?

4.108 This must be repeated for each delay event, in chronological order. Further, since the claim will be based on a retrospective analysis, the occurrence of a subsequent delay event can change the effect of an earlier delay event.

4.109 The process of obtaining factual witness statements and expert evidence to establish this case is discussed at paragraph 4.130, below. It will be noted that none of the above

Difficulties and complexities

4.110 Making or defending a delay claim is always complex as it is heavily fact-dependent and there is no quick way through the required level of detail. However, there are certain points which can add an additional level of complexity to the position.

Complex/multiple critical paths

4.111 On a retrospective basis, there should usually be only one critical path through the project (since there is generally only one longest path once it is known what actually happened). However, in a prospective analysis, or sometimes, rarely, in a retrospective analysis, it is possible that there is more than one critical path or (more likely) a second very near critical path which is so close to the actual critical path as to also be important in the delay analysis.

4.112 Concurrent delay (as now defined in the authorities) in principle requires there either to be two critical path activities impacted by different events (one employer-risk and one contractor-risk) causing delay over the same period, or that the same critical path activity is impacted by two different events (one employer-risk and one contractor-risk) causing delay over the same period. Put this way, it can easily be understood why it is rare in practice.

4.113 Projects where a double critical path is more likely include projects where there is more than one planned and actual work front (for example, where work is proceeding simultaneously on separate areas of a railway line or tunnel, or where a project involves the simultaneous construction of two tower blocks).

4.114 In such cases, it is possible that events impacting different areas of the project could both cause critical delay occurring over the same period of time. However, in particular in a retrospective analysis, it should be noted that the true single cause of critical delay can usually be identified with sufficiently clear analysis of the facts.

Relevance of as-planned critical path or near-critical paths at particular points during the project

4.115 The problems of a prospective delay analysis have been discussed above in the context of a trial taking place after the project is complete and the facts of what happened are known. In that context, the as-planned critical path and/or near critical paths are usually irrelevant, as the Court is only interested in matters which in fact caused critical delay.

4.116 However, the as-planned critical path and/or near critical paths can be relevant in a retrospective delay analysis, as they may explain why particular decisions were reasonably made at a particular time to focus on some specific aspect of the works. In this way, the as-planned critical path and/or near critical paths can affect the as-built critical path via the decision-making of the project manager. If that decision-making was a reasonable response to events on the project at the time (including delay events), then it is submitted that the consequences of that decision-making may well be factually attributable to a preceding delay event.

Frequent mistakes in practice

Introduction

4.117 This section will cover some of the more frequent mistakes that are made in practice, whether in advancing or defending a delay claim.

Focus on liability only

4.118 Perhaps the most frequent type of mistake seen is that of focussing on establishing or defeating liability for the relevant delay event, without any attempt at all to explain how that delay event *caused* critical delay. For example, the contractor might advance a claim for a variation, which focusses on liability for the change and simply assumes that if additional work was required, this will delay the completion date. This type of claim will not succeed in the TCC.

4.119 The contractor in a delay claim must establish liability (that the delay event was at the employer's contractual risk) and causation of the relevant period of delay (which involves all of the matters set out in 'Making or defending a delay claim in practice', above).[58] If the contractor only establishes liability, its claim will fail.

4.120 For a defendant to a delay claim, some concentration on liability is excusable since this is in principle a complete defence to the claim. However, it is often the case that a claimant contractor has a better case on liability than it does on causation of delay: and if the delay event caused no delay, this is also a complete defence to the claim.

Focus on delay caused to immediately affected activity only

4.121 Another version of an inadequate delay claim often seen in practice is that where there is a detailed description of the delay caused by the delay event to the immediately affected activity, but the crucial issues of (1) whether that activity is on the critical path and (2) whether delay to that activity in fact caused delay to the completion date (in other words, all the other matters discussed above) are entirely overlooked.

4.122 It is not enough to establish that (for example) a variation meant that work could not progress as planned in a specific area of the works. It must be shown that the delay to that area was on the critical path and as a matter of fact caused critical delay.

Focus on the last event which delayed completion

4.123 Another typical mistake is focussing only on the event which occurred last which also pushed out the completion date and seeking to attribute all the delay which occurred on the project to that event, on the basis that the works could not have been completed before the date on which they did because of the last-occurring event.

4.124 As a matter of authority, it was decided as long ago as 1993 in *Balfour Beatty* that this approach (referred to as the gross approach) is wrong in principle in a claim made

---

58 If time-related cost is claimed, the contractor must also establish causation for this head of loss. This is discussed in Chapter 5.

pursuant to the JCT Forms.[59] The same principle was held to apply to shipbuilding standard forms in *Adyard*.[60] It is submitted that any contract which requires proof of actual delay caused by the particular event to the completion date prohibits the use of this approach. Akenhead J discussed this issue in *Walter Lilly*:[61]

> 365. What one cannot do is to identify the last of a number of events which delayed completion and then say it was that last event at the end which caused the overall delay to the Works. One needs to consider what critically delayed the Works as they went along. For instance in this case, it would be wrong to say that the problem with the Courtyard Sliding Doors delayed the Works until it emerged as a problem in April 2008. Put another way, it did not delay the Works (if at all) until it emerged as a problem which needed to be addressed . . .
>
> 379. In the assessment of what events caused what overall or critical delay, one needs also to bear in mind that it is not necessarily the last item or area of work which is finished last which causes delay. Thus, often on building projects, the last item of work is the final clean up of the site. That may only take two people one day to do but it is (almost always) the job which must be done on the last day of the job. It is what delays that final operation which in itself takes no longer than it was always going to take which must be assessed. This is of some importance in this case because it is argued that snagging (or an excessive amount of it) itself delayed the project. It is, rightly, common ground that snagging always has to be done because, with the best will in the world, there will be minor deficiencies, blemishes or incomplete items of work which will be required to be completed before hand over. Obviously, if there is an excessive amount of snagging and therefore more time than would otherwise have been reasonably necessary to perform the de-snagging exercise has to be expended, it can potentially be a cause of delay in itself.

4.125 A practical application of this principle can also be seen in the *Bluewater v Mercon* case discussed above at paragraphs 4.92 and following. It was not until the structure was complete and ready to sail away that the lack of a barge was capable of causing delay to the progress of the works.

Ignoring contractual notice provisions

4.126 It is frequently the case that the contract provides that the contractor has to give notice to the employer in the event of a delay event occurring. The requirements of these forms of notice vary greatly between contracts. A discussion of the contractual significance and/or interpretation of such notice provisions is outside the scope of this book, but it is worth emphasising here that where the clause imposes or arguably imposes a notice condition precedent on any delay claim, it is rash to ignore it. The issue will not go away, and the lack of any attempt to deal with the requirement for notice in the claim gives the defendant the legitimate opportunity to point out that the claimant is presumably worried about its failure to comply with the clause.

4.127 In practical terms, it is rare that a notice provision imposes formal requirements on the notice which has to be given, although it often has to be in writing. This means that it may be possible to establish that notice was given within the required timescale by reference to meeting minutes, contemporaneous emails or sometimes progress reports.

---

59 (1993) 62 BLR 1.
60 [2011] BLR 384 (Comm).
61 [2012] BLR 503 (TCC).

Evidence at trial

4.128 Proving a delay claim at trial will require factual and, usually, expert evidence. The factual evidence should be the most important of these because it is the factual witness who is in a position to establish the story of the project, and thus the causation case discussed above. Causation is a matter of fact, not opinion, and is therefore for the factual witnesses to deal with rather than an expert. The role of a delay expert in TCC proceedings is discussed further below.

4.129 A frequent mistake is to allow the delay expert to recreate the history of the project via contemporaneous documents and without (obviously) any direct, personal knowledge of what happened. Often, the delay expert does not have sufficient technical expertise to comment on why particular activities constrained other activities, but is obliged to include this in his report since otherwise the claim does not make sense. As discussed in more detail below, this type of mistake will undermine the credibility of the delay expert.

Factual witness evidence

4.130 The aim of a factual witness statement dealing with delay is to explain, in clear and readily comprehensible terms, the chain of events which led from the delaying event to the delayed completion date (essentially following the steps above). This will usually include an explanation of why that factual witness understood particular activities to be on the critical path at relevant times – there should be no problem in obtaining this information from a factual witness, since in order properly to manage the project it is necessary to understand which activities are the most important/likely to affect the completion date.

4.131 Generally speaking, one factual witness should tell the story of the project and deal with the claims for delay. This has the advantage that there will be one person who had overall oversight of the project, such as a project manager. This is the natural person to talk about the problems which caused delay to the progress of the works overall. It is good tactics generally to limit the number of witnesses talking about a particular topic to the minimum possible: see discussion in Chapter 3 above.

4.132 As foreshadowed above, the relevant witness should be someone who had the relevant knowledge of the project at the time. Sometimes, it is not possible to limit this to one person – for example, because the project manager (PM) changed halfway through the project. In that case, the first PM should give evidence up to the point that she left, and the second PM should then take over.

4.133 A factual witness statement dealing with delay should invariably be written in chronological order. This will involve starting with an explanation in outline terms of what was *planned* to occur and when before explaining what went wrong and why, and why that affected the completed date in the case of each event. If the contractor's plans changed during the project (as they almost always do), then the relevant changes need to be identified at the time that they were made. The delay caused by any particular event should, of course, be measured against the latest plan in force prior to the event occurring, not against the original programme.

4.134 It is often sensible, depending on the size of the project and the period in dispute, to take the project in monthly or three-monthly intervals. A more detailed (even daily) review of what happened may be necessary when dealing with individual delay events.

4.135 Before dealing with any delay event, the witness should give a factual summary of progress on the project at the point just before the delay event occurred, in order to establish (if the contractor) that matters were proceeding to plan prior to the event or (if the employer) that the project and/or the affected activity were already in delay for other reasons. This summary will need to look at both the progress of the activity which is said to be immediately affected by the delay event, and at the progress of the works overall, including in particular whether the activity was on the critical path.

4.136 The witness can then discuss the effect of the relevant delay event, again both on the immediately affected activity and on the progress of the works overall. This will involve discussing why and how (or why not) the delayed activity affected the successor activity, and so on through the chain of activities on the critical path up to an effect on the completion date.

4.137 It must never be assumed that the nature of a constraint, or the lack of a constraint, between activities is obvious. It must be spelled out so that the Judge cannot possibly misunderstand.

4.138 If defending the claim, the aim will be to show that the project was delayed by other, contractor-risk, events and that the events relied on by the contractor did not cause any critical delay. The appropriate method is essentially identical to that set out above. In particular, the factual witness will want to identify the first-occurring delay event relied on by the contractor and provide a summary of progress on the project prior to that event. If possible, this should explain briefly how and why the project was already slipping behind during that period (there is no need to be exhaustively detailed, since the contractor does not claim he was delayed in this period, and under the contract unless he can establish an extension of time (EOT) for this period, liquidated damages are due). However, this narrative should pick up any matters which it is the employer's case continued to cause delay over the remainder of the project, in order to show that they are part of a recurring problem causing delay throughout.

4.139 In relation to each delay event which the employer relies on as being a contractor-risk event in fact causing the delay to the completion date, the factual witness will need to go through the same steps as set out above in order to explain how and why this occurred.

4.140 The factual witness will need to make extensive reference to the contemporaneous documents. The Court will not simply accept a factual witness's version of events. In order to prove that the story told by the factual witness is correct, she will need to refer to meeting minutes, progress reports, emails and often contemporaneous updated programmes in order to establish that she is correct as to the precise dates on which and sequence in which events unfolded on the project. However, the statement should not consist of quotations from documents: see further Chapter 3 above.

4.141 The factual witness may also be a quasi-expert witness who has relevant specialist technical knowledge which it is necessary to include in a witness statement to explain the reasoning behind a particular programme, or the specific constraint between particular activities. The factual witness should include his technical understanding in the witness statement where necessary: such 'opinion' evidence is admissible from a technical factual witness in appropriate circumstances.[62] In these circumstances, the Court will usually also expect to hear from an independent technical expert supporting the factual witness's explanation.

4.142 Overall, the emphasis should be on ensuring the explanation of what caused the delay and *how* the delay to the completion date was caused should be as clear as possible. A useful test is whether the legal team understand the explanation (given that the TCC Judge will be a lawyer). If the legal team cannot understand the causation story of the delay case, two consequences follow: there are no prospects that the Court will be able to understand and – significantly – there is a problem with the case!

Expert evidence

4.143 See the discussion in Chapter 3 with reference to general issues regarding expert evidence and in particular the areas of expertise that a delay expert can bring to a claim. In this chapter, the focus is upon a discussion of delay analysis carried out using a methodology which uses or relies on an electronic programme (usually using Primavera or Microsoft Project or similar software).

Electronic programme-based analysis

4.144 In relation to delay analysis using an electronic programme, the approach of the Court has changed over the past 10 to 15 years. In order to understand what has happened, it is necessary briefly to explain how such an analysis works.

Logic links

4.145 An electronic programme which has been prepared in a way which makes it suitable for use in delay analysis includes logic links between each activity on the programme. The logic links tell the software the nature of the physical relationship between the activities on the programme and are therefore intended to reflect the reality of the constraints (as discussed above) on the ground. For the purpose of this discussion, it is sufficient to explain the most common links:

- *Finish-to-start link*. This link tells the software that the second activity cannot start until the first activity has finished. A simple example would be the need to dig a hole before it is possible to fill that hole with concrete. In this case, the activity for digging the hole has a finish-to-start relationship with the activity for pouring concrete.
- *Finish-to-finish link*. This link tells the software that the second activity cannot finish until the first activity has finished. A simple example would be the need to complete preparation of O&M manuals before the project overall can be completed (assuming O&M manuals are contractually required prior to completion). In this case, the activity for preparation of the O&M manuals has a finish-to-finish relationship with the overall completion date.

---

62 See further the discussion in Chapter 3.

- *Start-to-start link.* This link tells the software that the second activity can only start once the first activity has started (it doesn't mean that the activities have to start at the same time). A simple example would be the need to have sufficiently progressed the building of a wall before the painting of that wall can start (assuming that on the specific technical facts of this wall and this paint that painting can progress in line with the progress of the wall; it is not necessary to complete construction of the whole wall before painting can start). In this case, the activity for building the wall has a start-to-start relationship with the activity for painting.

4.146 It will be appreciated that these logic links are only capable of reflecting either physical constraints or a contractor's preference. They cannot by themselves reflect any resource constraints. The software used in many electronic programmes is capable of including planned resource information. In practice, however, this is very rarely used and so the information will not be available in the programme for the delay claim.

4.147 It is also possible to instruct the software to 'fix' a start or end date of a particular activity using a variety of instructions such as 'Must Finish By' or 'Start On' which override the logic links described above. The software further does not require that every single activity is logic linked to another so that in principle a programme could show the planned sequence and duration of activities using only 'fixed' start and end dates without any logic links added at all.

4.148 The software uses the logic links and the 'fixed' dates to produce a critical path through the works. This is usually shown by colouring the critical activities red on the programme.

Methods of programme-based analysis

4.149 There are a number of different methods of programme-based delay analysis. A detailed discussion of these methods is outside the scope of this book.

4.150 Useful resources include the SCL Delay and Disruption Protocol (2nd edition) and *Beware the Dark Arts* by David Barry.[63] In every case, it is essential to ensure that the method of delay analysis chosen fulfils the requirements of the contract as discussed above.

Reliability of programme-based analysis

4.151 In any event, all the methods involve seeking to add to the delaying event or sequence of delaying events into the programme (whether into the baseline programme or into a programme updated for actual progress up to the time of the event), and relying on the delaying effect of that event *as shown on the programme* as being the actual effect. This relies on the logic links and other constraints on activities included within the programme accurately reflecting physical reality on the ground.

4.152 Nowadays, most contractors on projects of any size will produce an electronic programme showing their planned sequence and timing of the works (and this is often a contractual requirement). To be suitable for use in delay analysis (as opposed to managing the works), the programme should in principle have *all* its activities logically linked to each other, accurately reflecting the reality of the constraints on site, and none of the activities

---

63 See https://www.blackrockexpertservices.com/transmissions/beware-dark-arts/.

should be fixed (often referred to as constrained). This, in theory, means that when a delay event is added, all the activities affected move on the programme controlled only by their logic links (and thus reflecting real life). This is often referred to as dynamic delay analysis.

4.153 However, it is rare (if not impossible) to find such a programme. It is not necessary to produce a perfect dynamically linked programme for the purposes of managing a project, and most contractors take the approach of logic linking what they regard as key activities and simply fixing most others. This means that to be suitable even in principle for a dynamic delay analysis, the expert is invariably required to make extensive changes and improvements to the logic links. Given that many programmes include literally thousands of activities, this takes a very significant amount of time and is very rarely capable of being agreed with the other side.

4.154 If the logic in the programme is wrong, then the critical path shown and the delay analysis produced by it will also be wrong. One wrong logic link can have a major effect on the results of the analysis. The basis of the result is also often opaque, because the programme has run through hundreds or thousands of activities, each separately programmed, in reaching its result. For this reason, these are sometimes called 'black box' delay analyses.

4.155 It is emphasised again that causation of delay is a factual, common-sense matter. If the expert is asserting that a particular event caused x amount of delay, because the programme says so, but cannot explain in simple terms how or why, this should be a red flag. The problem can perhaps be summed up by a literary analogy. In Salman Rushdie's novel *Haroun and the Sea of Stories*, Haroun must get the story-tap turned back on for his father, a storyteller who has lost the ability to tell stories. He finds the person who has turned it off, and asks the reason why:

> 'Orders,' said Iff. 'All queries to be taken up with the Grand Comptroller.' 'Grand Comptroller of what?' Haroun wanted to know.
> 'Of the Processes Too Complicated To Explain, of course. At P2C2E House, Gup City, Kahani. All letters to be addressed to the Walrus.'

If the causation case as set out by the expert involves a P2C2E, it is very unlikely to stand up at trial.

4.156 For these reasons, the popularity of delay analysis based on an electronic programme has waned significantly over the past 15 years. In 2007, in *Mirant Asia-Pacific Construction (Hong Kong) Ltd v Ove Arup & Partners International Ltd*,[64] HHJ Toulmin CMG, QC set out at [119] to [130] a hymn of praise to the utility of a critical path identified using a programme (requiring 'detailed and sophisticated analysis' by a delay expert) and a delay analysis carried out in the same way.

4.157 However, even by the following year in 2008, Lord Drummond Young was commenting (correctly in the view of the editors) as follows:[65]

> 29. In my opinion the pursuers clearly went too far in suggesting that an expert could only give a meaningful opinion on the basis of an as-built critical path analysis. For reasons discussed below (at paragraphs [36]–[37]) I am of opinion that such an approach has serious dangers of its own. I further conclude, as explained in those paragraphs, that Mr Lowe's own use of an as-built critical path analysis is flawed in a significant number of important respects. On that

---

64 [2007] EWHC 918 (TCC) (not appealed).
65 *City Inn Ltd v Shepherd Construction Ltd* [2007] CSOH 190; [2008] BLR 269 (Outer House, Court of Session).

basis, I conclude that that approach to the issues in the present case is not helpful. The major difficulty, it seems to me, is that in the type of programme used to carry out a critical path analysis any significant error in the information that is fed into the programme is liable to invalidate the entire analysis. Moreover, for reasons explained by Mr Whitaker (paragraphs [36]–[37] below), I conclude that it is easy to make such errors. That seems to me to invalidate the use of an as-built critical path analysis to discover after the event where the critical path lay, at least in a case where full electronic records are not available from the contractor. That does not invalidate the use of a critical path analysis as a planning tool, but that is a different matter, because it is being used then for an entirely different purpose . . .

. . .

36. Mr Whitaker criticized the method of delay analysis that Mr Lowe had adopted; in particular, he was critical of the use of an as-built critical path analysis. He stated that a critical path analysis involves identification of the duration of the relevant activities, based on the as-built records, and the logic links between those activities. The identification of the correct logic links was of vital importance. Problems arose with a critical path analysis when logic links were incorporated when they should not be there, or if logic links were inserted which were not wholly correct, or if necessary links were omitted. If a mistake was made in one logic link, that was liable to produce an error in the identification of the activities that were critical to completion of the works, and that in turn could invalidate the critical path shown in the relevant programme. If a number of erroneous links were identified, Mr Whitaker stated that it would definitely be the case that the critical path identified in the programme would not be correct . . .

4.158 The learned Judge went on to give a very lengthy list of errors in the logic links in the programme used. Subsequently, the emphasis in the authorities has firmly been on the necessity to demonstrate delay on the facts.[66]

4.159 The editors' view is, therefore, that a solely electronic programme-based critical path analysis and/or delay analysis should be approached with caution.

---

66 See cases referred to at n 8, above.

CHAPTER 5

Delay and disruption money claims

Introduction

5.1 Delay-related money claims could be made by either the contractor or the employer. They could also be claims under the contract (made pursuant to a specific provision) or in damages at common law, for breach. Different considerations apply to each type of claim, but one important piece of practical advice applies to both: start with the money. In order to recover the claimed sum, it will be necessary to demonstrate that (1) the losses claimed have in fact been incurred[1] and (2) those losses were caused by the specific event or breach relied on. It is much easier to focus properly on those hurdles if one starts with the actual losses and works backwards to the event/breach, as further described below. Further, it cannot be over-emphasised that contemporaneous documentary evidence is essential. 'A party to a dispute, particularly if there is an arbitration will learn three lessons (often too late) the importance of records, the importance of records and the importance of records.'[2]

Contractor's delay-related money claims under the contract

Introduction

5.2 Most standard form contracts in use in the United Kingdom include a specific contractual provision governing the contractor's claim for the recovery of losses not dealt with elsewhere in the contract. In other standard forms, such as FIDIC, there is no such specific clause. In that contract money claims in addition to the variation account are brought under clause 20.[3]

Different tests for time and money

5.3 As is well known, the basis for recovery of delay-related money claims is different from the basis for recovery of an extension of time in most of the standard form contracts. In the JCT standard forms, the contractor must identify a Relevant Matter (a more restricted list than a Relevant Event) which has caused the relevant 'loss or expense'. The contractor must prove that he would not have incurred those losses 'but for' the occurrence of the

---

1 Save for a claim by the employer for liquidated damages.
2 Max Abrahamson, *Engineering Law and the ICE Contracts* (4th edn, 1979).
3 Notwithstanding that this is odd given the wording of clause 20 itself, which appears to govern the procedure for bringing claims made under other clauses of the contract.

Relevant Matter, and for money claims this test is not relaxed in the case of concurrent delay in contrast to time claims.[4]

Relevance of contractual provisions to valuation

5.4 Under the JCT standard forms, recovery of preliminaries associated with a particular variation can be recovered via the variations clause. Depending on which route is taken, a different basis of valuation applies:

- Under the Valuation Rules applicable to variation claims, the schedule of rates/bill of quantities is used to identify an applicable contractual rate to be used.
- Under the loss and expense clause, actual cost must be proved.

5.5 A similar regime applies under the NEC forms.

5.6 The fact that preliminaries can be recovered via individual variations is often overlooked in the contractor's claims for delay-related losses. It can in some circumstances be advantageous to the contractor to bring a rates-based claim, whether because the rates are easier to prove than actual losses, or because a rates-based claim gives rise to a higher recovery.

5.7 If some preliminaries are being claimed via the variations clause and some via the loss and expense clause (for example, if some of the delay was caused by a variation and some by weather), obviously credit has to be given in the loss and expense claim for periods of time recovered via the variation clause.

Relevance of tender pricing

5.8 Tender pricing and the level of resource planned at tender will often be relevant to demonstrating that a loss has been incurred: if the contractor would always have made a loss on the project because he under-priced the job or a particular aspect of the job, or if the contractor would always have had to incur additional cost in obtaining additional resource, it may not be possible for the contractor to show that the delaying or disruptive events relied on in fact caused a financial loss.

5.9 Contractors should expect to have to disclose their internal tender pricing (or risk adverse inference being drawn) if insufficient information is available from the contract bills of quantities/contract sum analysis itself.

Notice

5.10 The contract often requires notice to be given specifically for money claims (sometimes separately from time claims). Careful attention should be paid to the terms of the contract. In some cases, such as the JCT standard forms, notice is a condition precedent to making a claim.[5]

---

4 Usually known as the *Malmaison* principle. See chapter 7 of *Keating on Offshore Construction and Marine Engineering* for a discussion as to the contractual basis of this distinction.
5 See *Keating on JCT Contracts* (looseleaf) for commentary on the latest versions of the JCT forms.

Contractor's critical delay-related claims

Introduction

5.11 If a project is critically delayed, one head of cost which a contractor incurs is that relating to the extended duration of the project overall. These costs include matters such as the general cost of administering a project, management-level staff, general plant and overall site facilities (such as security or office facilities). Such costs are known as prolongation costs or preliminaries (the term is taken from the first part of a traditional bill of quantities 'where items of necessary cost are collected which do not usually become part of the finished works').[6] Sometimes, the contractor claims that as a result of events on the project, such costs have not only been prolonged, but have also been increased (for example, two project managers needed rather than one). Since the *increase* in such costs (as opposed to their prolonged duration) is not caused by critical delay, such claims are discussed under 'Disruption claims' below.

5.12 Where there is critical delay, the contractor also (in principle) incurs a loss of overheads: the reasoning goes that the contractor includes in her overall price for the work a fixed allowance for her head office costs of running the business (these are not preliminaries because they are not specifically related to the project itself), and if the project duration is prolonged, the contractor is prevented from moving on to the next project and recovering the relevant allowance on that project.

5.13 Claims for preliminaries and overheads are discussed in turn below.

Preliminaries/prolongation cost claims

5.14 As set out above, preliminaries are time-related costs relating to the site overall.

5.15 The time-related costs claimed should be those which were incurred at the time the relevant critical delay was incurred, not the average costs per day or per week over the whole contract.[7] This is because the overall management/plant resources tend to gradually increase and decrease on a bell curve as the project starts, is in full flow and then gets closer to completion; therefore, an overall average will not represent the actual cost caused by the relevant delay.

5.16 Further, where costs are claimed in relation to the whole site, it is essential to ensure that they really are time-related costs. In *Costain v Haswell*,[8] the Judge was considering a claim for prolongation costs in circumstances in which the relevant critical delay event affected two buildings specifically out of ten buildings on a site. The contractor claimed the weekly general site overheads. The judge said:[9]

> ... a claim for damages on account of delays to construction work is rather different [to a claim for an extension of time]. There, in order to recover substantial damages, the contractor needs to show what losses he has incurred as a result of the prolongation of the activity in question. Those losses will include the increased and additional costs of carrying out the delayed activity itself as well as the additional costs caused to other site activities as a result of the delaying

---

6 *Keating on Construction Contracts* (10th edn, 2016), para 9-049.
7 *Ascon Contracting Ltd v Alfred McAlpine Construction Isle of Man Ltd*, 66 Con LR 119 at [43].
8 [2009] EWHC B25 (TCC).
9 At [184].

event. But the contractor will not recover the general site overheads of carrying out all the activities on site as a matter of course unless he can establish that the delaying event to one activity in fact impacted on all the other site activities. Simply because the delaying event itself is on the critical path does not mean that in point of fact it impacted on any other site activity save for those immediately following and dependent upon the activities in question.

5.17 It is submitted that if the resources being claimed were genuinely time-related costs (and thus increased by the critical delay to the project), it would not matter where on the site they were based. For example, it would not matter if the project manager's office was off site altogether: he or she is still a purely time-related resource because he or she is required over the whole extended duration of the project. The better rationalisation of the decision in *Costain* may be that the Judge was not satisfied on the evidence that the claim was truly only for time-related costs, rather than other elements of site-activity-related cost.

5.18 As discussed above, the calculation of preliminaries costs will depend on whether they are being claimed via a variation or via the loss and expense clause.

5.19 If via the variation clause, in principle preliminaries should be valued on a contract rates basis, as discussed above. The difficulty here is that there is usually no specific rate in the contract for preliminaries which are usually priced as a lump-sum allowance within the overall price. This is often dealt with by calculating an average daily or weekly contractual rate by dividing the lump-sum allowance by the number of days or weeks in the original contract period. If there is no specific pricing in the contract for preliminaries at all, then this will usually mean that under the relevant valuation clause the position defaults to proof of actual cost.

5.20 If the claim for preliminaries is via the loss and expense clause, it will be necessary to demonstrate actual cost via staff payroll documents, etc. Contractors will want to include costs such as pension contributions, etc. which form part of overall salaries. It will be essential to provide relevant documentary evidence of these costs and this can involve a very large volume of documentation. A practical way through this type of problem is often for the parties' quantum experts to make a joint visit to the contractor's offices in order to interrogate the contractor's internal cost recording system and/or payroll information by way of sampling or tracking a particular cost through the system to check its reliability and/or comprehensiveness.

5.21 It can be harder to demonstrate actual costs for items such as contractor-owned plant since obviously there is no clear project-related cost for such an item. The usual approach is to calculate a value by taking into account the purchase price of the item, its likely useful life and depreciation and working out an average estimated cost for the relevant period of critical delay.

5.22 However, it may well be that the item has long since been written off in the contractor's accounts due to its age. In that case, the contractor is faced with a real problem. Often, the approach taken is to build up a notional hire cost using pricing books or estimates. However, a claim for notional hiring fees was rejected in *Alfred McAlpine Homes North Ltd v Property & Land Contractors Ltd*[10] on the basis that clause 26 (as it then was) of the JCT standard form required proof of actual cost to the contractor. The contractor may, therefore, need to consider whether as a result of the prolonged use of particular plant

---

10 [1996] 76 BLR 59 (TCC) at 90G–93F.

on the specific project, it was necessary to hire plant on a different project, and/or whether the contractor can prove that in some other way there was an actual cost to it relating to that plant.

Overheads claims

5.23 As stated above, overheads claims are for the fixed allowance notionally made in the contract price for the head office costs of running the business. If the project duration is prolonged, the contractor is prevented from moving on to the next project and recovering the relevant allowance on that project. It is well established that such claims are in principle recoverable.[11]

5.24 The relevant allowance for overheads is not always separately identified. The contract usually sets out the contractor's overheads and profit (OHP) percentage. The specific elements of overhead and profit within that overall number are often not stated. Further, since actual head office costs are not usually recorded in a way which makes it possible to identify which projects are defraying which head office costs, it is very difficult to demonstrate that the prolonged duration of one particular project actually caused any specific loss.

5.25 For this reason, the industry has developed various formulae. The best known in the United Kingdom are the *Hudson* and *Emden* formulae. These are formulae for calculating claims for loss of profit and overheads taken together. They calculate the loss as the contractor's OHP percentage based on a fair annual average multiplied by the contract sum and the period of delay and divided by the contract period. The *Hudson* formula uses the percentage for OHP stated in the contract, which can be criticised on the basis that this bears no necessary relationship to the contractor's actual overheads. The *Emden* formula is an attempt to improve on this by calculating the contractor's OHP percentage by dividing the total overhead cost and profit of the contractor's organisation as a whole by the total turnover.

5.26 The use of such formulae was considered in *Walter Lilly*.[12] Akenhead J said (in relation to a claim made under the loss and expense clause in the JCT standard form) at [543]:

(a) A contractor can recover head office overheads and profit lost as a result of delay on a construction project caused by factors which entitle it to loss and expense.

(b) It is necessary for the contractor to prove on a balance of probabilities that if the delay had not occurred it would have secured work or projects which would have produced a return (over and above costs) representing a profit and/or a contribution to head office overheads.

(c) The use of a formula, such as Emden or Hudson, is a legitimate and indeed helpful way of ascertaining, on a balance of probabilities, what that return can be calculated to be.

(d) The 'ascertainment' process under Clause 26 does not mean that the Architect/Quantity Surveyor or indeed the ultimate dispute resolution tribunal must be certain (that is sure beyond reasonable doubt) that the overheads and profit have been lost ... What one has to do is to be able to be confident that the loss or expense being allowed had actually been incurred as a result of the Clause 26 delay or disruption causing factors.

---

11 See *Walter Lilly v Mackay* [2012] BLR 503 (TCC) at [540].
12 [2012] BLR 503 (TCC).

5.27 It will be apparent from this that the most important practical consideration when bringing or defending such claims is the existence and/or soundness of the factual evidence adduced by the contractor as to the future projects which it would have been able to undertake and which would have produced a contribution to profit and/or head office overheads. It is essential that this evidence is cogent and logical. Such evidence might include the production of invitations to tender which it declined, or even negotiations which had to be abandoned. The contractor may also use its accounts to show a drop in turnover and establish that this resulted from the project-specific delay rather than other causes.

5.28 *Walter Lilly* also demonstrates that if this evidence is to be challenged, the relevant points should be put to the contractor's witnesses in cross-examination.[13]

5.29 It will further be important for an employer to check whether a contractor has already recovered any of this cost via the variation account as the valuation of variations usually includes a percentage for fixed overheads.

Loss of profit claims

5.30 Similar issues arise in relation to lost profit claims as they do in relation to lost overheads. See the discussion in *Walter Lilly* above.

Increased costs resulting from inflation

5.31 Contractors sometimes contend that they are entitled to any increased costs of labour and materials because they were bought at a later and more expensive time than planned at tender due to the delay to the project. Such claims are in principle recoverable,[14] but again in practice all will turn on whether the contractor can establish the relevant elements of the claim. The contractor would need to prove: (1) when it was originally planned to purchase such materials; (2) what the cost would have been at that time; (3) that this was a reasonable time to make the purchase; (4) that the contractor's tender pricing made sufficient allowance for that cost; (5) that the purchase was delayed as a result of the delay to the project; and (6) the difference in cost between the actual price and the tender allowance.

Disruption claims

Introduction

5.32 'Disruption' is the industry term for claims for losses caused by the 'disturbance of the contractor's regular and economic progress and/or delay to a non-critical activity even though, on occasion, there is no or only a small ultimate delay in completion'.[15]

5.33 The key practical difficulty experienced in bringing these claims is proving causation. Contractors often bring what are known as global or total cost claims, described in *Walter Lilly* as 'a contractor's claim which identifies numerous potential or actual causes of delay and/or disruption, a total cost on the job, a net payment from the employer and a

---

13 See paras [546]–[552] of the judgment.
14 Subject to the terms of any express clause dealing with inflationary increases; on any view double recovery on this head is not permitted.
15 *Keating on Construction Contracts* (10th edn, 2016), para 8-064.

claim for the balance between costs and payment which is attributed without more and by inference to the causes of delay and disruption relied on',[16] and in *London Underground v Citylink* as 'one that provides an inadequate explanation of the causal nexus between the breaches of contract or relevant events/matters relied upon and the alleged loss and damage or delay that relief is claimed for'.[17]

Authorities

5.34 Global claims have a long history in the Courts. Most of the relevant cases were reviewed in some detail in *Walter Lilly*,[18] which is therefore a convenient place to find a helpful summary of the development of the law. The learned Judge summarises the findings in the Scottish case of *John Doyle Construction Ltd v Laing Management (Scotland) Ltd*.[19] The real significance of this case was that it was held that even if a global claim fails as a whole, it may be possible to allocate some of the cost claimed to events which the employer is shown to be responsible for by way of examination of the evidence.[20] This was applied in England in *London Underground v Citylink*[21].

5.35 Following these cases, there were two common misapprehensions prevalent in the construction industry regarding global claims. These were that in order to bring a global claim:

– there was a requirement that it be impossible or at least impractical to separate the loss/delay and specify cause and effect; and
– there was a requirement that the contractor has not herself created the difficulty in establishing causation in the orthodox manner.

5.36 These issues were considered in detail in *Walter Lilly* (in the context of a claim under the 1998 version of the JCT Standard Form). The learned Judge summarised the relevant principles in an important passage from his judgment:[22]

> (a) Ultimately, claims by contractors for delay or disruption related loss and expense must be proved as a matter of fact. Thus, the Contractor has to demonstrate on a balance of probabilities that, first, events occurred which entitle it to loss and expense, secondly, that those events caused delay and/or disruption and thirdly that such delay or disruption caused it to incur loss and/or expense (or loss and damage as the case may be). I do not accept that, as a matter of principle, it has to be shown by a claimant contractor that it is impossible to plead and prove cause and effect in the normal way or that such impossibility is not the fault of the party seeking to advance the global claim. One needs to see of course what the contractual clause relied upon says to see if there are contractual restrictions on global cost or loss claims. Absent and subject to such restrictions, the claimant contractor simply has to prove its case on a balance of probabilities.

---

16 At [484].
17 At [142].
18 At [142].
19 [2002] BLR 393, at [479] in *Walter Lilly*.
20 At [38].
21 [2007] BLR 391. See also *Bluewater Energy Services BV v Mercon Steel Structures BV* (2014) 155 Con LR 85 at [1350]–[1367].
22 At [486].

...

(c) It is open to contractors to prove these three elements with whatever evidence will satisfy the tribunal and the requisite standard of proof. There is no set way for contractors to prove these three elements. For instance, such a claim may be supported or even established by admission evidence or by detailed factual evidence which precisely links reimbursable events with individual days or weeks of delay or with individual instances of disruption and which then demonstrates with precision to the nearest penny what that delay or disruption actually cost.

(d) There is nothing in principle 'wrong' with a 'total' or 'global' cost claim. However, there are added evidential difficulties (in many but not necessarily all cases) which a claimant contractor has to overcome. It will generally have to establish (on a balance of probabilities) that the loss which it has incurred (namely the difference between what it has cost the contractor and what it has been paid) would not have been incurred in any event. Thus, it will need to demonstrate that its accepted tender was sufficiently well priced that it would have made some net return. It will need to demonstrate in effect that there are no other matters which actually occurred (other than those relied upon in its pleaded case and which it has proved are likely to have caused the loss). It is wrong, as Counsel suggested, that the burden of proof in some way transfers to the defending party. It is of course open to that defending party to raise issues or adduce evidence that suggest or even show that the accepted tender was so low that the loss would have always occurred irrespective of the events relied upon by the claimant contractor or that other events (which are not relied upon by the claimant as causing or contributing to the loss or which are the 'fault' or 'risk' of the claimant contractor) occurred may have caused or did cause all or part of the loss.

(e) The fact that one or a series of events or factors (unpleaded or which are the risk or fault of the claimant contractor) caused or contributed (or cannot be proved not to have caused or contributed) to the total or global loss does not necessarily mean that the claimant contractor can recover nothing. It depends on what the impact of those events or factors is ... the overall claim will not be rejected save to the extent that those events caused some loss ... where the tribunal can take out of the 'rolled up award' or 'total' or 'global' loss elements for which the contractor cannot recover loss in the proceedings, it will generally be left with the loss attributable to the events which the contractor is entitled to recover loss.

(f) Obviously, there is no need for the Court to go down the global or total cost route if the actual cost attributable to individual loss causing events can be readily or practicably determined. I do not consider that ... a contractor should be debarred from pursuing what he called a 'rolled up award' if it could otherwise seek to prove its loss in another way. It may be that the tribunal will be more sceptical about the global cost claim if the direct linkage approach is readily available but is not deployed. That does not mean that the global cost claim should be rejected out of hand.

(g) DMW's Counsel's argument that a global award should not be allowed where the contractor has himself created the impossibility of disentanglement ... is not on analysis supported by [the] authorities and is wrong. Vinelott J [in Merton] was referring to unreasonable delay by the contractor in making its loss and/or expense claim; that delay would have led to their being non-compliance with the condition precedent but all that he was saying otherwise was that, if such delay created difficulty, the claim may not be allowed. He certainly was not saying that a global cost claim would be barred necessarily or at all if there was such delay ... In principle, unless the contract dictates that a global cost claim is not permissible if certain hurdles are not overcome, such a claim may be permissible on the facts and subject to proof.

5.37 These observations have subsequently been applied by the TCC[23] and represent the current approach of the Court.

---

23 *John Sisk & Son Ltd v Carmel Building Services Lt*d (in administration) [2016] BLR 283; and *William Clark Partnership Ltd v Dock St PCT Ltd* (2015) 163 Con LR 117.

Practicalities

5.38 In practical terms, the effect of this judgment can be summarised as follows:

- A claim for time/money (whether under the contract or for breach) has to be adequately pleaded, that is, so that the defendant can understand what is being alleged.
- This will normally mean that the claim event/breach will need to be pleaded in detail – as will the consequence, in terms of time/money, but the causal link will normally not have to be pleaded in detail.
- Causation will be considered and decided in light of the factual and expert evidence and may be inferred from the circumstances.
- A global claim will be viable even if it is not impossible/impractical to plead cause and effect in relation to discrete causes/losses and/or even if any such difficulty is due to the claimant's conduct.
- A global claim will probably fail (as a global claim) if a material cause of the loss is shown not to be the defendant's responsibility; but in this event a sub-claim or discrete lesser claim may be made out.
- Ultimately, the overriding question is simply whether or not the claimant has established breach/claim event, causation and loss on the balance of probabilities.

5.39 *Walter Lilly* is not, therefore, a licence for contractors to assert global or total cost claims and expect to make a full recovery. The editors' experience is that the TCC remains robust in relation to inadequate evidence of causation.

5.40 Contractors can improve their prospects of success by the following:

- Checking loss and expense claims to ensure that the heads of loss claimed are in principle capable of being caused by the event relied on. Common mistakes include claiming costs which were incurred either before or well after the event relied on, or for a different time period entirely, claiming costs which demonstrably relate to a completely different area of the site or different resource than that said to be affected by the event and more generally claiming costs relating to activities or resources which conceptually cannot have had anything to do with the alleged disruption event relied on.
- Ensuring that they provide some factual, as well as expert, evidence dealing with their loss and expense claim in order to explain the connection between the loss claimed and the event relied on. Such factual evidence should cover:
    o what the relevant employer-risk issues were;
    o what activity/activities they affected and why;
    o what the effect on those activities was (prolonged, additional resource, had to be re-sequenced meaning that other resource was retained on site, etc.); and
    o how the specific claim being made has been calculated so as to demonstrate to the Court that the costs claimed relate to that specific problem.

5.41 It is also sometimes appropriate to demonstrate a loss by using comparative productivity data. If a contractor can show that during a period when there were no delaying/disruptive events, it made progress as planned and at a certain cost, then this may well help to demonstrate that in a disrupted period the additional time taken and the additional cost incurred over that period and/or in relation to that activity were the consequence of the relevant disruptive event.

'Thickening' costs

5.42 'Thickening' is the industry term given to claims where it is alleged that the effect of the event relied on is not (or not only) to cause delay or disruption to the project, but to require the contractor to obtain increased resource than planned at time of tender.

5.43 In the usual way, it will be necessary to prove the event or breach relied on, causation and the loss itself. Causation evidence should be factual as discussed above in relation to disruption claims. In proving the loss, it will be necessary to provide evidence of what the tender allowance was for the particular resource, and that it was adequate for the project (so that the additional resource would not have been incurred in any event).

Subcontractor claims

5.44 Contractors often also include claims by their subcontractors within a loss and expense claim, both in relation to critical delay-related costs and in relation to disruption. There is nothing wrong with this approach in principle. The usual difficulties are, once again, those of causation.

5.45 It remains necessary for the contractor to persuade the Court, on the balance of probabilities, that the event/breach relied on under the main contract was a material cause of the delay or disruption to the subcontractor's works. Contractors will be in a better position if their subcontractors' claims are put forward in a detailed and sensible way, so that the causal nexus is at least clearly explained on the documents. Similar considerations arise to those relevant when claiming main contract disruption costs: if (for example) the main contractor is alleging that scaffolding was disrupted for three weeks, it is unlikely that the subcontractor's claim for eight weeks of additional scaffolding cost will be successful.

Acceleration claims

5.46 It is in practice rare for contractors to spend money on accelerating the works in the absence of an express instruction to do so. This is perhaps the reason why there is very little UK authority on acceleration claims. The point was discussed in *Ascon Contracting Ltd v Alfred McAlpine Isle of Man Ltd*:[24]

> 50. 'Acceleration' tends to be bandied about as if it were a term of art with a precise technical meaning, but I have found nothing to persuade me that that is the case. The root concept behind

---

[24] (2000) 66 Con LR 119 at [50]–[51]. There is another UK case, *Motherwell Bridge Construction Ltd v Micafil Vakuumtechnik* (2002) 81 Con LR 44 (TCC), in which a claim for constructive acceleration (no express instruction) was granted, but the judgment contains no legal reasoning explaining the decision, so must be regarded with caution.

the metaphor is no doubt that of increasing speed and therefore, in the context of a construction contract, of finishing earlier. On that basis 'accelerative measures' are steps taken, it is assumed at increased expense, with a view to achieving that end. If the other party is to be charged with that expense, however, that description gives no reason, so far, for such a charge. At least two further questions are relevant to any such issue. The first, implicit in the description itself, is 'earlier than what?' The second asks by whose decision the relevant steps were taken.

51. The answer to the first question will characteristically be either 'earlier than the contractual date' or 'earlier than the (delayed) date which will be achieved without the accelerative measures'. In the latter category there may be further questions as to responsibility for the delay and as to whether it confers entitlement to an extension of time. The answer to the second question may clearly be decisive, especially in the common case of contractual provisions for additional payment for variations, but it is closely linked with the first; acceleration not required to meet a contractor's existing obligations is likely to be the result of an instruction from the employer for which the latter must pay, whereas pressure from the employer to make good delay caused by the contractor's own default is unlikely to be so construed.

5.47 Standard form contracts tend to make express provision only for the employer/contract administrator to issue a formal instruction for the contractor to accelerate. In those cases, the contractual provisions will govern recovery. In most cases, no such formal instruction is given and/or there is a dispute about either of or both the instruction and responsibility for the underlying delays, but the contractor wishes to claim costs incurred in speeding up the works.

5.48 It is thought that there are in principle four potential routes for the contractor (assuming liability is disputed):

- Claiming that the acceleration was in fact instructed by the employer, so is either a variation or (if included in the contract) an instruction under the relevant acceleration clause.
- Claiming the acceleration costs via the loss and expense clause as a consequence of an employer-risk matter entitling the contractor to cost. However, it is thought that this depends on two issues:
  - The wording of the relevant loss and expense clause (if there is one), which may restrict the types of losses for which claim can be made.[25]
  - Whether it is possible to establish that the employer-risk matter *caused* the acceleration. If the contractor simply decides to accelerate to mitigate delay caused by an employer-risk event without any notification or agreement from the employer, such a claim is likely to be met with the argument that the cause of the acceleration costs was not the employer-risk event, but the contractor's unilateral decision. Any contractor seeking to establish a claim under this head would, therefore, it is submitted, need to notify the employer before taking any action and obtain agreement (whether expressly, impliedly or by conduct). Given this analysis, it may be that in fact there is little difference between this situation and a claim that the employer effectively instructed the acceleration.
- Claiming acceleration costs as damages for breach of contract. This might be possible where there is an express acceleration clause which the employer has used

---

25 For example, in FIDIC.

alleging that the relevant delay is the contractor's responsibility and has refused to pay the relevant additional costs. If it is eventually found that the delay was the employer's responsibility, so that the employer should under the clause have paid the contractor the additional costs, this would, it is suggested amount to a breach of contract. Otherwise, in some cases, the relevant delaying event may also be a breach of contract itself (such as a refusal to allow access to the site). It may also be possible to establish that the independent certifier or the employer has acted in such a way as to amount to a breach of contract.[26]

- If it is alleged that there has been an instruction, claiming damages in restitution on the basis that a benefit has been conferred on the employer and it would be unjust for the contractor to remain unpaid.

5.49 A claim for acceleration costs clearly will be very difficult where a contractor is accelerating to mitigate its own delay (whether critical or activity-related): under most standard forms, the contractor is obliged to take reasonable steps to mitigate any delay in any event (without additional remuneration); in the event that the contractor takes action over and above this standard, it is difficult to see how this could be claimed in the absence of an express instruction to do so.

5.50 In terms of establishing a claim for acceleration, slightly different considerations arise depending on whether it is contended that the acceleration mitigated critical delay or activity delay/disruption.

5.51 In relation to critical delay:

- It will be necessary to prove that in the absence of the acceleration measures undertaken, the project would have been critically delayed by an employer-risk event.
- It will likely be necessary to prove that the acceleration was successful (delay was mitigated) or that if unsuccessful/partially unsuccessful that this was also due to employer-risk events.
- If an extension of time is granted, this would mean that the delay was not in fact mitigated (because otherwise no extension of time would be required), so in principle the acceleration claim was unsuccessful.

5.52 If it is contended that specific activity delay was mitigated:

- It will be necessary to prove that in the absence of the acceleration measures undertaken, an activity/activities would have been prolonged by an employer-risk event.
- It will likely be necessary to prove that the acceleration was successful as above.

---

26 See the Australian case of *Perini Corp v Commonwealth of Australia* [1969] 2 NSWR 530 and the Canadian case of *Morrison-Knudsen v British Columbia Hydro and Power Authority (No 2)* (1978) 85 DLR (3d) 186 (BC Ct App). Note that the facts of both of these cases were unusual, with essentially a total refusal to operate the extension of time mechanism while demanding mitigation.

5.53 It is thought likely that a contractor will face significant challenges bringing such a claim in the absence of an instruction.

Employer's claims for delay

5.54 The employer's claim for damages for delay is usually subject to a provision for liquidated damages. These are pre-agreed sums which the contractor agrees to pay on a daily or weekly basis for the relevant period of delay to the contractual completion date. Subject to issues of penalties, the existence of a liquidated damages regime usually means that the employer's general right to claim damages for delay in relation to a breach of contract is entirely superseded.[27]

5.55 If there is no liquidated damages regime, the employer's right to claim damages for breach arises on the usual principles of contract law. The employer will have to identify the relevant breach and demonstrate causation and proof of actual loss (and that the claim is not too remote, etc.).

---

27 See *Keating on Construction Contracts* (10th edn, 2016).

CHAPTER 6

Defects claims

General nature of a defects claim

6.1 Conceptually, defects claims are very wide-ranging indeed. To the layman, a 'defect' will usually comprise some physical deficiency in the completed works, such as a leaking roof, or ill-fitting floorboards. Conversely, there may be nothing physically wrong with a structure, yet it is still 'defective' – for example, a building which is watertight yet has been finished in the wrong render (contrary to an agreed specification), or a door which has been painted in the wrong colour (against an employer's instructions). Some buildings may exhibit signs of physical 'defects' which are not in fact attributable to any underlying breach, the classic example being shrinkage cracks in a large concrete slab, which generally speaking are unavoidable.

6.2 Matters become complicated when defects emerge which are not readily attributable to any particular cause (for example, a warehouse floor which is suffering from cracking). Time and time again the same story emerges: the design and build contractor asserts that such cracks are down to shrinkage, and usually passes all of the claims down the line without offering up any properly substantiated defence; the slab subcontractor blames the foundations subcontractor; and the foundations subcontractor blames the slab subcontractor. The employer, of course, blames everyone, only to then find himself criticised for inadequate maintenance, or unrealistic expectations when it comes to the scope of the necessary remedial scheme.

6.3 Every construction practitioner will have come across defects claims. For some, they will be a bread-and-butter part of practice. Many litigators loathe them, and even the most energetic lawyer is unlikely to be particularly enthused by their study; see, for example, the first paragraph of the recent case of *Manorshow Ltd v Boots Opticians*:[1] 'This is a dilapidations claim.'

6.4 That said, defects claims form a central part of TCC business, and long will they continue to do so. Notwithstanding better design and construction teams, together with more efficient management and quality control, the human element in the process of construction means that defects are inevitable. As projects become larger and more complicated, sucking in construction professionals and consultants as well as contractors and their subcontractors, multi-party disputes are commonplace, and at times even the physical capacity of the Rolls Building Courts to accommodate the hearing is tested. In such circumstances, efficient management of such litigation is an important part of the TCC's role.

6.5 One of the difficulties in writing a chapter of this sort is the general absence of any reported cases concerning the case management and presentation of such claims. As to case management, almost all of the important procedural decisions are made at CMC stage, with

---

1 [2017] EWHC 2751 (TCC).

some spats continuing at (or developing by) the PTR. As to presentation, generally speaking, it is only where the process has gone wrong that comments will be made in the course of judgments to offer any 'official' insight into the presentational issues which often arise.

6.6 What follows, therefore, is a series of practical suggestions for the prosecution and defence of litigation concerning defects, together with the selection and deployment of appropriate expertise.

Prosecuting a defects claim

Structure of the statement of case

6.7 There is no right or wrong way to plead out a defects claim. Much will depend on the nature of the problems in question. For example, it may be apparent from an early stage that liability will not be a large issue in dispute, but scope of remedial works will be, in which case the primary focus of the draftsman may be on schemes of remediation, in telling the story as to how attempts to repair have failed, or in highlighting the intransigence of the defendants in attending to the problems. In other instances, liability will be hotly contested, but quantum more or less agreed.

6.8 There are, therefore, no hard and fast rules, but it is submitted that the following is a sensible structure which can be adapted as appropriate to suit the relevant dispute:

- *The parties.* Who to sue will be driven by a variety of considerations. A design and build contractor with full design responsibility will often suffice, but there may be a need to bring in further parties (such as subcontractors under warranties, or consultant professionals under warranties or in tort) in the event of a lack of insurance, parlous financial circumstances or even out of an abundance of caution, especially where knowledge of the claim is not as advanced as it might be.
- *Obligations.* This includes all relevant contracts and/or appointments and/or duties of care. Where contractual obligations are relied upon, and where appropriate, the scope of the relevant obligations should be identified. Often, documents such as the Employer's Requirements, or specifications, or even standalone express terms of the contract itself, will import fitness for purpose obligations, or other sorts of 'absolute' obligations or performance requirements, which may be unfettered by the normal obligation to take reasonable skill and care (whether express or implied). Aside from express 'fitness for purpose' obligations, such requirements might include obligations for a floor to take particular loadings, for a process plant to meet specified output parameters or for a building to satisfy a certain 'design life' or 'service life'. To this end see, for example, *MT Hojgaard AS v E.ON Climate and Renewables UK Robin Rigg East Ltd*[2] and *125 OBS (Nominees1) Ltd v Lend Lease Construction (Europe) Ltd.*[3] Contracts of this sort are often termed contracts of 'double obligation' and are a very powerful weapon to the claimant, as where absolute requirements can be made out, the reason why the requirements have not been satisfied is usually irrelevant.

---

2 [2017] UKSC 59.
3 [2017] EWHC 25 (TCC).

- *Narrative of performance* (i.e. in the case of a contractor, the works, and in the case of a designer or construction professional, performance of the relevant services). Where limitation is a potential problem, claimants may need to tread very carefully and it may be that this section is best left out if there are very real difficulties concerning dates of practical completion (regarding an action against a design and build contractor), breach (regarding an action in contract) or damage (regarding an action in tort). Limitation can always be addressed in reply if picked up by the defendant. That said, if limitation has already been flushed out in pre-action correspondence, it may be prudent to include material in the statement of case dealing with the issues to demonstrate confidence (even where there is little) in the claim.
- *Identification of the defects*, including a narrative of how and when they emerged or were discovered, together with any reaction to them and/or involvement in remedials/attempted remedials by the defendants. The reaction of particular defendants in these periods may well prove important in the event that a limitation defence is subsequently advanced, as sometimes the conduct of parties may operate so as to extend time for limitation purposes.
- *Breach.* These allegations should be set out 'hierarchically'. For example, where there are breaches of fitness for purpose obligations, or failures to meet any other absolute performance requirements, these breaches should logically be pleaded out first. Following those should be any further breaches of express or implied terms of the contract. In defects claims, these breaches will usually comprise: (1) failure to comply with express obligations set out in contract documents; or (2) failure to comply with any express or implied obligation to carry out works or services with reasonable skill and care (or any analogous wording). Normally, the breaches can be categorised thematically, and it is submitted that it is good practice to do so, importing sub-headings and signposting wherever possible. Such categories will usually include: (1) defective design/specification; (2) defective workmanship; and (3) defective materials. Depending on the problems in question, there may be room for other residual breaches (for example, failures to warn). Often, it will be necessary to work backwards from each of the defects to identify the relevant operative breach(es) of contract and/or duty. Only operative breaches should ever be pleaded. Where alleging breach, and in particular breaches of the obligation to carry out works with reasonable skill and care, the draftsman should always identify (1) the steps which were taken but should not have been and (2) the steps which were not taken but should have been. Simply asserting that a defendant was in breach for either doing something or not doing something is an incomplete allegation and will be countered by any sensible defendant with a request for further particulars.
- *Factual/technical causation of the defect.* This section should set out a description of how each of the breaches in question have caused and/or contributed to each of the defects in question. This is usually the most difficult and lengthy section of any defects statement of claim. Drafting it will often entail a detailed understanding and explanation as to how, for example, a breach led to particular forces or stresses being exerted on particular parts of the structure, such forces and/or stresses then being the cause of particular physical damage. Sometimes more

than one breach will cause and/or contribute to the force and/or stress in question, and by extension the relevant defect. Careful analysis with the assistance of the appointed technical experts is essential at pleadings stage and should not, as is regrettably too frequently the case, be the subject of investigation and development after close of pleadings, which leads to rounds of amendments, counter-amendments and unnecessary expenditure of costs.

- *Legal causation.* This section should explain how each of the breaches has caused and/or contributed to each of the losses in question, which will normally entail a description of how the defects have led to the need to remediate and/or a diminution in value of the asset. This section can usually be relatively concise, as tying in each of the defects to the breach(es) in question will have already been accomplished in the 'causation of the defect' section above.

- *Loss.* For a claimant, this will normally be the costs of reinstatement together with ancillary claims (for example, loss of rent, business disruption, wasted management time, professional fees, etc). In some instances, this section may need to include material anticipating and refuting any allegations of a failure to mitigate loss. One important tactical consideration for a claimant at this stage is whether or not to plead alternative remedial schemes, particularly where lesser or cheaper proposals have been historically advanced by the defendants. It is submitted that where proposals have been put forward, and they are unfeasible for technical or other reasons, claimants should deal with them upfront, even if further detail needs to follow in the Reply. Where the issue becomes a particularly acute consideration, however, is where limitation is in issue: see, for example, *Cooperative Group Ltd v Birse Developments Ltd*,[4] where the Court of Appeal had refused an earlier attempt to amend pleadings concerning the appropriate remedial scheme, and a further attempt to amend was refused on the basis that the claimant could and should have pleaded its true case much earlier in the proceedings. Where limitation is looming, one practical consideration might be to append a list of all facts and matters known to the claimant in relation to both the construction of the property and the defects, and to require the defendants to plead to it, so at the very least, there is a good chance that all relevant facts and matters concerning the problems will be the subject of the parties' pleaded cases, thus (with a fair wind) removing, or at least lessening, the risk that amendments to introduce and rely on alternative schemes will be refused on the basis that they do not arise out of the facts and matters in issue between the parties (any claim arising out of 'new' facts and matters being time-barred). The safest option, however, is always to plead properly and fully first time around.

6.9 Generally speaking, prolixity is to be discouraged. It is obviously necessary to plead full particulars, especially in relation to breach and causation, and where claims are complicated or involve multiple parties, length is often unavoidable. However, it will often be more appropriate to relegate certain matters to appendices in order for the statement of case to remain comprehensible and readily navigable by both the Court and the defendants.

---

4 [2013] EWHC 3145 (TCC).

Elements which can be appended include: lists of express terms from the contract (which are often lengthy); detailed narrative of the works and/or manifestation of the defects; and particulars of the relevant remedial scheme or schemes.

Defending the case

Liability defences

6.10 The starting point for any defendant is to resist a claim on the basis that breach is either not made out or any breach did not cause the damage complained of.

6.11 For contractual claims, building contracts frequently contain a myriad of obligations, some of which, on analysis, are conflicting, or incorporate performance requirements which are somewhat opaque (again, see *MT Hojgaard*). It may be that the obligations asserted by a claimant are not as extensive as the claimant might like, or that what are alleged to be performance requirements are in fact subject to some dilution (for example, being limited to the operation of a reasonable skill and care as opposed to the satisfaction of an absolute obligation).

6.12 To this end, there really is no substitute for careful analysis of all relevant contract documentation, which may (in the case of historic claims) necessitate disclosure requests from the claimant in order to obtain full copies of the contract itself.

6.13 Where the documentation does not reveal the existence of a stand-out contractual defence, investigation of the specific allegations with the assistance of experts is crucial. At the very least, this may give rise to the opportunity to pull in other parties by way of contribution proceedings – for example, if it transpires that the failure of a particular element can be attributed to both design and workmanship deficiencies.

6.14 Further, where claims are brought against construction professionals, the terms of the relevant appointment are, of course, paramount, and increasingly often will contain express limitations on liability, or net contribution clauses. The latter in particular may well give rise to a powerful defence even if breach cannot realistically be defended.

Quantum defences

6.15 In defects claims, quantum defences usually focus on two issues, namely that (1) the pleaded remedial scheme is disproportionate or otherwise excessive or (2) the claimant has failed to mitigate its loss.

6.16 Rival remedial schemes are almost inevitable where the claimed remedial scheme is extensive. They should, however, be investigated carefully, and ought not to be put forward where they are technically doubtful (see, for example, the Court's rejection of 'resin jacking' as a viable remedial scheme to a sinking floor slab in *Cooperative Group Ltd v John Allen Associates Ltd*).[5]

6.17 The credibility of any rival remedial scheme will, it is submitted, also suffer in the event that it is put forward in a defence either (1) as part of a large menu of alternative options or (2) without any adequate particulars. The first tends to suggest a certain level of desperation, and the latter a lack of belief in the suitability of the proposed solution.

---

5 [2010] EWHC 2300 (TCC).

6.18 That said, where a feasible and proportionate alternative remedial scheme does exist, and where it is properly pleaded out (ideally with an itemised and priced scheme prepared with the assistance of technical and quantum experts), a claimant who chooses to ignore it does so at its peril, particularly if it later seeks to adopt it, but its claim faces limitation problems (see *Coop v Birse*).

6.19 One word of caution, however. A properly advised claimant should be alert to any presentational deficiencies in an alternative remedial scheme put forward by defendants. Defendants should not expect to be granted indulgences by the Court to rely on alternative remedial schemes as and when their experts develop their thinking as the case progresses post close of pleadings. Any sensible claimant will insist on an amendment which, at the very least, will have costs consequences for the defendant in question. Finessing an alternative scheme during the course of the litigation (and following discussions between experts under CPR 35.12) is one thing, but a rambling development of different schemes not only poses a practical problem for the Court and the parties (in dealing with round after round of amendments and re-amendments), but will also affect credibility of that party's case (and the reliability of its expert) if the goalposts are continually moving.

6.20 Alleging a failure to mitigate will face complications in the event that the claimant has acted on apparently competent advice (see, for example, *Hospitals for Sick Children v McLaughlin & Harvey*[6]), or where the work has in fact been done (see, for example, *Banco de Portugal v Waterlow & Sons*[7] and *Linklaters v Sir Robert McAlpine Ltd*[8]). Nevertheless, even given the fact that the duty to mitigate is not a heavy one, there will be instances where points can legitimately be taken, and time will be wisely spent by a defendant in looking into what points might sensibly be advanced.

Limitation

6.21 One factor of which defendants should be acutely aware at all times is the possibility of a limitation defence. Many defects claims, particularly those involving multiple parties or those concerning chronic failures manifesting themselves over a long period of time, are by their nature pretty sterile, and often litigation is a last resort embarked upon to prevent claims becoming time-barred. Even then, deadlines are often missed. Indicators of potential weaknesses in a claimant's case in this regard might include reliance on a duty of care in tort (in an attempt to extend time to the date of damage, as opposed to the date of breach), or as intimated above, vague or woolly pleading concerning the dates upon which work or services were carried out and/or completed. Avenues for limitation defences may also appear where deeds are improperly executed or delivered.

6.22 Defendants should always be alert to the possibility of running such defences and should not treat the claimant's pleaded case as gospel. Further, in tort in particular, the case law in relation to limitation continues to develop (see, for example, *Coop v Birse*,[9] in which it was held that a contractor's cause of action in tort against its subcontractors accrued on the date of practical completion, when the building was handed over by the contractor to

---

6 (1990) 19 Con LR 25.
7 [1932] AC 452.
8 [2010] EWHC 1145 (TCC).
9 [2014] EWHC 530.

the employer, and not on the date that the contractor itself suffered financial loss (for example, when claims were in fact brought)).

6.23 To counter any such limitation defences, claimants should look, if they can, for indemnity provisions, to which different (and favourable) limitation rules apply. Sometimes wording amounting to an indemnity can be found in the text of collateral warranties (such as where an action is brought by a subsequent purchaser or tenant with the benefit of a direct or assigned warranty), or, again, upon careful scrutiny of the contract documents (and, in particular, material such as the Employer's Requirements and/or tender documentation which is commonly appended to and expressly incorporated into the contract). Where the date of completion of works is unclear (and often unknown to the claimant, particularly if it was not party to the original building contract), piecing together the precise chronology of events (accompanied by appropriate disclosure requests of the defendants) is essential, and more frequently than not may reveal an uncertainty over the actual date of completion which at the very least might permit a successful defence to any early strike out or summary judgment application prosecuted on limitation grounds.

Controlling, policing and challenging the presentation of defects claims

6.24 Defects claims frequently suffer from inadequate particularisation. There are many reasons for this: sometimes claims are issued in a rush, on account of limitation deadlines or other commercial considerations; on other occasions, the draftsman may lack sufficient information and/or an understanding as to the level of detail which is required to properly articulate a complicated claim for breach of contract.

6.25 A common occurrence in this regard is the eliding of the concepts of breach of contract on one hand and defects on the other. A defect, of course, is the physical manifestation of a breach or breaches of contract. But the breach still needs to be identified. All too frequently, defendants find themselves defending what is no more than a list of defects (and often a rudimentary one at that) which is presented as particulars of breach. In fact, that list is no more than what presumably it was originally intended to be, namely a list of problems with a building or facility. Such lists often disclose no discernible cause of action.

6.26 Another familiar tactic is to attach a schedule or report to the relevant pleading, usually one which has been prepared by a professional of sorts, and often for negotiation purposes. The report is then offered up in lieu of providing proper particulars of breach and/or causation, presumably from a (misguided) perception that costs can be saved in this way.

6.27 Finally, there will always be claimants who cut corners when it comes to pleading causation, leaving the defendant to unpick a generalised allegation such as 'The defects below were caused and/or contributed to by the breaches set out above', which is self-evidently unhelpful, but nevertheless commonplace.

6.28 Such practices have the potential to drive up unnecessary cost if they are not dealt with swiftly and robustly. The obvious time to do so formally is at the CMC, but it is submitted that the party facing a poorly articulated claim ought to prepare itself early by:

– issuing correspondence pointing out the failings in question and putting that party on notice in relation to costs (and this is the very least that should be done);

- issuing a Request for Further Information (RFI) prior to the CMC hearing, so that any inadequate responses to the RFI can be ventilated before the Judge, or, if no responses have been forthcoming, requesting an order that proper responses are submitted by a particular date.

6.29 One benefit of this technique is that it tends to flush out the likely approach of the Court at an early stage and, given the TCC's aspiration that the trial of each case will take place before the Judge who has managed the case since the first CMC (see paragraph 5.1.5 of the TCC Guide), any such application will provide a useful insight into that particular Judge's attitude to the claim in question. So, if the Court is satisfied that the complaints about poor presentation or particulars are merited, then it is likely to make noises in this regard in the friendly-ish atmosphere of the first CMC. By contrast, if a defendant is judged to be playing games, or as being overly pedantic, then its requests are likely to be treated with less sympathy.

6.30 Ultimately, it is a matter of balance. The Court has the power to order re-pleading of particular parts of a case if it will lead to inefficiency in the proceedings (see paragraphs 5.1.6 and 5.5.5 of the TCC Guide), and if a defects claim is truly obscure then parties should consider taking advantage of such powers, particularly where a party has tried without success to obtain further information.

6.31 Consideration should also be given to Scott Schedules, but, it is submitted, only on the basis that sensible and useful column headings can be agreed by the parties, and in the absence of any such agreement, it is essential that the Court is involved to adjudicate at the first CMC, given the tendency of such documents to spiral out of control in terms of content and costs if they are not carefully policed. See further at paragraphs 5.6.1 to 5.6.3 of the TCC Guide.

6.32 By contrast, in lower value cases, the Court may consider the pleading will suffice, despite a degree of vagueness, and the defendant will just have to do its best.

6.33 Where defects are manifest, parties should give strong thought to saving costs by agreeing a protocol to try defects by sample. Ultimately, this is a matter which the parties need to consent to, but practical (and, it is submitted, fair) ways to achieve a result might include:

- trying the highest value items and agreeing a process of pro rata extrapolation across the remainder;
- picking items at random and again agreeing a process of pro rata extrapolation across the remainder; and
- grouping defects into categories and trying a particular item or items in that category (again with some form of extrapolation across the remainder).

Instructing appropriate expertise

Appointment of experts

6.34 Expert evidence has been dealt with generally in Chapter 3. In this section, specific issues relating to expert evidence in defects cases are discussed.

6.35 Defects claims have a tendency to draw in a multiplicity of experts, with disciplines seemingly endless and ever more esoteric. That said, in the post-Jackson era, with increasing focus on cost-efficient litigation, the Court will expect proper justification at CMC stage before approving the instruction of such personnel. It goes without saying that parties should pay careful attention to which disciplines are in fact required. Sometimes the parties will find that they are not required at all (as was the case, for example, with delay experts in *Van Oord UK Ltd v Allseas UK Ltd*[10] – a discipline which many commentators consider is not an area of expertise in any event).

6.36 With a little thought, there will frequently be more parsimonious ways to deal with any issues requiring expert input than by individual instruction of multiple experts by each and every party. In the context of a defects claim, those might include:

- consideration of a jointly instructed expert or experts, particularly where there are multiple defendants who might usefully combine resources on specific issues (such as, for example, the sharing of valuation experts by defendants facing claims for diminution in value in the alternative to the costs of reinstatement);
- agreeing to dispense with quantum expert evidence and instead to source commercial quotations for particular remedial works;
- requesting liberty to apply at a later stage for expert evidence in a particular discipline in the event that it turns out to be required, its necessity not being readily apparent at CMC stage when the dispute is still relatively nascent; and
- appointing an expert who is capable of opining in more than one discipline, particularly where there is an overlap (as may be the case with disputes concerning both geotechnical and structural engineering, for example).

6.37 One factor which is frequently overlooked when it comes to the appointment of experts is the general needs of the Court. Putting the parties' requirements and wishes aside, Judges will nevertheless often expect to see particular matters dealt with by experts, and to be assisted by the same. For example, in *HSM Offshore BV v Aker Offshore Partner Ltd*[11] at [170], the Judge commented that the absence of quantity surveying (QS) expert evidence (which had not been requested by either party) was a 'grievous loss to comprehension and clarity'. In that case, this loss contributed to all of the claimant's claims failing for (among other things) want of proper substantiation and presentation in accordance with the terms of the contract, which are two matters which any decent QS expert would be expected to address in an expert report. A salutary tale indeed for the claimant in that case, but also a reminder that it should not be seen as impertinent to enquire at the CMC stage as to whether the Court would be helped by the instruction of particular experts.

Investigations

6.38 It is unusual for parties to defects litigation to be on an equal footing when it comes to the extent of any physical investigations. A claimant will almost always have the best knowledge, especially if they are living with the problems on a day-to-day basis. By contrast, some party-appointed experts may not have even visited the building in question, and

---

10 [2015] EWHC 3074 (TCC).
11 [2017] EWHC 2979 (TCC).

in other instances it may be impossible to do so as the defects no longer exist (whether on account of demolition or prior remediation).

6.39 From the claimant's perspective, it is obviously better if the defendants' experts have had an opportunity to physically inspect themselves, and approaches should be made to ensure that this happens at an early stage, ideally pursuant to an agreed protocol. If the defendant then refuses to do so, and an audit trail is available in this regard, then this may well be important at a later date.

6.40 It may be necessary to involve the Court at the CMC stage (or sooner) if one party faces a particularly recalcitrant opponent in this regard. The Court has power to order service of information not reasonably available to another party (see CPR 35.9) and can order inspection of and experiments with property (see, for example, CPR 25.1(1)(c)–(d)). Applications in this regard are not unheard of, particularly in claims where invasive investigation is required, and the asset in question is operational. The TCC will expect parties to have given consideration to the necessity and scope of any testing before the first CMC and at every subsequent pre-trial stage of the action (see paragraph 13.3.4 of the TCC Guide and paragraph 13.3.5, which empowers the TCC to make directions in this regard).

Independence of experts and quality of expert evidence

6.41 While it may be seen to be stating the obvious, the Court will rightly expect experts to act independently at all times, consistent with their overriding duty to the Court. In some cases, however, experts are found wanting in this area, which might be seen as somewhat surprising given the rapid expansion of the expert witness industry and, one would have thought, increased awareness on the part of such experts of their role in modern-day dispute resolution. See, for example, the relatively recent case of *Van Oord v Allseas* for an example of an expert who lost his way (in that case, quite literally, the gentleman in question leaving Court prior to the conclusion of his testimony, never to return).

6.42 The behaviour of experts in the witness box during a defects claim is obviously difficult to both predict and control, so for these reasons, personal reputations and recommendations do play, and will continue to play, a central role in the appointment of experts.

6.43 That said, it is submitted that experts who continue to play an active operational role in their relevant industry, as opposed to that of the 'career expert', make invariably more persuasive witnesses, even though they are likely to require more guidance or even hand-holding through the litigation process. See, again, *125 OBS (Nominees1) v Lend Lease Construction*, in which the claimant's expert (who had not testified previously) found considerable favour with the Court.

6.44 The above gives rise to inevitable questions as to where to find good people. Aside from the aforementioned personal recommendations, and the usual industry bodies, parties should not overlook that the answer may well best lie with the client, who will usually have day-to-day involvement in the relevant practice area or, if not, should have access to a professional team who can perhaps point the lawyers in the correct direction.

CHAPTER 7

Public procurement litigation in the TCC

Introduction

7.1 Procurement litigation is fast-moving and often somewhat fraught. The short time limit in which to bring claims (in most cases, 30 days from the date on which the claimant first knew or ought to have known of the facts amounting to breach)[1] and the somewhat one-sided nature of the process (whereby contracting authorities tend to hold the vast majority of disclosable information) mean that much Court time relating to procurement challenges is taken up with interlocutory applications, often prior to close of pleadings.

7.2 Applications by economic operators (typically for disclosure) are frequently met with cross-applications by authorities (typically for relief from the automatic injunction under Regulation 95(1), further information and strike out/summary judgment (often on limitation grounds)). Very few cases make it all the way to trial, but over the past six or seven years, the TCC has heard a growing number of cases in relation to public procurement challenges.

7.3 As a result, the TCC can now genuinely hold itself out as a pre-eminent Tribunal for the consideration of both final and interlocutory matters in the field. This reputation has recently been enhanced by the publication of the TCC Guidance Note on Procedures for Public Procurement Cases, launched in July 2017, and which now appears at Appendix H to the TCC Guide. Although it is described as guidance as opposed to a protocol, it is expected that it will be adopted in all procurement disputes going forward. A copy of the protocol is appended at Appendix 2 hereto.

7.4 A notable feature of procurement litigation is the ever-changing statutory regime pursuant to which claims are brought, namely the Public Contracts Regulations. At the time of writing, the 2015 Regulations are in force, which are the fourth iteration of the relevant legislation in the past 12 years. As well as keeping lawyers on their toes, the frequent revisions in the law introduce new concepts, many of which are relatively untested in litigation (e.g. the concept of 'ineffectiveness' introduced by the 2009 Regulations, and the codification of European jurisprudence in relation to 'material change' enshrined in the 2015 Regulations).

7.5 The 2016 referendum in the United Kingdom, which saw a majority of the British population vote to leave the European Union, imports further uncertainty over the direction in which the law might develop. To the editors, at least, it seems somewhat implausible that competitive tendering as a concept will be abandoned, not least on account of the fiduciary duties of public bodies, but also given that both contracting authorities and contractors have well-established processes for participating in competitions. Depending on the nature

---

1 See Regulation 92(2) of the Public Contracts Regulations 2015. References to the Regulations in this chapter are references to the 2015 Regulations unless expressly stated otherwise.

of the United Kingdom's relationship with the single market post-Brexit, it may well be the case that the legislation continues to be pegged to the relevant European directives in any event. Alternatively, if the United Kingdom were to subscribe to the World Trade Organization's Government Procurement Agreement, public contracting would be subject to a comparable regime.

7.6 The relatively recent introduction of the graduated issue fee in the High Court has led to some challengers thinking twice about commencing proceedings. For most procurement disputes, a fee of £10,000 will be payable on account of the level of damages ordinarily claimed. In some instances, this is enough to put off challengers unless they are confident in the strength of their case. Claimants sometimes seek a way around this charge by commencing proceedings for declaratory relief, in respect of which a lesser fee is payable, and subsequently amending the claim to include a claim for damages (and paying the increased fee). However, this approach risks being held to be an abuse of process unless the amendment arises because of new information which was not available when the claim was issued. This course of action may also give rise to a challenge to the damages claim on limitation grounds (given the short time limit in which to bring claims). The safest way to proceed is to issue proceedings for exhaustive relief in one go, even if this means committing to the full issue fee.

Applications to lift the automatic suspension

7.7 Prior to the coming into force of the Public Contracts (Amendment) Regulations 2009 which implemented the new Remedies Directive (2007/66), an aggrieved economic operator who wished to stop a procurement process (and thereby prevent contract award) needed to apply for an interim injunction.

7.8 Under the 2006 Regulations, the Courts approached the question of whether or not to grant an order restraining a contracting authority from entering into a contract by applying the test for an interim injunction set out in *American Cyanamid Co Ltd v Ethicon Ltd*[2], by considering: (1) if there is a serious issue to be tried; (2) if an award of damages would be an adequate remedy for the claimant if no injunction were granted; and (3) where the balance of convenience lies. The Court's application of the *American Cyanamid* test in procurement cases is a developing area of jurisprudence, with some Judges maintaining the three-stage analysis set out in *American Cyanamid* itself, while others take the view that the adequacy of an award of damages falls to be considered as part of the balance of convenience, which is likely to include the adequacy for the defendant of any cross-undertaking offered and protection of the public interest.

7.9 From the perspective of the aggrieved contractor who had missed out on the contract, the 'old' regime posed a practical problem: contracting authorities who became aware of an injunction application would immediately award the contract, leaving the challenger with a remedy in damages only. This became known as the 'race to contract' or 'race to signature'. The European Commission became concerned that: (1) contracts were being awarded before Tribunals had the chance to consider applications for injunctive relief (see the May 2006 impact assessment report (COM(2006)195); and (2) contracts were being awarded illegally, while the existing regime did not make it possible to prevent or correct

---

2 [1975] AC 396.

effectively the consequences of such illegal action (see the June 2006 proposal for the Remedies Directive (COM(2006) final/2)). This culminated in the adoption of a new Remedies Directive (2007/66).

7.10 The Public Contracts (Amendment) Regulations 2009 amended the 2006 Regulations, implementing the 2007 Remedies Directive. Under the new regime (see Regulation 47G of the 2006 Regulations as amended), upon commencement of proceedings by a challenger, the contracting authority was automatically prevented from entering into the contract (which has become known as the 'automatic injunction' or 'automatic suspension') unless the Court made an order bringing the suspension to an end on an application under Regulation 47H(1)(a). Under the 2015 Regulations, the relevant provisions are found at Regulations 95 (automatic injunction) and 96 (relief from the automatic injunction).

7.11 The drafting of the legislation is somewhat cumbersome. Pursuant to Regulation 96(1)(a), the Court may make an interim order bringing an end to the automatic suspension imposed by Regulation 95(1) if it considers that it would not be 'appropriate' to make an order requiring a contracting authority to refrain from entering into the contract (see Regulation 96(2)(b)).

7.12 Neither the 2006 Regulations nor the 2015 Regulations contain any specific guidance on the approach to be followed in this regard. Indeed, the Office of Government Commerce Response to the Second Public Consultation (paragraphs 46 to 48) in relation to the UK implementation of the 2007 Remedies Directive expressly concluded that it would be wrong for the Regulations to require the Court to adopt any particular approach (such as the *American Cyanamid* test), as this would be out of line with the general approach taken by legislation (including rules of Court) in relation to other proceedings. It does seem, however, that the Commission had in fact suggested its own guidance at Article 2(5) of the 2007 Remedies Directive, in the form of what might loosely be labelled a 'balance of interests' test, pursuant to which the review Tribunal (in this case the Court) should 'take into account the probable consequences of interim measures for all interests likely to be harmed, as well as the public interest, and may decide not to grant such measures when their negative consequences could exceed their benefits'. Article 2(5) of the Remedies Directive did not expressly find its way into the 2006 Regulations as amended in 2009 (although a 'balance of interests' type test was included in the comparable Scottish and Irish legislation). Somewhat inconsistently, a 'balance of interests' test was expressly included in the equivalent legislation for procurements in the defence sector, the Defence and Security Public Contracts Regulations 2011 at Regulation 57(2). The Defence Regulations seek to implement into UK law European Directive 2009/81 on the coordination of procedures for the award of certain works contracts, supply contracts and service contracts by contracting authorities or entities in the fields of defence and security. The reason for the inconsistency in drafting between the Defence Regulations and the Public Contracts Regulations is not clear.

7.13 There is a considerable body of opinion among lawyers that the *American Cyanamid* test, as applied, is not the most appropriate basis on which to decide whether the automatic suspension should be maintained or terminated, since it gives too little weight to the importance of reviewing public authorities' compliance with law and too much weight to the purely commercial question of whether an award of damages would adequately compensate a claimant.

7.14 Whether or not *American Cyanamid* was an appropriate test under the 'new' regime was first argued in *Exel Europe v University Hospitals Coventry & Warwickshire NHS Trust*,[3] the first automatic injunction case before the TCC. The argument adopted was that the three-stage test is incompatible with the 'balance of interests' test in the 2007 Remedies Directive. The Judge concluded that *Cyanamid* did apply. It has been applied since (albeit there is a range of approaches), and it is fair to say that the Courts have not been particularly impressed by subsequent attempts to argue that the *Cyanamid* test runs contrary to European law.[4]

7.15 In practical terms, the result has been to make it extremely difficult for challenging contractors to maintain the automatic suspension. That is either because a remedy in damages is almost always adequate compensation for a disgruntled tenderer if it transpires that the procurement was unlawful, or because the contractor is unwilling to give an undertaking in damages. Even if damages are found to be an adequate remedy for the authority as well as the contractor, this will not in itself be sufficient to persuade the Court to maintain the injunction (see *Openview Security Solutions v Merton LBC*[5]).

7.16 It seems, therefore, that *Cyanamid* is here to stay, and the overwhelming majority of challenges will not succeed.[6]

7.17 This is not always the case, and there are instances in which the Court has been persuaded to maintain the injunction, but these cases are very much confined to their own facts. Material factors in the Court's consideration in deciding not to grant relief from the injunction under Regulation 95(1) have been as follows:

- In *Counted4 Community Interest Co v Sunderland City Council*,[7] the first decision under the 2015 Regulations, the Court held that damages would not be an adequate remedy for the claimant: if the suspension were lifted, then the workforce would be lost and it would take years to develop skills which were not available on the wider market. Further, the current service being supplied for the duration of the suspension did not create a risk to users of the service such that the public interest outweighed the prejudice to the claimant if the suspension were lifted.
- In *Bristol Missing Link Ltd v Bristol City Council*,[8] damages were held not to be an adequate remedy because the claimant was a non-profit-making organisation and lifting the suspension would have caused it to lose a third of its turnover, which would have had a knock-on effect on the other services it provided. If the

---

3 [2010] EWHC 3332 (TCC).
4 See the discussion in *Bristol Missing Link Ltd v Bristol City Council* [2015] EWHC 876 (TCC).
5 [2015] EWHC 2694 (TCC).
6 For recent examples, see: *Exel*; *Openview*; *Fox Building and Engineering Ltd v Department of Finance and Personnel* [2015] NIQB 72; *Allpay Ltd v Northern Ireland Housing Executive* [2015] NIQB 54 (in that instance because there was (unusually) no serious issue to be tried); *Group M UK Ltd v Cabinet Office* [2014] EWHC 3659 (TCC) (ditto); *Rutledge Recruitment & Training Ltd v Department for Employment and Learning* [2011] NIQB 61 (ditto); *Halo Trust v Secretary of State for International Development* [2011] EWHC 87 (TCC) (ditto); *John Sisk & Son Holdings Ltd v Wester Health and Social Care Trust* [2014] NIQB 56; *Chigwell (Shepherds Bush) Ltd v ASRA Greater London Housing Association Ltd* [2012] EWHC 2746 (QB); *Newcastle Upon Tyne Hospital NHS Foundation Trust v Newcastle Primary Care Trust* [2012] EWHC 2093 (QB); *Metropolitan Resources North West Ltd v Secretary of State for the Home Department* [2011] EWHC 1186 (Ch); and *Indigo Services (UK) Ltd v Colchester Institute Corp* [2010] EWHC 3237 (QB).
7 [2015] EWHC 3898 (TCC).
8 [2015] EWHC 876 (TCC).

- suspension were lifted, then that would effectively have ended the claim, and the Judge held that there was a public interest in the law relating to procurement procedures being properly conducted.
- In *NATS (Services) Ltd v Gatwick Airport Ltd*,[9] the injunction was upheld because there would have been great difficulty in estimating the damages, and further the loss of the contract would have significantly impaired NATS's ability to secure international air traffic control contracts. There had already been a significant delay in the procurement process and a further delay had to be seen in that context. The authority's resulting position of uncertainty was not determinative in the balance of convenience.
- In *DWF LLP v Secretary of State for Business, Innovation and Skills*,[10] the Court of Appeal lifted the injunction with regard to all successful bidders except those with whom DWF had originally tied for last place. If DWF won at trial, damages would not be an adequate remedy because they would be impossible to quantify fairly. By contrast, if DWF lost, then the Secretary of State's damages would be easily quantified.
- Particularly where the suspension is maintained, the TCC is likely to support and impose a rapid progress to trial (and may well use powers to control and define the scope of disclosure in such cases – as to which see below). For the consideration of expedition principles before contract award, see *Joseph Gleave v Secretary of State for Defence*.[11]

7.18 The following guidance is offered to parties which find themselves prosecuting, or defending, an application for an order to lift the automatic suspension under Regulation 96.

- For economic operators, serious consideration should be given to whether or not the application brought by the authority to lift the suspension should even be contested. Starting proceedings (and the imposition of the injunction) does provide some commercial clout to a contractor looking to negotiate a solution, but the bulk of the jurisprudence suggests that this will be a hurdle which, more often than not, is overcome by the authority, with consequent costs sanctions imposed on the contractor (and the morale-boosting effect of an early win) if the application is contested. Moreover, consenting to the termination of the suspension may signal to the defendant that the claimant has confidence in their case.
- There are circumstances where money alone will not offer an adequate remedy due to other consequences stemming from the contract being awarded to another party – for example, redundancies, loss of human capital through TUPE transfers, loss of market share or loss of reputation (see the remarks of the Court in *John Sisk & Son Holdings Ltd v Wester Health and Social Care Trust*[12] (although the injunction was lifted in that case)). If contractors wish to contest applications, then these are

---

9 [2014] EWHC 3133 (TCC).
10 [2014] EWCA Civ 900.
11 [2017] EWHC 238 (TCC).
12 [2014] NIQB 56.

the areas upon which strong evidence should be adduced (although given the odds against a contractor, it may still not ultimately be enough to get over the line).
- Authorities should make the application early. Given the TCC's willingness to accommodate expedited trials, a late application may well be met by the submission that the balance of convenience militates against the injunction being lifted because: (1) most procurements are usually fairly long in the tooth by the stage that litigation is commenced; (2) the authority has delayed in making the application; (3) the Court is able to fix a hearing in a relatively short space of time; and (4) there is no discernible prejudice to the authority in waiting a few weeks or months longer for the conclusion of a trial and handing down of judgment before being permitted (or not) to award the contract in question.
- If authorities are sensitive about disclosure (as to which, see below), it is unwise to take the point that there is no serious issue to be tried unless the claimant's case is clearly unsustainable on its face, without the need for evidence. The requirement that there be a serious issue is sometimes described as a low threshold, so in most cases (but not all, as identified in the cases cited above) the claimant will satisfy the requirement; an assertion that there is no serious issue may attract a successful application for early specific disclosure so that the contractor can rebut the allegation. Many authorities, ultimately, will concede the point (even if the concession is not made until exchange of skeleton arguments) rather than risk being ordered to provide documents that they would rather hold back for the time being. It is submitted that this is a sensible approach (apart from in the most extreme cases where the challenge is fanciful) and consistent with authority. For example, in *Pearson Driving Assessments Ltd v The Minister for the Cabinet and The Secretary of State for Transport*,[13] the Court considered an application for early specific disclosure in the context of a pending section 47(H). At paragraph 15, the judgment states:

> The court, on the application of Section 47 (H), will simply not be in a position to find facts which are controversial or at the very least, which are not supported clearly by uncontroversial, contemporaneous documentation. Therefore, insofar as there is reliance by the defendants on those sorts of facts, those are facts which cannot properly be deployed as grounds for deciding that there is no serious issue to be tried.

Disclosure

Introductory matters

7.19 A recurring theme in procurement litigation – and one upon which contracting authorities and economic operators will never see eye to eye – concerns disclosure of documents held by the authority as part of the tender process. Public procurement is one of the very few areas of law in which one party essentially holds all the cards, and in the first instance at least, can decide whether or not it wishes to deploy them. In the meantime, all that the economic operator generally knows is that it has lost. It is often the case that only

---

13 [2013] EWHC 2082 (TCC).

the contracting authority is able to provide precise details of what happened during the procurement, the extent of any breaches and the factors which led to its decisions.

7.20 Often, documentation which is in the hands of the authority is necessary to enable a claimant to understand what has happened and identify the relevant breaches and fully to plead its allegations. However, there is also a tight time limit for the commencement of procurement cases. This means that, where documents are not disclosed at the outset of a procurement case, it may be necessary for a claimant to amend its case at a later date. This is clearly not desirable or cost-effective nor in accordance with the overriding objective.

7.21 Sometimes authorities will refuse to disclose documents and hope that the (short) time limit for bringing a challenge expires. Others often offer selective disclosure in an attempt to show willing. All will generally refuse to disclose material documents concerning the evaluation (and in particular tender returns from the winning bidder) without at the very least a skirmish in correspondence, but usually will only do so if required by the provisions of a Court order.

The approach of the TCC to early disclosure in procurement litigation

7.22 Applications for disclosure in public procurement cases often take the form of a 'hybrid' application for (1) early disclosure and (2) specific disclosure. The Court may make an order for specific disclosure at any time, irrespective of whether standard disclosure has occurred (see CPR 31.12 and *Alstom v Eurostar*[14] at [19]) and, if required, the Court will adopt the tests under CPR 31.16 for pre-action disclosure even though the action has already been commenced (see *Alstom* at [22], [32], [37]). Thus, material considerations for the Court may include whether disclosure of the documents requested is desirable to dispose fairly of the anticipated proceedings, and whether disclosure of the documents requested may well assist the dispute to be resolved without proceedings and to save costs. In *Alstom*, Vos J held that there was 'much force' in the applicant's submission that it required early disclosure of documents to both properly plead its case and to avoid limitation problems (see *Alstom* at [52]–[53]).

7.23 The leading case in relation to disclosure in procurement litigation is now widely recognised as being the decision of Coulson J (as he then was) in *Roche Diagnostics Ltd v The Mid Yorkshire Hospitals NHS Trust*,[15] in particular paragraph 20. The relevant principles can be summarised as follows:

- Paragraph 20(a) – the Court recognises the 'uniquely difficult position' of a challenger in procurement disputes. The presumption is that essential information and documentation relating to the evaluation process should be provided promptly.
- Paragraph 20(b) – the (very) short time limits in procurement confirm the general approach above.
- Paragraph 20(c) – each case must be judged on its merits. There is a distinction between cases where a prima facie case has been made out, and where an unsuccessful tenderer is simply aggrieved.

---

14 [2010] EWHC B32 (Ch).
15 [2013] EWHC 933 (TCC).

- Paragraph 20(d) – the application must be focussed, and the information likely to be sought is 'that which demonstrates how the evaluation was actually performed and therefore why the claiming party lost'.
- Paragraph 20(e) – the Court will undertake a balancing exercise, balancing (1) the claimant's lack of knowledge and thus the importance of prompt provision of disclosure, with (2) the need to guard against a 'fishing exercise'.

7.24 More recent cases continue to follow in this vein (for example, *Group M UK Ltd v Cabinet Office*[16] and *Gem Environmental Building Services Ltd v London Borough of Tower Hamlets*,[17] which expressly recognises the importance of 'making the playing field as level as possible' so as to prevent any injustice or detriment to contractors who are essentially in the dark as to the legality of the procurement in question.

7.25 After the decision in *Roche* referred to above, some practitioners considered that the more accommodating approach of the TCC to disclosure in procurement cases might signal a more open approach on the part of the authorities to provision of material documents at an early stage. However, authorities continue to contest disclosure applications and success on the part of contractors is far from guaranteed (see, for example, the decisions in *Gem Environmental* – where disclosure was refused primarily because the abandonment of the procurement was subject to a further review by the defendant which was to be completed only 72 hours after the hearing (and one can detect some irritation towards the claimant contractor in the judgment for persisting with the application) – and *Covanta Energy Ltd v Merseyside Waste Disposal Authority*[18] (decided under the 2009 Regulations) where the Court (applying *Roche*) considered that the documents requested were either not reasonably necessary to enable the claimant to understand the merits of its case, or were insufficiently focussed and in some instances amounted to 'fishing').

7.26 Nevertheless, subject of course to issues of proportionality and relevance, it is submitted that the TCC Judges will probably look unfavourably on an authority which does not (1) retain basic evaluation documentation and (2) provide the same when requested by a challenging contractor (see, for example, the criticism of the Court in *Geodesign Barriers Ltd v The Environment Agency*,[19] in which the Judge was surprised by the defendant authority's paucity of documentary evidence relating to the selection and evaluation of tenders and ordered disclosure of the other parties' bid documents notwithstanding the fact that the claimant was only placed sixth out of ten bidders).

7.27 Under the 2015 Regulations, authorities are now required to keep records: they are obliged draw up a written tender report in relation to the procurement (Regulation 84(1)), to document the progress of procurement procedures (Regulation 84(7)) and to keep sufficient documentation to justify decisions taken in all stages of the procurement procedure (Regulation 84(8)). These new provisions should afford contractors some hope that relevant documentation in relation to a failed bid will at the very least exist (or ought to), and authorities should probably expect short shrift from the Court if Regulation 84 is not complied with. Failure to keep such documentation is itself a substantive breach of the

---

16 [2014] EWHC 3401 (TCC).
17 [2016] EWHC 3045 (TCC).
18 [2013] EWHC 2964 (TCC).
19 [2015] EWHC 1121 (TCC).

Regulations, although how it could be said to cause the claimant to have suffered loss is not clear; in the General Court of the Court of Justice of the European Union it is thought that it would be likely to lead to the annulment of the authority's decision. Further, it would seem now to be difficult for a contracting authority sensibly to assert that it will be inconvenienced or disproportionately prejudiced by searching for documents which it has a statutory obligation to generate and maintain.

Tactical considerations

7.28 In view of the recent developments in the legislation, the starting point for a contractor which feels that inadequate documentation or information has been supplied in relation to a procurement might be a formal request for sight of documents generated by the authority as part of its obligations under Regulation 84.[20]

7.29 Failing that, if a formal application is necessary, the authorities indicate that it is imperative that any such application should be focussed on documents which (1) are necessary to enable the contractor to understand the strength of its case and (2) form part of tightly drawn categories. If the contractor can point to any obvious inadequacies in the authority's record-keeping process (as was the case in *Geodesign*), then this may well assist in persuading the Court to grant disclosure. It is also suggested that applications are made at the earliest opportunity; the later the application is made, the less likely it is to be granted, given that the Court will set down a timetable for standard disclosure in the normal manner at the CMC, and delay in bringing the application might tend to suggest that provision of the requested documents is not that important.

7.30 For authorities facing disclosure requests, where a notice communicating an authority's decision to award a contract has been given, the starting point is to ensure that the information required by Regulation 86(2) – namely the losing bidder's score, the winning bidder's score and the reasons for the decision, including the 'characteristics and relative advantages of the successful tender', has been provided.

7.31 In practice, it is not uncommon to find that the requirements of Regulation 86(2) – or its previous guise in the superseded legislation – are not met. Further, there is no guidance on the meaning of the phrase 'characteristics and relative advantages of the successful tender', and unsurprisingly this tends to lead to disputes, as contractors complain that insufficient information has been provided. It is suggested that, at the very least, authorities should provide details of the characteristics and relative advantages of the winning tender in relation to each of the criteria against which bids were marked, as opposed to more generally. Authorities may wish to consider providing the following in order to stave off a disclosure application and, ideally, full proceedings:

- provision of score sheets relating to the losing bid;
- concise summary reasons relating to the losing bidder's scores against each criterion, perhaps in tabular format; and
- a copy of the internal tender report (redacted where appropriate).

---

20 Note, however, that Regulation 84 does not require that these documents be disclosed, only that they be created and maintained.

7.32 Where information in relation to rival bids is sought, and the same appears to be material and relevant to the allegations in question, the authority should give careful consideration to redaction (while bearing in mind that redacting documents generally provokes suspicion) and provision of documents into a confidentiality ring (as to which, see below). Appendix H to the TCC Guide provides guidance in relation to redactions generally, involving (1) the production of a schedule (identifying the locations and reasons for any redaction) and (2) with the exception of irrelevant documents, provision to the Court of unredacted versions, with the redactions highlighted in a prominent colour which does not obscure the information beneath it.

7.33 It is suggested, however, that the rival bidder is kept fully informed of the nature and progress of the application at all times so that the authority does not face criticism (or worse) that it is improperly handling confidential and commercially sensitive information.

7.34 One thing which authorities might wish to consider is inviting the winning bidder to obtain its own representation and attend the disclosure hearing. Indeed, Appendix H to the TCC Guide now recognises that the interests of a third party should be considered by the Court, and that the Court will expect to hear from such persons.

7.35 Permission from the Court will therefore be required if the third party wishes to make submissions (unless, of course, it applies to join itself as a party) but, in practice, TCC Judges have generally permitted the third party to be heard. However, it seems that more formality is now to be expected; paragraph 56 of Appendix H to the TCC Guide advises that a formal application should be made by the interested party as soon as possible. From the contractor's perspective, this introduces inconvenience, as the third party will inevitably insist on any of its sensitive material to be disclosed into a tightly controlled confidentiality ring (see below). From the authority's perspective, it may well be the case that the third party does some or all of the running in defending the application itself, as well as facilitating the submission that the reason why documents have not been shared results from its obligations to protect confidential information, as opposed to any unwillingness to provide them (even though such unwillingness may well have featured heavily in the authority's decision-making process).

Handling confidential information

7.36 The issue of handling confidential information can be of great concern in procurements under the Regulations. There is no fixed description of what constitutes confidential information, but it may be very wide indeed. It will usually include details regarding prices, proposals put forward in competitive dialogue, sensitive technical information and possibly some personal information. Generally speaking, it can cover anything which might have contributed to the commercial edge of a winning bid. In the most recent Regulations, the requirement imposed by the old Regulations, that a tenderer designate those parts of its tender which it regards as confidential, has been replaced by a rule that the whole tender is confidential by default.

7.37 Where disputes arise, an authority may be required to disclose a wide array of documents to the winning bidder about how the procurement was conducted and how bids were evaluated. Very often, although not always, this will include information in relation to the winning tenderer's bid. The losing bidder will obviously want to see why another bid is apparently better than its own and may well distrust the information supplied by the authority as part of the debriefing process absent sight of documentary evidence (if indeed any information has been supplied at all).

7.38 The concern to protect commercial confidence generally comes from two sources. The first is from the winning bidder. Naturally, such parties will be extremely sensitive over what they have submitted. The second is from contracting authorities, which often demonstrate an institutional reluctance to reveal such information. This might be justified on the basis that disclosure will remove an element of competition if there is a similar procurement ongoing, or if there is a possibility of a forced or consensual re-run of the existing procurement. More likely, however, those authorities find themselves under extreme pressure from winning bidders to not disclose anything. As discussed above, such parties may seek to defend their interest in maintaining the confidentiality of their tender by turning up to Court or adding themselves as parties to the litigation.

7.39 Confidential information is usually asked for as part of the debrief process following the notice of award. A disappointed tenderer will want to know where it has gone wrong, or what was considered to be so special about the other bid. As set out above, an authority is required under the Regulations to provide comparative scores of the winning and losing bids, together with information concerning the reasons for its decision and the characteristics and relative advantages/disadvantages of the tenders. This can give rise to a need to disclose wide-ranging comparative information, and in practice is interpreted in very different ways by contracting authorities: some provide little or no information at all; others provide arguably too much. But there will almost inevitably be a request to see the winning tenderer's bid and the evaluation information associated with that bid.

7.40 Pursuant to Regulation 86(6), an authority can withhold the provision of information if it considers that: (1) it would impede law enforcement or is contrary to the public interest; (2) it would prejudice the legitimate commercial interests of a particular economic operator; or (3) it might prejudice fair competition between economic operators.

7.41 If an authority hides behind Regulation 86(6), contractors may attempt to make freedom of information requests under the Freedom of Information Act 2000 ('FIA'). It is not unheard of for losing bidders to put in anonymous requests for information – and sometimes to be given it. However, in recent years, such requests have assumed less importance because of the very short time limits for bringing claims introduced in 2011. This means that proceedings will often be issued before information is provided through freedom-of-information channels. In any event, many requests are refused if the authority takes advantage of section 43(2) of FIA, which exempts information from being disclosed where its provision would, or would be likely to, prejudice the commercial interests of any person and the public interest in maintaining confidentiality outweighs the public interest in disclosure.

7.42 The only option open to a contractor where an authority hides behind Regulation 86(6) or section 43(2) of FIA is to make a disclosure request under the CPR. This will either entail an application for pre-action disclosure (before proceedings have started) or specific disclosure (after proceedings have started), although in practice most applications are 'blended' (as explained above) because the short time limits mean that litigation is often afoot before the contractor is in possession of any documents.

7.43 There is an obvious conflict between the protection of confidentiality and competition on the one hand, and transparency on the other hand – a fundamental principle of our justice system is, of course, the entitlement to a fair trial.

7.44 Several English cases have grappled with the problem of disclosure of confidential information (see, for example, *Amaryllis No 2*,[21] *Veolia ES Nottinghamshire Ltd v Nottinghamshire County Council*,[22] *Mears v Leeds*[23] and *Bombardier Transportation Ltd v Merseytravel*[24]).

7.45 A useful authority on the issue is the decision of the TCC in *Croft House Care Ltd v Durham County Council*.[25] That judgment makes clear that the fact that documents might contain confidential information is not in itself a reason for not providing such documents on disclosure and inspection. What the Court needs to do is to balance one party's right to confidentiality with the need for claims to be disposed of fairly.

7.46 As set out above, the case law in relation to disclosure in procurement litigation is pretty well developed, and the generally accepted position is set out in the case of *Roche*. Paragraphs 20(a) and 30 of the judgment deal with confidential information as follows:

> ... in general terms, and always subject to issues of proportionality and confidentiality, the challenger ought to be provided promptly with the essential information and documentation relating to the evaluation process actually carried out, so that an informed view can be taken of its fairness and legality;[26]
>
> ...
>
> there is no difficulty relating to confidentiality because the parties are agreed that the specific disclosure should take place into the confidentiality ring.[27]

7.47 The widespread adoption of confidentiality rings as a means of handling confidential information has practically ended the argument in relation to disclosure, particularly when coupled with the Court's own initiative in protecting such information for the purposes of the litigation (for example, by handing down open judgments with confidential annexes – see *EnergySolutions EU Ltd v Nuclear Decommissioning Agency*[28]). Where confidentiality is asserted in procurement challenges, the Court will almost certainly order disclosure into rings as a matter of routine, with liberty to apply to take documents out of the ring if, on analysis, they are not in fact confidential as asserted and/or at all. For examples of other recent cases where confidentiality rings were adopted, see *Group M Ltd v Cabinet Office* and *Geodesign*.

7.48 However, before rings are established, it is reiterated that it must be demonstrated by the applicant that the confidential information is relevant. It will not be necessary to see the winning bid if the complaints are about how the losing tender was marked (as opposed

---

21 [2009] EWHC 1666 (TCC).
22 [2010] EWCA Civ 1214.
23 [2011] EWHC 40 (QB).
24 [2017] EWHC 575 (TCC).
25 [2010] EWHC 909 (TCC).
26 At paragraph 20(a).
27 At paragraph 30.
28 [2016] EWHC 1988 (TCC).

to it being unfairly marked in comparison with the winning bidder), or about being disqualified at an early stage in the process.

7.49 There are no set rules as to how confidentiality rings should be set up. Some useful (and welcome) guidance appears at paragraphs 34 to 48 of Appendix H to the TCC Guide.

7.50 The basic principle of rings is, normally, to establish a 'tiered' access to documents. Access is usually requested on behalf of solicitors, Counsel, and a party-appointed expert (where expert assistance is required in order to understand the documents disclosed (to this end, see *Geodesign* at [53])) together with a representative from the lay client. Different persons may have different levels of access to documents depending on the nature of the confidential information itself. All such persons are ordinarily required to sign confidentiality undertakings. The inclusion of a client representative in the ring frequently causes the most controversy, and in practical terms it is usually necessary to appoint a person who has had nothing to do with the procurement and who will undertake not to participate in relevant future procurements. This is because there is an obvious reluctance to allow someone who was on the bidding team, or who may be involved in future bids in the same area, to see the rival documentation, particularly if there will be a re-run. This is not to say it will never happen, but if it does, it will almost certainly only be permitted on condition that the individual in question undertakes not to involve himself in any rerun and/or in any competitions for the same or similar contracts for a period of years going forward.

7.51 Once disclosed, there remain very real problems in dealing with confidential information. The most immediately obvious for a contractor's lawyers is the taking of instructions, which is difficult if decision-makers with knowledge of the procurement underlying the dispute are not in the ring. But there are other practical considerations. Difficulties often arise with obtaining an expert to assist with reviewing documents disclosed into the confidentiality ring, especially where the subject matter of the contract is specialised. Experts may be unable to assist either because of a genuine conflict, or because of their own personal considerations (for example, not wanting to jeopardise commercial relationships with particular authorities or in the industry/with particular contractors). Further, during the hearing, it may be necessary for persons outside the ring to leave the Court at particular times, and extreme care needs to be taken when referring to such documents in oral submissions.

7.52 Problems are not limited to the challenger. It is more difficult to settle a case when the contractor's legal team cannot properly talk to their clients about the merits of the case (which will frequently involve analysis of the confidential information) apart from in the most general of terms.

7.53 In terms of practical guidance, it is submitted that the authorities should adopt a sensible approach to confidentiality rings and look to accommodate them without troubling the Court. This is supported by paragraphs 7 and 35 of Appendix H to the TCC Guide.

7.54 This may not be possible if the winning bidder digs its heels in, but the authorities suggest that the Court, in the interests of justice, will naturally favour disclosure of documents into a ring as opposed to ordering no disclosure at all. Contractors should also be realistic; any attempt to appoint members of the procurement team into the ring will inevitably be contested (and likely to fail).

7.55 Appendix H to the TCC Guide contains the following further guidance in relation to the use of confidential information:

- If any statement of case contains confidential information, the serving party should lodge non-confidential and confidential versions (the latter unredacted and sealed in an envelope), using annexes where possible (paragraph 11).
- The parties should make use of coloured paper so that confidential status is immediately apparent (paragraph 30).
- Parties may apply to the Court for an order restricting inspection of the Court file (paragraph 31).

CHAPTER 8

Costs budgeting in the TCC

Introduction

8.1 Costs budgeting is a creature of the Jackson reforms and is now well established in TCC litigation. It applies automatically to all cases commenced after 22 April 2014 of a value up to £10 million (see CPR 3.12, 3.13 and PD 3E.1 – up from £2 million under the old regime for cases commenced before 1 April 2013 but before 22 April 2014), and at the Court's discretion thereover (see CPR 3.12(1A) and *CIP Properties (AIPT) Ltd v Galliford Try Infrastructure Ltd*[1]).

8.2 Undoubtedly, the motivation behind the introduction of costs budgeting was sound. Clearly, it is in the interest of all parties to litigation that proceedings are undertaken expeditiously and proportionately. All practitioners will have had experience of cases which have become unmanageable and frequently incapable of settlement on account of costs. Given that (1) the Court will rarely depart from the costs budget at assessment stage (see CPR 3.18(b)) and (2) changes to costs budgets have to be the subject of an application to the Court (see PD 3E, paragraph 7.6), it is obviously helpful to parties to have a clear understanding of their exposure in relation to costs at all relevant stages of the proceedings.

8.3 Notwithstanding the good intentions behind the reforms, it is probably fair to say that costs budgeting is not a popular procedure, at least among Court users. This is for a number of reasons.

8.4 Firstly, the recoverable costs of preparing Precedent H schedules – the complexity of which is a task not to be underestimated – is capped at the higher of £1,000 or 1 per cent of the agreed/approved budget, save in exceptional circumstances (see PD 3E, paragraph 7.2). In addition (and understandably), lawyers may well find the procedure of preparing and submitting costs budgets difficult to 'sell' to clients (if indeed it is commercially feasible to charge at all). In practical terms, therefore, and particularly in relation to complex cases, the preparation and consideration of costs budgets is likely to be (at best) a loss leader.

8.5 Secondly, in light of *Mitchell v News Group Newspapers Ltd*[2] (as to which, see further below), the issue of costs budgeting is frequently the subject matter of tactical manoeuvring and threats ahead of the first CMC, as the prima facie sanction is that a failure to serve a budget on time is to limit recovery of costs to applicable Court fees (see CPR 3.14). Despite the guidance from the Court of Appeal in *Denton v T H White Ltd*[3]

---

1 [2014] EWHC 3546 (TCC).
2 [2013] EWCA Civ 1537.
3 [2014] EWCA Civ 906.

emphasising that deadlines should not be treated as 'tripwires', this does not, in practice, prevent parties taking points, often of dubious merit.

8.6 Thirdly, there remains a tendency to use (or rather abuse) the costs budgeting process so as to apply pressure to other parties to the litigation. One common example is for one particular party, commonly insurance backed, to lowball its budget, in a somewhat artificial effort to enable it to raise criticisms against other parties' budgets (either for being disproportionate generally, or too high at one or more specific stage(s)). Recent jurisprudence suggests that this approach will not be tolerated (see *Findcharm Ltd v Churchill Group Ltd*[4]), but it would be premature to say that the practice is dead.

8.7 Finally, the approach of the TCC to costs budgeting may well come down to which particular Judge has been assigned to the costs CMC, particularly in the absence of any further guidance, be it from the Court of Appeal or from appropriate revisions to the CPR. In practical terms, this makes advising clients as to the likely outcome of the costs budgeting hearing somewhat difficult.

8.8 From the perspective of the Court, the procedure also gives rise to various headaches, aside from the somewhat unattractive proposition of the Friday list becoming exclusively congested by contested costs budget hearings. Principal among these, it is suggested, are: (1) inconsistencies in presentation of costs budgets, meaning that sensible comparison and analysis of rival budgets is made more difficult than it might be; and (2) where budgets are in issue, insufficient time being set aside in the Court's diary for consideration of the same. If the parties, by sensible cooperation, can avoid these headaches for the Court, the more likely it is that a decision can be made efficiently.

Presentation of costs budgets

8.9 One common problem for practitioners, particularly at costs CMC stage, is that of presentation. It is often difficult to fully digest and understand costs budgets given the multitude of different parameters in play (for example, differing hourly rates (although rates should not now be considered at costs budgeting hearings – see the recently revised PD 3E, paragraph 7.10); different ways of presenting time, the delphic issue of brief fees and differing contingencies).

8.10 At the time of writing, it is understood that moves are afoot to standardise the presentation of costs budgets to enable them to be dealt with more efficiently by the Court.

8.11 In the absence of any standardised template, the authors offer the following schedules as an example of how one might sensibly present rival costs budgets. These are put forward as examples only and may not be appropriate in all cases. They assume five-party litigation.

8.12 The first schedule, which is basic, sets out an overview of the parties' positions in Precedent H forms. It covers the scenario where, as is often the case, different parties have allowed for different contingencies, and examples of 'outlier' budgets which

---

4 [2017] EWHC 1108 (TCC).

may be thought of as being (1) disproportionately high and (2) deliberately low. See Table 8.1.

8.13 The second schedule, which is more detailed, is a suggested format of how a party may present a summary of the challenges to a particular party's costs budget, while comparing costs at each stage against its own budget, as well as recording any offers contained in the Precedent R forms. It is suggested that the numbers which are italicised should be presented to the Court in a different colour for ease of reference. See Table 8.2.

8.14 Perhaps the best guidance that can be offered is to liaise with the Court at an early stage if there is any preference as to how the issues concerning costs budgets should be presented. As is apparent from the relevant jurisprudence, it would appear that the approach of the Court to costs budgeting matters is likely to depend on the preferences of the assigned

Table 8.1 Suggested sample presentation table for costs budgets

Stage	C	D1	D2	3P	4P
Pre-action	55,532.00	84,475.18	86,273.17	4,675.00	10,576.67
Statements of Case	94,166.30	74,180.36	89,450.94	44,107.00	54,045.50
CMC	35,387.20	10,695.50	9,688.20	8,975.00	0.00
Disclosure	221,593.00	158,945.00	88,300.00	112,570.22	178,120.00
Witness Statements	99,965.00	85,950.00	29,860.00	45,000.00	67,055.00
Expert Reports	381,553.00	333,975.00	120,393.00	191,409.00	105,830.00
PTR	51,752.50	32,000.00	11,995.00	15,950.00	23,335.00
Trial Preparation	224,150.00	152,300.00	60,910.00	75,450.00	85,515.00
Trial	774,600.00	375,150.00	125,910.00	158,820.00	291,350.00
ADR	24,113.00	19,375.00	10,940.00	47,005.60	28,388.00
Contingency A – Mediation	100,966.00	44,475.00	40,679.00	35,725.00	40,608.00
Contingency B – Amendments to Pleadings	16,700.00	16,650.00	9,000.00		
Contingency B – Leading Counsel					275,000.00
TOTAL	**2,080,478.00**	**1,388,171.04**	**683,399.31**	**739,686.82**	**1,159,823.17**
1% for costs budget prep	20,804.78	13,881.71	6,833.99	7,396.87	11,598.23
2% for other costs budgeting costs	41,609.56	27,763.42	13,667.99	14,793.74	23,196.46

Table 8.2 Suggested sample comparative presentation table for costs budgets

Stage		C	D1	D2	3P	4P
Pre-action	Own	55,532.00	84,475.18	86,273.17	4,675.00	10,576.67
	Offer to Cl.		55,532.00	55,532.00		55,532.00
	Difference		0.00	0.00		0.00
Statements of Case	Own	94,166.30	74,180.36	89,450.94	44,107.00	54,045.50
	Offer to Cl.		94,166.30	92,806.30		94,166.30
	Difference		0.00	*1,360.00*		0.00
CMC	Own	35,387.20	10,695.50	9,688.20	8,975.00	0.00
	Offer to Cl.		35,387.20	35,387.20		35,387.20
	Difference		0.00	0.00		0.00
Disclosure	Own	221,593.00	158,945.00	88,300.00	112,570.22	178,120.00
	Offer to Cl.		158,520.00	117,683.00		206,593.00
	Difference		*63,073.00*	*103,910.00*		*15,000.00*
Witness Statements	Own	99,965.00	85,950.00	29,860.00	45,000.00	67,055.00
	Offer to Cl.		99,965.00	71,600.00		69,575.00
	Difference		0.00	*28,365.00*		*30,390.00*
Expert Reports	Own	381,553.00	333,975.00	120,393.00	191,409.00	105,830.00
	Offer to Cl.		297,715.50	284,870.00		219,053.00
	Difference		*83,837.50*	*96,683.00*		*162,500.00*
PTR	Own	51,752.50	32,000.00	11,995.00	15,950.00	23,335.00
	Offer to Cl.		40,152.50	29,422.50		43,242.50
	Difference		*11,600.00*	*22,330.00*		*8,510.00*
Trial Preparation	Own	224,150.00	152,300.00	60,910.00	75,450.00	85,515.00
	Offer to Cl.		191,650.00	163,750.00		124,150.00
	Difference		*32,500.00*	*60,400.00*		*100,000.00*
Trial	Own	774,600.00	375,150.00	125,910.00	158,820.00	291,350.00
	Offer to Cl.		414,100.00	425,100.00		597,600.00
	Difference		*360,500.00*	*349,500.00*		*177,000.00*
ADR	Own	24,113.00	19,375.00	10,940.00	47,005.60	28,388.00
	Offer to Cl.		24,113.00	16,733.00		24,113.00
	Difference		0.00	*7,380.00*		0.00
Contingency A – Mediation	Own	100,966.00	44,475.00	40,679.00	35,725.00	40,608.00
	Offer to Cl.		54,950.00	76,816.00		49,906.00
	Difference		*46,016.00*	*24,150.00*		*51,060.00*
Contingency B – Amended Pleadings	Own	16,700.00	16,650.00	9,000.00	0.00	0.00
	Offer to Cl.		16,700.00	16,700.00		16,700.00
	Difference		0.00	0.00		0.00
Contingency B – Leading Counsel	Own					
	Offer to Cl.					
	Difference					
Total Claimed/ Offered		2,080,478.00	1,482,951.50	1,386,400.00		1,536,018.00

Judge. Parties are well advised to get on the right side of the Court from the outset so as to make the Judge's job, which may well be heavy and somewhat tedious in relation to costs budgeting, as painless as possible.

Timing of costs budgets

8.15 Pursuant to CPR 3.13(1)(b), a party is required to file its costs budget 21 days before the first CMC. Failure to do so attracts a significant sanction under CPR 3.14, namely to be treated as if its budget is comprised of only the applicable Court fees.

8.16 Since the decision of the Court of Appeal in *Mitchell*, which brought CPR 3.14 sharply into focus, there have been various decisions of the High Court and the Court of Appeal in relation to the exercise of the Court's discretion when it comes to considering applications for relief from sanctions under CPR 3.9.

8.17 The majority of these cases are not concerned with costs budgets, but concern parties' failure to serve statements of case and witness statements by the prescribed dates.[5]

8.18 Cases directly on point suggest that if the delay in filing the costs budget can be measured in (a low number of) days, the breach will probably be treated as insignificant, and relief from sanctions will generally be granted.[6] That said, the case of *Bari and others v Alternative Finance Ltd* makes clear that cavalier attitudes on the part of legal teams when there has been a breach will not be well received. In that case, the solicitors had attempted to conceal the fact that the budget had been served late. While relief was allowed, it was coupled with costs consequences on the indemnity basis.

The TCC's approach to consideration of costs budgets

8.19 Partly because the rules are relatively new, and partly because of human nature and differing personal attitudes towards costs generally, it is perhaps not surprising that the approach of the Courts, including the TCC, to the issue of costs budgeting and costs management will vary from Judge to Judge. Some Judges take great interest in costs budgeting as a matter of principle. Others do not.

8.20 There is authority for the principle that the Court should take a relatively broad-brush approach when it comes to assessing costs budgets, unless it is being asserted that any particular budget is disproportionate (see, for example, *GSK Project Management Ltd v QPR Holdings Ltd*,[7] per Stuart Smith J). For examples of disproportionate budgets, see

---

5 See, for example, *Denton v TH White Ltd* [2014] EWCA Civ 906; *Clearway Drainage Systems Ltd v Miles Smith Ltd* [2016] EWCA Civ 1258; *O'Connor v The Pennine Acute Hospitals NHS Trust* [2015] EWCA Civ 1244; *LBI HF v Stanford* [2014] EWHC 3385; *Dukanovic v QBE Insurance Co (UK) Ltd*, 2 January 2015 (Stoke on Trent County Court); *Devon & Cornwall Autistic Community Trust v Cornwall Council* [2015] EWHC 129 (QB); *Buswell v Symes* [2015] EWHC 2262 (QB); *Fouda v Southwark LBC* [2015] EWHC 1128 (QB); and *British Airways Plc v Spencer* [2015] EWHC 2477 (Ch).

6 See, for example, *Murray v BAE Systems Ltd* (unreported, 17 February 2016) – seven days late); *Azure East Midlands Ltd v Manchester Airport Group* [2014] EWHC 1644 (TCC) – two days late; *Bari and others v Alternative Finance Ltd* (2 April 2014) – one day late; *Wain v Gloucestershire County Council* [2014] EWHC 1274 (TCC) – one day late; *Utilise TDS Ltd v Davies* [2014] EWHC 834 (Ch) – 45 minutes late).

7 [2015] EWHC 2274 (TCC).

CIP Properties (AIPT) Ltd v Galliford Try Infrastructure Ltd,[8] *Bloomberg LP v Sandberg*[9] and *Group Seven Ltd v Nasir*.[10]

8.21 Further, following the 2016 amendments to the relevant rules, Judges should not now approve or disapprove of hourly rates at costs budgeting stage (see PD 3E, paragraph 7.10). This might suggest that the intention of the legislature is for points of detail which ordinarily arise at detailed assessment stage to remain points of detail for that stage, as opposed to being matters for the costs CMC Judge. However, there is evidence that Judges will nevertheless look into the hourly rates for the purposes of approving a budget (see, for example, *JSC Mezhdunarodniy Promyshlenniy Bank v Pugachev*).[11]

8.22 However, lurking in the background and contrary to the 'broad-brush' school of thought is CPR 3.18(b) and the comments of the Court of Appeal in relation to the same (for example, in *Henry v News Group Newspapers Ltd*[12] and *Harrison v University Hospitals Coventry and Warwickshire NHS Trust*[13]). TCC Judges may well be at pains to stress that costs management is not detailed assessment (see, for example, *Merrix v Heart of England NHS Foundation Trust*[14] at [78] and [84], per Carr J), but in view of (1) the appellate jurisprudence in relation to CPR 3.18(b) referred to above and (2) the intention of CPR 3.18(b) to reduce the costs of the detailed assessment process by treating agreed/approved costs budgets as binding, absent good reason, it seems inevitable that certain Judges may well be tempted in particular circumstances to approach the costs budgeting process in a more involved, rather than broad-brush, fashion.

8.23 In view of the above uncertainties, the only really worthwhile guidance which can be suggested is as follows:

- Be familiar with every aspect of the budgets, whether contested or not, and be ready for any eventuality which might arise at the hearing.
- Keep points of challenge/defence concise. Combing through costs budgets is mentally fatiguing and often requires intensive cross referencing to different documents in the bundle. Remember that the Judge will have very limited knowledge of the case and will not have had time to digest all (or any) of the idiosyncratic points raised by the parties in advance.
- Do not assume that the Court will be willing to undertake approval of budgets on paper if they are not agreed. Experience would suggest that, in the event of contention, a hearing will almost always be ordered, and invitations to dispense with a hearing (and, to a large extent, leave the hard work to the Judge) are unlikely to find favour with the Court.
- Keep the budget under review at all stages and make any and all necessary applications to revise the budget as the litigation proceeds.

---

8 [2015] EWHC 481 (TCC).
9 [2016] EWHC 488 (TCC).
10 [2016] EWHC 620 (Ch).
11 [2013] EWHC 1983 (Ch).
12 [2013] EWCA Civ 19.
13 [2017] EWCA Civ 792.
14 [2017] EWHC 346 (QB).

Costs budgets and interim payments

8.24 One important impact of the introduction of costs budgeting has been on the level of any interim payment on account in relation to costs which will be recoverable by a successful party at trial. The relevant provision of the CPR is Rule 44.2(8), which provides: 'where the court orders a party to pay costs subject to detailed assessment, it will order that party to pay a reasonable sum on account of costs, unless there is a good reason not to do so'.

8.25 In circumstances where the Court has the benefit of a costs budget, generally speaking, the Court will be satisfied that the approved budget is an appropriate benchmark for the costs to be recovered, and that any interim award should operate on the basis that recoverable costs are unlikely to be much less (see, for example, *Elvanite Full Circle Ltd v AMEC Earth & Environmental (UK) Ltd*[15]). This is consistent with the overriding principle that there is no good reason to depart from the costs budget (see CPR 3.18 and the subsequent case of *Thomas Pink v Victoria's Secret*[16]).

8.26 The practical effect of the above is that a successful party can expect a considerably higher payment on account than previously might have been the case, at least in relation to forecast costs.

Practical considerations

8.27 In light of the somewhat inconsistent (and developing) approach of the Courts to costs management, it is difficult to provide detailed practical guidance in relation to the preparation and contestation of costs budgets.

8.28 However, the following points are offered by way of general pointers:

- If in doubt, submit a budget. Disputes may arise: (1) over the value of the claim (for example, if the Claim Form is not clear (see, for example, *Sharp v Blank*,[17] where the wording on the Claim Form of 'in excess of £300,000' was held to trigger the need for costs budgets as it did not specify that the claim was for more than £10 million); or (2) if there is another issue as to whether or not costs budgeting applies (see, for example, *Jamadar v Bradford Teaching Hospitals NHS Foundations Trust*,[18] where there was confusion (albeit somewhat hard to comprehend) over whether or not the case was a multi-track case). It is suggested that in such circumstances, it is much better to have prepared and submitted a budget under protest, even if is merely an outline budget, rather than to incur the costs of protracted correspondence in dealing with *Mitchell*-type points and/or any relevant protective applications.
- If the deadline for a costs budget has been missed, even if by a short period of time, apply for relief from sanctions under CPR 3.9 immediately. If caught in time, and accompanied with appropriate contrition and/or explanation in the form of a witness statement, it is more unlikely that any such application will be

---

15 [2013] EWHC 1643 (TCC).
16 [2015] 3 Costs LR 463.
17 [2015] EWHC 2685 (Ch).
18 [2016] EWCA Civ.

contested. If a deadline is looming and it becomes apparent that the last time for filing will not be met, it is submitted that it is sensible to apply for an extension of time for filing the budget, in addition to applying for relief from sanctions, given that different considerations apply.
– If possible, seek to agree a homogenous format for presenting the parties' rival budgets for the sake of speed and consistency at the hearing.
– Ensure that the application is listed for sufficient time. In multi-party litigation, the one hour routinely set aside for CMC is unlikely to be long enough in the event that budgets are contested. If no time is available in the Court's diary, then parties should seek agreement for a separate listing of a costs CMC. That in itself may assist the parties in focussing minds and narrowing issues in relation to costs budgets, given that it may well be possible to persuade the Court that the costs of a stand-alone costs budgeting hearing should not be subject to the normal CMC order of costs in the case where one or more parties has taken bad points in relation to the budgeting matters in issue.

8.29 Costs budgeting has certainly had a significant impact on TCC litigation, and it is likely to stay for the foreseeable future. In the meantime, practitioners can only wait to see how far the costs reforms will ultimately go. It may not be long before full-scale fixed costs for all forms of litigation are introduced and, in the event that this does occur, one wonders whether this will trigger a resurgence in domestic arbitration.

CHAPTER 9

The TCC and adjudication

Introduction

9.1 The Housing Grants Construction and Regeneration Act 1996 ('the Act') changed the landscape of construction dispute resolution beyond recognition. Many disputes, big and small, which otherwise would have been litigation through the TCC have been resolved through adjudication processes which, while non-binding, have led the parties to accept the result as a final decision, or arrive at settlement. While this has had the inevitable effect of reducing the number of substantive disputes being litigated, it also spawned a seemingly ceaseless flow of satellite claims relating to the enforcement of adjudication decisions, or disputes resulting from the payment process requirements of the Act. There are now over 600 cases which deal with adjudication, and countless articles and publications. This chapter is not intended as a substitute for more in-depth books,[1] but rather focusses on the nexus between the Court function and adjudication.

Before the adjudication

9.2 In adjudication, each side bears its own costs unless the parties agree otherwise. Obtaining an adjudication award which is not capable of being enforced is expensive. Some grounds to challenge a decision arise only from the conduct of the adjudication or from the decision, and can only really be dealt with by the Courts following the issue of the award. However, some grounds to challenge enforcement can be anticipated. In some circumstances, the referring party is able to prevent otherwise good enforcement points by obtaining agreement, either expressly or tacitly, so that the point does not survive. For example, if the contract specifies an incorrect appointing body or a defective procedure, the parties can obviously agree a particular course of action. It may be that by participating in a particular procedure without protest, a party is taken to have waived any jurisdictional challenge which might otherwise have existed. However, some potential challenges may not be overcome where one of the parties does not agree, or wishes generally to reserve its rights and await the outcome of the adjudication. The types of challenge which may exist in advance of the referral to adjudication include whether there is a 'construction contract' (the question may be whether a particular entity is a party to a construction contract, or whether the contract is a 'construction' contract for the purposes of the Act) or whether there is a dispute which has 'crystallised'.

9.3 Taking the first of these examples – whether there is a construction contract to which the Act applies – a party will have to consider strategically the best course of action if there is dispute between the parties about the nature of the contract. If, for example, there is a

---

[1] Notably, *Coulson on Adjudication* (3rd edn, 2015).

question of whether there was a contract at all, then commencing an adjudication will be risky because the question of the validity of the contract might always be a matter which the Court will be required to resolved; and if and to the extent that the resolution of the issue would involve substantial issues of fact, the award will not be capable of summary enforcement (see, for example, *Pegram Shopfitters Ltd v Tally Weijl (UK) Ltd*[2]). However, if the issue is capable of being determined summarily, it may be sensible to obtain clarity from the Court before the adjudication is commenced, rather than afterwards on enforcement. This can be achieved by commencing Part 8 proceedings for a declaration. This is a tactic which is open, of course, not just to the prospective referring party, but also the prospective responding party. If the Court determines that there is a construction contract, then the parties can adjudicate in the knowledge that the award will not be subject to successful challenge on grounds that no construction contract existed; if the Court determines otherwise, the parties know that they will most likely have to resort to litigation to resolve their dispute.

9.4 Questions about whether a dispute exists are much less likely to succeed; generally the Court will look broadly at whether a claim has been made and whether it has been rejected. Strategically, the cost of seeking a declaration prior to the adjudication is unlikely to be sensible if the ground for objecting to the adjudication is weak. Such arguments are better made (if made at all) in the adjudication itself (albeit probably to be rejected by the adjudicator) under a reservation of rights. The point can then be argued on the question of enforcement, if relevant. The only advantage of taking the point in advance of an adjudication is the added credibility the point may be perceived to have if the argument is not being run in the face of an unfavourable adjudication award.

During the adjudication

9.5 In theory, it is open to a party to obtain injunctive relief to restrain the adjudication process once it has started on grounds which otherwise would give reason to refuse to enforce the decision (for example, where there is no construction contract or where the adjudicator has not been appointed properly). However, caution should be exercised: it is to be noted that injunctive relief is a discretionary remedy and therefore the existence of a potential 'jurisdictional' argument may not, of itself, be sufficient to persuade a Judge in the TCC to exercise that discretion. In *Workplace Technologies Plc v E Squared Ltd*,[3] HHJ Wilcox held, in face of an argument that an injunction should be granted to prevent a potentially void adjudication procedure continuing, that the balance of convenience favoured allowing the adjudication process to continue. The Court considered that if it granted an injunction without determining the issue of the date of the contract (and whether the scheme for adjudication under the Act applied), then it inexorably followed that it may be interfering in a valid adjudication to its detriment, frustrating the statutory scheme of the giving of an early decision as to who shall hold the money pending litigation or arbitration. By contrast, if the defendant was right about the date of the contract, it would at the most mean that he or she was subjected to a pointless adjudication (which it could choose not to participate in, if it considered its arguments about validity sound), but in any event the

---

2 [2003] EWCA Civ 1750.
3 [2000] CILL 1607.

adjudication decision would then be unenforceable. In the more recent decision of *Twintec Ltd v Volkerfitzpatrick Ltd*,[4] the Court concluded that the appointment was made under a purported provision of a contract which had not in fact been incorporated into the agreement, and thus was invalid. While stating that it was only in 'exceptional' circumstances that the Court would injunct a party, Edwards-Stuart J considered that this was a proper case for the power to be exercised, concluding that it was difficult to see how it could be either just or convenient to permit an adjudication to continue in circumstances where the decision of the adjudicator will be incapable of enforcement. The Court therefore rejected the submission that the appropriate time for the Court to intervene is at the enforcement stage. While it may be uncommon, therefore, it does seem that if the Court is satisfied that the appointment is invalid, it will take the 'exceptional' course of injuncting the adjudication from continuing. This is a different 'default' position from that taken by HHJ Wilcox, and took express account of the diversion of valuable resources and substantial irrecoverable expenditure dealing with the issues in the adjudication. Where the question is one of validity, this is likely to be the approach of the Court.

9.6 More difficult is the situation where a party argues that the adjudication should be restrained by the Court because it is oppressive and unreasonable. Alternative arguments on these grounds were advanced before Edwards-Stuart J in *Twintec* and they were rejected. The Court emphasised that these two requirements are disjunctive.

> A referral to adjudication may be unreasonable (for example, if deliberately delayed until shortly before Christmas) without necessarily being oppressive. Alternatively, it may prove to be oppressive – perhaps because, unknown to the referring party, the relevant personnel within the responding party have just been posted abroad – without having been unreasonably started. Both elements must be present and, in my judgment, to a fairly high degree.

9.7 Edwards-Stuart J considered the authorities and identified the following propositions:

- The fact that a referral to adjudication is brought in parallel with existing litigation raising the same issue is not in itself a ground for restraining the referral: see Herschell Engineering v Breen Property.[5]
- The mischief at which the 1996 Act is aimed is the delays in achieving finality in arbitration or litigation: see *Herschell* at [20].
- The right to refer a dispute to adjudication at any time confers a commercial advantage on the referring party and this must be taken to have been known by Parliament when the 1996 Act was passed: see *London Borough of Camden v Makers*[6] at [32]. One aspect of this advantage is the fact that the responding party will in most cases incur irrecoverable costs in defending the adjudication, and this can operate as a bargaining lever in favour of the referring party.
- A party should not be prevented from pursuing its right to refer a dispute to adjudication save in the most exceptional circumstances: see *Makers* at [35].

9.8 In practice, it will be difficult to identify circumstances where it is considered that the bringing of an adjudication pursuant to the statutory (or contractually agreed) right

---

4 [2014] EWHC 10 (TCC).
5 [2000] BLR 272.
6 [2009] EWHC 605 (TCC).

is both unreasonable and oppressive in circumstances where, as the Judge pointed out, Parliament has in effect expressly approved a party's right to start an adjudication in circumstances that can effectively amount to an ambush of the responding party.[7] The matter has recently been discussed by O'Farrell J in *Jacobs UK Ltd v Skanska Construction UK Ltd*.[8] She rejected the submission that it is open to a party to start and stop serial adjudications at will, but held that it is a question of fact in each case.[9]

9.9 If an injunction is to be sought, the applicant will need to follow CPR Part 25 and the accompanying practice direction.[10] The application will usually be urgent if it is being brought in the context of an adjudication which has already commenced, but it is unlikely that circumstances exist in which the application should be made without notice. The applicant will need to support the application notice with evidence in the form of a witness statement setting out the circumstances in which the injunction is sought, setting out the reasons why the Court's discretion should be exercised.

After the adjudication

9.10 The much more usual time for the TCC Judges to become involved in adjudication is when the successful party seeks to enforce the Award. It would be open to a party to seek to enforce the award by mandatory injunction, but, as pointed out in *Coulson on Adjudication*, while this theoretical approach is available, the TCC has procedures in place for dealing with enforcement through the summary judgment process under CPR Part 24. Indeed, parties will ignore this advice at their peril and, potentially, cost. In one case,[11] the claimant had brought a statutory demand and pursued bankruptcy Court proceedings. Some six months later, the matter was referred to the TCC after the statutory demand was set aside, and the decision was enforced by the TCC summarily. In relation to the application for costs of the bankruptcy proceedings, Coulson J (as he then was) stated:

> Of course I quite accept . . . that the issue of a bankruptcy petition was not of itself the wrong way of enforcing these proceedings. On the other hand, given that there is a procedure expressly tailored by the TCC to allow the prompt and efficient enforcement of adjudicators' decisions, the court has to consider very carefully an application for the costs of other proceedings, commenced in addition to the enforcement claim, particularly in circumstances where, in the end, it was the enforcement route that has proved to be the right course for the Claimant to take.

The Judge did not allow the claimant's application for costs of the earlier bankruptcy proceedings.

9.11 The party wishing to enforce an award needs to commence proceedings using Part proceedings. The Claim Form can be short, identifying the construction contract and/or the terms of the contract, or by reference to the statute, the basis of the adjudicator's jurisdiction. The Claim Form should then set out the fact of the adjudication, and the decision, the fact that the sum due pursuant to the decision remains unpaid, and make a claim for that

---

7 See also *T Clarke (Scotland) v MMAXX Underfloor Heating Ltd* [2014] CSOH 62, in which an injunction was refused.
8 [2017] EWHC 2395 (TCC).
9 Ibid at [33].
10 See *Coulson on Adjudication*, para 16.42.
11 *Harlow & Milner Ltd v Linda Teasdale (No 1)* [2006] EWHC 54 (TCC).

sum together with interest or any other sums sought (for example, if there is a claim for the adjudicator's fees which have been paid in lieu of payment by the unsuccessful party). In addition to the Claim Form, the claiming party should prepare an application notice setting out the directions that are sought, a pro-forma for which is found at Appendix F to the TCC Guide. In essence, the standard directions abridge the time for acknowledgement of service from 14 days to a much shorter period (say, four working days). There is then a timetable for the service of evidence by the defendant and, in response, the claimant. The draft directions suggest 14 and seven days respectively. When permission is granted for the claimant to issue an application for summary judgment, the TCC sets out the time and date for an oral hearing, and directions relating to a bundle and skeleton arguments. The TCC endeavours to list such a hearing within one month of the date of the issue of the Claim Form. It is rare for the hearings to involve any oral evidence, and usually the matter will be determined on the basis of argument and submission, with judgment given immediately after the hearing or, if reserved, a few days later.

9.12 The recipient of such a Claim Form can, of course, admit liability for the claim within the acknowledgement of service, or respond by way of evidence and submission pursuant to the Court's order. If the defendant does nothing, which is not uncommon, the claimant should look to a default judgment being entered rather than waiting for the listed hearing (even if only a matter of weeks away). Challenging an adjudicator's award without justification may result in an award of indemnity costs against the defendant.[12]

9.13 It has become increasingly common for the unsuccessful party to issue proceedings for a declaration in advance of enforcement proceedings, through Part 8. This would involve a pre-emptive declaration of the (in)validity of the adjudication procedure, on grounds that the adjudicator lacked jurisdiction, or that the procedure adopted was in breach of the rules of natural justice. Another route open to the unsuccessful party would be to have the, or an, issue determined in the adjudication decided finally by the Court in Part 8 proceedings in short order, which, if successful, would have the effect of overriding the adjudicator's decision. Indeed, if the issue is a short and self-contained point, which requires no oral evidence or any other elaboration than that which is capable of being provided during a relatively short interlocutory hearing, then it had been considered until recently that the defendant may be entitled to have the point decided by way of a claim for a declaration *without* having started separate Part 8 proceedings. In *Caledonian Modular Ltd v Mar City Developments Ltd*,[13] Coulson J (as he then was) pointed out that it is envisaged at paragraph 9.4.3 of the TCC Guide that separate Part 8 proceedings will not always be required in order for such an issue to be decided at the enforcement hearing. Paragraph 9.4.3 states:

> It sometimes happens that one party to an adjudication commences enforcement proceedings, whilst the other commences proceedings under Part 8, in order to challenge the validity of the adjudicator's award. This duplication of effort is unnecessary and it involves the parties in extra costs, especially if the two actions are commenced at different Court Centres. Accordingly, there should be sensible discussions between the parties or their lawyers, in order to agree the appropriate venue and also to agree who shall be claimant and who defendant. All the issues raised by each party can and should be raised in a single action. However, in cases where an adjudicator has made a clear error (but has acted within his jurisdiction), it may on occasions be

---

12 See, for example, *JG Walker Groundworks Ltd v Pior Homes (East) Ltd* [2013] EWHC 3723 (TCC).
13 [2015] EWHC 1855 (TCC).

appropriate to bring proceedings under Part 8 for a declaration as a pre-emptive response to an anticipated application to enforce the decision.

However, as discussed further below, this guidance has now been superseded.

9.14 Clearly, Part 8 proceedings parallel with enforcement have never been available if the subject matter of the adjudicated dispute involves significant factual issues requiring investigation. Coulson J (as he then was) commented, in 2015, in *Mar City*: 'It needs to be emphasised that this procedure will rarely be used, because it is very uncommon for the point at issue to be capable of being so confined'; however, since then, there have been a number of proceedings demonstrating the Court's ability and willingness to deal with somewhat complex issues, including waiver and estoppel (i.e. factual) determined in parallel Part 8 proceedings. For example, the questions that have been considered have related to the validity of an interim application,[14] the timing and content of payment notices, including questions of estoppel,[15] and the proper construction of the contract.[16] Other issues that might be readily susceptible to such a strategy may be where there is a question relating to the enforceability of liquidated damages provisions, or whether a limitation clause applies. Of course, one tactic in this situation may be for the parties to agree in advance of the adjudication that the most sensible route would be a short Part 8 procedure instead of the adjudication. As noted by Coulson J (as he then was) in *Hutton Construction Ltd v Wilson Properties (London) Ltd*,[17] many of the Part 8 declaration proceedings after adjudication had been brought 'consensually', but – this being the case – might not the parties in such cases sensibly have had the matters decided in the first instance, in a binding manner, in front of a High Court Judge? The costs of doing so are successfully recovered, and if neither side plans to accept the adjudicator's decision on the point if defeated, this route saves both sides time and cost.

9.15 While, in relation to an appropriate issue, the TCC Judge is likely to be willing to assist in final resolution of issues in a cost-effective way, they will not squeeze disputes into Part 8 solely for the purposes of allowing a party to obtain a decision in the same time frame as enforcement proceedings. If the matters in dispute should properly be heard in the wider context of other evidence or issues, the Court will refuse to adopt a Part 8 procedure or allow the point to be decided at the enforcement hearing. Moreover, in *Hutton*, Coulson J's (as he then was) judgment reflected a reigning in of the Court's willingness to allow Part 8 proceedings to determine matters following an adjudication, unless the parties were agreed that the Court should do so. The Judge stated in terms that the guidance at paragraph 9.4.3, quoted above, ought to be considered superseded by the guidance given in his judgment. This guidance stated that, where the parties were not agreed on the way forward, any defendant (to prospective enforcement proceedings) must, in bringing separate Part 8 proceedings to have an issue determined, be able to demonstrate that:

— there is a short and self-contained issue which arose in the adjudication and which the defendant continues to contest;

---

14 *Leeds City Council v Waco UK Ltd* [2015] EWHC 1400 (TCC).
15 *Kersfield Developments (Bridge Road) Ltd v Bray and Slaughter Ltd* [2017] EWHC 15 (TCC).
16 For example, *Manor Asset Ltd v Demolition Services Ltd* [2016] EWHC 222 (TCC); *Bouygues (UK) Ltd v Febrey Structures Ltd* [2016] EWHC 1333 (TCC).
17 [2017] EWHC 517 (TCC).

- the issue requires no oral evidence, or any other elaboration beyond that which is capable of being provided during the interlocutory hearing set aside for the enforcement;
- the issue is one which, on a summary judgment application, it would be unconscionable for the Court to ignore.

9.16 The Court went on to indicate that in practice this would mean demonstrating that, for example, the adjudicator's construction of a contract clause is 'beyond any rational justification', or that the adjudicator's calculation of the relevant time periods is 'obviously wrong', or that the adjudicator's categorisation of a document as, say, a payment notice when, 'on any view', it was not capable of being described as such a document. Coulson J (as he then was) remarked that many of the applications which are currently being made by way of Part 8 proceedings following an adjudication 'are an abuse of the court process', and went on to state that the TCC does not have the resources to allow defendants to re-run large parts of an adjudication at a disputed enforcement hearing, particularly in circumstances where the adjudication may have taken 28 days or 42 days, while the Judge might have available no more than two hours pre-reading and a two-hour hearing in which to dispose of the dispute. Finally, the Court made clear that because it is a potential abuse of the Court process:

> ... a defendant who unsuccessfully raises this sort of challenge on enforcement will almost certainly have to pay the claimant's costs of the entire action on an indemnity basis. Of course, the other side of the coin is that, if the claimant does not agree to the defendant's proposal to deal with the issue on enforcement, but the court concludes that the issue does fall within the limited exception to which I have referred, it is the claimant who runs the risk of being penalised in costs.

9.17 It might be thought regrettable that the run of cases arising out of 'smash and grab' adjudications[18] appears to have soured the TCC's appetite for resolving substantive disputes. In practice, the remarks may be no more than an underlining of the relatively limited scope of type of dispute ordinarily suited to Part 8 proceedings. In the right case, there is no doubt that resolving any straightforward issue of contractual construction is sensible, and the editors of this book consider, indeed, that the parties ought to consider whether to bring such issues direct to the TCC rather than have the matters adjudicated first.

9.18 Finally, while the TCC has also suggested that there may exist a 'hybrid' procedure between Part 7 and Part 8, Coulson J's (as he then was) remarks in *Hutton* make it very clear that this is not the sort of procedure which the Court would be happy to conclude within the very short time frame allowed by the Part 24 summary judgment procedure. The Court will generally not slow that procedure to allow it, and any relevant Part 8 procedure on a slightly slower track, to run in parallel with a simultaneous conclusion: the unsuccessful party must generally pay up, as intended by the statute, pending final resolution.

---

18 Since the 2011 changes to the Act, where an employer fails to issue the appropriate notice required by the Act, the sum applied for may become due to the contractor. There have been a string of cases in which parties, usually contractors, have sought to take advantage of the statutory provisions by adjudicating the question of entitlement, and then seeking enforcement in the Courts. However, the TCC has played a vital role in overseeing these cases. In *Hutton*, Coulson J (as he then was) commented that the significant increase in these sorts of claims arose principally from the 'ill-considered amendments to the 1996 Act, and the over-prescription of the payment terms included in the standard forms of contract, which have led to provisions of unnecessary complexity'.

Stays of execution

9.19 An adjudication award is intended, pursuant to the Act, to have a temporarily binding nature. It is a decision which is binding until the substantive issues are finally decided by the Courts. It is now long settled that a party cannot set off a competing cross-claim against an adjudicator's decision, and contractual clauses which purport to do so will either be construed otherwise or, if necessary, struck down. The (temporarily) binding nature of the award, pursuant to the Act, will be given effect to.[19]

9.20 The difficulty that this gives rise to in some cases is that the party in receipt of the proceeds of the award is financially unstable, or even insolvent, so that the reality is that the decision is, or may not be, not temporary – it is final: the money can never be paid back to the responding party. In these circumstances, the TCC has given guidance as to the extent of its powers to prevent the purported injustice this could give rise to.

9.21 Rules of Supreme Court Order 47, preserved in Section A of the Civil Procedure Rules 1998, provides that, where a judgment is given or an order made for the payment of money and the Court is satisfied that there are special circumstances which render it inexpedient to enforce the judgment, the Court may by order stay the execution of the judgment for such period and subject to such conditions as the Court thinks fit.

9.22 In *Straw Realisations (No 1) Ltd v Shaftsbury House (Developments) Ltd*,[20] Edwards-Stuart J provided a good guide to the modern approach of the Courts to the interrelationship of enforcement and insolvency, setting out the following principles, having considered the relevant authorities:

- A clause in a contract that purports to supersede the obligation to comply with an adjudicator's decision, in this case the provision for a mutual setting off of the accounts between the parties on the happening of certain events as set out in clause 8.5 and an obligation only to pay the balance and the restriction on any further payments, cannot prevail over an obligation to comply with the decision of an adjudicator: see *Ferson v Levolux* and *Verry v Camden*.
- If, at the date of the hearing of the application to enforce an adjudicator's decision, the successful party is in liquidation, then the adjudicator's decision will not be enforced by way of summary judgment: see *Bouygues v Dahl Jensen*[21] and *Melville Dundas Ltd v George Wimpey UK Ltd*.[22] The same result follows if a party is the subject of the appointment of administrative receivers: see *Melville Dundas*.
- For the same reason, if a party is in administration and a notice of distribution has been given, an adjudicator's decision will not be enforced.
- If a party is in administration, but no notice of distribution has been given, an adjudicator's decision which has not become final (pursuant to a contractual provision – for example, notice must be given that the award is disputed within a certain period if the decision is not to become binding) will not be enforced by

---

19 See *William Verry Ltd v The London Borough of Camden* [2006] EWHC 761 (TCC); *Ferson Contractors v Levolux AT Ltd* [2003] BLR 118.
20 [2010] EWHC 2597 (TCC). See also *FG Skerritt Ltd v Caledonian Building Systems Ltd* [2013] EWHC 1898 (TCC).
21 [2000] BLR 522.
22 [2007] BLR 257.

way of summary judgment. This follows from the decision in *Melville Dundas*, as well as being consistent with the reasoning in *Integrated Building Services v PIHL UK Ltd*.[23]

- If a party is in administration, and no notice of distribution has been given, but the adjudicator's decision has, by agreement of the parties or operation of the contract, become final, the decision may be enforced by way of summary judgment (subject to the imposition of a stay).
- Unlike the law in Scotland, there is no rule of English law that the fact that a party is on the verge of insolvency (*vergens ad inopiam*) triggers the operation of bankruptcy set-off: see *Melville Dundas*, per Lord Hope at [33].
- If a party is insolvent in a real sense, or its financial circumstances are such that if an adjudicator's decision is complied with the paying party is unlikely to recover its money, or at least a substantial part of it, the Court *may* grant summary judgment, but stay the enforcement of that judgment.

9.23 Thus, if a responding party cannot show that the judgment creditor is in liquidation, or in administration where the decision has not become binding, but where the judgment creditor is in financial difficulties, what are the factors which the TCC will take into account when deciding whether or not to exercise its general discretion to order a stay of execution? A useful commentary on the development of the law, which had given rise to a number of decisions, is set out in *Coulson on Construction Adjudication*.[24] For the purposes of this book, it is sufficient to note that the appropriate principles were effectively settled in *Wimbledon Construction Co 2000 Ltd v Derek Vago*,[25] and those principles have in a relatively limited number of cases been shown to have been satisfied in subsequent cases. The principles are as follows:

- The probable inability of the claimant to repay the judgment sum (awarded by the adjudicator and enforced by way of summary judgment) at the end of the substantive trial, or arbitration hearing, may constitute special circumstances within the meaning of Order 47 rule 1(1)(a) rendering it appropriate to grant a stay (see *Herschell Engineering Ltd v Breen Property Ltd*[26]).
- If the claimant is in insolvent liquidation, or there is no dispute on the evidence that the claimant is insolvent, then a stay of execution will usually be granted (see *Bouygues*[27] and *Rainford House Ltd v Cadogan Ltd*[28]).

---

23 [2010] CSOH 80.
24 3rd edn, pp 467–470.
25 [2005] EWHC 1086 (TCC). See also *Gosvenor London Ltd v Aygun Aluminium UK Ltd* [2018] EWHC 227 (TCC), in which Fraser J added a further principle relating to the risk of asset dissipation.
26 [2000] BLR 272.
27 See above.
28 [2001] BLR 416.

- Even if the evidence of the claimant's present financial position suggested that it is probable that it would be unable to repay the judgment sum when it fell due, that would not usually justify the grant of a stay if:
    o the claimant's financial position is the same or similar to its financial position at the time that the relevant contract was made (see *Herschell*); or
    o the claimant's financial position is due, either wholly or in significant part, to the defendant's failure to pay those sums which were awarded by the adjudicator (see *Absolute Rentals v Glencor Enterprises Ltd*[29]).

9.24 In practice, it is the latter two points which usually see off applications for a stay of execution: it is often the case (particularly in smaller construction projects or where sub-contracts are concerned) that small companies had limited cash flow at the point of contract, and/or that the deprivation of substantial sums itself is the cause of the financial predicament. It is to be noted that not having access to the relevant accounts at the time of contracting does not alter this position.[30] Given that the matter is one of discretion weighing all relevant factors, some cases demonstrate other factors which may be at play – (unusual) examples include the overall conduct of the parties (for example, trading while insolvent)[31] and the judgment debtor's inability to pay.[32]

9.25 If a party intends to seek a stay of execution, it should produce witness evidence which deals in terms with the criteria set out in *Wimbledon v Vago*. It is for the party applying for a stay to decide whether there were grounds for a stay and to adduce the relevant evidence. It was pointed out by Ramsey J in *O'Donnell Developments Ltd v Build Ability Ltd*[33] that while the parties must cooperate, there is no obligation on the judgment creditor to give widespread disclosure of all of its financial and business information so that the other party can see whether there is something which gives grounds for an application to stay. Applying this reasoning in another judgment,[34] Ramsey J further commented that if there were such an obligation it would mean that parties could gain the benefit of that confidential information which in the competitive construction industry would have serious consequences in relation to the ability of contractors and subcontractors when tendering or dealing with disputes.

9.26 It must also be borne in mind that the insolvency procedure cannot be used cynically to try to avoid having an award enforced. In *Bernard Sport Surfaces Ltd v Astrosoccer4U Ltd*,[35] Coulson J (as he then was) held that 'the notice of intention to appoint an administration [was] entirely bogus' and was made with the intention of circumventing the enforcement regime. He therefore refused to grant a stay.

---

29 [2000] CILL 1639.
30 See *Air Design (Kent) Ltd v Deerglen (Jersey) Ltd* [2008] EWHC 3047.
31 *Partner Projects Ltd v Corinthian Nominees Ltd* [2011] EWHC 2989.
32 *Bewley Homes Plc v CNM Estates (Surbiton) Ltd* [2010] EWHC 2619.
33 [2009] EWHC 3388 (TCC).
34 *Farrelly (MNE) Building Services Ltd v Byrne Bros (Formwork) Ltd* [2013] EWHC 1186 (TCC).
35 [2017] EWHC 2425 (TCC).

CHAPTER 10

The TCC and ADR

Introduction

10.1 The Courts seek actively to encourage parties to settle their disputes in numerous ways. The Pre-Action Protocol's (Appendix 2) origins lie in an attempt to front-load preparation and make settlement prior to commencement of an action more likely. In the standard Court form submitted prior to the first CMC, the parties are required to indicate whether any form of alternative dispute resolution (ADR) has been attempted or whether a stay should be imposed for a period to allow ADR. As will be explored later, the Court will also consider, to some extent, the parties' wishes when it comes to a timetable to the final hearing which can accommodate commercial negotiations, and the Court has the power to impose sanctions in costs if a party does not engage meaningfully in ADR. These tools are put to good effect: on the basis of the TCC annual reports, while there is no data which specifically identifies the number of cases which end by negotiated settlement, each year the number of fought trials equates to a relatively constant figure of around 10 per cent of the number of claims commenced. It is clear that, whatever the precise number, the very vast majority of claims commenced do not proceed to judgment.

10.2 This chapter explores the interrelationship between the Court and ADR, and the practical approach generally taken by the TCC in balancing the policy of encouraging negotiation and settlement, with the management of the progression of a dispute to trial.

What is ADR?

10.3 The term 'ADR' covers all types of dispute resolution other than litigation. This therefore includes arbitration, although given the many similarities (and some disadvantages) of the arbitral process to the Court process particularly in the UK domestic context, nowadays ADR is more commonly used as a term to refer to mediation, conciliation, early neutral evaluation or other hybrid procedures designed to encourage or facilitate settlement of the dispute. It also covers the use of dispute adjudication or resolution boards, which in recent years have become commonplace in large infrastructure and engineering projects.

10.4 'Mediation' involves an independent and impartial third party who helps the parties reach agreement. It is often useful in the context of the type of disputes which come to the TCC for the mediator to understand the types of issues and risks which arise in TCC litigation; not because it is necessary for the mediator to provide an evaluation of the claim to the party, but so that they can with some authority identify for the parties the range of outcomes and risks faced in litigation. 'Conciliation' is a similar beast to mediation, but the principal difference is that, at some point, the conciliator is usually asked to provide the parties with a non-binding recommendation for the settlement. 'Early Neutral Evaluation' is a process in which more of the focus is upon the provision of a view by a trusted independent third party, sometimes on the potential outcome to the entirety of the dispute should the matter fight, but often on key contractual or legal points which the parties believe may unlock the wider case. It is now commonplace for parties to mix and match these procedures, so that there may be an early neutral evaluation followed (sometimes the following day or week) by a commercially focussed mediation. A Dispute Adjudication Board (DAB), or Dispute Resolution Board (DRB), is a panel, usually of three people often including engineering and legal expertise, retained by the parties to a significant construction project to provide recommendations or decisions on disputes as they arise. Sometimes the decisions are binding, or, like adjudications temporarily binding but subject always to final Court or arbitration proceedings; sometimes the board make recommendations which are not binding at all, although the recommendation carries with it some obvious benefit in the context of the parties' ongoing project management and commercial negotiations. Because DABs/DRBs exist for the lifetime of the project, there is less interaction between the Court process and these forms of ADR, although disputes can arise if the DRB is part of a mandatory tiered resolution process with which the parties are required to comply prior to commencing litigation, considered in the following section.

Enforcement of contractual ADR schemes

10.5 Some contracts have tiered stages of ADR which the parties are either required or encouraged to engage with prior to Court proceedings being commenced, in relation to a particular dispute. If the contract does no more than encourage steps to be taken, by the use of permissive rather than mandatory language (for example, 'may'), then there is obviously no bar to commencing litigation without having taken steps in accordance with the contractual structure. However, where the contract mandates that certain steps be taken, the common question faced by the TCC is: What does the Court do if a party to the contract commences litigation without having complied, or complied properly, with the required steps?

10.6 Traditionally, a simple agreement to negotiate, in broad and unspecific terms, is not enforceable. This is because it is regarded as too uncertain. Even an agreement to negotiate 'in good faith' is unlikely to be enforceable without more.[1] It is considered to be unworkable in practice as it is inherently inconsistent with the position of a negotiating party; therefore, it provides uncertainty. Similarly, an agreement to 'seek to have the dispute resolved amicably by mediation' was held to be unenforceable.[2] However, more recent cases have demonstrated that where some further definition of the obligation to negotiate is provided, the Court will strive to uphold the obligation. In *Cable & Wireless Plc v IBM United Kingdom*,[3] the Court determined that the prescription of a particular procedure to an obligation to attempt in good faith to settle a dispute was the characteristic which turned an unenforceable obligation into one with sufficient certainty to be enforceable. That was the case notwithstanding that the description of the procedure, while not vague, was somewhat less than detailed: it was simply to follow whatever ADR was 'recommended to the parties by the Centre for Dispute Resolution'.

10.7 The Court noted that in the face of a clear breach of the obligation to participate in ADR, there was an entitlement, prima facie, to enforcement of the obligation. However,

---

1 *Courtney & Fairbairn Ltd v Tolaini Bros* [1975] 1 WLR 297; *Watford v Miles* [1992] 2 AC 128.
2 *Sul America v Enesa Engenharis* [2012] 1 Ll R 671 (CA).
3 [2002] EWHC 2059.

the remedy was equitable and therefore discretionary, and while strong cause would have to be shown in order to justify declining to enforce an agreement, once determined as sufficiently certain, it was suggested that there may be cases where 'a reference to ADR would be obviously futile and where the likelihood of a productive mediation taking place would be so slight as not to justify enforcing the agreement. Even in such circumstances ADR would have to be a completely hopeless exercise'.[4] In the recent case of *Astor Management AG v Atalaya Mining Plc*,[5] Leggatt J held (albeit in the context of the construction of a reasonable endeavours clause) that there was no 'principle of futility' (whether as a principle of law of interpretative presumption) which enabled the disapplication of a contractual precondition just because the Court considered that compliance served no useful purpose. It is unlikely that this is determinative against the Court's ability to refuse to provide discretionary equitable relief on grounds of futility, it is in line with the general direction of travel which makes it increasingly improbable that the Court will sanction non-compliance with dispute resolution condition precedent clauses.

10.8 In *Holloway v Chancery Mead Ltd*,[6] Ramsey J held that the ADR clause must meet at least the following three requirements:

- the process must be sufficiently certain in that there should not be the need for an agreement at any stage before matters can proceed;
- the administrative processes for selecting a party to resolve the dispute and to pay that person should also be defined;
- the process or at least a model of the process should be set out so that the detail of the process is sufficiently certain.

10.9 In line with this approach, a clause which required disputes to be resolved by a senior officer 'in an amicable fashion' within a period of up to one month, following consideration by a panel of three executives, again within a defined period, was considered 'too equivocal in terms of the process required and too nebulous in terms of the content of the parties' respective obligations to be given legal effect'.[7] Of particular concern was the absence of 'guidance as to the quality or nature of the attempts to be made'.

10.10 However, even these criteria are in doubt. In *Emirates Trading Agency LLC v Prime Mineral Exports Private Ltd*,[8] Teare J considered the effect of a requirement[9] for the parties to 'first seek to resolve the dispute or claim by friendly discussion', in circumstances where a party can then invoke the arbitration clause 'if no solution can be arrived at in between the Parties for a continuous period of 4 weeks'. Teare J inventively distinguished the Court of Appeal's decision in *Sul America* on the basis that as the reference to mediation did not go on further to define that process (for example, a particular overseeing body), it was 'incomplete'; and recognised implicitly that other first instance authorities may have provided requirements for greater certainty – such as Ramsey J's decision in *Chancery Mead* – but that, as first instance decisions, were not binding upon him. Teare

---

4 Per Colman J, above.
5 [2017] EWHC 425 (Comm).
6 [2007] EWHC 2495 (TCC).
7 *Wah v Grant Thornton and others* [2012] EWHC 3198.
8 [2014] EWHC 2104 (Comm).
9 Described as 'very open-ended language' in *Astor Management*.

J found that the requirement was sufficiently certain to be enforced, when coupled with an implied obligation to resolve by friendly discussions 'in good faith' – thus providing the identifiable standard 'namely fair, honest and genuine discussions'. His decision was explicitly driven by public policy concerns: enforcement of such an agreement when found as part of a dispute resolution clause was in the public interest, firstly, because commercial men expect the Court to enforce obligations which they have freely undertaken and, secondly, because the object of the agreement is to avoid what might otherwise be an expensive and time-consuming arbitration. This case certainly represents the high-water mark in enforceability of a loosely drafted requirement to negotiation. While it contained a temporal limit, which no doubt helped, it is far from clear from Teare J's reasoning that this was determinative; rather, his rationale as regards certainty rested more on the 'friendly discussions' themselves being sufficiently certain, when benchmarked against good faith. It is obvious that the Courts have, in developing the law in light of changed public policy, effected a U-turn from the early authorities; and enforcing a requirement for 'friendly discussions' while determining that a clause requiring 'mediation' is uncertain would, objectively, appear to be in conflict. There is no modern appellate decision resolving these differences, so it is, presently, unclear whether the TCC would adopt Ramsey J's criteria from *Chancery Mead*, or move from them in the way the Commercial Court has done. The authors' view is that the public policy appetite for encouraging dispute resolution outside of the Courts is likely to be the overwhelming criteria and clauses with looser and looser language may well be enforceable.

10.11 It might also be noted that the original rationale for the absence of sufficient certainty in the older authorities related not just to an ability to determine whether the obligation might have been breached, but, because, per Lord Denning, 'no court could estimate damages'.[10] The line of authorities including *Cable & Wireless* consider the question of certainty in the context of, in effect, injunctive relief staying Court proceedings pending compliance, rather than in the context of a claim for damages. Lord Denning's fundamental objection has not been cured by the introduction of more certainty as to the procedure that must be followed for the negotiations: it remains the case that it would be in many cases impossible for the Court to determine what damages might flow from breach. However, plainly for the same policy reasons aligning the law with the modern judicial approach to encouraging ADR,[11] the question of certainty in the context of damages is no longer troubling. In *Emirates Trading*, Teare J seemed less concerned about the damages point, commenting only that if a party were to seek damages for breach of the obligation it might be difficult to establish what the outcome of the discussions would have been, but in such a case damages could, in appropriate cases, be awarded for loss of a chance.

Jurisdiction, adjournment or stay?

10.12 A failure to partake in a contractually stipulated ADR procedure does not affect the jurisdiction of the Court. It is possible, therefore, to commence proceedings. The question is whether the proceedings would then be adjourned or stayed. One issue which

---

10 Per Lord Denning MR in *Courtney*.
11 Colman J said in *Cable and Wireless* that: 'For the courts now to decline to enforce contractual references to ADR on the grounds of intrinsic uncertainty would be to fly in the face of public policy.'

potentially arises is where an action is commenced in flagrant breach of a dispute resolution procedure solely to issue proceedings in time, for limitation purposes. There does not appear to be any reported authority directly on point; it seems to the authors that it is more likely that the Court would conclude that the proceedings have been validly commenced for limitation purposes (providing the cause of action itself has accrued, obviously), and that the appropriate course is to stay or adjourn the proceedings pending the parties' compliance with the contractual procedure.

10.13 The concepts of 'adjourning', or pausing, proceedings to give effect to required ADR provisions or 'staying' those proceedings are used somewhat interchangeably. Indeed, the TCC Guide effectively elides the two when, at 7.2.2, it states, 'the court will not necessarily grant a stay of proceedings upon demand and it will always need to be satisfied that an adjournment is actually necessary to enable ADR to take place'.

10.14 One commonly perceived distinction is that costs incurred during the stay of proceedings are not recoverable, whereas costs during adjourned proceedings are. It is difficult to identify the rationale for this distinction, in light of section 51 of the Supreme Court Act 1981, which provides that 'the costs of and incidental to the proceedings ... shall be in the discretion of the Court'. It is clear that this can include pre-action costs where the matter is not resolved and proceedings are begun.[12] There is no reason in principle why costs incurred during a stay might themselves not be regarded as 'incidental' to the proceedings and thus fall within the discretion of the Court. It may be that, in its discretion, a Court refuses to allow costs incurred during a stay which have only fallen to be incurred during the proceedings themselves because of a failure to comply with a contractual precondition. So, if the costs of a senior executive negotiation would not themselves have fallen to be recovered as part of litigation costs,[13] the failure to have instituted that procedure until after commencing proceedings does not necessarily have the effect of making those costs recoverable.

10.15 In the case of *Roundstone Nurseries Ltd v Stephenson Holdings Ltd*,[14] the parties asked the TCC to stay the proceedings while they endeavoured to comply with the Pre-Action Protocol, into which they wanted to incorporate a mediation hearing. The mediation was cancelled at the last minute, but one of the parties then entered judgment in default of defence against the other, because a mix up over dates had led to a failure to have served the defence within the automatic dates required by the CPR. Ultimately, the application to set aside judgment pursuant to CPR Part 13 was allowed by consent, albeit on the basis that, it was argued, the costs of the application be paid by the party in default. However, the Court determined that judgment should not have been entered in default, given the knowledge of the claimant of the existence of a substantive defence, and the claimant was made to pay the costs of the application to set aside. The case was referred to by Coulson J (as he then was) in his judgment in *CIP Properties (AIPT) Ltd v Galliford Try Infrastructures Ltd*[15] as

---

12 See further discussions at Chapter 2, above.
13 The costs of a separate, stand-alone alternative dispute resolution process, particularly where it took place before proceedings were commenced, did not usually form part of the costs of, or incidental to, litigation: *Roundstone Nurseries Ltd v Stephenson Holdings Ltd* [2009] EWHC 1431 (TCC).
14 [2009] EWHC 1431 (TCC).
15 [2014] EWHC 3546 (TCC).

a reason why staying proceedings for the purposes of ADR may lead to unnecessary complication, given there is little practical difference between the two.[16]

10.16 Appendix E to the TCC Guide, however, still contains a draft order in respect of ADR which stays proceedings, rather than adjourns them. The order provides for a specific date by which the parties are to inform the Court as to whether or not the case has been finally settled, and that, if it has not been settled, the parties are to comply with all outstanding directions made by the Court.

ADR and the Pre-Action Protocol

10.17 ADR will often be appropriate before the proceedings have begun, or at any subsequent stage. It is generally regarded that the later ADR takes place, the more the costs which will have been incurred, often unnecessarily. The TCC encourages parties actively to consider the best timing of ADR.

10.18 As pointed out by Section 8 of the TCC Guide, the TCC Pre-Action Protocol[17] itself provides for a type of ADR, because it requires there to be at least one face-to-face meeting between the parties before the commencement of proceedings. At this meeting, there should be sufficient time to discuss and resolve the dispute. However, *Higginson Securities (Developments) Ltd and another v Hodson*[18] concerned an application for a stay to enable without prejudice meetings to occur as part of the Pre-Action Protocol. The Protocol provides at paragraph 5.1:

> The overriding objective (CPR rule 1.1) applies to the pre-action period. The Protocol must not be used as a tactical device to secure advantage for one party or to generate unnecessary costs. In many cases, including those of modest value, the letter of claim and the response can be simple and the costs of both sides should be kept to a modest level. In all cases, the costs incurred at the Protocol stage should be proportionate to the complexity of the case and the amount of money which is at stake. The Protocol is not intended to impose a requirement on the parties to marshal and disclose all the supporting details and evidence that may ultimately be required if the case proceeds to litigation.

10.19 The case concerned a low-value architect's negligence claim in which around £70,000 was in dispute. A short Protocol letter was issued and, following the provision of some further information, a similarly short response some eight months later was provided. This letter denied liability and required the claim to be withdrawn. The letter did not suggest a meeting. The prospective claimant did not suggest a meeting either. A Claim Form was issued two months later, and the defendant threatened an application for a stay on grounds that the pre-action procedure had not been exhausted. The claimant responded that there was no merit in a without-prejudice meeting in the light of the defendant's position. Proceedings were served, and although there were then discussions about whether a stay for mediation would be appropriate and, if so, when, no agreement was reached. The respondent then pursued its application for a stay.

---

16 See also *Russell v Stone* [2017] EWHC 1555 (TCC) for the complications that can arise when a standstill agreement is used instead of a stay or adjournment.
17 See Chapter 2; see also Appendix 2.
18 [2012] EWHC 1052 (TCC) (26 April 2012).

10.20 Akenhead J remarked generally that it was vitally important that practitioners in the field of construction claims, particularly in low-value claims, consider pragmatic and cost-saving responses in the circumstances in which they find themselves at the given time. Considering that the costs of the application itself were around £10,000 for the two sides, the Judge observed that it was obvious that the defendant's approach had been disproportionate, both in terms of avoiding time being wasted and in keeping costs down. The application for a stay was rejected. It might be noted, however, that the Judge went on to require a stay of four weeks to permit a without-prejudice meeting or mediation following the service of defence.

10.21 While it is unlikely that in a higher value claim, the Court would be as ready to conclude that, as things stood, a meeting would be unproductive, the Court is likely always to take a pragmatic approach in light of the circumstances which exist at the time. It may well be that if, on the basis of the pre-action correspondence, it was clear that there was little prospect of settlement until a particular stage in the procedure (for example, disclosure), the Court may have some sympathy with a party's genuine attempt to keep costs down by suggesting that the parties proceed in the litigation to the relevant point. That said, the Court is likely to be unimpressed if disagreement about such an approach itself leads to the unnecessary expenditure of costs in determining the appropriate course of action: a short application in writing to the Judge to decide on the basis of brief correspondence might be one way in which such a point might be swiftly resolved.

ADR and general case management

10.22 The TCC Guide states that at the first CMC, the TCC should be addressed on the parties' views as to the likely efficacy of ADR, the appropriate timing of ADR, and the advantages and disadvantages of a short stay of proceedings to allow ADR to take place. Having considered the representations of the parties, it is suggested that the Court may order a short stay to facilitate ADR at that stage. Alternatively, the Court may simply encourage the parties to seek ADR and allow it to occur within the timetable for the resolution of the proceedings set down by the Court.

10.23 The TCC Guide should potentially be read subject to the observations by Coulson J (as he then was) in *CIP Properties*. At the first CMC, the parties could not agree whether or when there should be a mediation, or what period of stay or adjournment should be inserted so as to allow for ADR. The Judge stated that, when setting directions for the trial of a large TCC case, the Court will allow a reasonable period between each step in the process, so that the parties not only have sufficient time to take that step, but also have an opportunity to reflect and consider their positions before incurring the next tranche of costs. By way of example, the Judge noted (in the context of a multi-party, high value defects claim: fairly standard TCC fare) that the Court will commonly identify a period of two months or so between, say, disclosure and the exchange of witness statements, or between the exchange of witness statements and the production of the experts' joint statement. Such a period should be usually long enough, in all but the most complex cases, to allow the parties to engage in ADR between those two steps, if they are agreed that this is a sensible course. Thus, the Judge observed, the TCC endeavours to facilitate the ADR process at each stage of the litigation, while also keeping at the forefront of its consideration the requirement to put in place a cost-efficient and sensible timetable to lead up to a fixed trial date (on the assumption – which the Court must make for these purposes – that there will be an effective trial). For these reasons, the Court found in terms that it is usually inappropriate for the Court at a CMC to build in some sort of special 'window' of three or four months in order that the Court proceedings can be put on hold whilst the parties engage in ADR, and that the fixing of any lengthy 'window', for purposes unconnected with the preparation for trial, is bad case management.

10.24 At any stage after the first CMC and prior to the commencement of the trial, the Court will, either on its own initiative or if requested to do so by one or both of the parties, consider afresh the likely efficacy of ADR and whether or not a short stay or adjournment of the proceedings should be granted, in order to facilitate ADR. However, in line with the observations of Coulson J (as he then was), it is likely to be a rare case that a trial once set down will be adjourned solely for the purposes of ADR. Absent agreement of all the parties, the TCC would almost certainly refuse such an application; even if all the parties were agreed, the interests of the Court in the wider business and efficacy of the TCC will mean that the Court is likely to be very reluctant to do so.

Cost sanctions

10.25 The TCC has the power to impose cost sanctions if a party has unreasonably refused to take part in ADR. The key decision of the Court of Appeal in this regard remains *Halsey v Milton Keynes General NHS Trust*,[19] in which it was indicated that such a costs order would be the exception to the general rule that costs follow the event, but the Court must look at all the circumstances of the case to determine whether a party's conduct can be regarded as unreasonable. The circumstances will include: (1) the nature of the case; (2) the merits of the case; (3) the extent to which other settlement methods have been attempted; (4) whether the costs of the ADR would be disproportionately high; (5) whether any delay in setting up and attending the ADR would have been prejudicial; (6) whether the ADR had a reasonable prospect of success.

10.26 The TCC Guide indicates that further guidance can be found in the more recent TCC case of *PGF II SA v OMFS Co 1 Ltd*,[20] particularly in relation to silence in the face of a request to mediate. In that case, the Court of Appeal considered the first instance judgment of Mr Recorder Furst QC, sitting as a deputy Judge of the TCC, who acceded in part to the claimant's application for a costs sanction on the ground that the defendant had unreasonably refused to mediate, by depriving the defendant of the costs to which it would otherwise have been entitled under Part 36, but he declined to take the further step of making the defendant pay the claimant's costs, incurred during the same period. Recorder Furst QC decided firstly that the defendant's silence amounted to a refusal and, secondly, applying the *Halsey* guidelines, that its refusal had been unreasonable.

10.27 The Court of Appeal upheld the first instance decision, and specifically endorsed a passage in the ADR Handbook[21] in which the authors had drawn heavily from the first

---

19 [2004] EWCA Civ 576.
20 [2014] 152 Con LR 72.
21 *The Jackson ADR Handbook* by Messrs Blake, Brown and Sime, supported by an editorial advisory board, and endorsed by the Judicial College, the Civil Justice Council and the Civil Mediation Council. An edition updated from that referred to by the Court has been since published, in November 2016.

instance decision. Paragraph 11.63 sets out the steps which a party should follow when faced with a request to engage in ADR but which believes that it has reasonable grounds for refusing to participate in at that stage. These include:

- not ignoring an offer to engage in ADR;
- responding promptly in writing, giving clear and full reasons why ADR is not appropriate at the stage, based if possible on the *Halsey* guidelines;
- raising with the opposing party any shortage of information or evidence believed to be an obstacle to successful ADR, together with consideration of how that shortage might be overcome;
- not closing off ADR of any kind, and for all time, in case some other method than that proposed, or ADR at some later date, might prove to be worth pursuing.

10.28 The Court of Appeal emphasised, however, that refusing to accept an invitation to participate in ADR (or, worse – as pointed out by Briggs LJ – refusing even to engage in whether there should be any form of ADR) would inevitably generally lead to a finding of unreasonable conduct. In terms of imposing a sanction, however, it is just one aspect of conduct overall which is to be assessed. The power of the Court would range from no sanction (albeit unlikely where there has been an intentional refusal to engage, absent very specific circumstances) through to the reduction of the successful parties' costs in whole or in part (most likely); in turn through to an order by which the successful party pays some or all of the unsuccessful party's costs (albeit only in the case of the most serious and flagrant failures to engage – for example, where the Court had taken it on itself to encourage the parties to do so).

10.29 One circumstance in which a refusal to mediate may not result in a particular sanction was demonstrated in the TCC in *Northrop Grumman Mission Systems Europe Ltd v BAE Systems*.[22] Ramsey J found that the fact that BAE considered it had a strong case was a factor which provided some limited justification for not mediating, while also observing that the ADR Handbook pointed out that mediation can have a positive effect in resolving disputes even if the claims have no merit. However, on the whole it was a case where the nature of the case was susceptible to mediation and where mediation had reasonable prospects of success, such that the defendant's refusal to mediate was unreasonable. However, there was an admissible without-prejudice offer which, while itself not a reason to refuse to mediate, was also a factor to be taken into account when considering the costs position overall. The Judge concluded that the failure to accept the offer (ultimately beaten) equally meant that the parties had lost the opportunity of resolving the case without a hearing. In the circumstances, the fair outcome was determined to be that neither party's conduct should be taken into account to modify what would otherwise be the general rule on costs. It is doubtful that this case, in itself, would support a proposition in principle that making a WP offer then permits a party to refuse to mediate; however, it will obviously be a relevant factor: where, for example, the offer has only just been beaten, it might be thought that a mediation would (or should) have had some prospect of success; where the unsuccessful party fell a long way short, it might be concluded that the mediation would never have succeeded in bridging the gap in expectations (one of the relevant questions in *Halsey*).[23]

---

22 [2014] 156 Con LR 141.
23 See also *Graham Gore v Kishwar Naheed* [2017] EWCA Civ 369 at [49].

The TCC and early neutral evaluation

10.30 The TCC Guide, at Section 7.5, provides that the TCC Judges may provide an early neutral evaluation (ENE) either in respect of a full case or of particular issues arising within it. Given the consensual nature of ADR, the Court will expect the parties generally to agree directions, and will be reluctant to impose steps on the parties and would not direct (for example) key attributes such as whether the process is without prejudice or binding. Therefore, the parties need to consider and agree not just the timing of submissions, but, for example, whether limited disclosure or documentation is needed, whether there will be witness evidence, and if so whether written or oral hearing, or whether there will be a (usually limited) opportunity for oral submissions.[24] Importantly, the parties need to consider whether the ENE procedure and the documents, submissions or evidence produced in relation to the ENE are to be without prejudice, or, alternatively, that the whole or part of those items are not without prejudice and can be referred to at any subsequent trial or hearing. The Court will also require a statement regarding whether the parties agree that the Judge's evaluation after the ENE process will be binding on the parties or binding in certain circumstances (for example, if not disputed within a period) or temporarily binding subject to a final decision in arbitration, litigation or final agreement.

10.31 Once a Judge has carried out an ENE, that Judge plays no further part in the proceedings unless the parties agree. The Judge undertaking the ENE will give appropriate directions for the preparation and conduct of the ENE.

The TCC and mediation

10.32 Similarly, the TCC provides what it terms a 'Court Settlement Process', which is a form of mediation carried out by TCC Judges. The TCC Guide provides a draft order which the parties need to seek providing suitable directions (Appendix G). As with Judges assisting parties with ENE, having been involved in the Court Settlement Process, the Judge will play no further part in the litigation. This factor may influence parties who have issued in regional TCC Court Centres where there is only one full-time TCC Judge: in these circumstances, it would make sense to have a TCC Judge from a different centre appointed as the Settlement Judge so that, should the mediation not be successful, the trial can continue to be managed and heard at the issuing regional centre.

---

[24] The TCC Guide suggests that the hearing would not last more than one day.

CHAPTER 11

The TCC and arbitration

11.1 Arbitration is seen more as a rival to litigation as a means of dispute resolution than complementary to it, as might mediation, ENE and the like be considered. The comparative advantages and disadvantages are explained in Chapter 1. Although effectively competing for work, there are aspects in which the TCC retains a role in the supervision and regulation of arbitration, and appeals from arbitration. Much like in its approach to other ADR, the policy which drives the TCC approach is one of supporting the arbitral process if that is how parties have decided to resolve their disputes. This chapter explains some of the key aspects in which the TCC supports the arbitral process, and the involvement of the TCC in appealing the decision of an arbitrator.

11.2 Arbitration claims are applications made to the Court under the Arbitration Act 1996. Where the underlying arbitration relates to matters of construction or engineering, or themselves the sort of claim which would be, if litigated, heard in the TCC, then the related claim should be commenced in the TCC. Applications under section 9 of the Arbitration Act 1996 to stay proceedings to arbitration should be started by application notice in the TCC, following the general CPR procedure for applications.[1] All other arbitration-related business in the TCC should be commenced as an 'Arbitration Claim' under CPR 62.2(1).

Stay of proceedings

11.3 Unlike the position in relation to other forms of ADR, where the Court can exercise an equitable discretion to stay litigation for a period so as to enforce a contractual requirement to participate in ADR, there is a statutory obligation to do in the context of arbitration. Section 9 of the Arbitration Act 1996 provides that, where a party to an arbitration agreement against whom legal proceedings are brought applies to have those proceedings stayed, the Court *shall* grant a stay unless satisfied that the arbitration agreement is null and void, inoperative or incapable of being performed.

11.4 Generally, arguments raised on such applications therefore involve questions as to whether there is a binding and operative arbitration agreement[2] or whether there is a basis upon which it is not possible to operate the clause as required by the contract.[3] The other

---

1 CPR Part 23. See the TCC Guide Part 6 for further guidance.
2 Even if there is not, then the Court may still stay proceedings pursuant to its inherent jurisdiction to do so: see, for example, *Turville Heath Inc v Chartis Insurance UK Ltd* [2012] EWHC 3019 (TCC), in which it was determined that on its proper construction, the dispute resolution provision did not fall to be construed as an arbitration agreement for the purposes of section 9 of the Arbitration Act 1996, but by reason of the steps the parties had in fact taken to that point in engaging in the procedure, the Court nevertheless agreed to stay litigation so that the process may conclude. Cf *Costain Ltd v Tarmac Holdings Ltd* [2017] EWHC 319 (TCC), where Coulson J (as he then was) held that there was a valid arbitration agreement despite the existence of two dispute resolution mechanisms for different parts of the contract.
3 For example, where a named arbitrator is no longer capable of acting because of a conflict.

category of arguments relates to whether a party has taken a step in the proceedings, with the effect that it is no longer open to a party to apply under section 9 for a stay.[4]

11.5 In terms of the requirements for a valid arbitration agreement, a clause must be incorporated into the agreement: this may cause particular difficulties where obligations are said to be stepped down from a main contract to a sub-contract.[5] It is also necessary that the attributes of 'arbitration' are present in the procedure envisaged by the parties. The Court of Appeal[6] has approved the list of attributes which must be present, and others which may be relevant, as set out in *Mustill & Boyd: Commercial Arbitration* (2nd edn, 2001). Those which must be present are as follows:

- The agreement pursuant to which the process is, or is to be, carried on ('the procedural agreement') must contemplate that the tribunal which carries on the process will make a decision which is binding on the parties to the procedural agreement.
- The procedural agreement must contemplate that the process will be carried on between those persons whose substantive rights are determined by the tribunal.
- The jurisdiction of the tribunal to carry on the process and to decide the rights of the parties must derive either from the consent of the parties or from an order of the court or from a statute the terms of which make it clear that the process is to be an arbitration.
- The tribunal must be chosen, either by the parties, or by a method to which they have consented.
- The procedural agreement must contemplate that the tribunal will determine the rights of the parties in an impartial manner, with the tribunal owning an equal obligation of fairness towards both sides.
- The agreement of the parties to refer their disputes to the decision of the tribunal must be intended to be enforceable in law.
- The procedural agreement must contemplate a process whereby the tribunal will make a decision upon a dispute which has already formulated at the time when the tribunal is appointed.

Those which may be relevant are as follows:

- Whether the procedural agreement contemplates that the tribunal will receive evidence and contentions, or at least give the parties the opportunity to put them forward;
- Whether the wording of the agreement is consistent or inconsistent with the view that the process was intended to be an arbitration;
- Whether the identity of the chosen tribunal, or the method prescribed for choosing the tribunal, shows that the process was intended to be an arbitration;
- Whether the procedural agreement requires the tribunal to decide the dispute according to law.

11.6 An arbitration agreement, properly incorporated, may nevertheless be unenforceable in a consumer context (for example, which would include many of the types of low-value domestic construction projects dealt with by the TCC) by reference to the Unfair Terms in Consumer Contracts Regulations 1999.[7] A clause will be unenforceable if, by the requirement to refer to arbitration, there is significant imbalance in the parties' rights, to the consumer's detriment.

---

4 Arbitration Act 1996 s 9(3).
5 See, for example, *Yorkshire Water Services Ltd v Taylor Woodrow Construction Northern Ltd* [2002] 90 Con LR 86.
6 *David Wilson Homes Ltd v Survey Services Ltd (in liquidation)* [2001] 1 All ER (Comm) 449, approving principles set out in *Mustill & Boyd: Commercial Arbitration* (2nd edn, 2001).
7 *Mclcrist v Buck* [2008] EWHC 2172 (TCC).

11.7 A party can (and indeed must) take the proper procedural step to acknowledge legal proceedings, an application under Section 9 cannot be made after the party has taken any step in the proceedings to answer the claim itself.

Jurisdiction of the arbitrator

11.8 The Arbitration Act 1996[8] provides that unless otherwise agreed by the parties, the Arbitral Tribunal may rule on its own substantive jurisdiction, that is, as to whether there is a valid arbitration agreement, whether the Tribunal is properly constituted and what matters have been submitted to arbitration in accordance with the arbitration agreement. Prior to the Arbitration Act 1996, questions of jurisdiction would be dealt with routinely by the Courts, but the question must now be determined in the first instance by the Tribunal in the arbitration itself, unless certain criteria are satisfied. The TCC will only determine any question as to the jurisdiction in the first instance if the parties agree or where the arbitrator(s) agree and the TCC is satisfied that the determination of the question is likely to produce substantial savings in costs, that the application was made without delay and that there is good reason why the matter should be decided by the TCC.[9]

11.9 If the party disputing jurisdiction is unable to bring itself with section 32, it remains open to it to appeal the decision of the arbitrator(s) on the question of jurisdiction to the TCC under section 67 of the Arbitration Act 1996.[10] Such an appeal should be brought as an Arbitration Claim, and would involve a re-hearing, rather than review, of the jurisdiction argument, but the grounds of objection must be the same as those raised in front of the Tribunal.[11] It is essential that a party objecting to substantive jurisdiction does so in good time, or it will otherwise lose its right to object. This relates both to objection prior to the arbitrator's determination and to any appeal under section 67.[12] Any appeal from an arbitral award relating to jurisdiction must be brought within 28 days of the date of the award or, if there has been any arbitral process of appeal or review, of the date when the applicant or appellant was notified of the result of that process.[13]

Extension of time limits for the referral of disputes

11.10 Applications to the TCC can be made to extend time in circumstances where an arbitration agreement to refer future disputes to arbitration provides that a claim shall be barred or extinguished unless a particular step is taken within a particular time. The Court can only intervene in this way if it is satisfied that the circumstances are such as were outside the reasonable contemplation of the parties when they agreed the provision in

---

8 See s 30.
9 Arbitration Act 1996 s 32.
10 For a recent example of such a challenge failing, see *Petroleum Co of Trinidad and Tobago Ltd v Samsung Engineering Trinidad Co Ltd* [2017] EWHC 3055 (TCC).
11 *Habas Sinai Ve Tibbi Gazlar Istihsal Endustrisi AS v VSC Steel Co Ltd* [2013] EWHC 4071 (Comm) (19 December 2013).
12 Arbitration Act 1996 s 73.
13 Arbitration Act 1996 s 70.

question, and that it would be just to extend time, or that the conduct of one party makes it unjust to hold the other party to the strict terms of the provision.[14]

11.11 In *Harbour & General v Environment Agency*,[15] Waller LJ provided an explanation of the purpose and extent of this provision. It was made clear that, in contrast to section 27 of the Arbitration Act 1950, section 12 was intended to reflect the underlying philosophy of the Act of party autonomy, which meant, among other things, that any power given to the Court to override the bargain that the parties have made must be fully justified. The idea that the Court has some general supervisory jurisdiction over arbitration has, since 1996, been abandoned. This explanation was elaborated by Toulson J in *Korbetis v Transgrain*,[16] who confirmed that it should be restricted to circumstances which were not only beyond the reasonable contemplation of the parties, but were also such that if the parties had contemplated them, they would also have contemplated that the time bar might not apply in such circumstances.

11.12 In *William McIlroy Swindon Ltd v Quinn Insurance Ltd*,[17] the TCC did not consider the substantive application of the section to the facts, finding instead that because the insurance policy was governed by Irish law, the Court did not have jurisdiction to extend time under the Act. An example of circumstances which did not justify an extension was the failure to have sent an acceptance fax to the correct number or follow up a response.

Powers of the TCC in relation to procedural aspects of arbitration

11.13 The TCC has the power, in limited circumstances, to involve itself in the appointment of arbitrators. Under section 17 of the Arbitration Act 1996, in circumstances where both parties were required to appoint an arbitrator and one party does not do so, the non-defaulting party can upon notice appoint an arbitrator, and that arbitrator can be the sole arbitrator. However, under section 17(3), the defaulting party can then apply to the Court to set aside the appointment.

11.14 If there is no agreement as to what should happen on failure of the procedure for the appointment of the Arbitral Tribunal, then any party to the arbitration agreement may on notice to the other parties apply to the TCC to exercise its powers pursuant to section 18 of the Arbitration Act 1996: to give directions as to the making of any necessary appointments; to direct that the Tribunal shall be constituted by such appointments (or any one or more of them) as have been made; to revoke any appointments already made; and to make any necessary appointments itself. In deciding whether to exercise its powers, the TCC is required to have regard to any agreement between the parties as to the qualifications required of the parties.[18]

11.15 Section 24 of the Arbitration Act 1996 gives the parties the right (upon notice to the other parties and the arbitrator(s)) to apply to the TCC to remove an arbitrator on various grounds: justifiable doubts about impartiality; lack of qualifications required by the

---

14 Arbitration Act 1996 s 12.
15 [2000] 1 Lloyd's Rep 65.
16 [2005] EWHC 1345 (QB) at [21]. See also Hamblin J in *SOS Corporacion Alimentaria, SA and others v Inerco Trade SA* [2010] EWHC 162 (Comm), making clear that the test is whether they would contemplate that the time limit 'might not' apply rather than it 'would not' or 'must not' apply (at [67]).
17 [2010] EWHC 2448 (TCC), appeal allowed but issue of extending time not considered on appeal.
18 Arbitration Act 1996 s 19.

arbitration agreement; physical or mental incapacity; and a failure to have conducted the proceedings properly or use reasonable dispatch in relation to the proceedings or award, such that substantial injustice has been or will be caused. If there is an institution vested with the power to remove an arbitrator, the TCC will not intervene until all relevant avenues under the institution have been exhausted. On removing an arbitrator, the question of fees or expenses (whether due or to be repaid) is a matter the TCC can deal with.

11.16 In demonstrating justifiable doubts about impartiality for the purposes of section 24, it is not necessary to show actual bias. It is necessary only to demonstrate that a fair-minded and informed observer, having considered the facts, would conclude that there was a real possibility that the Tribunal was biased. In *Cofely Ltd v Bingham & Knowles Ltd*,[19] there was evidence that the arbitrator had received 18 per cent of his appointments and 25 per cent of his income from cases involving Knowles, and that it had been accepted in *Eurocom Ltd v Siemens Plc*[20] that Knowles steered the appointment process towards its desired appointees, as a matter of general practice. Cofely had reasonably sought to obtain further information about the relationship between the first and second defendants, but the first defendant's response involved avoiding addressing the requests and instead gave the appearance of seeking to foreclose further enquiry by demonstrating their irrelevance and doing so in an aggressive manner. Considered together, the evidence supported the grounds relied upon by Cofely and raised the real possibility of apparent bias, establishing a valid ground for removal of an arbitrator. If the arbitrator would not resign, an order for his removal would be made.

11.17 Analogy can be made to cases regularly determined in the TCC relating to the conduct of adjudications. So, for example, lengthy telephone calls between the Tribunal and one of the parties is likely to give rise to claim of apparent bias.[21] The involvement of the adjudicator in simultaneous adjudications involving one of the parties without disclosing the fact to the other party was held to be a material breach of the rules of natural justice. This behaviour would, if replicated in the context of an arbitration, be likely to give rise to justifiable doubts about impartiality for the purposes of section 24 of the Arbitration Act 1996.

11.18 Other powers include the provision of relief in relation to fees and expenses, and any liability if an arbitrator resigns their appointment;[22] the adjustment of the arbitrators fees;[23] making an order requiring a party to comply with a peremptory order made by the Tribunal;[24] and whether the parties, or the arbitrator, agree, using the same Court procedures as are available in relation to legal proceedings to secure the attendance of a witness to give oral testimony or to produce documents or other evidence.[25] However, it is clear from section 44 of the Arbitration Act 1996 that wider powers to influence or control the procedure of the arbitration is extremely limited. In urgent cases, where necessary to preserve

---

19 [2016] BLR 187; 164 Con LR 39.
20 [2014] EWHC 3710 (TCC).
21 See Paice and Springall v MJ Harding Contractors [2015] EWHC 661 (TCC), involving a lengthy telephone conversation between Mr Paice and the adjudicator's wife, who acted as his office manager; *Discain Project Services Ltd v Opecprime Developments Ltd (No 1)* [2000] BLR 402, based upon unilateral telephone conversations between one party and the adjudicator.
22 Arbitration Act 1996 s 25.
23 Arbitration Act 1996 s 28.
24 Arbitration Act 1996 s 42.
25 Arbitration Act 1996 s 43.

evidence, the Court has the same powers it would have in legal proceedings with regard to taking of evidence, preserving it, allowing inspection, the sale of goods and the granting of injunctions. However, if the case is not one of urgency, applications to Court can only be made with the permission of the Tribunal or agreement of the parties. If an (urgent) order is made, it ceases to have effect when the matter is considered by the relevant Tribunal.

11.19 There is a power to extend time limits agreed by the parties (save where section 12 applies) in relation to any matter relating to the arbitral proceedings or specified in any provision of the Arbitration Act 1996 having effect in default of such agreement in circumstances where any available recourse to the arbitrator or institution has been exhausted. This could, therefore, include, for example, the time limits relating to the appointment of an arbitrator or an appeal from an award. The TCC would have to be persuaded that a substantial injustice would be done otherwise.

Appeal

11.20 Appeals against arbitration awards are considered by the TCC pursuant to section 67 (dealing with jurisdiction, considered above), section 68 (serious irregularity) or section 69 (points of law). The list of serious irregularities is set out in section 68(2), and must be one which has caused or will cause substantial injustice to the application:

- failure by the Tribunal to comply with section 33 (general duty of Tribunal);
- the Tribunal exceeding its powers (otherwise than by exceeding its substantive jurisdiction: see section 67);
- failure by the Tribunal to conduct the p]roceedings in accordance with the procedure agreed by the parties;
- failure by the Tribunal to deal with all the issues that were put to it;
- any arbitral or other institution or person vested by the parties with powers in relation to the proceedings or the award exceeding its powers;
- uncertainty or ambiguity as to the effect of the award;
- the award being obtained by fraud or the way in which it was procured being contrary to public policy;
- failure to comply with the requirements as to the form of the award; or
- any irregularity in the conduct of the proceedings or in the award which is admitted by the Tribunal or by any arbitral or other institution or person vested by the parties with powers in relation to the proceedings or the award.

11.21 It is only in the clearest of cases that the Court will determine that there has been a serious irregularity which has or will cause substantial injustice. By far the more common approach of the TCC on appeal is to uphold the arbitration award.

11.22 Similarly, leave to appeal on a point of law is granted extremely sparingly. It must be demonstrated that: the determination of the question will substantially affect the rights of one or more of the parties; the question is one which the Tribunal was asked to determine; on the basis of the findings of fact in the award:

- the decision of the Tribunal on the question is obviously wrong; or

- the question is one of general public importance and the decision of the Tribunal is at least open to serious doubt; and
- despite the agreement of the parties to resolve the matter by arbitration, it is just and proper in all the circumstances for the Court to determine the question.[26]

11.23 Of central importance to the limitation on the right of appeal are the words, 'on the basis of the findings of fact in the award'. Unlike appeals from the High Court to the Court of Appeal where there is a (limited) right to appeal factual questions, appeals to the TCC in respect of arbitration awards must take all factual findings as they stand: the TCC is astute to the strategy of dressing up factual questions as questions of law or mixed fact and law, and will not entertain such an approach.[27]

11.24 The party applying for permission to appeal must follow PD62, supplementing CPR Part 62, paragraph 12.1 onwards. The arbitration Claim Form must identify the question of law, and state the grounds (but not the argument) on which the party challenges the award. It must be accompanied by a skeleton argument no longer than 15 pages and printed in 12-point font and 1.5 line spacing. It should indicate how long it is likely to deal with the application on the papers and, generally, the Court will determine an application for permission to appeal without a hearing unless it appears that a hearing is required.

11.25 In reality, the TCC determines the same question on leave to appeal as it does on the substantive appeal. Generally, therefore, the TCC will either dispose of the matter on paper (generally by dismissing the application), or if the Judge considers that the appeal has sufficient merit to warrant a hearing for leave to appeal, then – unless there are good reasons not to – the substantive appeal can be heard at the same time as the oral hearing for permission to appeal.[28]

---

26 Arbitration Act 1996 s 69.
27 This approach is not limited to the TCC, but for TCC cases, see, for example, *London Underground Ltd v Citylink Telecommunications Ltd* [2007] EWHC 1749 (TCC).
28 See *HOK Sport Ltd v Aintree Racecourse Co Ltd* [2003] BLR 155.

Appendix 1

The Technology and Construction Court Guide

Section 1. Introduction

1.1 Purpose of Guide

1.1.1 The Technology and Construction Court ("TCC") Guide is intended to provide straightforward, practical guidance on the conduct of litigation in the TCC. Whilst it is intended to be comprehensive, it naturally concentrates on the most important aspects of such litigation. It therefore cannot cover all the procedural points that may arise. It does, however, describe the main elements of the practice that is likely to be followed in most TCC cases. This Guide does not and cannot add to or amend the CPR or the relevant practice directions. The purpose and function of this Guide is to explain how the substantive law, rules and practice directions are applied in the TCC and cannot affect their proper interpretation and effect: see *Secretary of State for Communities and Local Government v Bovale* [2009] 1 WLR 2274 at [36].

1.1.2 The Guide reflects the flexible framework within which litigation in the TCC is habitually conducted. The guidance set out in the Guide is designed to ensure effective management of proceedings in the TCC. It must always be remembered that, if parties fail to comply with these requirements, the court may impose sanctions including orders for costs and, following the implementation of the Jackson reforms, will be more ready to do so.

1.1.3 In respect of those procedural areas for which specific provision is not made in this Guide, the parties, together with their advisors, will be expected to act reasonably and in accordance with both the spirit of the Guide and the overriding objective at **CPR 1.1**

1.1.4 It is not the function of the Guide to summarise the Civil Procedure Rules ("the CPR"), and it should not be regarded as a substitute for the CPR. The parties and their advisors are expected to familiarise themselves with the CPR and, in particular, to understand the importance of the "overriding objective" of the CPR. The TCC endeavours to ensure that all its cases are dealt with justly and at proportionate cost. This includes ensuring that the parties are on an equal footing; taking all practicable steps to save expenditure; dealing with the dispute in ways which are proportionate to the size of the claim and cross-claim and the importance of the case to the parties; and managing the case throughout in a way that takes proper account of its complexity and the different financial positions of the parties. The court will also endeavour to ensure expedition, and to allot to each case an appropriate share of the court's resources.

1.1.5 The TCC Guide has been prepared in consultation with the judges of the TCC in London, Cardiff, Birmingham, Manchester and Leeds, and with the advice and support of TECBAR, TeCSA, the Society for Construction Law, the Society for Computers and Law and the TCC Users' Committees in London, Cardiff, Birmingham, Manchester, Liverpool and Leeds. The TCC Guide is published with the approval of the Head of Civil Justice and the deputy Head of Civil Justice.

1.2 The CPR

1.2.1 Proceedings in the TCC are governed by the CPR and the supplementary Practice Directions. **CPR Part 60** and its associated **Practice Direction** deal specifically with the practice and procedure of the TCC.

1.2.2 Other parts of the CPR that frequently arise in TCC cases include **Part 3** (Case Management Powers); **Part 8** (Alternative Procedure for Claims); **Parts 12 and 13** (Default Judgment and Setting Aside); **Part 17** (Amendments); **Part 20** (Counterclaims and Other Additional Claims); **Part 24** (Summary Judgment); **Part 25** (Interim Remedies and Security for Costs); **Part 26** (Case Management); **Part 32** (Evidence); **Part 35** (Experts and Assessors); **Part 44** (Costs); and **Part 62** (Arbitration Claims).

1.3 The TCC

1.3.1 <u>What are TCC Claims?</u> **CPR 60.1 (2)** and **(3)** provide that a TCC claim is a claim which (i) involves technically complex issues or questions (or for which trial by a TCC judge is desirable) and (ii) has been issued in or transferred into the TCC specialist list. Paragraph 2.1 of the TCC Practice Direction identifies the following as examples of the types of claim which it may be appropriate to bring as TCC claims –

(a) building or other construction disputes, including claims for the enforcement of the decisions of adjudicators under the Housing Grants, Construction and Regeneration Act 1996;

(b) engineering disputes;

(c) claims by and against engineers, architects, surveyors, accountants and other specialised advisors relating to the services they provide;

(d) claims by and against local authorities relating to their statutory duties concerning the development of land or the construction of buildings;

(e) claims relating to the design, supply and installation of computers, computer software and related network systems;

(f) claims relating to the quality of goods sold or hired, and work done, materials supplied or services rendered;

(g) claims between landlord and tenant for breach of a repairing covenant;

(h) claims between neighbours, owners and occupiers of land in trespass, nuisance, etc.

(i) claims relating to the environment (for example, pollution cases);

(j) claims arising out of fires;

(k) claims involving taking of accounts where these are complicated; and

(l) challenges to decisions of arbitrators in construction and engineering disputes including applications for permission to appeal and appeals.

It should be noted that this list is not exhaustive and many other types of claim might well be appropriate for resolution in the TCC. In recent years the range of work in the TCC has become increasingly diverse, and many civil claims which are factually or technically complex are now heard in the TCC. This has included group actions for personal injury and public nuisance, and a number of procurement disputes arising in connection with the Public Contracts Regulations 2006. In addition, the TCC regularly deals with allegations of lawyers' negligence arising in connection with planning, property, construction and other technical disputes and with applications under the Arbitration Act 1996. However, with the exception of claims to enforce adjudicators' decisions or other claims with special features that justify a hearing before a High Court Judge, the TCC will not usually accept cases with a value of less than £250,000 (see paragraph 1.3.6 below) unless there is good reason for it to do so. A non-exhaustive list of special features which will usually justify listing the case in the High Court is:

(a) Adjudication and arbitration cases of any value;

(b) International cases whatever their value (international cases will generally involve one or more parties resident outside the UK and/or involve an overseas project or development);

(c) Cases involving new or difficult points of law in TCC cases;

(d) Any test case or case which will be joined with others which will be treated as test cases;

(e) Public procurement cases;

(f) Part 8 claims and other claims for declarations;

(g) Complex nuisance claims brought by a number of parties, even where the sums claimed are small;

(h) Claims which cannot readily be dealt with effectively in a County Court or Civil Justice centre by a designated TCC judge;

(i) Claims for injunctions.

For further guidance, see *West Country Renovations v McDowell* [2013] 1 WLR 416.

1.3.2 The Court. Both the High Court and the County Courts deal with TCC business. TCC business is conducted by TCC judges unless a TCC judge directs otherwise: see CPR 60.1(5)(b)(ii).

TCC business in the High Court is conducted by TCC judges who are High Court judges (who sit principally in the Rolls Building), and by designated circuit judges and recorders. Circuit judges and recorders only have jurisdiction to manage and try TCC cases if they have been nominated by the Lord Chancellor pursuant to section 68(1)(a) of the Senior Courts Act 1981 or are authorised to sit in the TCC as High Court judges under section 9 of that Act.

TCC business in the County Court is conducted by TCC judges who include circuit judges and recorders. TCC business may also be conducted by certain district judges ("TCC liaison district judges") provided that: (1) a TCC judge has so directed under CPR 60.1(5)(b)(ii); (2) the designated civil judge for the court has so directed in accordance with the Practice Direction at CPR 2BPD11.1(d).

It should be noted that those circuit judges who have been nominated pursuant to section 68(1)(a) of the Senior Courts Act 1981 fall into two categories: "full time" TCC judges and "part time" TCC judges. "Full time" TCC judges spend most of their time dealing with TCC business, although they will do other work when there is no TCC business requiring their immediate attention. "Part time" TCC judges are circuit judges who are only available to sit in the TCC for part of their time. They have substantial responsibilities outside the TCC.

In respect of a court centre where there is no full time TCC judge, the term "principal TCC judge" is used in this Guide to denote the circuit judge who has principal responsibility for TCC work.

Section 1. Introduction

The phrase "Technology and Construction Court" or "TCC" or "the court" is used in this Guide to denote any court which deals with TCC claims. All of the courts which deal with TCC claims form a composite group of courts. When those courts are dealing with TCC business, **CPR Part 60, its accompanying Practice Direction and this Guide** govern the procedures of those courts. The High Court judge in charge of the TCC ("the Judge in Charge"), although based principally in London, has overall responsibility for the judicial supervision of TCC business in those courts

1.3.3 <u>The TCC in London.</u> The principal centre for TCC work is the High Court in London at the Rolls Building, Fetter Lane, London, EC4. 1NL. The Rolls Building is a new specialist court building off Fetter Lane. The Judge in Charge of the TCC sits principally at the Rolls Building together with other High Court judges who are TCC judges. Subject to paragraph 3.7.1 below, any communication or enquiry concerning a TCC case, which is proceeding at the Rolls Building, should be directed to the clerk of the judge who is assigned to that case and, if by email, copied to the TCC Registry. The various contact details for the judges' clerks are set out in **Appendix D**.

The TCC judges who are based at the Rolls Building will, when appropriate, sit at court centres outside London.

TCC County Court cases in London are brought in (or transferred to) the Central London Civil Justice Centre, 13-14 Park Crescent, London W1N 4HT. This court is shortly to move into new accommodation in the Royal Courts of Justice.

1.3.4 <u>District Registries.</u> TCC claims can be brought in the High Court outside London in any District Registry, although the Practice Direction states that it is preferable that, wherever possible, such claims should be issued in one of the following District Registries: Birmingham, Bristol, Cardiff, Chester, Exeter, Leeds, Liverpool, Newcastle, Nottingham and Manchester. There are currently full-time TCC Judges in Birmingham, Manchester and Leeds. Contact details are again set out in **Appendix D**. There are part time TCC judges and/or recorders nominated to deal with TCC business available at most court centres throughout England and Wales.

In a number of regions a "TCC liaison district judge" has been appointed. It is the function of the TCC liaison district judge:

(a) To keep other district judges in that region well informed about the role and remit of the TCC (in order that appropriate cases may be transferred to the TCC at an early, rather than late, stage).

(b) To deal with any queries from colleagues concerning the TCC or cases which might merit transfer to the TCC.

(c) To deal with any subsidiary matter which a TCC judge directs should be determined by a district judge pursuant to rule 60.1 (5) (b) (ii).

(d) To deal with urgent applications in TCC cases pursuant to paragraph 7.2 of the Practice Direction (i.e. no TCC judge is available and the matter is of a kind that falls within the district judge's jurisdiction).

(e) to hear TCC cases when a TCC judge has so directed under CPR 60.1(5)(b)(ii) and when the designated civil judge for the court has so directed in accordance with the Practice Direction at CPR 2BPD11.1(d).

1.3.5   County Courts outside London. TCC claims may also be brought in those county courts which are specified in the **Part 60 Practice Direction**. The specified county courts are: Birmingham, Bristol, Cardiff, Chester, Exeter, Leeds, Liverpool, Newcastle, Nottingham and Manchester. Contact details are again set out in **Appendix D**.

Where TCC proceedings are brought in a county court, statements of case and applications should be headed:

"In the ... County Court

Technology and Construction Court"

1.3.6   The division between High Court and County Court TCC cases. As a general rule TCC claims for more than £250,000 are brought in the High Court, whilst claims for lower sums are brought in the County Court. However, this is not a rigid dividing line (see paragraph 1.3.1 above). The monetary threshold for High Court TCC claims tends to be higher in London than in the regions. Regard must also be had to the complexity of the case and all other circumstances. Arbitration claims and claims to enforce or challenge adjudicators' decisions are generally (but not invariably) brought in the High Court. The scale of fees differs in the High Court and the county court. This is a factor which should be borne in mind in borderline cases.

1.4   The TCC Users' Committees

1.4.1   The continuing ability of the TCC to meet the changing needs of all those involved in TCC litigation depends in large part upon a close working relationship between the TCC and its users.

1.4.2   London. The Judge in Charge chairs meetings of the London TCC Users' Committee (usually two meetings a year). The judge's clerk acts as secretary to the Committee and takes the minutes of meetings. That Committee is made up of representatives of the London TCC judges, the barristers and solicitors who regularly use the Court, the professional bodies, such as architects, engineers and arbitrators, whose members are affected by the decisions of the Court, and representatives of both employers and contractors' groups.

1.4.3   Outside London. There are similar meetings of TCC Users' Committees in Birmingham, Manchester, Liverpool, Cardiff and Leeds. Each Users' Committee is chaired by the full time TCC judge or the principal TCC judge in that location.

1.4.4   The TCC regards these channels of communication as extremely important and all those who are concerned with the work of the Court are encouraged to make full use of these meetings. Any suggestions or other correspondence raising matters for consideration by the Users' Committee should, in the first instance, be addressed to the clerk to the Judge in Charge at the Rolls Building or to the clerk to the appropriate TCC judge outside London.

1.5   Specialist Associations

1.5.1   There are a number of associations of legal representatives which are represented on the Users' Committees and which also liaise closely with the Court. These contacts ensure that the Court remains responsive to the opinions and requirements of the professional users of the Court.

Section 1. Introduction

1.5.2 The relevant professional organisations are the TCC Bar Association ("TECBAR") and the TCC Solicitors Association ("TeCSA"). Details of the relevant contacts at these organisations are set out on their respective websites, namely www.tecbar.org and www.tecsa.org.uk.

Section 2. Pre-Action Protocol and conduct

2.1 Introduction

2.1.1 There is a Pre-Action Protocol for Construction and Engineering Disputes. Where the dispute involves a claim against architects, engineers or quantity surveyors, this Protocol prevails over the Professional Negligence Pre-Action Protocol: see paragraph 1.1 of the Protocol for Construction and Engineering Disputes and paragraph A.1 of the Professional Negligence Pre-Action Protocol. The current version of the Construction and Engineering Pre-Action Protocol ("the Protocol") is set out in volume 1 of the White Book at section C5.

2.1.2 The purpose of the Protocol is to encourage the frank and early exchange of information about the prospective claim and any defence to it; to enable parties to avoid litigation by agreeing a settlement of the claim before the commencement of proceedings; and to support the efficient management of proceedings where litigation cannot be avoided.

2.1.3 Proportionality. The overriding objective (CPR rule 1.1) applies to the pre-action period. The Protocol must not be used as a tactical device to secure advantage for one party or to generate unnecessary costs. In lower value TCC claims (such as those likely to proceed in the county court), the letter of claim and the response should be simple and the costs of both sides should be kept to a modest level. In all cases the costs incurred at the Protocol stage should be proportionate to the complexity of the case and the amount of money which is at stake. The Protocol does not impose a requirement on the parties to produce a detailed pleading as a letter of claim or response or to marshal and disclose all the supporting details and evidence or to provide witness statements or expert reports that may ultimately be required if the case proceeds to litigation. Where a party has serious concerns that the approach of the other party to the Pre-Action Protocol is not proportionate, then it is open for that party to issue a claim form and/or make an application (see **Paragraph 4.1.5** below) to seek the assistance of the court.

2.2 To Which Claims Does The Protocol Apply?

2.2.1 The court will expect all parties to have complied in substance with the provisions of the Protocol in all construction and engineering disputes. The only exceptions to this are identified in paragraph 2.3 below.

2.2.2 The court regards the Protocol as setting out normal and reasonable pre-action conduct. Accordingly, whilst the Protocol is not mandatory for a number of the claims noted by way of example in **paragraph 1.3.1** above, such as computer cases or dilapidations claims, the court would, in the absence of a specific reason to the contrary, expect the Protocol generally to be followed in such cases prior to the commencement of proceedings in the TCC.

2.3 What Are The Exceptions?

2.3.1 A claimant does not have to comply with the Protocol if his claim:

(a) is to enforce the decision of an adjudicator;

(b) is to seek an urgent declaration or injunction in relation to adjudication (whether ongoing or concluded);

(c) includes a claim for interim injunctive relief;

(d) will be the subject of a claim for summary judgment pursuant to **Part 24** of the CPR; or

(e) relates to the same or substantially the same issues as have been the subject of a recent adjudication or some other formal alternative dispute resolution procedure; or

(f) relates to a public procurement dispute.

The protocol does not contemplate an extended process and it should not be drawn out. Thus, the letter of claim should be concise and it is usually sufficient to explain the proposed claim(s), identifying key dates, so as to enable the potential defendant to understand and to investigate the allegations. Only essential documents need be supplied, and the period specified for a response should not be longer than one month without good reason. In particular, where a claim is brought by an litigant based outside the UK it will generally be appropriate to confine the steps to the time limits provided by the Protocol and, in many cases, to dispense with the meeting referred to in paragraph 5.1 of the Protocol. In any event, such a meeting is not mandatory and may be dispensed with if it would involve disproportionate time and cost or it is clear that it would be unlikely to serve any useful purpose.

2.3.2 In addition, a claimant need not comply with any part of the Protocol if, by so doing, his claim may become time-barred under the Limitation Act 1980. In those circumstances, a claimant should commence proceedings without complying with the Protocol and must, at the same time, apply for directions as to the timetable and form of procedure to be adopted. The court may order a stay of those proceedings pending completion of the steps set out in the Protocol.

2.4 What Are The Essential Ingredients Of The Protocol?

2.4.1 The Letter of Claim. The letter of claim must comply with Section 3 of the Protocol. Amongst other things, it must contain a clear and concise summary of the facts on which each claim is based; the basis on which each claim is made; and details of the relief claimed, including a breakdown showing how any damages have been quantified. The claimant must also provide the names of experts already instructed and on whom he intends to rely.

2.4.2 The Defendant's Response. The defendant has 14 days to acknowledge the letter of claim and 28 days (from receipt of the letter of claim) either to take any jurisdiction objection or to respond in substance to the letter of claim. Paragraph 4.3.1 of the Protocol enables the parties to agree an extension of the 28 day period up to a maximum of 3 months. In any case of substance it is quite usual for an extension of time to be agreed for the defendant's response. The letter of response must comply with section 4 of the Protocol. Amongst other things, it must state which claims are accepted, which claims are rejected and on what basis. It must set out any counterclaim to be advanced by the defendant. The defendant should also provide the names of experts who have been instructed and on whom he intends to rely. If the defendant fails either to acknowledge or to respond to the letter of claim in time, the claimant is entitled to commence proceedings.

2.4.3 Pre-action Meeting. The Construction and Engineering Protocol is the only Protocol under the CPR that generally requires the parties to meet, without prejudice, at least once, in order to identify the main issues and the root causes of their disagreement on those issues. The purpose of the meeting is to see whether, and if so how, those issues might be resolved without recourse to litigation or, if litigation is unavoidable, what steps should be taken to ensure that it is conducted in accordance with the overriding objective. At or as a result of the meeting, the parties should consider whether some form of alternative dispute resolution ("ADR") would be more suitable than litigation and if so, they should endeavour to agree which form of ADR to adopt. Although the meeting is "without prejudice", any party who attended the meeting is at liberty to disclose to the Court at a later stage that the meeting took place; who attended and who refused to attend, together with the grounds for their refusal; and any agreements concluded between the parties. (See also paragraph 2.3.1 above in relation to claims brought by claimants based ouside the UK).

2.5 What Happens To The Material Generated By The Protocol?

2.5.1 The letter of claim, the defendant's response, and the information relating to attendance (or otherwise) at the meeting are not confidential or 'without prejudice' and can therefore be referred to by the parties in any subsequent litigation. The detail of any discussion at the meeting(s) and/or any note of the meeting cannot be referred to the court unless all parties agree.

2.5.2 Normally the parties should include in the bundle for the first case management conference: (a) the letter of claim, (b) the response, and (c) if the parties agree, any agreed note of the pre-action meeting: see **Section 5** below. The documents attached to or enclosed with the letter and the response should not be included in the bundle.

2.6 What If One Party Has Not Complied With The Protocol?

2.6.1 There can often be a complaint that one or other party has not complied with the Protocol. The court will consider any such complaints once proceedings have been commenced. If the court finds that the claimant has not complied with one part of the Protocol, then the court may stay the proceedings until the steps set out in the Protocol have been taken or impose such other conditions as the court thinks appropriate pursuant to **CPR 3.1(3)**.

2.6.2 **The Practice Direction in respect of Protocols** (section C of volume 1 of the White Book) makes plain that the court may make adverse costs orders against a party who has failed to comply with the Protocol. The court will exercise any sanctions available with the object of placing the innocent party in no worse a position than he would have been if the Protocol had been complied with.

2.6.3 The court is unlikely to be concerned with minor infringements of the Protocol or to engage in lengthy debates as to the precise quality of the information provided by one party to the other during the Protocol stages. The court will principally be concerned to ensure that, as a result of the Protocol stage, each party to any subsequent litigation has a clear understanding of the nature of the case that it has to meet at the commencement of those proceedings.

2.7 Costs of compliance with the Protocol.

2.7.1 If compliance with the Protocol results in settlement, the costs incurred will not be recoverable from the paying party, unless this is specifically agreed.

2.7.2 If compliance with the Protocol does not result in settlement, then the costs of the exercise cannot be recovered as costs, unless:

- those costs fall within the principles stated by Sir Robert Megarry V-C in *Re Gibson's Settlement Trusts* [1981] Ch 179; or

- the steps taken in compliance with the Protocol can properly be attributable to the conduct of the action: see the judgment of Coulson J in *Roundstone Nurseries v Stephenson* [2009] EWHC 1431 (TCC) where he held at [48]: ". . . as a matter of principle, it seems to me that costs incurred during the Pre-Action Protocol process may, in principle, be recoverable as costs incidental to the litigation: see *McGlinn v. Waltham (No. 1)* [2005] 3 All ER1126.

Section 3. Commencement and transfer

3.1 Claim Forms

3.1.1 All proceedings must be started using a claim form under **CPR Part 7** or **CPR Part 8** or an arbitration claim form under **CPR Part 62**: see **paragraph 10.1** below. All claims allocated to the TCC are assigned to the Multi-Track: see **CPR 60.6(1)**.

3.2 Part 7 Claims

3.2.1 The **Part 7** claim form must be marked "Technology and Construction Court" in the appropriate place on the form.

3.2.2 Particulars of Claim may be served with the claim form, but this is not a mandatory requirement. If the Particulars of Claim are not contained in or served with the claim form, they must be served within **14 days** after service of the claim form.

3.2.3 A claim form must be verified by a statement of truth, and this includes any amendment to a claim form, unless the court otherwise orders.

3.3 Part 8 Claims

3.3.1 The **Part 8** claim form must be marked "Technology and Construction Court" in the appropriate place on the form.

3.3.2 A **Part 8** claim form will normally be used where there is no substantial dispute of fact, such as the situation where the dispute turns on the construction of the contract or the interpretation of statute. For example, claims challenging the jurisdiction of an adjudicator or the validity of his decision are sometimes brought under **Part 8**. In those cases the relevant primary facts are often not in dispute. **Part 8** claims will generally be disposed of on written evidence and oral submissions.

3.3.3 It is important that, where a claimant uses the **Part 8** procedure, his claim form states that **Part 8** applies and that the claimant wishes the claim to proceed under **Part 8**.

3.3.4 A statement of truth is again required on a **Part 8** claim form.

3.4 Service

3.4.1 Claim forms issued in the TCC at the Rolls Building in London are to be served by the claimant, not by the Registry. In some other court centres claim forms are served by the court, unless the claimant specifically requests otherwise.

3.4.2 The different methods of service are set out in **CPR Part 6** and the accompanying Practice Direction.

3.4.3 Applications for an extension of time in which to serve a claim form are governed by **CPR 7.6** and there are only limited grounds on which such extensions of time are granted. The evidence required on an application for an extension of time is set out in **paragraph 8.2 of Practice Direction A supplementing CPR Part 7**.

3.4.4 When the claimant has served the claim form, he must file a certificate of service: **CPR 6.17 (2)**. This is necessary if, for instance, the claimant wishes to obtain judgment in default (**CPR Part 12**).

Section 3. Commencement and transfer

3.4.5 Applications for permission to serve a claim form out of the jurisdiction are subject to **CPR 6.30-6.47** inclusive.

3.5 Acknowledgment of Service

3.5.1 A defendant must file an acknowledgment of service in response to both **Part 7** and **Part 8** claims. Save in the special circumstances that arise when the claim form has been served out of the jurisdiction, the period for filing an acknowledgment of service is **14 days** after service of the claim form.

3.6 Transfer

3.6.1 Proceedings may be transferred from any Division of the High Court or from any specialist list to the TCC pursuant to **CPR 30.5**. The order made by the transferring court should be expressed as being subject to the approval of a TCC judge. The decision whether to accept such a transfer must be made by a TCC judge: see **CPR 30.5 (3)**. Many of these applications are uncontested, and may conveniently be dealt with on paper. Transfers from the TCC to other Divisions of the High Court or other specialist lists are also governed by **CPR 30.5**. In London there are sometimes transfers between the Chancery Division, the Commercial Court and the TCC, in order to ensure that cases are dealt with by the most appropriate judge. Outside London there are quite often transfers between the TCC and the mercantile and chancery lists. It should be noted that transfers from the Chancery Division may become subject to a requirement for permission from the Chancellor.

3.6.2 A TCC claim may be transferred from the High Court to a County Court or a County Court hearing centre, and from any County Court or County Court hearing centre to the High Court, if the criteria stated in **CPR 30.3** are satisfied. In ordinary circumstances, proceedings will be transferred from the TCC in the High Court to the TCC in an appropriate County Court if the amount of the claim does not exceed £250,000.

3.6.3 Where no TCC judge is available to deal with a TCC claim which has been issued in a district registry or one of the county courts noted above, the claim may be transferred to another district registry or county court or to the High Court TCC in London (depending upon which court is appropriate).

3.6.4 On an application to transfer the case to the TCC from another court or Division of the High Court, there are a number of relevant considerations:

(a) Is the claim broadly one of the types of claim identified in paragraph 2.1 of the Part 60 Practice Direction?

(b) Is the financial value of the claim and/or its complexity such that, in accordance with the overriding objective, the case should be transferred into the TCC?

(c) What effect would transfer have on the likely costs, the speed with which the matter can be resolved, and any other broader questions of convenience for the parties?

3.6.5 On an application to transfer into the TCC, when considering the relative appropriateness of different courts or divisions, the judge will ascertain where and in what areas of judicial expertise and experience the bulk or preponderance of the issues may lie. If there was little significant difference between the appropriateness of the two venues, and the claimant, having started in one court or division, was anxious to remain there, then the application to transfer in by another party is likely to be unsuccessful.

3.6.6   Where a TCC Claim is proceeding in a District Registry and it becomes apparent that the case would merit case management or trial before a High Court judge, the matter should be raised with the TCC judge at the District Registry who will consult the Judge in Charge: see paragraph 3.7.3 below. If the case does merit the involvement of a High Court judge it is not necessary for the case to be transferred to London but rather a High Court judge can in appropriate cases sit outside London to deal with the case in the District Registry.

3.7 Assignment

3.7.1   Where a claim has been issued at or transferred to the TCC in London, the Judge in Charge of the TCC ("the Judge in Charge") shall assign it to a particular TCC judge.

3.7.2   In general the assigned TCC judge who case manages a case will also try that case. Although this continuity of judge is regarded as important, it is sometimes necessary for there to be a change of assigned judge to case manage or try a case because all High Court Judges in the Queen's Bench Division have other judicial duties.

3.7.3   (a) When a TCC case has been assigned to a named High Court judge, all communications about case management should be made to the assigned High Court judge's clerk with email communications copied to the TCC Registry at tcc@hmcourts-service.gsi.gov.uk.

   (b) All communications in respect of the issue of claims or applications and all communications about fees, however, should be sent to the TCC Registry.

   (c) All statements of case and applications should be marked with the name of the assigned judge.

3.7.4   There are currently full time TCC judges at Birmingham, Manchester and Leeds. There are principal TCC judges at other court centres outside London. TCC cases at these court centres are assigned to judges either (a) by direction of the full time or principal TCC judge or (b) by operation of a rota. It will not generally be appropriate for the Judge in Charge (who is based in London) to consider TCC cases which are commenced in, or transferred to, court centres outside London. Nevertheless, if any TCC case brought in a court centre outside London appears to require management and trial by a High Court judge, then the full time or principal TCC judge at that court centre should refer the case to the Judge in Charge for a decision as to its future management and trial.

3.7.5   When a TCC case has been assigned to a named circuit judge at a court centre other than in London, all communications to the court about the case (save for communications in respect of fees) shall be made to that judge's clerk. All communications in respect of fees should be sent to the relevant registry. All statements of case and applications should be marked with the name of the assigned judge.

3.8 Electronic Working in London

3.8.1   At the time of writing this guide claims in the TCC and Commercial Court Registry in London cannot be issued electronically.

3.8.2   It is planned that eworking in the TCC will be resumed in the near future when suitable software becomes available and that it will then be extended to courts outside London.

Section 4. Access to the court

4.1 General Approach

4.1.1 There may be a number of stages during the case management phase when the parties will make applications to the court for particular orders: see **Section 6** below. There will also be the need for the court to give or vary directions, so as to enable the case to progress to trial.

4.1.2 The court is acutely aware of the costs that may be incurred when both parties prepare for an oral hearing in respect of such interlocutory matters and is always prepared to consider alternative, and less expensive, ways in which the parties may seek the court's assistance.

4.1.3 There are certain stages in the case management phase when it will generally be better for the parties to appear before the assigned judge. Those are identified at **Section 4.2** below. But there are other stages, and/or particular applications which a party may wish to make, which could conveniently be dealt with by way of a telephone hearing (**Section 4.3** below) or by way of a paper application (**Section 4.4** below).

4.1.4 Access prior to the issue of proceedings. Under **paragraph 4.1 of the Practice Direction supplementing CPR Part 60** it is provided that a party who intends to issue a TCC claim must make any application before the claim form is issued to a TCC judge. This provision allows a party, for instance, to issue an application for pre-action disclosure.

4.1.5 As a party will have issued a TCC claim in circumstances where **paragraph 6 of the Pre-Action Protocol for Construction and Engineering Disputes** applies (limitation or time bar by complying with the pre-action protocol), this provision does not apply to that situation. The court might however be persuaded to deal with an application concerned with the pre-action protocol process under this provision although it may be necessary to insist on a claim form being issued.

4.1.6 Sometimes parties wish to use the TCC procedures for **Early Neutral Evaluation (see section 7.5)** or the **Court Settlement Process (see section 7.6)** prior to issuing a TCC claim, often as part of the pre-action protocol. The court will seek to accommodate the parties' wishes but again may have to insist on a claim form being issued.

4.2 Hearings in Court

4.2.1 First Case Management Conference. The court will normally require the parties to attend an oral hearing for the purposes of the first Case Management Conference. This is because there may be matters which the judge would wish to raise with the parties arising out of the answers to the case management information sheets and the parties' proposed directions: see section 5.4 below. Even in circumstances where the directions and the case management timetable may be capable of being agreed by the parties and the court, the assigned judge may still wish to consider a range of case management matters face-to-face with the parties, including cost budgeting and ADR. See **paragraphs 7.2.3**, **7.3.2**, **8.1.3**, **11.1-11.2.4**, **13.3**, **13.4**, **15.4.2** and **16.3.2** below. For these reasons **CPR 29.4** may be applied more sparingly in the TCC.

4.2.2 Whilst the previous paragraph sets out the ideal position, it is recognised that in low value cases the benefits of personal attendance might be outweighed by the costs involved. This is particularly so at court centres outside London, where the parties may have to travel substantial distances to court. Ultimately, the question whether personal attendance should be dispensed with at any particular case management conference must be decided by the judge, after considering any representations made and the circumstances of that particular case.

4.2.3   Pre-trial Review. It will normally be helpful for the parties to attend before the judge on a Pre-trial Review ("PTR"). It is always preferable for Counsel or other advocates who will be appearing at the trial to attend the PTR. Again, even if the parties can agree beforehand any outstanding directions and the detailed requirements for the management of the trial, it is still of assistance for the judge to raise matters of detailed trial management with the parties at an oral hearing. In appropriate cases, e.g. where the amount in issue is disproportionate to the costs of a full trial, the judge may wish to consider with the parties whether there are other ways in which the dispute might be resolved. See **paragraphs 14.1 to 14.5** below for detailed provisions relating to the PTR.

4.2.4   Interim Applications. Whether or not other interim applications require an oral hearing will depend on the nature and effect of the application being made. Disputed applications for interim payments, summary judgment and security for costs will almost always require an oral hearing. Likewise, the resolution of a contested application to enforce an adjudicator's decision will normally be heard orally. At the other end of the scale, applications for extensions of time for the service of pleadings or to comply with other orders of the court can almost always be dealt with by way of a telephone hearing or in writing and, indeed, orders sometimes expressly provide for this.

4.3   Telephone Hearings

4.3.1   Depending on the nature of the application and the extent of any dispute between the parties, the Court is content to deal with many case management matters and other interlocutory applications by way of a telephone conference.

4.3.2   Whilst it is not possible to lay down mandatory rules as to what applications should be dealt with in this way (rather than by way of an oral hearing in court), it may be helpful to identify certain situations which commonly arise and which can conveniently be dealt with by way of a telephone conference.

(a) If the location of the court is inconvenient for one or more of the parties then the CMC and the PTR could, in the alternative to the procedure set out in **Section 4.2** above, take place by way of a telephone conference. The judge's permission for such a procedure must be sought in advance.

(b) If the parties are broadly agreed on the orders to be made by the court, but they are in dispute in respect of one or two particular matters, then a telephone hearing is a convenient way in which those outstanding matters can be dealt with by the parties and the assigned judge.

(c) Similarly, specific arguments about costs, once a substantive application has been disposed of, or arguments consequential on a particular judgment or order having been handed down, may also conveniently be dealt with by way of telephone hearing.

(d) Other applications which, depending on their size and importance, may conveniently be dealt with by way of a telephone hearing include limited applications in respect of disclosure and specific applications as to the scope and content of factual or expert evidence exchanged by the parties.

Section 4. Access to the court

4.3.3 Telephone hearings are not generally suitable for matters which are likely to last for more than an hour (although the judge may be prepared, in an appropriate case, to list a longer application for a telephone hearing) or which require extensive reference to documents.

4.3.4 Practical matters. Telephone hearings can be listed at any time between 8.30 a.m. and 5.30 pm, subject to the convenience of the parties and the availability of the judge. It is not essential that all parties are on the telephone when those that are not find it more convenient to come to court. Any party, who wishes to have an application dealt with by telephone, should make such request by letter or e-mail to the judge's clerk, sending copies to all other parties. Except in cases of urgency, the judge will allow a period of two working days for the other parties to comment upon that request before deciding whether to deal with the application by telephone.

4.3.5 If permission is given for a telephone hearing, the court will normally indicate which party is to make all the necessary arrangements. In most cases, it will be the applicant. The procedure to be followed in setting up and holding a telephone hearing is generally that set out in **section 6 of the Practice Direction 23A supplementing CPR Part 23** and the TCC in London and at Regional Centres are "telephone conference enabled courts" for the purposes of that section. The party making arrangements for the telephone hearing must ensure that all parties and the judge have a bundle for that hearing with identical pagination.

It is vital that the judge has all the necessary papers, in good time before the telephone conference, in order that it can be conducted efficiently and effectively. Save in very simple cases involving no or only minimal amounts of documentation, it is usually essential that any bundle provided be paginated for a telephone hearing, failing which the judge may cancel it.

4.4 Paper Applications

4.4.1 **CPR 23.8 and paragraphs 11.1-11.2 of Practice Direction 23A** enable certain applications to be dealt with in writing. Parties in a TCC case are encouraged to deal with applications in writing, whenever practicable. Applications for abridgments of time, extensions of time and to reduce the trial time estimate can generally be dealt with in writing, as well as all other variations to existing directions which are wholly or largely agreed. Disputes over particular aspects of disclosure and evidence may also be capable of being resolved in this way.

4.4.2 If a party wishes to make an application to the court, it should ask itself the question: "Can this application be conveniently dealt with in writing?" If it can, then the party should issue the application and make its (short) written submissions both in support of its application and why it should be dealt with on paper. The application, any supporting evidence and the written submissions should be provided to all parties, as well as the court. These must include a draft of the precise order sought. There are some paper applications which can be made without notice to the other party or parties: see **CPR 23.4(2), 23.9 and 23.10**.

4.4.3 The party against whom the application is made, and any other interested party, should respond within **3 days** dealing both with the substantive application and the request for it to be dealt with in writing.

4.4.4 The court can then decide whether or not to deal with the application in writing. If the parties are agreed that the court should deal with it in writing, it will be rare for the court to take a different view. If the parties disagree as to whether or not the application should be dealt with in writing, the court can decide that issue and, if it decides to deal with it in writing can go on to resolve the substantive point on the basis of the parties' written submissions.

4.4.5   Further guidance in respect of paper applications is set out in **Section 6.7** below.

4.4.6   It is important for the parties to ensure that all documents provided to the court are also provided to all the other parties, so as to ensure that both the court and the parties are working on the basis of the same documentation. The pagination of any bundle which is provided to the court and the parties must be identical.

4.5   E-mail Communications

4.5.1   Electronic Working under the provisions of CPR Part 5, Practice Direction 5C is not currently available.

4.5.2   The judges' clerks all have e-mail addresses identified in **Appendix D**. They welcome communication from the parties electronically. In addition, by agreement with the judge's clerk, it is also possible to provide documents to the Court electronically. However, it should be noted that HM Court Service imposes a restriction on the size of any e-mail, including its attachments. Larger attachments can be submitted by CD/DVD. Further, the provision of substantial documents electronically is to be used only with the permission of the judge and when time is short. The Court Service is not to be used as an outsource for printing.

4.5.3   Depending on the particular circumstances of an individual trial, the assigned judge may ask for an e-mail contact address for each of the parties and may send e-mail communications to that address. In addition, the judge may provide a direct contact e-mail address so that the parties can communicate directly with him out of court hours. In such circumstances, the judge and the parties should agree the times at which the respective e-mail addresses can be used.

4.5.4   Every e-mail communication to and from the court or a judge must be copied simultaneously to all the other parties. The subject line of every e-mail should include the name of the case (abbreviated if necessary) and the claim number.

4.6   Video Conferencing

4.6.1   In appropriate cases, particularly where there are important matters in dispute and the parties' representatives are a long distance from one another and/or the court, the hearing may be conducted by way of a Video Conference ("VC"). Prior arrangements will be necessary for any such hearing.

4.6.2   In London, a VC can be arranged through the VC facilities in the Rolls Building, but there is significant demand for these, so parties must notify the court well ahead In some cases, it may be possible to use Skype or other commercially viable software as a suitable alternative to VC facilities (but the parties must bear in mind that such software usually only provides an insecure link, and it will be essential in any event to ensure that all of the parties and the judge in question have access to the software and a relevant account).

4.6.3   Outside London, a VC can be arranged at the following TCC courts with the requisite facilities: Birmingham, Bristol, Cardiff, Central London, Chester, Exeter, Leeds, Liverpool, Newcastle-upon-Tyne, Nottingham, Manchester and Winchester.

4.7 Contacting the court out of hours

4.7.1 Occasionally it is necessary to contact a TCC judge out of hours. For example, it may be necessary to apply for an injunction to prevent the commencement of building works which will damage adjoining property; or for an order to preserve evidence. A case may have settled and it may be necessary to inform the judge, before he/she spends an evening or a weekend reading the papers.

4.7.2 At the Rolls Building. RCJ Security has been provided with the telephone numbers and other contact information of all the clerks to the TCC judges based at the Rolls Building and and their clerks and of the court manager. If contact is required with a judge out of hours, the initial approach should be to RCJ Security on 020-7947-6000. Security will then contact the judge's clerk and/or the court manager and pass on the message or other information. If direct contact with the judge or court manager is sought, RCJ Security must be provided with an appropriate contact number. This number will then be passed to the judge's clerk and/or the court manager, who will seek directions from the judge whether it is appropriate for the judge to speak directly with the contacting party.

4.7.3 At other court centres. At the Central London Civil Justice Centre and at all court centres outside London there is a court officer who deals with out of hours applications.

4.8 Lodging documents

4.8.1 In general documents should be lodged in hard copy only and not sent by email or fax. This causes unnecessary duplication as well as additional work for hard-pressed court staff. Fax communication with the court, in particular, is discouraged. If the court or judge's clerk agrees, some documents may be sent by email but otherwise only if matters are urgent may documents be sent by either email or fax, with a hard copy sent by way of confirmation and marked as such. In certain cases, the court may ask for documents to be submitted in electronic form by email or otherwise, where that is appropriate. The judge may ask for certain documents to be lodged in a particular form, such as pdf or Microsoft Word or Excel.

Section 5. Costs and Case management and the first CMC

5.1 General

5.1.1 The general approach of the TCC to costs and case management is to give directions at the outset for the conduct of the case, up to trial, and then throughout the proceedings to serve the overriding objective of dealing with cases justly and at proportionate cost. Since the introduction of costs management the control of costs will be an important factor in how cases are managed from the outset: the parties must read this section in conjunction with **Section 16**, which concerns costs management and cost capping. The judge to whom the case has been assigned has wide case management powers, which will be exercised to ensure that:

- the real issues are identified early on and remain the focus of the ongoing proceedings;

- a realistic timetable is ordered which will allow for the fair and prompt resolution of the action;

- appropriate steps are taken to ensure that there is in place a suitable protocol for conducting e-disclosure (this should have been discussed by the parties at an early stage in the litigation and the parties may wish to use the TeCSA e-disclosure protocol (which can be found on its website).

- in document heavy cases the parties will be invited to consider the use of an electronic document management system; it is important that this is considered at an early stage because it will be closely linked to e-disclosure;

- costs are properly controlled and reflect the value of the issues to the parties and their respective financial positions. In cases commenced before 22 April 2014 and below the value set by the relevant Practice Direction (£2 million), this will be done by way of Costs Management Orders. For cases commenced after 22 April 2014, this limit is increased to £10 million by **CPR 3.12** (as amended). The attention of the parties is drawn to the amended rule.

5.1.2 In order to assist the judge in the exercise of his costs and case management functions, the parties will be expected to co-operate with one another at all times. See **CPR 1.3**. Costs sanctions may be applied, if the judge concludes that one party is not reasonably co-operating with the other parties.

5.1.3 A hearing at which the judge gives general procedural directions is a case management conference ("CMC"). CMCs are relatively informal and business-like occasions. Representatives may sit when addressing the judge.

5.1.4 The following procedures apply in order to facilitate effective case management:

- Upon commencement of a case in the TCC, it is allocated automatically to the multi-track. The provisions of **CPR Part 29** apply to all TCC cases (but see paragraph 4.2.1 above).

Section 5. Case management and the first CMC

- The TCC encourages a structured exchange of proposals and submissions for CMCs in advance of the hearing, including costs budgets, so as to enable the parties to respond on an informed basis to proposals made.

- The judges of the TCC operate pro-active case management. In order to avoid the parties being taken by surprise by any judicial initiative, the judge will consider giving prior notification of specific or unusual case management proposals to be raised at a case management conference.

5.1.5 The TCC's aim is to ensure that where possible the trial of each case takes place before the judge who has managed the case since the first CMC. Whilst continuity of judge is not always possible, because of the need to double- or triple-book judges and the need for High Court Judges to be deployed on other duties, or because cases can sometimes overrun their estimated length through no fault of the parties, this remains an aspiration of case management within the TCC.

5.1.6 To ensure that costs are properly controlled the judge will consider at all stages of case management whether there are ways in which costs can be reduced. If the judge considers that any particular aspect has unnecessarily increased costs, such as prolix pleadings or witness statements, the judge may make a costs order disallowing costs or ordering costs to be paid, either on the basis of a summary assessment, or by giving a direction to the costs judge as to what costs should be disallowed or paid on a detailed assessment: see also **paragraph 5.5.5** below.

5.2 The Fixing of the First CMC

5.2.1 Where a claim has been started in the TCC, or where it has been transferred into the TCC, **paragraph 8.1 of the Part 60 Practice Direction** requires the court within **14 days** of the earliest of

- the filing by the defendant of an acknowledgement of service, or

- the filing by the defendant of the defence, or

- the date of the order transferring the case to the TCC

to fix the first CMC.

If some defendants but not others are served with proceedings, the claimant's solicitors should so inform the court and liaise about the fixing of the first CMC. See also **paragraph 4.2.1** above.

5.2.2 The first CMC will usually be fixed sufficiently far ahead to allow the parties time to discuss both e-disclosure and costs budgets. If any of the parties wishes to delay the first CMC for any reason, it can write to the judge's clerk explaining why a delayed CMC is appropriate (for example, in cases where the CMC would not otherwise take place until after service of the defence or the defences, it may be appropriate to postpone the first CMC until these are available). If such a request is agreed by the other party or parties, it is likely that the judge will grant the request.

5.3 The Case Management Information Sheet and Other Documents

It should be noted that for proceedings in the TCC, being a specialist court, the standard directions that can be found on line are not always appropriate.

5.3.1   All parties are expected to complete a detailed response to the case management information sheet sent out by the Registry when the case is commenced/transferred. A copy of a blank case management information sheet is attached as **Appendix A**. It is important that all parts of the form are completed, particularly those sections (eg. concerned with estimated costs) that enable the judge to give directions in accordance with the overriding objective.

5.3.2   The Registry will also send out a blank standard directions form to each party. A copy is attached at **Appendix B**. This provides an example of the usual directions made on the first CMC. The parties may either fill it in, indicating the directions and timetable sought, or, preferably, provide draft directions in a similar format. The parties should return both the questionnaire and the proposed directions to the court, so that the areas (if any) of potential debate at the CMC can be identified. The parties are encouraged to exchange proposals for directions and the timetable sought, with a view to agreeing the same before the CMC for consideration by the court. The parties should note that **CPR 31.5** requires the parties no less than 14 days before the first CMC to file and serve a disclosure report and no less than 7 days before to discuss and seek to agree proposals for disclosure and file costs budgets. Failure to do the last may result in a party's recoverable costs being limited to the court fee.

5.3.3   If the case is large or complex, it is helpful for the advocates to prepare a Note to be provided to the judge the day before the CMC which can address the issues in the case, the suggested directions, and the principal areas of dispute between the parties. If such a Note is provided, it is unnecessary for the claimant also to prepare a Case Summary as well.

5.3.4   In smaller cases, a Case Summary for the CMC, explaining briefly the likely issues, can be helpful. Such Case Summaries should be non-contentious and should (if this is possible without incurring disproportionate cost) be agreed /between the parties in advance of the hearing.

5.4   Checklist of Matters likely to be considered at the first CMC

5.4.1   The following checklist identifies the matters which the judge is likely to want to consider at the first CMC, although it is not exhaustive:

- The need for, and content of, any further statements of case to be served. This is dealt with in **Section 5.5** below.

- The outcome of the Protocol process, and the possible further need for ADR. ADR is dealt with in **Section 7** below.

- The desirability of dealing with particular disputes by way of a Preliminary Issue hearing. This is dealt with in **Section 8** below.

- The court may require a list of issues to be provided and updated during the course of the procedural steps, but this is often left to the pre-trial review.

- Whether the trial should be in stages (eg. stage 1 liability and causation, stage 2 quantum). In very heavy cases this may be necessary in order to make the trial manageable. In more modest cases, where the quantum evidence will be extensive, a staged trial may be in the interest of all parties.

- The appropriate orders in respect of the disclosure of documents and for a protocol to manage e-disclosure. This is dealt with in **Section 11** below.

- The appropriate orders as to the exchange of written witness statements. This is dealt with in **Section 12** below. It should be noted that, although it is normal for evidence-in-chief to be given by way of the written statements in the TCC, the judge may direct that evidence about particular disputes (such as what was said at an important meeting) should be given orally without reference to such statements.

- Whether it is appropriate for the parties to rely on expert evidence and, if so, what disciplines of experts should give evidence, on what issues, and whether any issues can be conveniently dealt with by single joint experts. This may be coupled with an order relating to the carrying out of inspections, the obtaining of samples, the conducting of experiments, or the performance of calculations. Considerations relating to expert evidence are dealt with in **Section 13** below. The parties must be aware that, in accordance with the overriding objective, the judge will only give the parties permission to rely on expert evidence if it is both necessary and appropriate, and, even then, will wish to ensure that the scope of any such evidence is limited as far as possible.

- Review of the parties' costs budgets and the making of a Costs Management Order (subject to any financial threshold relevant to the case). In certain cases there is the possibility of making a costs capping order. See **section 16.3** below.

- Whether there will be any additional claims under Part 20. See section 5.5.4 below.

- The appropriate timetable for the taking of the various interim steps noted above, and the fixing of dates for both the PTR and the trial itself (subject to **paragraph 5.4.2** below). The parties will therefore need to provide the judge with an estimate for the length of the trial, assuming all issues remain in dispute. Unless there is good reason not to, the trial date will generally be fixed at the first CMC (although this may be more difficult at court centres with only one TCC judge). Therefore, to the extent that there are any relevant concerns as to availability of either witnesses or legal representatives, they need to be brought to the attention of the court on that occasion. The length of time fixed for the trial will depend on the parties' estimates, and also the judge's own view. If the parties' estimate of trial length subsequently changes, they should inform the clerk of the assigned judge immediately.

5.4.2 The fixing of the trial date at the CMC is usually as a provisional fixture. Therefore no trial fee is payable at this stage. The court should at the same time specify a date upon which the fixture will cease to be "provisional" and, therefore, the trial fee will become payable. This should ordinarily be two months before the trial date. It should be noted that:

- if the trial fee is not paid within 14 days of the due date, then the whole claim will be struck out: see **CPR 3.7 (1) (a) and (4)**;

- if the court is notified at least 14 days before the trial date that the case is settled or discontinued, then the trial fee, which has been paid, shall be refunded: see **fee 2.2 in Schedule 1 to the Civil Proceedings Fees Order 2004**.

For all purposes other than payment of the trial fee, the provisional date fixed at the CMC shall be regarded as a firm date.

5.4.3 Essentially, the judge's aim at the first CMC is to set down a detailed timetable which, in the majority of cases, will ensure that the parties need not return to court until the PTR.

5.5 Further statements of case

5.5.1 **Defence.** If no defence has been served prior to the first CMC, then (except in cases where judgment in default is appropriate) the court will usually make an order for service of the defence within a specified period. The defendant must plead its positive case. Bare denials and non-admissions are, save in exceptional circumstances, unacceptable.

5.5.2 **Further Information.** If the defendant wants to request further information of the Particulars of Claim, the request should, if possible, be formulated prior to the first CMC, so that it can be considered on that occasion. All requests for further information should be kept within reasonable limits, and concentrate on the important parts of the case.

5.5.3 **Reply.** A reply to the defence is not always necessary. However, where the defendant has raised a positive defence on a particular issue, it may be appropriate for the claimant to set out in a reply how it answers such a defence. If the defendant makes a counterclaim, the claimant's defence to counterclaim and its reply (if any) should be in the same document.

5.5.4 **Additional or Part 20 Claims.** The defendant should, at the first CMC, indicate (so far as possible) any additional (Part 20) claims that it is proposing to make, whether against the claimant or any other party. Additional (Part 20) claims are required to be pleaded in the same detail as the original claim. They are a very common feature of TCC cases, because the widespread use of sub-contractors in the UK construction industry often makes it necessary to pass claims down a contractual chain. Defendants are encouraged to start any necessary Part 20 proceedings to join additional parties as soon as possible. It is undesirable for applications to join additional defendants to be made late in the proceedings.

5.5.5 **Costs.** If at any stage the judge considers that the way in which the case has been pleaded, particularly through the inclusion of extensive irrelevant material or obscurity, is likely to lead or has led to inefficiency in the conduct of the proceedings or to unnecessary time or costs being spent, the judge may order that the party should re-plead the whole or part of the case and may make a costs order disallowing costs or ordering costs to be paid, either on the basis of a summary assessment or by giving a direction to the costs judge as to what costs should be disallowed or paid on a detailed assessment: see also **paragraph 5.1.6** above and **paragraph 12.1.4** below.

5.6 Scott Schedules

5.6.1 It can sometimes be appropriate for elements of the claim, or any additional (Part 20) claim, to be set out by way of a Scott Schedule (ie. by a table, often in landscape format, in which the Claimant's case on liability and quantum is set out item by item in the first few columns and the Defendant's response is set out in the adjacent columns). For example, claims involving a final account or numerous alleged defects or items of disrepair, may be best formulated in this way, which then allows for a detailed response from the defendant. Sometimes, even where all the damage has been caused by one event, such as a fire, it can be helpful for the individual items of loss and damage to be set out in a Scott Schedule. The secret of an effective Scott Schedule lies in the information that is to be provided and its brevity: excessive repetition is to be avoided. This is defined by the column headings. The judge may give directions for the relevant column headings for any Schedule ordered by the court. It is important that the defendant's responses to any such Schedule are as detailed as possible. Each party's entries on a Scott Schedule should be supported by a statement of truth.

Section 5. Case management and the first CMC

5.6.2   Nevertheless, before any order is made or agreement is reached for the preparation of a Scott Schedule, both the parties and the court should consider whether this course (a) will genuinely lead to a saving of cost and time or (b) will lead to a wastage of costs and effort (because the Scott Schedule will simply be duplicating earlier schedules, pleadings or expert reports). A Scott Schedule should only be ordered by the court, or agreed by the parties, in those cases where it is appropriate and proportionate.

5.6.3   When a Scott Schedule is ordered by the court or agreed by the parties, the format must always be specified. The parties must co-operate in the physical task of preparation. Electronic transfer between the parties of their respective entries in the columns will enable a clear and user-friendly Scott Schedule to be prepared, for the benefit of all involved in the trial.

5.7   Agreement Between the Parties

5.7.1   Many, perhaps most, of the required directions at the first CMC may be agreed by the parties. If so, the judge will endeavour to make orders in the terms which have been agreed pursuant to **CPR 29.4**, unless he considers that the agreed terms fail to take into account important features of the case as a whole, or the principles of the CPR. The agreed terms will always, at the very least, form the starting-point of the judge's consideration of the orders to be made at the CMC. If the agreed terms are submitted to the judge 3 days in advance of the hearing date, it may be possible to avoid the need for a hearing altogether, although it is normally necessary for the Court to consider the case with the parties (either at an oral hearing or by way of a telephone conference) in any event.

5.7.2   The approach outlined in **paragraph 5.7.1** above is equally applicable to all other occasions when the parties come before the court with a draft order that is wholly or partly agreed.

5.8   Drawing Up of Orders

5.8.1   Unless the court itself draws up the order, it may direct one party (usually the claimant or applicant) to do so within a specified time. If no such direction is given, then the advocate appearing for the Claimant (or applicant) must prepare and seek to agree a draft order and submit it for the judge's approval within 7 days of the conclusion of the hearing. This is to ensure that the draft is presented to the court whilst the case is still fresh in the judge's mind and he can satisfy himself that the draft is accurate to carry his order into effect. The party charged with drawing up the order must draw up the order and lodge it with the court for approval. Once approved, the order will be stamped by the court and returned to that party for service upon all other parties. The order should refer to the date on which the order was made by stating "Date order made: [date]". Orders should be referred to by this date, rather than later dates which reflect the process of submission of the draft order, approval by the judge and sealing by the court.

5.8.2   In exceptional cases where the parties cannot agree a minute of order (whether within the specified time or at all), then the party with carriage of the order should submit the order, so far as it has been agreed, to the judge together with a summary of those elements of those parts of the order which are not agreed, and setting out any rival wording proposed by the other side, within the specified time. That communication must be in an agreed form as far as possible stating neutrally the other parties' objections, and it must be copied to the other parties when it is submitted to the court. The court heavily discourages extended satellite correspondence over the precise form of order. If, exceptionally, the judge wishes to hear further submissions on the draft form of order before he approves it he will ask for those submissions. Unilateral further submissions to the court as to the minute of order are only to be made in exceptional circumstances (eg. where a party considers that there is a real risk that the court is being misled or its position is being seriously misrepresented). Parties who unreasonably refuse to agree a minute of order, or who take up court time arguing over the precise form of minute can expect to have costs orders made against them.

5.8.3 It is often the case that the parties, after the hearing, decide that it is sensible to include other directions in the draft order by consent, or to vary the timetable to accommodate such matters. Any such agreement must be clearly indicated in both the draft order (eg. by adding in the matters under a separate heading stating that such matters are being made "By Consent") and in an explanatory note for the judge submitted with the proposed order.

5.9 Further CMC

5.9.1 In an appropriate case, the judge will fix a review CMC, to take place part way through the timetable that has been set down, in order to allow the court to review progress, and to allow the parties to raise any matters arising out of the steps that have been taken up to that point. However, this will not be ordered automatically and will be confined to cases of significant complexity.

5.9.2 Each party will be required to give notice in writing to the other parties and the court of any directions which it will be seeking at the review CMC, two days in advance of the hearing.

5.10 The Permanent Case Management Bundle

5.10.1 In conjunction with the judge's clerk, the claimant's solicitor is responsible for ensuring that, for the first CMC and at all times thereafter, there is a permanent bundle of copy documents available to the judge, which contains:

- any relevant documents resulting from the Pre-Action Protocol;
- the claim form and all statements of case;
- all orders;
- all completed case management information sheets;
- all costs budgets;
- any proposed protocol for e-disclosure (if agreed);
- Disclosure Reports/Statements as required by **CPR 31.5.3**;
- Any case summaries (see **sections 5.3.3 and 5.3.4** above).

5.10.2 The permanent case management bundle can then be supplemented by the specific documents relevant to any particular application that may be made. Whether these supplementary documents should (a) become a permanent addition to the case management bundle or (b) be set on one side, will depend upon their nature. The permanent case management bundle may remain at court and be marked up by the judge; alternatively, the judge may direct that the permanent case management bundle be maintained at the offices of the claimant's solicitors and provided to the court when required.

Section 6. Applications after the first CMC

6.1 Relevant parts of the CPR

6.1.1 The basic rules relating to all applications that any party may wish to make are set out in **CPR Part 23** and its accompanying Practice Directions.

6.1.2 **Part 7** of the **Practice Direction** accompanying **CPR Part 60** is also of particular relevance.

6.2 Application Notice

6.2.1 As a general rule, any party to proceedings in the TCC wishing to make an application of any sort must file an application notice (**CPR 23.3**) and serve that application notice on all relevant parties as soon as practicable after it has been filed (**CPR 23.4**). Application notices should be served by the parties, unless (as happens in some court centres outside London) service is undertaken by the court. Where the circumstances may justify an application being made without notice, see **section 6.10** below.

6.2.2 The application notice must set out in clear terms what order is sought and, more briefly, the reasons for seeking that order: see **CPR 23.6**.

6.2.3 The application notice must be served at least **3 days** before the hearing at which the Court deals with the application: **CPR 23.7 (1).** Such a short notice period is only appropriate for the most straight-forward type of application.

6.2.4 Most applications, in particular applications for summary judgment under **CPR Part 24** or to strike out a statement of case under **CPR 3.4,** will necessitate a much longer notice period than **3 days**. In such cases, it is imperative that the applicant obtain a suitable date and time for the hearing of the application from the assigned judge's clerk before the application notice is issued. The applicant must then serve his application notice and evidence in support sufficiently far ahead of the date fixed for the hearing of the application for there to be time to enable the respondent to serve evidence in response. Save in exceptional circumstances, there should be a minimum period of **10 working days** between the service of the notice (and supporting evidence) and the hearing date. If any party considers that there is insufficient time before the hearing of the application or if the time estimate for the application itself is too short, that party must notify the Judge's clerk and the hearing may then be refixed by agreement.

6.2.5 When considering the application notice, the judge may give directions in writing as to the dates for the provision or exchange of evidence and any written submissions or skeleton arguments for the hearing.

6.2.6 In cases of great urgency applications may be made without formal notice to the other party, but that party should (save in exceptional cases) be informed of the hearing sufficiently in advance to enable him to instruct a representative to attend.

6.3 Evidence in Support

6.3.1 The application notice when it is served must be accompanied by all evidence in support: **CPR 23.7 (2)**.

6.3.2 Unless the CPR expressly requires otherwise, evidence will be given by way of witness statements. Such statements must be verified by a statement of truth signed by the maker of the statement: **CPR 22.1.**

6.4 Evidence in opposition and Evidence in reply

6.4.1 Likewise, any evidence in opposition to the application should, unless the rules expressly provide otherwise, be given by way of witness statement verified by a statement of truth.

6.4.2 It is important to ensure that the evidence in opposition to the application is served in good time before the hearing so as to enable:

- the court to read and note up the evidence;
- the applicant to put in any further evidence in reply that may be considered necessary.

Such evidence should be served at least **5 working days** before the hearing.

6.4.3 Any evidence in reply should be served not less than **3 working days** before the hearing. Again, if there are disputes as to the time taken or to be taken for the preparation of evidence prior to a hearing, or any other matters in respect of a suitable timetable for that hearing, the court will consider the written positions of both parties and decide such disputes on paper. It will not normally be necessary for either a separate application to be issued or a hearing to be held for such a purpose.

6.4.4 If the hearing of an application has to be adjourned because of delays by one or other of the parties in serving evidence, the court is likely to order that party to pay the costs straight away, and to make a summary assessment of those costs.

6.5 Application Bundle

6.5.1 The bundle for the hearing of anything other than the most simple and straightforward application should consist of:

- the permanent case management bundle (see **Section 5.8** above);
- the witness statements provided in support of the application, together with any exhibits;
- the witness statements provided in opposition to the application together with exhibits;
- any witness statements in reply, together with exhibits.

6.5.2 The permanent case management bundle will either be with the court or with the claimant's solicitors, depending on the order made at the first CMC: see **paragraph 5.9** above. If it is with the claimant's solicitors, it should be provided to the court not less than **2 working days** before the hearing. In any event, a paginated bundle (see **paragraph 6.5.4** below) containing any material specific to the application should also be provided to the court not less than **2 working days** before the hearing, unless otherwise directed by

Section 6. Applications after the first CMC

the judge. A failure to comply with this deadline may result in the adjournment of the hearing, and the costs thrown away being paid by the defaulting party.

6.5.3 In all but the simplest applications, the court will expect the parties to provide skeleton arguments and copies of any authorities to be relied on. The form and content of the skeleton argument is principally a matter for the author, although the judge will expect it to identify the issues that arise on the application, the important parts of the evidence relied on, and the applicable legal principles. For detailed guidance as to the form, content and length of skeleton arguments, please see paragraph 7.11.12 of the Queen's Bench Guide; Appendix 3 of the Chancery Guide; and Appendix 9 of the Commercial Court Guide.

6.5.4 For an application that is estimated to last ½ day or less, the skeleton should be provided no later than **1 pm on the last working day before the hearing**. It should be accompanied by photocopies of the authorities relied on (preferably in the form of a common agreed bundle). An electronic copy of each skeleton argument (in Microsoft Word compatible format) should be sent to the clerk of the judge hearing the application: if a party is reluctant for other parties to be provided with its skeleton argument in Word, it may serve it in pdf (or other readable) form provided that it certifies that the version sent to the judge is identical in content to that served on the other party(ies).

6.5.5 For an application that is estimated to last more than ½ day, the skeleton should be provided no later than **4 pm one clear working day before the hearing**. It should be accompanied by photocopies of the authorities relied on (again, preferably in the form of a common agreed bundle).

6.5.6 The time limits at **paragraphs 6.5.4** and **6.5.5** above will be regarded as the latest times by which such skeletons should be provided to the court. Save in exceptional circumstances, no extension to these periods will be permitted.

6.5.7 Pagination. It is generally necessary for there to be a paginated bundle for the hearing. Where the parties have produced skeleton arguments, these should be cross-referred to the bundle page numbers. Where possible bundles should be paginated right through, but this may be dispensed with where a document within a discrete section of the bundle has its own internal pagination.

6.6 Hearings

6.6.1 Arbitration applications may be heard in private: see **CPR 62.10**. All other applications will be heard in public in accordance with **CPR 39.2**, save where otherwise ordered.

6.6.2 Provided that the application bundle and the skeletons have been lodged in accordance with the time limits set out above, the parties can assume that the court will have a good understanding of the points in issue. However, the court will expect to be taken to particular documents relied on by the parties and will also expect to be addressed on any important legal principles that arise.

6.6.3 It is important that the parties ensure that every application is dealt with in the estimated time period. Since many applications are dealt with on Fridays, it causes major disruption if application hearings are not disposed of within the estimated period. If the parties take too long in making their submissions, the application may be adjourned, part heard, and the Court may impose appropriate costs sanctions.

6.6.4 At the conclusion of the hearing, unless the court itself draws up the order, it will direct the applicant to do so within a specified period.

6.7 Paper Applications

6.7.1 As noted in **Section 4** above some applications may be suitable for determination on paper under the procedure set out in **paragraph 4.4** above.

6.7.2 In addition, certain simple applications (particularly in lower value cases) arising out of the management of the proceedings may be capable of being dealt with by correspondence without the need for any formal application or order of the court. This is particularly true of applications to vary procedural orders, which variations are wholly or largely agreed, or proposals to vary the estimated length of the trial. In such cases, the applicant should write to the other parties indicating the nature of its application and to seek their agreement to it. If, however, it emerges that there is an issue to be resolved by the court, then a formal application must be issued and dealt with as a paper application or, possibly, at an oral hearing.

6.7.3 It is essential that <u>any</u> communication by a party to the judge or the court is copied to all other parties, subject to **section 6.10** below (applications without notice).

6.8 Consent Orders

6.8.1 Consent Orders may be submitted to the Court in draft for approval without the need for attendance.

6.8.2 Two copies of the draft order should be lodged, at least one of which should be signed. The copies should be undated as the Court will set out the date the order is made: see **paragraph 5.8.1** above.

6.8.3 As noted elsewhere, whilst the parties can agree between themselves the orders to be made either at the Case Management Conference or the Pre-Trial Review, it is normally necessary for the Court to consider the case with the parties (either at an oral hearing or by way of a telephone conference) on those occasions in any event.

6.8.4 Generally, when giving directions, the court will endeavour to identify the date by which the relevant step must be taken, and will not simply provide a period during which that task should be performed. The parties should therefore ensure that any proposed consent order also identifies particular dates, rather than periods, by which the relevant steps must be taken.

6.9 Costs

6.9.1 Costs are dealt with generally at **Section 16** below.

6.9.2 The costs of any application which took a day or less to be heard and disposed of will be dealt with summarily, unless there is a good reason for the court not to exercise its powers as to the summary assessment of costs.

6.9.3 Accordingly, it is necessary for parties to provide to the court and to one another their draft statements of costs no later than **24 hours** before the start of the application hearing. Any costs which are incurred after these draft statements have been prepared, but which have not been allowed for (e.g. because the hearing has exceeded its anticipated length), can be mentioned at the hearing.

6.10 Applications without notice

6.10.1 All applications should be made on notice, even if that notice has to be short, unless:

- any rule or Practice Direction provides that the application may be made without notice; or

- there are good reasons for making the application without notice, for example, because notice would might defeat the object of the application.

6.10.2 Where an application without notice does not involve giving undertakings to the court, it will normally be made and dealt with on paper, as, for example, applications for permission to serve the claim form out of the jurisdiction, and applications for an extension of time in which to serve a claim form.

6.10.3 Any application for an interim injunction or similar remedy will require an oral hearing.

6.10.4 A party wishing to make an application without notice which requires an oral hearing before a judge should contact the TCC Registry at the earliest opportunity.

6.10.5 If a party wishes to make an application without notice at a time when no TCC judge is available, he should apply to the Queen's Bench Judge Chambers.

6.10.6 On all applications without notice it is the duty of the applicant and those representing him:

- to make full and frank disclosure of all matters relevant to the application;

- to ensure that a note of the hearing of the without notice application, the evidence and skeleton argument in support and any order made all be served with the order or as soon as possible thereafter.

6.10.7 The papers lodged the application should include two copies of a draft of the order sought. Save in exceptional circumstances where time is not met, all the evidence relied upon in support of the application and any other relevant documents must be lodged in advance with the TCC Registry. If the application is urgent, the Registry should be informed of the fact and of the reasons for the urgency. Counsel's estimate of reading time likely to be required by the court should also be provided.

Section 7. ADR

7.1 General

7.1.1 The court will provide encouragement to the parties to use alternative dispute resolution ("ADR") and will, whenever appropriate, facilitate the use of such a procedure. In this Guide, ADR is taken to mean any process through which the parties attempt to resolve their dispute, which is voluntary. In most cases, ADR takes the form of inter-party negotiations or a mediation conducted by a neutral mediator. Alternative forms of ADR include early neutral evaluation either by a judge or some other neutral person who receives a concise presentation from each party and then provides his or her own evaluation of the case. The parties are advised to refer to the ADR Handbook.

7.1.2 Although the TCC is an appropriate forum for the resolution of all IT and construction/engineering disputes, the use of ADR can lead to a significant saving of costs and may result in a settlement which is satisfactory to all parties.

7.1.3 Legal representatives in all TCC cases should ensure that their clients are fully aware of the benefits of ADR and that the use of ADR has been carefully considered prior to the first CMC.

7.2 Timing

7.2.1 ADR may be appropriate before the proceedings have begun or at any subsequent stage. However the later ADR takes place, the more the costs which will have been incurred, often unnecessarily. The timing of ADR needs careful consideration.

7.2.2 The TCC Pre-Action Protocol (**Section 2** above) itself provides for a type of ADR, because it requires there to be at least one face-to-face meeting between the parties before the commencement of proceedings. At this meeting, there should be sufficient time to discuss and resolve the dispute. As a result of this procedure having taken place, the court will not necessarily grant a stay of proceedings upon demand and it will always need to be satisfied that an adjournment is actually necessary to enable ADR to take place.

7.2.3 However, at the first CMC, the court will want to be addressed on the parties' views as to the likely efficacy of ADR, the appropriate timing of ADR, and the advantages and disadvantages of a short stay of proceedings to allow ADR to take place. Having considered the representations of the parties, the court may order a short stay to facilitate ADR at that stage. Alternatively, the court may simply encourage the parties to seek ADR and allow for it to occur within the timetable for the resolution of the proceedings set down by the court.

7.2.4 At any stage after the first CMC and prior to the commencement of the trial, the court, will, either on its own initiative or if requested to do so by one or both of the parties, consider afresh the likely efficacy of ADR and whether or not a short stay of the proceedings should be granted, in order to facilitate ADR.

7.3 Procedure

7.3.1 In an appropriate case, the court may indicate the type of ADR that it considers suitable, but the decision in this regard must be made by the parties. In most cases, the appropriate ADR procedure will be mediation.

7.3.2 If at any stage in the proceedings the court considers it appropriate, an ADR order in the terms of **Appendix E** may be made. If such an order is made at the first CMC, the court may go on to give directions for the conduct of the action up to trial (in the event that the ADR fails). Such directions may include provision for a review CMC.

7.3.3 The court will not ordinarily recommend any individual or body to act as mediator or to perform any other ADR procedure. In the event that the parties fail to agree the identity of a mediator or other neutral person pursuant to an order in the terms of **Appendix E**, the court may select such a person from the lists provided by the parties. To facilitate this process, the court would also need to be furnished with the CVs of each of the individuals on the lists.

7.3.4 Information as to the types of ADR procedures available and the individuals able to undertake such procedures is available from TeCSA, TECBAR, the Civil Mediation Council, and from some TCC court centres outside London.

7.4 Non-Cooperation

7.4.1 Generally. At the end of the trial, there may be costs arguments on the basis that one or more parties unreasonably refused to take part in ADR. The court will determine such issues having regard to all the circumstances of the particular case. In *Halsey v Milton Keynes General NHS Trust* [2004] EWCA Civ 576; [2004] 1 WLR 3002, the Court of Appeal identified six factors that may be relevant to any such consideration:

(a) the nature of the dispute;

(b) the merits of the case;

(c) the extent to which other settlement methods have been attempted;

(d) whether the costs of the ADR would be disproportionately high;

(e) whether any delay in setting up and attending the ADR would have been prejudicial;

(f) whether the ADR had a reasonable prospect of success.

This case is the subject of extensive discussion in Civil Procedure, Volume 2, at Section 14. See also *PGF II SA v OMFS Company 1 Ltd* [2013] EWCA Civ 1288, [2014] BLR 1, particularly in relation to silence in the face of a request to mediate.

7.4.2 If an ADR Order Has Been Made. The court will expect each party to co-operate fully with any ADR procedure which takes place following an order of the court. If any other party considers that there has not been proper co-operation in relation to arrangements for mediation or any other ADR Procedure, the complaint will be considered by the court and cost orders and/or other sanctions may be ordered against the defaulting party in consequence. However, nothing in this paragraph should be understood as modifying the rights of all parties to a mediation or any other ADR Procedure to keep confidential all that is said or done in the course of that ADR Procedure.

7.5 Early Neutral Evaluation

7.5.1 An early neutral evaluation ("ENE") may be carried out by any appropriately qualified person, whose opinion is likely to be respected by the parties. In an appropriate case, and with the consent of all parties, a TCC judge may provide an early neutral evaluation either in respect of the full case or of particular issues arising within it. Unless the parties otherwise agree the ENE will be produced in writing and will set out conclusions and brief reasons. Such an ENE will not, save with the agreement of the parties, be binding on the parties.

7.5.2 If the parties would like an ENE to be carried out by the court, then they can seek an appropriate order from the assigned judge either at the first CMC or at any time prior to the commencement of the trial.

7.5.3 The assigned judge may choose to do the ENE himself. In such instance, the judge will take no further part in the proceedings once he has produced the ENE, unless the parties expressly agree otherwise. Alternatively, the assigned judge will select another available TCC judge to undertake the ENE.

7.5.4 The judge undertaking the ENE will give appropriate directions for the preparation and conduct of the ENE. These directions will generally be agreed by the parties and may include:

- a stay of the substantive proceedings whilst the ENE is carried out.

- a direction that the ENE is to be carried out entirely on paper with dates for the exchange of submissions.

- a direction that particular documents or information should be provided by a party.

- a direction that there will be an oral hearing (either with or without evidence), with dates for all the necessary steps for submissions, witness statements and expert evidence leading to that hearing. If there is an oral hearing the ENE will generally not last more than one day.

- a statement that the parties agree or do not agree that the ENE procedure and the documents, submissions or evidence produced in relation to the ENE are to be without prejudice, or, alternatively, that the whole or part of those items are not without prejudice and can be referred to at any subsequent trial or hearing.

- a statement whether the parties agree that the judge's evaluation after the ENE process will be binding on the parties or binding in certain circumstances (e.g. if not disputed within a period) or temporarily binding subject to a final decision in arbitration, litigation or final agreement.

7.6 Court Settlement Process

7.6.1 The Court Settlement Process is a form of mediation carried out by TCC judges. Whilst mediation may be carried out by any appropriately qualified person, in an appropriate case, and with the consent of all parties, a TCC judge may act as a Settlement Judge pursuant to a Court Settlement Order in the terms set out in **Appendix G**. This has proved to be successful in many cases.

7.6.2   If the parties would like to consider the use of the Court Settlement Process or would like further information, they should contact the TCC Registry in London or the TCC Liaison District Judges in the court centres outside London.

7.6.3   Where, following a request from the parties, the assigned TCC judge considers that the parties might be able to achieve an amicable settlement and that a TCC judge is particularly able to assist in achieving that settlement, that judge or another TCC judge, with the agreement of the parties, will make a Court Settlement Order (**Appendix G**) embodying the parties' agreement and fixing a date for the Court Settlement Conference to take place with an estimated duration proportionate to the issues in the case.

7.6.4   The TCC judge appointed as the Settlement Judge will then conduct the Court Settlement Process in accordance with that Court Settlement Order in a similar manner to that of a mediator. If no settlement is achieved then the case would proceed but, if the assigned judge carried out the Court Settlement Process, then the case would be assigned to another TCC judge. In any event, the Settlement Judge would take no further part in the court proceedings.

Section 8. Preliminary issues

8.1 General

8.1.1 The hearing of Preliminary Issues ("PI"), at which the court considers and delivers a binding judgment on particular issues in advance of the main trial, can be an extremely cost-effective and efficient way of narrowing the issues between the parties and, in certain cases, of resolving disputes altogether.

8.1.2 Some cases listed in the TCC lend themselves particularly well to this procedure. A PI hearing can address particular points which may be decisive of the whole proceedings; even if that is not the position, it is often possible for a PI hearing to cut down significantly on the scope (and therefore the costs) of the main trial.

8.1.3 At the first CMC the court will expect to be addressed on whether or not there are matters which should be taken by way of Preliminary Issues in advance of the main trial. Subject to **paragraph 8.5** below, it is not generally appropriate for the court to make an order for the trial of preliminary issues until after the defence has been served. After the first CMC, and at any time during the litigation, any party is at liberty to raise with any other party the possibility of a PI hearing and the court will consider any application for the hearing of such Preliminary Issues. In many cases, although not invariably, a PI order will be made with the support of all parties.

8.1.4 Whilst, for obvious reasons, it is not possible to set out hard and fast rules for what is and what is not suitable for a PI hearing, the criteria set out in **Section 8.2** below should assist the parties in deciding whether or not some or all of the disputes between them will be suitable for a PI hearing.

8.1.5 <u>Drawbacks of preliminary issues in inappropriate cases.</u> If preliminary issues are ordered inappropriately, they can have adverse effect. Evidence may be duplicated. The same witnesses may give evidence before different judges, in the event that there is a switch of assigned judge. Findings may be made at the PI hearing, which are affected by evidence called at the main hearing. The prospect of a PI hearing may delay the commencement of ADR or settlement negotiations. Also two trials are more expensive than one. For all these reasons, any proposal for preliminary issues needs to be examined carefully, so that the benefits and drawbacks can be evaluated. Also the court should give due weight to the views of the parties when deciding whether a PI hearing would be beneficial.

8.1.6 <u>Staged trials.</u> The breaking down of a long trial into stages should be differentiated from the trial of preliminary issues. Sometimes it is sensible for liability (including causation) to be tried before quantum of damages. Occasionally the subject matter of the litigation is so extensive that for reasons of case management the trial needs to be broken down into separate stages.

8.2 Guidelines

8.2.1 <u>The Significance of the Preliminary Issues.</u> The court would expect that any issue proposed as a suitable PI would, if decided in a particular way, be capable of:

- resolving the whole proceedings or a significant element of the proceedings; or

- significantly reducing the scope, and therefore the costs, of the main trial; or

- significantly improving the possibility of a settlement of the whole proceedings.

Section 8. Preliminary issues

8.2.2 <u>Oral Evidence.</u> The court would ordinarily expect that, if issues are to be dealt with by way of a PI hearing, there would be either no or relatively limited oral evidence. If extensive oral evidence was required on any proposed PI, then it may not be suitable for a PI hearing. Although it is difficult to give specific guidance on this point, it is generally considered that a PI hearing in a smaller case should not take more than about 2 days, and in a larger and more complex case, should not take more than about 4 days.

8.3 Common Types of Preliminary Issue

The following are commonly resolved by way of a PI hearing:

(a) Disputes as to whether or not there was a binding contract between the parties.

(b) Disputes as to what documents make up or are incorporated within the contract between the parties and disputes as to the contents or relevance of any conversations relied on as having contractual status or effect.

(c) Disputes as to the proper construction of the contract documents or the effect of an exclusion or similar clause.

(d) Disputes as to the correct application of a statute or binding authority to a situation where there is little or no factual dispute.

(e) Disputes as to the existence and/or scope of a statutory duty.

(f) Disputes as to the existence and/or scope of a duty of care at common law in circumstances where there is no or little dispute about the relevant facts.

8.4 Other Possible Preliminary Issues

The following can sometimes be resolved by way of a preliminary issue hearing, although a decision as to whether or not to have such a hearing will always depend on the facts of the individual case:

8.4.1 <u>A Limitation Defence.</u> It is often tempting to have limitation issues resolved in advance of the main trial. This can be a good idea because, if a complex claim is statute-barred, a decision to that effect will lead to a significant saving of costs. However, there is also a risk that extensive evidence relevant to the limitation defence (relating to matters such as when the damage occurred or whether or not there has been deliberate concealment) may also be relevant to the liability issues within the main trial. In such a case, a preliminary issue hearing may lead to a) extensive duplication of evidence and therefore costs and b) give rise to difficulty if the main trial is heard by a different judge.

8.4.2 <u>Causation and 'No Loss' Points.</u> Causation and 'No Loss' points may be suitable for a PI hearing, but again their suitability will diminish if it is necessary for the court to resolve numerous factual disputes as part of the proposed PI hearing. The most appropriate disputes of this type for a PI hearing are those where the defendant contends that, even accepting all the facts alleged by the claimant, the claim must fail by reason of causation or the absence of recoverable loss.

8.4.3 <u>'One-Off' Issues.</u> Issues which do not fall into any obvious category, like economic duress, or misrepresentation, may be suitable for resolution by way of a PI hearing, particularly if the whole case can be shown to turn on them.

Section 8. Preliminary issues

8.5 Use of PI as an adjunct to ADR

8.5.1 Sometimes parties wish to resolve their dispute by ADR, but there is one major issue which is a sticking point in any negotiation or mediation. The parties may wish to obtain the court's final decision on that single issue, in the expectation that after that they can resolve their differences without further litigation.

8.5.2 In such a situation the parties may wish to bring proceedings under **CPR Part 8**, in order to obtain the court's decision on that issue. Such proceedings can be rapidly progressed. Alternatively, if the issue is not suitable for **Part 8** proceedings, the parties may bring proceedings under **Part 7** and then seek determination of the critical question as a preliminary issue. At the first CMC the position can be explained and the judge can be asked to order early trial of the proposed preliminary issue, possibly without the need for a defence or any further pleadings.

8.6 Precise Wording of PI

8.6.1 If a party wishes to seek a PI hearing, either at the first CMC or thereafter, that party must circulate a precise draft of the proposed preliminary issues to the other parties and to the court well in advance of the relevant hearing.

8.6.2 If the court orders a PI hearing, it is likely to make such an order only by reference to specific and formulated issues, in order to avoid later debate as to the precise scope of the issues that have been ordered. Of course, the parties are at liberty to propose amendments to the issues before the PI hearing itself, but if such later amendments are not agreed by all parties, they are unlikely to be ordered.

8.7 Appeals

8.7.1 When considering whether or not to order a PI hearing, the court will take into account the effect of any possible appeal against the PI judgment, and the concomitant delay caused.

8.7.2 At the time of ordering preliminary issues, both the parties and the court should specifically consider whether, in the event of an appeal against the PI judgment, it is desirable that the trial of the main action should (a) precede or (b) follow such appeal. It should be noted, however, that the first instance court has no power to control the timetable for an appeal. The question whether an appeal should be (a) expedited or (b) stayed is entirely a matter for the Court of Appeal. Nevertheless, the Court of Appeal will take notice of any "indication" given by the lower court in this regard.

Section 9. Adjudication business

9.1 Introduction

9.1.1 The TCC is ordinarily the court in which the enforcement of an adjudicator's decision and any other business connected with adjudication is undertaken. Adjudicators' decisions predominantly arise out of adjudications which are governed by the mandatory provisions of the Housing Grants, Construction and Regeneration Act 1996 (as amended by the Local Democracy, Economic Development and Construction Act 2009 for contracts entered into on or after 1 October 2011) relating to the carrying out of construction operations in England and Wales ("HGCRA"). These provisions apply automatically to any construction contract as defined in the legislation. Some Adjudicators' decisions arise out of standard form contracts which contain adjudication provisions, and others arise from *ad hoc* agreements to adjudicate. The TCC enforcement procedure is the same for all kinds of adjudication.

9.1.2 In addition to enforcement applications, declaratory relief is sometimes sought in the TCC at the outset of or during an adjudication in respect of matters such as the jurisdiction of the adjudicator or the validity of the adjudication. This kind of application is dealt with in **Paragraph 9.4** below.

9.1.3 The HGCRA provides for a mandatory 28-day period within which the entire adjudication process must be completed, unless a) the referring party agrees to an additional 14 days, or b) both parties agree to a longer period. In consequence, the TCC has moulded a rapid procedure for enforcing an adjudication decision that has not been honoured. Other adjudication proceedings are ordinarily subject to similar rapidity.

9.2 Procedure in Enforcement Proceedings

9.2.1 Unlike arbitration business, there is neither a practice direction nor a claim form concerned with adjudication business. The enforcement proceedings normally seek a monetary judgment so that **CPR Part 7** proceedings are usually appropriate. However, if the enforcement proceedings are known to raise a question which is unlikely to involve a substantial dispute of fact and no monetary judgment is sought, **CPR Part 8** proceedings may be used instead.

9.2.2 The TCC has fashioned a procedure whereby enforcement applications are dealt with promptly. The details of this procedure are set out below.

9.2.3 The claim form should identify the construction contract, the jurisdiction of the adjudicator, the procedural rules under which the adjudication was conducted, the adjudicator's decision, the relief sought and the grounds for seeking that relief.

9.2.4 The claim form should be accompanied by an application notice that sets out the procedural directions that are sought. Commonly, the claimant's application will seek an abridgement of time for the various procedural steps, and summary judgment under **CPR Part 24**. The claim form and the application should be accompanied by a witness statement or statements setting out the evidence relied on in support of both the adjudication enforcement claim and the associated procedural application. This evidence should ordinarily include a copy of the Notice of Intention to Refer and the adjudicator's decision. Further pleadings in the adjudication may be required where questions of the adjudicator's jurisdiction are being raised.

Section 9. Adjudication business

9.2.5 The claim form, application notice and accompanying documents should be lodged in the appropriate registry or court centre clearly marked as being a "paper without notice adjudication enforcement claim and application for the urgent attention of a TCC judge". A TCC judge will ordinarily provide directions in connection with the procedural application within **3 working days** of the receipt of the application notice at the courts.

9.2.6 The procedural application is dealt with by a TCC judge on paper, without notice. The paper application and the consequent directions should deal with:

(a) the abridged period of time in which the defendant is to file an acknowledgement of service;

(b) the time for service by the defendant of any witness statement in opposition to the relief being sought;

(c) an early return date for the hearing of the summary judgment application and a note of the time required or allowed for that hearing; and

(d) identification of the judgment, order or other relief being sought at the hearing of the adjudication claim.

The order made at this stage will always give the defendant liberty to apply.

9.2.7 A direction providing that the claim form, supporting evidence and court order providing for the hearing are to be served on the defendant as soon as practicable, or sometimes by a particular date, will ordinarily also be given when the judge deals with the paper procedural application.

9.2.8 The directions will ordinarily provide for an enforcement hearing within about **28 days** of the directions being made and for the defendant to be given at least **14 days** from the date of service for the serving of any evidence in opposition to the adjudication application. In more straightforward cases, the abridged periods may be less.

9.2.9 Draft standard directions of the kind commonly made by the court on a procedural application by the claimant in an action to enforce the decision of an adjudicator are attached as **Appendix F**.

9.2.10 The claimant should, with the application, provide an estimate of the time needed for the hearing of the application. This estimate will be taken into account by the judge when fixing the date and length of the hearing. The parties should, if possible jointly, communicate any revised time estimate to the court promptly and the judge to whom the case has been allocated will consider whether to refix the hearing date or alter the time period that has been allocated for the hearing.

9.2.11 If the parties cannot agree on the date or time fixed for the hearing, a paper application must be made to the judge to whom the hearing has been allocated for directions.

9.2.12 Parties seeking to enforce adjudication decisions are reminded that they might be able to obtain judgment in default of service of an acknowledgment of service or, if the other party does not file any evidence in response, they might be able to obtain an expedited hearing of the Part 24 application. Generally, it is preferable for a party to enter default judgment rather than seek an expedited hearing, because that reduces the costs involved (the terms of the order usually mention this explicitly).

Section 9. Adjudication business

9.3 The Enforcement Hearing

9.3.1 Where there is any dispute to be resolved at the hearing, the judge should be provided with copies of the relevant sections of the HGCRA, the adjudication procedural rules under which the adjudication was conducted, the adjudicator's decision and copies of any adjudication provisions in the contract underlying the adjudication.

9.3.2 Subject to any more specific directions given by the court, the parties should lodge, **by 4.00 pm one clear working day before the hearing**, a bundle containing the documents that will be required at the hearing. The parties should also file and serve short skeleton arguments and copies of any authorities which are to be relied on (preferably as an agreed joint bundle), summarising their respective contentions as to why the adjudicator's decision is or is not enforceable or as to any other relief being sought. For a hearing that is expected to last half a day or less, the skeletons should be provided **no later than 1 pm on the last working day before the hearing.** For a hearing that is estimated to last more than half a day, the skeletons should be provided **no later than 4 pm one clear working day before the hearing**.

9.3.3 The parties should be ready to address the court on the limited grounds on which a defendant may resist an application seeking to enforce an adjudicator's decision or on which a court may provide any other relief to any party in relation to an adjudication or an adjudicator's decision.

9.4 Other Proceedings Arising Out Of Adjudication

9.4.1 As noted above, the TCC will also hear any applications for declaratory relief arising out of the commencement of a disputed adjudication. Commonly, these will concern:

- Disputes over the jurisdiction of an adjudicator. It can sometimes be appropriate to seek a declaration as to jurisdiction at the outset of an adjudication, rather than both parties incurring considerable costs in the adjudication itself, only for the jurisdiction point to emerge again at the enforcement hearing.

- Disputes over whether there is a construction contract within the meaning of the Act (and, in older contracts, whether there was a written contract between the parties).

- Disputes over the permissible scope of the adjudication, and, in particular, whether the matters which the claimant seeks to raise in the adjudication are the subject of a pre-existing dispute between the parties.

9.4.2 Any such application will be immediately assigned to a named judge. In such circumstances, given the probable urgency of the application, the judge will usually require the parties to attend a CMC **within 2 working days** of the assignment of the case to him, and he will then give the necessary directions to ensure the speedy resolution of the dispute.

9.4.3 It sometimes happens that one party to an adjudication commences enforcement proceedings, whilst the other commences proceedings under Part 8, in order to challenge the validity of the adjudicator's award. This duplication of effort is unnecessary and it involves the parties in extra costs, especially if the two actions are commenced at different court centres. Accordingly there should be sensible discussions between the parties or their lawyers, in order to agree the appropriate venue and also to agree who shall be claimant and who defendant. All the issues raised by each party can and should be raised in a single action. However, in cases where an adjudicator has made a clear error (but has acted within his jurisdiction), it may on occasions be appropriate to bring proceedings under Part 8 for a declaration as a pre-emptive response to an anticipated application to enforce the decision.

Section 10. Arbitration

10.1 Arbitration Claims in the TCC

10.1.1 "Arbitration claims" are any application to the court under the Arbitration Act 1996 and any other claim concerned with an arbitration that is referred to in **CPR 62.2(1)**. Common examples of arbitration claims are challenges to an award on grounds of jurisdiction under section 67, challenges to an award for serious irregularity under section 68 or appeals on points of law under section 69 of the Arbitration Act 1996. Arbitration claims may be started in the TCC, as is provided for in **paragraph 2.3 of the Practice Direction – Arbitration** which supplements **CPR Part 62**.

10.1.2 In practice, arbitration claims arising out of or connected with a construction or engineering arbitration (or any other arbitration where the subject matter involved one or more of the categories of work set out in **paragraph 1.3.1 above**) should be started in the TCC. The only arbitration claims that must be started in the Commercial Court are those (increasingly rare) claims to which the old law (i.e. the pre-1996 Act provisions) apply: see **CPR 62.12**.

10.1.3 The TCC follows the practice and procedure for arbitration claims established by **CPR Part 62** and (broadly) the practice of the Commercial Court as summarised by **Section O of the Admiralty and Commercial Court Guide.** In the absence of any specific directions given by the court, the automatic directions set out in **section 6 of the Practice Direction supplementing CPR Part 62** govern the procedures to be followed in any arbitration claim from the date of service up to the substantive hearing.

10.2 Leave to appeal

10.2.1 Where a party is seeking to appeal a question of law arising out of an award pursuant to section 69 of the Arbitration Act 1996 and the parties have not in their underlying contract agreed that such an appeal may be brought, the party seeking to appeal must apply for leave to appeal pursuant to sections 69(2), 69(3) and 69(4) of that Act. That application must be included in the arbitration claim form as explained in **paragraph 12 of the Practice Direction**.

10.2.2 In conformity with the practice of the Commercial Court, the TCC will normally consider any application for permission to appeal on paper after the defendant has had an appropriate opportunity to answer in writing the application being raised.

10.2.3 The claimant must include within the claim form an application for permission to appeal. No separate application notice is required.

10.2.4 The claim form and supporting documents must be served on the defendant. The judge will not consider the merits of the application for permission to appeal until (a) a certificate of service has been filed at the appropriate TCC registry or court centre and (b), subject to any order for specific directions, a further **28 days** have elapsed, so as to enable the defendant to file written evidence in opposition. Save in exceptional circumstances, the only material admissible on an application for permission to appeal is (a) the award itself and any documents annexed to or necessary to understand the award and (b) evidence relevant to the issue whether any identified question of law is of general public importance: see the requirements of **paragraph 12 of the Practice Direction**.

10.2.5 If necessary, the judge dealing with the application will direct an oral hearing with a date for the hearing. That hearing will, ordinarily, consist of brief submissions by each party. The judge dealing with the application will announce his decision in writing or, if a hearing has been directed, at the conclusion of the hearing with brief reasons if the application is refused.

10.2.6 Where the permission has been allowed in part and refused in part:

(a) Only those questions for which permission has been granted may be raised at the hearing of the appeal.

(b) Brief reasons will be given for refusing permission in respect of the other questions.

10.2.7 If the application is granted, the judge will fix the date for the appeal, and direct whether the same judge or a different judge shall hear the appeal.

10.3 Appeals where leave to appeal is not required

10.3.1 Parties to a construction contract should check whether they have agreed in the underlying contract that an appeal may be brought without leave, since some construction and engineering standard forms of contract so provide. If that is the case, the appeal may be set down for a substantive hearing without leave being sought. The arbitration claim form should set out the clause or provision which it is contended provides for such agreement and the claim form should be marked "Arbitration Appeal – Leave not required".

10.3.2 Where leave is not required, the claimant should identify each question of law that it is contended arises out of the award and which it seeks to raise in an appeal under section 69. If the defendant does not accept that the questions thus identified are questions of law or maintains that they do not arise out of the award or that the appeal on those questions may not be brought for any other reason, then the defendant should notify the claimant and the court of its contentions and apply for a directions hearing before the judge nominated to hear the appeal on a date prior to the date fixed for the hearing of the appeal. Unless the judge hearing the appeal otherwise directs, the appeal will be confined to the questions of law identified in the arbitration claim form.

10.3.3 In an appropriate case, the judge may direct that the question of law to be raised and decided on the appeal should be reworded, so as to identify more accurately the real legal issue between the parties.

10.4 The hearing of the appeal

10.4.1 Parties should ensure that the court is provided only with material that is relevant and admissible to the point of law. This will usually be limited to the award and any documents annexed to the award: see *Hok Sport Ltd v Aintree Racecourse Ltd* [2003] BLR 155 at 160. However, the court should also receive any document referred to in the award, which the court needs to read in order to determine a question of law arising out of the award: see *Kershaw Mechanical Services Ltd v Kendrick Construction Ltd* [2006] EWHC (TCC).

10.4.2 On receiving notice of permission being granted, or on issuing an arbitration claim form in a case where leave to appeal is not required, the parties should notify the court of their joint estimate or differing estimates of the time needed for the hearing of the appeal.

10.4.3 The hearing of the appeal is to be in open court unless an application (with notice) has previously been made that the hearing should be wholly or in part held in private and the court has directed that this course should be followed.

10.5 Section 68 applications – Serious Irregularity

10.5.1 In some arbitration claims arising out of construction and engineering arbitrations, a party will seek to appeal a question of law and, at the same time, seek to challenge the award under section 68 of the Arbitration Act 1996 on the grounds of serious irregularity. This raises questions of procedure, since material may be admissible in a section 68 application which is inadmissible on an application or appeal under section 69. Similarly, it may not be appropriate for all applications to be heard together. A decision is needed as to the order in which the applications should be heard, whether there should be one or more separate hearings to deal with them and whether or not the same judge should deal with all applications. Where a party intends to raise applications under both sections of the Arbitration Act 1996, they should be issued in the same arbitration claim form or in separate claim forms issued together. The court should be informed that separate applications are intended and asked for directions as to how to proceed.

10.5.2 The court will give directions as to how the section 68 and section 69 applications will be dealt with before hearing or determining any application. These directions will normally be given in writing but, where necessary or if such is applied for by a party, the court will hold a directions hearing at which directions will be given. The directions will be given following the service of any documentation by the defendant in answer to all applications raised by the claimant.

10.6 Successive awards and successive applications

10.6.1 Some construction and engineering arbitrations give rise to two or more separate awards issued at different times. Where arbitration applications arise under more than one of these awards, any second or subsequent application, whether arising from the same or a different award, should be referred to the same judge who has heard previous applications. Where more than one judge has heard previous applications, the court should be asked to direct to which judge any subsequent application is to be referred.

10.7 Other applications and Enforcement

10.7.1 All other arbitration claims, and any other matter arising in an appeal or an application concerning alleged serious irregularity, will be dealt with by the TCC in the same manner as is provided for in **CPR Part 62, Practice Direction – Arbitration** and **Section O of The Admiralty and Commercial Courts Guide**.

10.7.2 All applications for permission to enforce arbitration awards are governed by **Section III of Part 62 (rules 62.17- 62.19)**.

10.7.3 An application for permission to enforce an award in the same manner as a judgment or order of the court may be made in an arbitration claim form without notice and must be supported by written evidence in accordance with **CPR 62.18(6)**. Two copies of the draft order must accompany the application, and the form of the order sought must correspond to the terms of the award.

10.7.4 An order made without notice giving permission to enforce the award:

- must give the defendant 14 days after service of the order (or longer, if the order is to be served outside the jurisdiction) to apply to set it aside;

- must state that it may not be enforced until after the expiry of the 14 days (or any longer period specified) or until any application to set aside the order has been finally disposed of: **CPR 62.18(9) and (10)**.

10.7.5 On considering an application to enforce without notice, the judge may direct that, instead, the arbitration claim form must be served on specified parties, with the result that the application will then continue as an arbitration claim in accordance with the procedure set out in **Section I of Part 62**: see **CPR 62.18(1)-(3)**.

Section 11. Disclosure

11.1 General

11.1.1 **CPR 31.5** now provides a menu of different disclosure options, of which standard disclosure is but one.

11.1.2 What order is for disclosure is appropriate will normally be considered and made at the first case management conference. This is governed by **CPR Part 31** and the Practice Direction supplementing it. This provides for various alternatives: (a) no disclosure (b) an order that a party discloses the documents on which it relies and at the same time requests any specific disclosure that it requires from the other parties (c) disclosure on an issue by issue basis (d) an order that each party discloses documents that it is reasonable to suppose will support its own case or damage that of another party (e) standard disclosure or any other form of disclosure..

In relation to electronic disclosure, see the provisions requiring the exchange of Electronic Documents Questionnaires (**CPR 31.22** and **PD13B**).

11.2 Limiting disclosure and the cost of disclosure

11.2.1 In many cases being conducted in the TCC, standard disclosure will not be appropriate. This may for any one or more of the following reasons:

- The amount of documentation may be considerable, given the complexity of the dispute and the underlying contract or contracts, and the process of giving standard disclosure may consequently be disproportionate to the issues and sums in dispute.

- The parties may have many of the documents in common from their previous dealings so that disclosure is not necessary or desirable.

- The parties may have provided informal disclosure and inspection of the majority of these documents, for example when complying with the pre-action Protocol.

- The cost of providing standard disclosure may be disproportionate.

- In such cases, the parties should seek to agree upon a more limited form of disclosure, whether in one of the forms set out in CPR 31.5 or otherwise, or to dispense with formal disclosure altogether.

11.2.2 Where disclosure is to be provided, the parties should consider whether it is necessary for lists of documents to be prepared or whether special arrangements should be agreed as to the form of listing and identifying disclosable documents, the method, timing and location of inspection and the manner of copying or providing copies of documents. Where documents are scattered over several locations, or are located overseas or are in a foreign language, special arrangements will also need to be considered. Thought should also be given to providing disclosure in stages or to reducing the scope of disclosure by providing the relevant material in other forms.

11.2.3 Electronic data and documents give rise to particular problems as to searching, preserving, listing, inspecting and other aspects of discovery and inspection. These problems should be considered and, if necessary made the subject of special directions. Furthermore, in many cases disclosure, inspection and the provision of documents in electronic form or electronic copies of hard copies may be undertaken using information technology. Attention is drawn to the relevant provisions in **CPR Part 31** and **Practice Direction 31B: Disclosure of Electronic Documents** A protocol for e-disclosure prepared by TeCSA, TECBAR and the Society for Computers and Law was launched on 1 November 2013 which provides a procedure and guidance in relation to these matters. The protocol was developed in consultation with the judges of the TCC, and is likely to be ordered by the court if the parties have not agreed on any alternative by the time of the first CMC. It is available on the TeCSA website.

11.2.4 All these matters should be agreed between the parties. If it is necessary to raise any of these matters with the court they should be raised, if possible, at the first CMC. If points arise on disclosure after the first CMC, they may well be capable of being dealt with by the court on paper.

Section 12. Witness statements and factual evidence for use at trial

12.1 Witness statements

12.1.1 Witness statements should be prepared generally in accordance with **CPR Part 22.1** (documents verified by a statement of truth) and **CPR Part 32** (provisions governing the evidence of witnesses) and their practice directions, particularly **paragraphs 17 to 22 of the Practice Direction supplementing CPR Part 32**.

12.1.2 Unless otherwise directed by the court, witness statements should not have annexed to them copies of other documents and should not reproduce or paraphrase at length passages from other documents. The only exception arises where a specific document needs to be annexed to the statement in order to make that statement reasonably intelligible.

12.1.3 When preparing witness statements, attention should be paid to the following matters:

- Even when prepared by a legal representative or other professional, the witness statement should be, so far as practicable, in the witness's own words.

- The witness statement should indicate which matters are within the witness's own knowledge and which are matters of information and belief. Where the witness is stating matters of hearsay or of either information or belief, the source of that evidence should also be stated.

- A witness statement should be no longer than necessary and should not be argumentative.

- A witness statement should not contain extensive reference to contemporaneous documents by way of narrative.

- The witness statement must include a statement by the witness that he believes the facts stated to be true.

12.1.4 Costs. If at any stage the judge considers that the way in which witness statements have been prepared, particularly by the inclusion of extensive irrelevant or peripheral material, is likely to lead or has led to inefficiency in the conduct of the proceedings or to unnecessary time or costs being spent, the judge may order that the witness should re-submit the witness statement in whole or part and may make a costs order disallowing costs or ordering costs to be paid, either on the basis of a summary assessment or by giving a direction to the costs judge as to what costs should be disallowed or paid on a detailed assessment: see **paragraph 5.5.5** above.

12.2 Other matters concerned with witness statements

12.2.1 Foreign language. If a witness is not sufficiently fluent in English to give his evidence in English, the witness statement should be in his or her own language and an authenticated translation provided. Where the witness has a broken command of English, the statement may be drafted by others so as to express the witness's evidence as accurately as possible. In that situation, however, the witness statement should indicate that this process of interpolation has occurred and also should explain the extent of the witness's command of English and how and to what parts of the witness statement the process of interpolation has occurred.

12.2.2 Reluctant witness. Sometimes a witness is unwilling or not permitted or is unavailable to provide a witness statement before the trial. The party seeking to adduce this evidence should comply with the provisions of **CPR 32.9** concerned with the provision of witness summaries.

12.2.3 Hearsay. Parties should keep in mind the need to give appropriate notice of their intention to rely on hearsay evidence or the contents of documents without serving a witness statement from their maker or from the originator of the evidence contained in those documents. The appropriate procedure is contained in **CPR 33.1 – 33.5**.

12.2.4 Supplementary Witness Statements. The general principle is that a witness should set out in their witness statement their complete evidence relevant to the issues in the case. The witness statement should not include evidence on the basis that it might be needed depending on what the other party's witnesses might say. The correct procedure in such cases is for the witness to provide a supplementary witness statement or, as necessary, for a new witness to provide a witness statement limited to responding to particular matters contained in the other party's witness statement and to seek permission accordingly. In some cases it might be appropriate for the court to provide for the service of supplementary witness statements as part of the order at the first case management conference.

12.2.5 Supplementary Evidence in Chief. The relevant witness evidence should be contained in the witness statements, or if appropriate witness summaries, served in advance of the hearing. Where, for whatever reason, this has not happened and the witness has relevant important evidence to give, particularly where the need for such evidence has only become apparent during the trial, the judge has a discretion to permit supplementary evidence in chief.

12.3 Cross-referencing

12.3.1 Where a substantial number of documents will be adduced in evidence or contained in the trial bundles, it is of considerable assistance to the court and to all concerned if the relevant page references are annotated in the margins of the copy witness statements. It is accepted that this is a time-consuming exercise, the need for which will be considered at the PTR, and it will only be ordered where it is both appropriate and proportionate to do so. See further **paragraphs 14.5.1** and **15.2.3** below.

12.4 Video link

12.4.1 If any witness (whose witness statement has been served and who is required to give oral evidence) is located outside England and Wales or would find a journey to court inconvenient or impracticable, his evidence might be given via a video link. Thought should be given before the PTR to the question whether this course would be appropriate and proportionate. Such evidence is regularly received by the TCC and facilities for its reception, whether in appropriate court premises or at a convenient venue outside the court building, are now readily available.

12.4.2 Any application for a video link direction and any question relating to the manner in which such evidence is to be given should be dealt with at the PTR. Attention is drawn to the Video-conferencing Protocol set out at Annex 3 to the **Practice Direction supplementing CPR Part 32 - Evidence**. The procedure described in Annex 3 is followed by the TCC.

Section 13. Expert evidence

13.1 Nature of expert evidence

13.1.1 Expert evidence is evidence as to matters of a technical or scientific nature and will generally include the opinions of the expert. The quality and reliability of expert evidence will depend upon (a) the experience and the technical or scientific qualifications of the expert and (b) the accuracy of the factual material that is used by the expert for his assessment. Expert evidence is dealt with in detail in **CPR Part 35** ("Experts and Assessors") and in the **Practice Direction supplementing Part 35**. Particular attention should be paid to all these provisions, given the detailed reliance on expert evidence in most TCC actions. Particular attention should also be paid to the "Protocol for the instruction of experts to give evidence in civil claims" annexed to **Practice Direction 35 – Experts and Assessors** (it should be noted that this Protocol is expected to be replaced at some point with the "Guidance for the instruction of experts to give evidence in Civil claims").

13.1.2 The attention of the parties is drawn to the specific requirements in relation to the terms of the expert's declaration at the conclusion of the report.

13.1.3 The provisions in **CPR Part 35** are concerned with the terms upon which the court may receive expert evidence. These provisions are principally applicable to independently instructed expert witnesses. In cases where a party is a professional or a professional has played a significant part in the subject matter of the action, opinion evidence will almost inevitably be included in the witness statements. Any points arising from such evidence (if they cannot be resolved by agreement) can be dealt with by the judge on an application or at the PTR.

13.2 Control of expert evidence

13.2.1 Expert evidence is frequently needed and used in TCC cases. Experts are often appointed at an early stage. Most types of case heard in the TCC involve more than one expertise and some, even when the dispute is concerned with relatively small sums, involve several different experts. Such disputes include those concerned with building failures and defects, delay and disruption, dilapidations, subsidence caused by tree roots and the supply of software systems. However, given the cost of preparing such evidence, the parties and the court must, from the earliest pre-action phase of a dispute until the conclusion of the trial, seek to make effective and proportionate use of experts. The scope of any expert evidence must be limited to what is necessary for the requirements of the particular case.

13.2.2 At the first CMC, or thereafter, the court may be asked to determine whether the cost of instructing experts is proportionate to the amount at issue in the proceedings, and the importance of the case to the parties. When considering an application for permission to call an expert, the court is to be provided with estimates of the experts' costs: see **CPR 35.4(2)**. The permission may limit the issues to be considered by the experts: see **CPR 35.4(3)**. This should ordinarily be linked to the party's costs budget.

13.2.3 The parties should also be aware that the court has the power to limit the amount of the expert's fees that a party may recover pursuant to **CPR 35.4 (4)**.

Section 13. Expert evidence

13.3 Prior to and at the first CMC

13.3.1 There is an unresolved tension arising from the need for parties to instruct and rely on expert opinions from an early pre-action stage and the need for the court to seek, wherever possible, to reduce the cost of expert evidence by dispensing with it altogether or by encouraging the appointment of jointly instructed experts. This tension arises because the court can only consider directing joint appointments or limiting expert evidence long after a party may have incurred the cost of obtaining expert evidence and have already relied on it. Parties should be aware of this tension. So far as possible, the parties should avoid incurring the costs of expert evidence on uncontroversial matters or matters of the kind referred to in paragraph 13.4.3 below, before the first CMC has been held.

13.3.2 In cases where it is not appropriate for the court to order a single joint expert, it is imperative that, wherever possible, the parties' experts co-operate fully with one another. This is particularly important where tests, surveys, investigations, sample gathering or other technical methods of obtaining primary factual evidence are needed. It is often critical to ensure that any laboratory testing or experiments are carried out by the experts together, pursuant to an agreed procedure. Alternatively, the respective experts may agree that a particular firm or laboratory shall carry out specified tests or analyses on behalf of all parties.

13.3.3 Parties should, where possible, disclose initial or preliminary reports to opposing parties prior to any pre-action protocol meeting, if only on a without prejudice basis. Such early disclosure will assist in early settlement or mediation discussions and in helping the parties to define and confine the issues in dispute with a corresponding saving in costs.

13.3.4 Before and at the first CMC and at each subsequent pre-trial stage of the action, the parties should give careful thought to the following matters:

- The number, disciplines and identity of the expert witnesses they are considering instructing as their own experts or as single joint experts.

- The precise issues which each expert is to address in his/her reports, to discuss without prejudice with opposing parties' experts and give evidence about at the trial.

- The timing of any meeting, agreed statement or report.

- Any appropriate or necessary tests, inspections, sampling or investigations that could be undertaken jointly or in collaboration with other experts. Any such measures should be preceded by a meeting of relevant experts at which an appropriate testing or other protocol is devised. This would cover (i) all matters connected with the process in question and its recording and (ii) the sharing and agreement of any resulting data or evidence.

- Any common method of analysis, investigation or reporting where it is appropriate or proportionate that such should be adopted by all relevant experts. An example of this would be an agreement as to the method to be used to analyse the cause and extent of any relevant period of delay in a construction project, where such is in issue in the case.

- The availability and length of time that experts will realistically require to complete the tasks assigned to them.

(Note that the amendment to **CPR 35.4(3)** permits the order granting permission to specify the issues which the expert evidence should address.)

13.3.5 In so far as the matters set out in the previous paragraph cannot be agreed, the court will give appropriate directions. In giving permission for the reception of any expert evidence, the court will ordinarily order the exchange of such evidence, with a definition of the expert's area of expertise and a clear description of the issues about which that expert is permitted to give evidence. It is preferable that, at the first CMC or as soon as possible thereafter, the parties should provide the court with the name(s) of their expert(s).

13.4 Single joint experts

13.4.1 An order may be made, at the first CMC or thereafter, that a single joint expert should address particular issues between the parties. Such an order would be made pursuant to **CPR Parts 35.7 and 35.8**.

13.4.2 Single joint experts are not usually appropriate for the principal liability disputes in a large case, or in a case where considerable sums have been spent on an expert in the pre-action stage. They are generally inappropriate where the issue involves questions of risk assessment or professional competence.

13.4.3 On the other hand, single joint experts can often be appropriate:

- in low value cases, where technical evidence is required but the cost of adversarial expert evidence may be prohibitive;
- where the topic with which the single joint expert's report deals is a separate and self-contained part of the case, such as the valuation of particular heads of claim;
- where there is a subsidiary issue, which requires particular expertise of a relatively uncontroversial nature to resolve;
- where testing or analysis is required, and this can conveniently be done by one laboratory or firm on behalf of all parties.

13.4.4 Where a single joint expert is to be appointed or is to be directed by the court, the parties should attempt to devise a protocol covering all relevant aspects of the appointment (save for those matters specifically provided for by **CPR 35.6, 35.7 and 35.8**).

13.4.5 The matters to be considered should include: any ceiling on fees and disbursements that are to be charged and payable by the parties; how, when and by whom fees will be paid to the expert on an interim basis pending any costs order in the proceedings; how the expert's fees will be secured; how the terms of reference are to be agreed; what is to happen if terms of reference cannot be agreed; how and to whom the jointly appointed expert may address further enquiries and from whom he should seek further information and documents; the timetable for preparing any report or for undertaking any other preparatory step; the possible effect on such timetable of any supplementary or further instructions. Where these matters cannot be agreed, an application to the court, which may often be capable of being dealt with as a paper application, will be necessary.

13.4.6 The usual procedure for a single joint expert will involve:

- The preparation of the expert's instructions. These instructions should clearly identify those issues or matters where the parties are in conflict, whether on the facts or on matters of opinion. If the parties can agree joint instructions, then a single set of

Section 13. Expert evidence

instructions should be delivered to the expert. However, rule 35.8 expressly permits separate instructions and these are necessary where joint instructions cannot be agreed

- The preparation of the agreed bundle, which is to be provided to the expert. This bundle must include CPR Part 35, the Practice Direction supplementing Part 35 and the section 13 of the TCC Guide.

- The preparation and production of the expert's report.

- The provision to the expert of any written questions from the parties, which the expert must answer in writing.

13.4.7 In most cases the single joint expert's report, supplemented by any written answers to questions from the parties, will be sufficient for the purposes of the trial. Sometimes, however, it is necessary for a single joint expert to be called to give oral evidence. In those circumstances, the usual practice is for the judge to call the expert and then allow each party the opportunity to cross-examine. Such cross-examination should be conducted with appropriate restraint, since the witness has been instructed by the parties. Where the expert's report is strongly in favour of one party's position, it may be appropriate to allow only the other party to cross-examine.

13.5 Meetings of experts

13.5.1 The desirability of holding without prejudice meetings between experts at all stages of the pre-trial preparation should be kept in mind. The desired outcome of such meetings is to produce a document whose contents are agreed and which defines common positions or each expert's differing position. The purpose of such meetings includes the following:

- The provision to the expert of any written questions from the parties, which the expert must answer in writing.

- to define a party's technical case and to inform opposing parties of the details of that case;

- to clear up confusion and to remedy any lack of information or understanding of a party's technical case in the minds of opposing experts;

- to identify the issues about which any expert is to give evidence;

- to narrow differences and to reach agreement on as many "expert" issues as possible; and

- to assist in providing an agenda for the trial and for cross examination of expert witnesses, and to limit the scope and length of the trial as much as possible.

13.5.2 In many cases it will be helpful for the parties' respective legal advisors to provide assistance as to the agenda and topics to be discussed at an experts' meeting. However, (save in exceptional circumstances and with the permission of the judge) the legal advisors must not attend the meeting. They must not attempt to dictate what the experts say at the meeting.

13.5.3 Experts' meetings can sometimes usefully take place at the site of the dispute. Thought is needed as to who is to make the necessary arrangements for access, particularly where the site is occupied or in the control of a non-party. Expert meetings are often more productive, if (a) the expert of one party (usually the claimant) is appointed as chairman and (b) the experts exchange in advance agendas listing the topics each wishes to raise and identifying any relevant material which they intend to introduce or rely on during the meeting.

13.5.4 It is generally sensible for the experts to meet at least once before they exchange their reports.

13.6 Experts' Joint Statements

13.6.1 Following the experts' meetings, and pursuant to **CPR 35.12 (3)**, the judge will almost always require the experts to produce a signed statement setting out the issues which have been agreed, and those issues which have not been agreed, together with a short summary of the reasons for their disagreement. In any TCC case in which expert evidence has an important role to play, this statement is a critical document and it must be as clear as possible.

13.6.2 It should be noted that, even where experts have been unable to agree very much, it is of considerable importance that the statement sets out their disagreements and the reasons for them. Such disagreements as formulated in the joint statement are likely to form an important element of the agenda for the trial of the action.

13.6.3 Whilst the parties' legal advisors may assist in identifying issues which the statement should address, those legal advisors must not be involved in either negotiating or drafting the experts' joint statement. Legal advisors should only invite the experts to consider amending any draft joint statement in exceptional circumstances where there are serious concerns that the court may misunderstand or be misled by the terms of that joint statement. Any such concerns should be raised with all experts involved in the joint statement.

13.7 Experts' Reports

13.7.1 It is the duty of an expert to help the court on matters within his expertise. This duty overrides any duty to his client: **CPR 35.3**. Each expert's report must be independent and unbiased. **Paragraphs 3(vii), 3.3.1(vi) and 5.5(i) of the Pre-Action Protocol for Construction and Engineering Disputes** contain provisions as to experts in TCC cases and accordingly **Annex C to the Practice Direction – Pre-Action Conduct** does not apply: see **The Practice Direction – Pre-Action Conduct.**

13.7.2 The parties must identify the issues with which each expert should deal in his or her report. Thereafter, it is for the expert to draft and decide upon the detailed contents and format of the report, so as to conform to **the Practice Direction supplementing CPR Part 35** and **the Protocol for the Instruction of Experts to give Evidence in Civil Claims**. It is appropriate, however, for the party instructing an expert to indicate that the report (a) should be as short as is reasonably possible; (b) should not set out copious extracts from other documents; (c) should identify the source of any opinion or data relied upon; and (d) should not annex or exhibit more than is reasonably necessary to support the opinions expressed in the report. In addition, as set out in **paragraph 15.2 of the Protocol for the Instruction of Experts to give Evidence in Civil Claims**, legal advisors may also invite experts to consider amendments to their reports to ensure accuracy, internal consistency, completeness, relevance to the issues or clarity of reports.

13.8 Presentation of Expert Evidence

13.8.1 The purpose of expert evidence is to assist the court on matters of a technical or scientific nature. Particularly in large and complex cases where the evidence has developed through a number of experts' joint statements and reports, it is often helpful for the expert at the commencement of his or her evidence to provide the court with a summary of their views on the main issues. This can be done orally or by way of a PowerPoint or similar presentation. The purpose is not to introduce new evidence but to explain the existing evidence.

13.8.2 The way in which expert evidence is given is a matter to be considered at the PTR. However where there are a number of experts of different disciplines the court will consider the best way for the expert evidence to be given. It is now quite usual for all expert evidence to follow the completion of the witness evidence from all parties. At that stage there are a number of possible ways of presenting evidence including:

- For one party to call all its expert evidence, followed by each party calling all of its expert evidence.

- For one party to call its expert in a particular discipline, followed by the other parties calling their experts in that discipline. This process would then be repeated for the experts of all disciplines.

- For one party to call its expert or experts to deal with a particular issue, followed by the other parties calling their expert or experts to deal with that issues. This process would then be repeated for all the expert issues.

- For the experts for all parties to be called to give concurrent evidence, colloquially referred to as "hot-tubbing". When this method is adopted there is generally a need for experts to be cross-examined on general matters and key issues before they are invited to give evidence concurrently on particular issues. Procedures vary but, for instance, a party may ask its expert to explain his or her view on an issue, then ask the other party's expert for his or her view on that issue and then return to that party's expert for a comment on that view. Alternatively, or in addition, questions may be asked by the judge or the experts themselves may each ask the other questions. The process is often most useful where there are a large number of items to be dealt with and the procedure allows the court to have the evidence on each item dealt with on the same occasion rather than having the evidence divided with the inability to have each expert's views expressed clearly. Frequently, it allows the extent of agreement and reason for disagreement to be seen more clearly. The giving of concurrent evidence may be consented to by the parties and the judge will consider whether, in the absence of consent, any modification is required to the procedure for giving concurrent evidence set out in the CPR (at **PD35, paragraph 11)**.

Section 14. The Pre-Trial Review

14.1 Timing and Attendance

14.1.1 The Pre-Trial Review ("PTR") will usually be fixed for a date that is 4-6 weeks in advance of the commencement of the trial itself. It is vital that the advocates, who are going to conduct the trial, should attend the PTR and every effort should be made to achieve this. It is usually appropriate for the PTR to be conducted by way of an oral hearing or, at the very least, a telephone conference, so that the judge may raise matters of trial management even if the parties can agree beforehand any outstanding directions and the detailed requirements for the management of the trial. In appropriate cases, e.g. where the amount in issue is disproportionate to the costs of a full trial, the judge may wish to consider with the parties whether there are other ways in which the dispute might be resolved.

14.2 Documents

14.2.1 The parties must complete the PTR Questionnaire (a copy of which is at **Appendix C** attached) and return it in good time to the court. In addition, the judge may order the parties to provide other documents for the particular purposes of the PTR.

14.2.2 In an appropriate case, the advocates for each party should prepare a Note for the PTR, which addresses:

- any outstanding directions or interlocutory steps still to be taken;
- the issues for determination at the trial;
- the most efficient way in which those issues might be dealt with at the trial, including all questions of timetabling of witnesses.

These Notes should be provided to the court **by 4 pm one clear working day before the PTR**.

14.2.3 The parties should also ensure that, for the PTR, the court has an up-to-date permanent case management bundle, together with a bundle of the evidence (factual and expert) that has been exchanged. This Bundle should also be made available to the court **by 4 pm one clear day before the PTR**.

14.3 Outstanding Directions

14.3.1 It can sometimes be the case that there are still outstanding interlocutory steps to be taken at the time of the PTR. That will usually mean that one, or more, of the parties has not complied with an earlier direction of the court. In that event, the court is likely to require prompt compliance, and may make costs orders to reflect the delays.

14.3.2 Sometimes a party will wish to make an application to be heard at the same time as the PTR. Such a practice is unsatisfactory, because it uses up time allocated for the PTR, and it gives rise to potential uncertainty close to the trial date. It is always better for a party, if it possibly can, to make all necessary applications well in advance of the PTR. If that is not practicable, the court should be asked to allocate additional time for the PTR, in order to accommodate specific applications. If additional time is not available, such applications will not generally be entertained.

14.4 Issues

14.4.1 The parties should, if possible, provide the judge at the PTR with an agreed list of the main issues for the forthcoming trial (including, where appropriate, a separate list of technical issues to be covered by the experts). The list of issues should not be extensive and should focus on the key issues. It is provided as a working document to assist in the management of the trial and not as a substitute for the pleadings.

14.4.2 If the parties are unable to agree the precise formulation of the issues, they should provide to the court their respective formulations. Because the list of issues should focus on the key issues the opportunity for disagreement should be minimised. The judge will note the parties' formulations, but, because the issues are those which arise on the pleadings, is unlikely to give a ruling on this matter at the PTR unless the different formulations show that there is a dispute as to the pleaded case.

14.5 Timetabling and Trial Logistics

14.5.1 Much of the PTR will be devoted to a consideration of the appropriate timetable for the trial, and other logistical matters. These will commonly include:

- Directions in respect of oral and written openings and any necessary reading time for the judge.

- Sequence of oral evidence; for example, whether all the factual evidence should be called before the expert evidence.

- Timetabling of oral evidence. To facilitate this exercise, the advocates should, after discussing the matter and whether some evidence can be agreed, provide a draft timetable indicating which witnesses need to be cross-examined and the periods during it is proposed that they should attend. Such timetables are working documents.

- The manner in which expert evidence is to be presented: see **paragraph 13.8** above.

- Whether any form of time limits should be imposed. (Since the purpose of time limits is to ensure that that the costs incurred and the resources devoted to the trial are proportionate, this is for the benefit of the parties. The judge will endeavour to secure agreement to any time limits imposed.)

- Directions in respect of the trial bundle: when it should be agreed and lodged; the contents and structure of the bundle; avoidance of duplication; whether witness statements and/or expert reports should be annotated with cross references to page numbers in the main bundle (see **paragraph 12.3** above); and similar matters.

- Whether there should be a core bundle; if so how it should be prepared and what it should contain. (The court will order a core bundle in any case where (a) there is substantial documentation and (b) having regard to the issues it is appropriate and proportionate to put the parties to cost of preparing a core bundle).

- Rules governing any email communication during trial between the parties and the court.

- Any directions relating to the use of electronic document management systems at trial (this subject to agreement between the parties).

Section 14. The Pre-Trial Review

- Any directions relating to the use of simultaneous transcription at trial (this subject to agreement between the parties).
- Whether there should be a view by the judge.
- The form and timing of closing submissions.
- Whether there is a need for a special court (because of the number of parties or any particular facilities required).
- Whether there is need for evidence by video link.
- Any applications for review or variation of costs budgets.

14.5.2 The topics identified in paragraph 14.5.1 are discussed in greater detail in section 15 below.

Section 15. The trial

15.1 Arrangements prior to the trial – witnesses

15.1.1 Prior to the trial the parties' legal representatives should seek to agree on the following matters, in so far as they have not been resolved at the PTR: the order in which witnesses are to be called to give evidence; which witnesses are not required for cross examination and whose evidence in consequence may be adduced entirely from their witness statements; the timetable for the trial and the length of time each advocate is to be allowed for a brief opening speech. When planning the timetable, it should be noted that trials normally take place on Mondays to Thursdays, since Fridays are reserved for applications.

15.1.2 The witnesses should be notified in advance of the trial as to: (a) when each is required to attend court and (b) the approximate period of time for which he or she will be required to attend.

15.1.3 It is the parties' responsibility to ensure that their respective witnesses are ready to attend court at the appropriate time. It is never satisfactory for witnesses to be interposed, out of their proper place. It would require exceptional circumstances for the trial to be adjourned for any period of time because of the unavailability of a witness.

15.2 Opening notes, trial bundle and oral openings

15.2.1 Opening notes. Unless the court has ordered otherwise, each party's advocate should provide an opening note, which outlines that party's case in relation to each of the issues identified at the PTR. Each opening note should indicate which documents (giving their page numbers in the trial bundle) that party considers that the judge should pre-read. The claimant's opening note should include a neutral summary of the background facts, as well as a chronology and cast list. The other parties' opening notes should be shorter and should assume familiarity with the factual background. In general terms, all opening notes should be of modest length and proportionate to the size and complexity of the case. Subject to any specific directions at the PTR, the claimant's opening note should be served two clear working days before the start of the trial; the other parties opening notes should be served by 1 pm on the last working day before the trial.

15.2.2 Trial bundles. Subject to any specific directions at the PTR, the trial bundles should be delivered to court at least three working days before the hearing. It is helpful for the party delivering the trial bundles to liaise in advance with the judge's clerk, in order to discuss practical arrangements, particularly when a large number of bundles are to be delivered. The parties should provide for the court an agreed index of all trial bundles. There should also be an index at the front of each bundle. This should be a helpful guide to the contents of that bundle. (An interminable list, itemising every letter or sheet of paper is not a helpful guide. Nor are bland descriptions, such as "exhibit "JT3", of much help to the bundle user.) The spines and inside covers of bundles should be clearly labelled with the bundle number and brief description.

15.2.3 As a general rule the trial bundles should be clearly divided between statements of case, orders, contracts, witness statements, expert reports and correspondence/minutes of meetings. The correspondence/minutes of meetings should be in a separate bundle or bundles and in chronological order. Documents should only be included if they are relevant to the issues in the case or helpful as background material. Documents should not be duplicated, and unnecessary duplication of e-mail threads should be avoided where possible. Exhibits to witness statements should generally be omitted, since the documents to which the witnesses are referring will be found elsewhere in the bundles. The bundles of contract documents and correspondence/minutes of meetings should be paginated, so that every page has a discrete number. The other bundles could be dealt with in one of two ways:

- The statements of case, witness statements and expert reports could be placed in bundles and continuously paginated.

- Alternatively, the statements of case, witness statements and expert reports could be placed behind tabbed divider cards, and then the internal numbering of each such document can be used at trial. If the latter course is adopted, it is vital that the internal page numbering of each expert report continues sequentially through the appendices to that report.

The court encourages the parties to provide original copies of expert reports in this way so that any photographs, plans or charts are legible in their original size and, where appropriate, in colour. In such cases sequential numbering of every page including appendices is essential.

The ultimate objective is to create trial bundles, which are user friendly and in which any page can be identified with clarity and brevity (e.g. "bundle G page 273" or "defence page 3" or "Dr Smith page 12"). The core bundle, if there is one (as to which see **paragraph 14.5.1** above), will be a separate bundle with its own pagination or contain documents from other bundles retaining the original bundle number behind a divider marked with the bundle number.

15.2.4   In document heavy cases the parties should consider the use of an electronic document management system that can be used at the trial. In order for the most effective use to be made of such a system, it is a matter that may require consideration at an early stage in the litigation.

15.2.5   Opening speeches. Subject to any directions made at the PTR, each party will be permitted to make an opening speech. These speeches should be prepared and presented on the basis that the judge will have pre-read the opening notes and the documents identified by the parties for pre-reading. The claimant's advocate may wish to highlight the main features of the claimant's case and/or to deal with matters raised in the other parties' opening notes. The other parties' advocates will then make shorter opening speeches, emphasising the main features of their own cases and/or responding to matters raised in the claimant's opening speech.

15.2.6   It is not usually necessary or desirable to embark upon legal argument during opening speeches. It is, however, helpful to foreshadow those legal arguments which (a) explain the relevance of particular parts of the evidence or (b) will assist the judge in following a party's case that is to be presented during the trial.

15.2.7   Narrowing of issues. Experience shows that often the issues between the parties progressively narrow as the trial advances. Sometimes this process begins during the course of opening speeches. Weaker contentions may be abandoned and responses to those contentions may become irrelevant. The advocates will co-operate in focussing their submissions and the evidence on the true issues between the parties, as those issues are thrown into sharper relief by the adversarial process.

15.3 Simultaneous transcription

15.3.1 Many trials in the TCC, including the great majority of the longer trials, are conducted with simultaneous transcripts of the evidence being provided. There are a number of transcribing systems available. It is now common for a system to be used involving simultaneous transcription onto screens situated in court. However, systems involving the production of the transcript in hard or electronic form at the end of the day or even after a longer period of time are also used. The parties must make the necessary arrangements with one of the companies who provide this service. The court can provide a list, on request, of all companies who offer such a service.

15.3.2 In long trials or those which involve any significant amount of detailed or technical evidence, simultaneous transcripts are helpful. Furthermore, they enable all but the shortest trials to be conducted so as to reduce the overall length of the trial appreciably, since the judge does not have to note the evidence or submissions in longhand as the trial proceeds. Finally, a simultaneous transcript makes the task of summarising a case in closing submissions and preparing the judgment somewhat easier. It reduces both the risk of error or omission and the amount of time needed to prepare a reserved judgment.

15.3.3 If possible, the parties should have agreed at or before the PTR whether a simultaneous transcript is to be employed. It is usual for parties to agree to share the cost of a simultaneous transcript as an interim measure pending the assessment or agreement of costs, when this cost is assessable and payable as part of the costs in the case. Sometimes, a party cannot or will not agree to an interim cost sharing arrangement. If so, it is permissible for one party to bear the cost, but the court cannot be provided with a transcript unless all parties have equal access to the transcript. Unlike transcripts for use during an appeal, there is no available means of obtaining from public funds the cost of a transcript for use at the trial.

15.4 Time limits

15.4.1 Generally trials in the TCC are conducted under some form of time limit arrangement. Several variants of time limit arrangements are available, but the TCC has developed the practice of imposing flexible guidelines in the form of directions as to the sharing of the time allotted for the trial. These are not mandatory but an advocate should ordinarily be expected to comply with them.

15.4.2 The practice is, in the usual case, for the court to fix, or for the parties to agree, at the PTR or before trial an overall length of time for the trial and overall lengths of time within that period for the evidence and submissions. The part of those overall lengths of time that will be allocated to each party must then be agreed or directed.

15.4.3 The amount of time to be allotted to each party will not usually be the same. The guide is that each party should have as much time as is reasonably needed for it to present its case and to test and cross examine any opposing case, but no longer.

15.4.4 Before the trial, the parties should agree a running order of the witnesses and the approximate length of time required for each witness. A trial timetable should be provided to the court when the trial starts and, in long trials, regularly updated.

15.4.5 The practice of imposing a strict guillotine on the examination or cross examination of witnesses, is not normally appropriate. Flexibility is encouraged, but the agreed or directed time limits should not ordinarily be exceeded without good reason. It is unfair on a party, if that party's advocate has confined cross-examination to the agreed time limits, but an opposing party then greatly exceeds the corresponding time limits that it has been allocated.

15.4.6 An alternative form of time limit, which is sometimes agreed between the parties and approved by the court, is the "chess clock arrangement". The available time is divided equally between the parties, to be used by the parties as they see fit. Thus each side has X hours. One representative on each side operates the chess clock. The judge has discretion "to stop the clock" in exceptional circumstances. A chess clock arrangement is only practicable in a two-party case.

15.5 Oral evidence

15.5.1 Evidence in chief is ordinarily adduced by the witness confirming on oath the truth and accuracy of the previously served witness statement or statements. A limited number of supplementary oral questions will usually be allowed (a) to give the witness an opportunity to become familiar with the procedure and (b) to cover points omitted by mistake from the witness statement or which have arisen subsequent to its preparation.

15.5.2 In some cases, particularly those involving allegations of dishonest, disreputable or culpable conduct or where significant disputes of fact are not documented or evidenced in writing, it is desirable that the core elements of a witness's evidence-in-chief are given orally. The giving of such evidence orally will often assist the court in assessing the credibility or reliability of a witness.

15.5.3 If any party wishes such evidence to be given orally, a direction should be sought either at the PTR or during the openings to that effect. Where evidence in chief is given orally, the rules relating to the use of witness statements in cross-examination and to the adducing of the statement in evidence at any subsequent stage of the trial remain in force and may be relied on by any party.

15.5.4 It is usual for all evidence of fact from all parties to be adduced before expert evidence and for the experts to give evidence in groups with all experts in a particular discipline giving their evidence in sequence: see **paragraph 13.8.2** above for ways for expert evidence to be given. Usually, but not invariably, the order of witnesses will be such that the claimant's witnesses give their evidence first, followed by all the witnesses for each of the other parties in turn. If a party wishes a different order of witnesses to that normally followed, the agreement of the parties or a direction from the judge must be obtained in advance.

15.5.5 In a multi-party case, attention should be given (when the timetable is being discussed) to the order of cross-examination and to the extent to which particular topics will be covered by particular cross-examiners. Where these matters cannot be agreed, the order of cross-examination will (subject to any direction of the judge) follow the order in which the parties are set out in the pleadings. The judge will seek to limit cross examination on a topic which has been covered in detail by a preceding cross examination.

15.5.6 In preparing witness statements and in ascertaining what evidence a witness might give in an original or supplementary witness statement or as supplementary evidence-in-chief, lawyers may discuss the evidence to be given by a witness with that witness. The coaching of witnesses or the suggestion of answers that may be given, either in the preparation of witness statements or before a witness starts to give evidence, is not permitted. In relation to the process of giving evidence, witness familiarisation is permissible, but witness coaching is not. The boundary between witness familiarisation and witness coaching is discussed in the context of criminal proceedings by the Court of Appeal in *R v Momodou* [2005] EWCA Crim 177 at [61] – [62]. Once a witness has started giving evidence, that witness cannot discuss the case or their evidence either with the lawyers or with anyone else until they have finally left the witness box. Occasionally a dispensation is needed (for example, an expert may need to participate in an experts' meeting about some new development). In those circumstances the necessary dispensation will either be agreed between the advocates or ordered by the judge.

15.6 Submissions during the trial

15.6.1 Submissions and legal argument should be kept to a minimum during the course of the trial. Where these are necessary, (a) they should, where possible, take place when a witness is not giving evidence and (b) the judge should be given forewarning of the need for submissions or legal argument. Where possible, the judge will fix a time for these submissions outside the agreed timetable for the evidence.

15.7 Closing submissions

15.7.1 The appropriate form of closing submissions can be determined during the course of the trial. Those submissions may take the form of (a) oral closing speeches or (b) written submission alone or (c) written submissions supplemented by oral closing speeches. In shorter or lower value cases, oral closing speeches immediately after the evidence may be the most cost effective way to proceed. Alternatively, if the evidence finishes in the late afternoon, a direction for written closing submissions to be delivered by specified (early) dates may avoid the cost of a further day's court hearing. In longer and heavier cases the judge may (in consultation with the advocates) set a timetable for the delivery of sequential written submissions (alternatively, an exchange of written submissions) followed by an oral hearing. In giving directions for oral and/or written closing submissions, the judge will have regard to the circumstances of the case and the overriding objective.

15.7.2 It is helpful if, in advance of preparing closing submissions, the parties can agree on the principal topics or issues that are to be covered. It is also helpful for the written and oral submissions of each party to be structured so as to cover those topics in the same order.

15.7.3 It is both customary and helpful for the judge to be provided with a photocopy of each authority and statutory provision that is to be cited in closing submissions.

15.8 Views

15.8.1 It is sometimes necessary or desirable for the judge to be taken to view the subject-matter of the case. In normal circumstances, such a view is best arranged to take place immediately after the openings and before the evidence is called. However, if the subject matter of the case is going to be covered up or altered prior to the trial, the view must be arranged earlier. In that event, it becomes particularly important to avoid a change of judge. Accordingly, the court staff will note on the trial diary the fact that the assigned judge has attended a view. In all subsequent communications between the parties and court concerning trial date, the need to avoid a change of judge must be borne firmly in mind.

15.8.2 The matters viewed by the judge form part of the evidence that is received and may be relied on in deciding the case. However, nothing said during the view to (or in the earshot of) the judge, has any evidential status, unless there has been an agreement or order to that effect.

15.8.3 The parties should agree the arrangements for the view and then make those arrangements themselves. The judge will ordinarily travel to the view unaccompanied and, save in exceptional circumstances when the cost will be shared by all parties, will not require any travelling costs to be met by the parties.

15.9 Judgments

15.9.1 Depending on the length and complexity of the trial, the judge may (a) give judgment orally immediately after closing speeches; (b) give judgment orally on the following day or soon afterwards; or (c) deliver a reserved judgment in writing at a later date.

15.9.2 If a party wishes to obtain a transcript of an oral judgment, it should notify the judge's clerk so that any notes made by the judge can be retained in order to assist the judge when correcting the transcript.

15.9.3 <u>Where judgment is reserved.</u> The judge will normally indicate at the conclusion of the trial what arrangements will be followed in relation to (a) the making available of any draft reserved judgment and (b) the handing down of the reserved judgment in open court. If a judgment is reserved, it will be handed down as soon as possible. Save in exceptional circumstances, any reserved judgment will be handed down within 3 months of the conclusion of the trial. Any enquiries as to the progress of a reserved judgment should be addressed in the first instance to the judge's clerk, with notice of that enquiry being given to other parties. If concerns remain following the judge's response to the parties, further enquiries or communication should be addressed to the judge in charge of the TCC.

15.9.4 If the judge decides to release a draft judgment in advance of the formal hand down, this draft judgment will be confidential to the parties and their legal advisers. Solicitors and counsel on each side should send to the judge a note (if possible, agreed) of any clerical errors or slips which they note in the judgment. However, this is not to be taken as an opportunity to re-argue the issues in the case.

15.10 Disposal of judge's bundle after conclusion of the case

15.10.1 The judge will have made notes and annotations on the bundle during the course of the trial. Accordingly, the normal practice is that the entire contents of the judge's bundle are disposed of as confidential waste. The empty ring files can be recovered by arrangement with the judge's clerk.

15.10.2 If any party wishes to retrieve from the judge's bundle any particular items of value which it has supplied (e.g. plans or photographs), a request for these items should be made to the judge's clerk promptly at the conclusion of the case. If the judge has not made annotations on those particular items, they will be released to the requesting party.

Section 16. Costs and Costs Management

16.1 General

16.1.1 All disputes as to costs will be resolved in accordance with **CPR Part 44**, and in particular **CPR 44.2**.

16.1.2 The judge's usual approach will be to determine which party can be properly described as 'the successful party', and then to investigate whether there are any good reasons why that party should be deprived of some or all of their costs.

16.1.3 It should be noted that, in view of the complex nature of TCC cases, a consideration of the outcome on particular issues or areas of dispute can sometimes be an appropriate starting point for any decision on costs.

16.1.4 As set out in **paragraphs 5.1.6, 5.5.5 and 12.1.4** above, if the judge considers that any particular aspect is likely to or has led to unnecessarily increased costs, the judge may make a costs order disallowing costs or ordering costs to be paid, either on the basis of a summary assessment, or by giving a direction to the costs judge as to what costs should be disallowed or paid on a detailed assessment.

16.2 Summary Assessment of Costs

16.2.1 Interlocutory hearings that last one day or less will usually be the subject of a summary assessment of costs in accordance with **CPR 44.6** and **section 9 of PD44**. The parties must ensure that their statements of costs, on which the summary assessment will be based, are provided to each other party, and the Court, no later than **24 hours** before the hearing in question: see **paragraph 6.9.3** above.

16.2.2 The Senior Courts Costs Office Guide to the Summary Assessment of Costs sets out clear advice and guidance as to the principles to be followed in any summary assessment. Generally summary assessment proceeds on the standard basis. In making an assessment on the standard basis, the court will only allow a reasonable amount in respect of costs reasonably incurred and any doubts must be resolved in favour of the paying party.

16.2.3 In arguments about the hourly rates claimed, the judge will have regard to the principles set out by the Court of Appeal in *Wraith v Sheffield Forgemasters Ltd* [1998] 1 WLR 132: ie. the judge will consider whether the successful party acted reasonably in employing the solicitors who had been instructed and whether the costs they charged were reasonable compared with the broad average of charges made by similar firms practising in the same area.

16.2.4 When considering hourly rates, the judge in the TCC may have regard to any relevant guideline rates.

16.2.5 The court will also consider whether unnecessary work was done or an unnecessary amount of time was spent on the work.

16.2.6 It may be that, because of pressures of time, and/or the nature and extent of the disputes about the level of costs incurred, the court is unable to carry out a satisfactory summary assessment of the costs. In those circumstances, the court will direct that costs be assessed on the standard (or indemnity) basis and will order an amount to be paid on account of costs under **CPR 44.3 (8)**.

16.3 Costs Management

16.3.1 Following a pilot scheme in the TCC and elsewhere, **Section II of CPR 3** introduces the new regime of Costs Management. This implements the recommendations of the Jackson Report.

16.3.2 The rules now require each party to file a costs budget in the prescribed form at the outset of the litigation (before the first CMC). Although not expressly stated in **Practice Direction 3E**, the budgets should be discussed between the parties prior to the budgets being filed with the court. The court will fix the first CMC sufficiently far ahead to enable this to be done.

16.3.3 At the first CMC the court will consider the costs budgets. If they are agreed, the court will make an order recording the extent to which the budgets have been agreed: see **CPR 3.15(2)(a)**. In such cases the parties' costs will be subject to detailed assessment as in the pre costs management regime. The penalty for failure to serve a budget is draconian: the party will be limited to recovering the court fees only (see CPR 3.14), as applied by the Court of Appeal in *Mitchell v News Group Newspapers* [2013] EWCA Civ 1537.

16.3.4 Where a budget or parts of a budget are not agreed, the court will consider the budget and make such revisions as it thinks fit. These will then be recorded in a Costs Management Order: see **CPR 3.15(2)(b)**.

16.3.5 Precedent H is the form for a costs budget. This divides the litigation into different phases, and the court will consider the amount of the fees and disbursements for each phase separately. Costs budgets are to be supported by a statement of truth (see **CPR 3EPD.1**).

16.3.6 Once approved, the costs shown in each phase of the costs budget will usually be recoverable on a detailed assessment if they have been incurred. Recovery will not usually be permitted where a party has overspent its budget for a particular phase, even though it may have underspent on another phase. The court will not depart from the approved figure in the budget unless satisfied that there is good reason to do so: see **CPR 3.18**.

16.3.7 Precedent H allows a party to provide an allowance for certain contingencies, but these must be set out in the budget and the reason for them given. It is open to a party to apply to the court to amend its costs budget if there is good reason to do so.

16.3.8 In cases where items in the costs budgets are in issue, it of great help to the court if counsel can prepare a brief summary of the differences (if necessary, there is available on the market an Excel programme that can do this).

16.3.9 The parties should note that a different regime applied to cases commenced before 1 April 2013: see **PD51G** (Costs Management in Mercantile Courts and Technology and Construction Courts – Pilot Scheme). For cases commenced on or after 1 April 2013: see **CPR 3.11-3.18** and **PD3E**, including the current £2 million cap (a revised Precedent H has been in force since 1 October 2013). For cases commencing after 22 April 2014 the costs management regime will apply where the value of the case is below £10 million: see **CPR 3.12** (as amended).

16.4 Costs Capping Orders

16.4.1 In exercising case management powers, the judge may make costs cap orders which, in normal circumstances, will be prospective only. New rules are set out in **CPR 3, Section III**. The judge should only do so, however, where:

- it is in the interests of justice to do so;
- there is a substantial risk that without such an order costs will be disproportionately incurred; and
- the court is not satisfied that the risk can be adequately controlled by case management and detailed assessment of costs after a trial.

See **CPR 3 Section III "Costs Capping"**.

16.4.2 The possibility of a costs cap order should be considered at the first CMC. The later such an order is sought, the more difficult it may be to impose an effective costs cap.

16.4.3 The procedure for making an application for a costs capping order are set out in **CPR 3.20** and **PD3F Costs Capping** (these include a new requirement that parties must file a costs budget rather than an estimate of costs with any application for a costs capping order).

16.5 Costs: Miscellaneous

16.5.1 Pursuant to **CPR 44.8** and **Section 10 PD44**, solicitors have a duty to tell their clients within 7 days if an order for costs was made against the clients and they were not present at the hearing, explaining how the order came to be made. They must also give the same information to anyone else who has instructed them to act on the case or who is liable to pay their fees.

Section 17. Enforcement

17.1 General

17.1.1 The TCC is concerned with the enforcement of judgments and orders given by the TCC and with the enforcement of adjudicators' decisions and arbitrators' awards. Adjudication and arbitration enforcement have been dealt with in, respectively, sections 9 and 10 above.

17.2 High Court

17.2.1 London. A party wishing to make use of any provision of the **CPR** concerned with the enforcement of judgments and orders made in the TCC in London can use the TCC Registry in London or any other convenient TCC District Registry listed in **Appendix A**.

17.2.2 Outside London. Where the judgment or order in respect of which enforcement is sought was made by a judge of the TCC out of London, the party seeking enforcement should use the Registry of the court in which the judgment or order was made.

17.2.3 Where orders are required or sought to support enforcement of a TCC judgment or order, a judge of the TCC is the appropriate judge for that purpose. If available, the judge who gave the relevant judgment or made the relevant order is the appropriate judge to whom all applications should be addressed.

17.3 County Court

17.3.1 A TCC County Court judgment (like any other County Court judgment):

- if for less than £600, must be enforced in the County Court;
- if for between £600 and £4999, can be enforced in either the County Court or the High Court, at the option of the judgment creditor;
- if for £5,000 or more, must be enforced in the High Court.

17.3.2 If a judgment creditor in a TCC County Court wishes to transfer any enforcement proceedings to any other County Court hearing centre (whether a TCC County Court or not), he must make a written request to do so pursuant to **section 2 of the Practice Direction supplementing Part 70**. Alternatively, at the end of the trial the successful party may make an oral application to the trial judge to transfer the proceedings to some other specified County Court or County Court hearing centre for the purposes of enforcement.

17.4 Enforcement on paper

17.4.1 Where the application or order is unopposed or does not involve any substantial dispute, the necessary order should be sought by way of a paper application.

Section 17. Enforcement

17.5 Charging Orders and Orders For Sale

17.5.1 One of the most common methods of enforcement involves the making of a charging order over the judgment debtor's property. There are three stages in the process.

17.5.2 The judgment creditor can apply to the TCC for a charging order pursuant to CPR 73.3 and 73.4. The application is in Form N379 in which the judgment creditor must identify the relevant judgment and the property in question. The application is initially dealt with by the judge without a hearing, and he may make an interim charging order imposing a charge over the judgment debtor's interest in the property and fixing a hearing to consider whether or not to make the charging order final.

17.5.3 The interim charging order must be served in accordance with CPR 73.5. If the judgment debtor or any other person objects to the making of a final charging order, then he must set out his objection in accordance with CPR 73.8. There will then be a hearing at which the court will decide whether or not to make the charging order final.

17.5.4 Ultimately, if the judgment remains unsatisfied, the party who has obtained the final charging order may seek an order for the sale of the property in accordance with CPR 73.10. Although paragraph 4.2 of PD 73 might suggest that a claim for an order for sale to enforce a charging order must be started in the Chancery Division, there is no such restriction in the rule itself and practical difficulties have arisen for parties who have obtained a judgment, an interim charging order and a final charging order in the TCC and who do not want to have to transfer or commence fresh proceedings in another division in order to obtain an order for sale. The TCC will, in appropriate circumstances, in accordance with the overriding objective, make orders for sale in such circumstances, particularly if the parties are agreed that is the most convenient cost-effective course: see *Packman Lucas Limited v Mentmore Towers Ltd* [2010] EWHC 1037 (TCC).

17.5.5 In deciding whether or not to make an order for sale, the court will consider, amongst other things, the size of the debt, and the value of the property relative to that debt, the conduct of the parties and the absence of any other enforcement option on the part of the judgment creditor.

Section 18. The TCC judge as arbitrator

18.1 General

18.1.1 Section 93(1) of the Arbitration Act 1996 ("the 1996 Act") provides that a judge of the TCC (previously an Official Referee) may "if in all the circumstances he thinks fit, accept appointment as a sole arbitrator or as an umpire by or by virtue of an arbitration agreement." Judges of the TCC may accept appointments as sole arbitrators or umpires pursuant to these statutory provisions. The 1996 Act does not limit the appointments to arbitrations with the seat in England and Wales.

18.1.2 However, a TCC judge cannot accept such an appointment unless the Lord Chief Justice "has informed him that, having regard to the state of (TCC) business, he can be made available": see section 93(3) of the 1996 Act. In exceptional cases a judge of the TCC may also accept an appointment as a member of a three-member panel of arbitrators if the Lord Chief Justice consents but such arbitrations cannot be under section 93 of the 1996 Act because section 93(6) of the 1996 Act modifies the provisions of the 1996 Act where there is a judge-arbitrator and this could not apply to arbitral tribunals with three arbitrators, one of whom was a judge-arbitrator.

18.1.3 Application should be made in the first instance to the judge whose acceptance of the appointment is sought. If the judge is willing to accept the appointment, he will make application on behalf of the appointing party or parties, through the judge in charge of the TCC, to the Lord Chief Justice for his necessary approval. He will inform the party or parties applying for his appointment once the consent or refusal of consent has been obtained.

18.1.4 Subject to the workload of the court and the consent of the Lord Chief Justice, the TCC judges will generally be willing to accept such requests, particularly in short cases or where an important principle or point of law is concerned. Particular advantages have been noted by both TECBAR and TeCSA in the appointment of a TCC judge to act as arbitrator where the dispute centres on the proper interpretation of a clause or clauses within one of the standard forms of building and engineering contracts.

18.2 Arbitration Management and Fees

18.2.1 Following the appointment of the judge-arbitrator, the rules governing the arbitration will be decided upon, or directed, at the First Preliminary Meeting, when other appropriate directions will be given. The judge-arbitrator will manage the reference to arbitration in a similar way to a TCC case.

18.2.2 The judge sitting as an arbitrator will sit in a TCC court room (suitably rearranged) unless the parties and the judge-arbitrator agree to some other arrangement.

18.2.3 Fees are payable to the Court Service for the judge-arbitrator's services and for any accommodation provided. The appropriate fee for the judge-arbitrator, being a daily rate, is published in the Fees Order and should be paid through the TCC Registry.

18.3 Modifications to the Arbitration Act 1996 for judge-arbitrators

18.3.1 As section 93 envisages that appointments of judge-arbitrators will be in arbitrations where the seat of the arbitration is in England and Wales, Schedule 2 of the 1996 Act modifies the provisions of the Act which apply to arbitrations where the seat is in England and Wales.

Section 18. The TCC judge as arbitrator

18.3.2 In relation to arbitrations before judge-arbitrators, **paragraph 2 of Schedule 2 to the Arbitration Act 1996** provides that references in Part I of the 1996 Act to "the court" shall be construed in relation to a judge-arbitrator, or in relation to the appointment of a judge-arbitrator, as references to "the Court of Appeal". This means that, for instance, any appeal from a judge-arbitrator under section 69 of the 1996 Act is therefore heard, in the first instance, by the Court of Appeal.

Appendices

Appendix A – Case management information sheet — 221
Appendix B – Case management directions form — 222
Appendix C – Pre-trial review questionnaire — 224
Appendix D – Contact details for Technology and Construction Court — 225
Appendix E – Draft ADR Order — 231
Appendix F – Draft directions order in adjudication enforcement proceedings — 232
Appendix G – Draft Court Settlement Order — 233

Appendix A – Case management information sheet

This Appendix is the same as Appendix A to the Part 60 Practice Direction.

Appendix B – Case management directions form

CASE MANAGEMENT DIRECTIONS FORM

Action no   HT-............   [*Insert name of judge in title of order*]

[*Delete or amend the following directions, as appropriate to the circumstances of the case*]

1. Trial date .... For the purposes of payment of the trial fee, but for no other purposes, this date is provisional. This date will cease to be provisional and the trial fee will become payable on ... [*usually 2 months before the trial date*].

2. Estimated length of trial ....

3. Directions, if appropriate, (a) for the trial of any preliminary issues or (b) for the trial to be divided into stages ...

4. This action is to be [consolidated] [managed and tried with] action no ... The lead action shall be ... All directions given in the lead action shall apply to both actions, unless otherwise stated.

5. Further statements of case shall be filed and served as follows:
   - Defence and any counterclaim by 4 pm on ...
   - Reply (if any) and defence to counterclaim (if any) by 4 pm on ...

6. Permission to make the following amendments ...

7. Disclosure
   - By 5 pm on ...
   - To be standard disclosure/on the basis set out in CPR 31(5)(7) ...
   - On the basis set out in CPR 31(5)(7) ...
   - Specific directions in respect of electronic disclosure ... [where appropriate the TeCSA/TECBAR/SCL e-disclosure protocol is to be followed]

8. There shall be a Scott Schedule in respect of defects/ items of damage/ other ...
   - The column headings shall be as follows ...
   - Claimant/ defendant to serve Scott Schedule by 5 pm on ...
   - Defendant/ claimant to respond to Scott Schedule by 5 pm on ...

9. Signed statements of witnesses of fact to be served by 5 pm on ...

   [Supplementary statements of witnesses of fact to be served by 5 pm on ...]

10. The parties have permission to call the following expert witnesses in respect of the following issues:
    - ...
    - ...
    - ...

Appendix B – Case management directions form

11. In respect of any expert evidence permitted under paragraph 10:
    - Directions for carrying out inspections/ taking samples/ conducting experiments/ performance of calculations shall be …
    - Experts in like fields to hold discussions in accordance with rule 35.12 by …
    - Experts' statements rule 35.12 (3) to be prepared and filed by 5 pm on …
    - Experts' reports to be served by 5 pm on …

12. A single joint expert shall be appointed by the parties to report on the following issue(s) …. The following directions shall govern the appointment of the single joint expert:
    - ….
    - ….

13. The following documents shall be provided to the court electronically or in computer readable form, as well as in hard copy …

14. Costs Management
    - The costs budgets filed by the parties are approved.
    - The costs budget filed by the Claimant/Defendant is approved.
    - The following parties' costs budgets are approved subject to the following revisions:
        - …
        - …

15. A review case management conference shall be held on … at … am/pm. Time allowed …

16. The pre-trial review shall be held on … at … am/pm. Time allowed …

17. The above dates and time limits may be extended by agreement between the parties. Nevertheless:
    - The dates and time limits specified in paragraphs … may not be extended by more than [14] days without the permission of the court.
    - The dates specified in paragraph 1 (trial) and paragraph 15 (pre-trial review) cannot be varied without the permission of the court.

18. Costs in the case.

DATED this   day of   201

Appendix C – Pre-trial review questionnaire

This Appendix is the same as Appendix C to the Part 60 Practice Direction.

Appendix D – Contact details for Technology and Construction Court

The High Court of Justice, Queen's Bench Division, Technology and Construction Court
The Rolls Building
7 Rolls Buildings
Fetter Lane
London EC4A 1NL

Management
Court Manager: Mr Wilf Lusty (wilf.lusty@hmcts.gsi.gov.uk)
List Officer: Mr Steven Gibbon (steven.gibbon@hmcts.gsi.gov.uk)

Court Manager: Tel: 020 7947 7427
Listing: Tel: 020 7947 7156
Registry Tel: 020 7947 7591
Fax: 0870 761 7724 (Goldfax)

TCC Judges
Mr Justice Edwards-Stuart (Judge in Charge of the TCC from 1 September 2013)
Clerk: Philip Morris (philip.morris@hmcts.gsi.gov.uk)
Tel: 020 7947 7205
Fax: 0870 761 7694 (Goldfax)

Mr Justice Ramsey
Clerk: Mr David Hamilton (david.hamilton5@hmcts.gsi.gov.uk)
Tel: 020 7947 6331
Fax: 0870 761 7694 (Goldfax)

Mr Justice Akenhead
Clerk: Mr Sam Taylor (sam.taylor1@hmcts.gsi.gov.uk)
Tel: 020 7947 7445
Fax: 0870 761 7694 (Goldfax)

Mr Justice Coulson
Clerk: Mr Simon Smith (simon.smith@hmcts.gsi.gov.uk)
Tel: 020 7947 6547
Fax: 0870 761 7694 (Goldfax)

Mr Justice Stuart-Smith
Clerk: Maxine Barfoot (maxine.barfoot@hmcts.gsi.gov.uk)
Tel: 020 7073 4837

The following High Court Judges may be available, when necessary and by arrangement with the President of the Queen's Bench Division, to sit in the TCC:

Mr Justice Burton
Mrs Justice Carr
Mr Justice Field
Mr Justice Foskett
Mr Justice Ouseley
Mr Justice Simon
Mr Justice Teare

The following judges are also TCC judges who may be available when necessary and by arrangement with the President of the Queen's Bench Division, to sit in the TCC:

His Honour Judge Anthony Thornton QC
His Honour Judge David Mackie QC

Birmingham District Registry: Birmingham County Court

33 Bull Street
Birmingham
West Midlands B4 6DS

TCC listing and clerk to His Honour Judge David Grant: Peter Duke (Peter.Duke@hmcts.gsi.gov.uk)
birmingham.tcc@hmcts.gsi.gov.uk
Tel: 0121 681 4441
Fax: 0121 250 6437

TCC Judges
His Honour Judge David Grant (principal TCC Judge)
His Honour Judge Simon Brown QC (Mercantile Judge)
His Honour Judge Charles Purle QC (Chancery Judge)
His Honour Judge David Cooke
His Honour Martin McKenna
His Honour Judge Simon Barker QC

Bristol District Registry: Bristol County Court

TCC Listing Office
Bristol Civil Justice Centre
2 Redcliff Street
Bristol BS1 6GR

TCC Listing Officer: Steven Stafford
Tel: 0117 366 4866
Email: bristoltcclisting@hmcts.gsi.gov.uk
Switchboard Tel: 0117 366 4800

TCC Judges
His Honour Judge Mark Havelock-Allan QC (principal TCC judge)

His Honour Judge Patrick McCahill QC
District Judge Brian Watson (TCC Liaison Judge)

Appendix D – Contact details for Technology and Construction Court

Cardiff District Registry: Cardiff County Court
Cardiff Civil Justice Centre
2 Park Street
Cardiff CF10 1ET

Main switchboard: 029 2037 6400
Fax: 029 2037 6475
Listing office: 029 2037 6412

Circuit Judges Listing Manager: Tracey Davies
Tel: 029 2037 6483, tracey.davies2@hmcts.gsi.gov.uk

Specialist Listing Officer: Amanda Thomas
Tel: 029 2037 6412, amanda.thomas6@hmcts.gsi.gov.uk

TCC Judges
His Honour Judge Andrew Keyser QC (principal TCC judge)
His Honour Judge Milwyn Jarman QC
His Honour Judge Anthony Seys Llewellyn QC

Central London Civil Justice Centre
Thomas More Building
Royal Courts of Justice
Strand
London
WC2 2LL

TCC/Chancery Section: Geanette Rodney
Tel: 0207 917 7821
(from 20 May 2014: 020 7947 7800; and for counter appointments 020 7947 7502)
Fax: 020 7917 7935
Goldfax: 0970 330 571
Email for e-applications: CLCCTCC@hmcts.gsi.gov.uk

Circuit Judge Listing: 020 7917 7932
Email: hearingsatcentrallondon.countycourt@hmcts.gsi.gov.uk
Email for skeleton arguments: CentralLondonCJSKEL@hmcts.gsi.gov.uk

TCC Judges
His Honour Judge Edward Bailey (principal TCC Judge)
His Honour Judge John Hand QC
His Honour Judge Timothy Lamb
Her Honour Judge Deborah Taylor
His Honour Judge Marc Dight

Chester District Registry: Chester County Court
The Chester Civil Justice Centre
Trident House
Little St John Street
Chester CH1 1SN

Tel: 01244 404200
Fax: 0870 324 0311
email: hearings@chester.countycourt.gsi.gov.uk

TCC Judge
His Honour Judge Derek Halbert

Exeter District Registry: Exeter County Court
Southernhay Gardens
Exeter
Devon EX1 1UH

Tel: 01392 415 350
Fax: 01392 415645
email: hearings@exeter.countycourt.gsi.gov.uk

TCC Judge
His Honour Judge Barry Cotter QC

Leeds Combined Court Centre
The Courthouse
1 Oxford Row
Leeds LS1 3BG

TCC Chancery and Mercantile Listing Officer: Richard Marsland
Tel: 0113 306 2440 / 2441
Fax: 08707617740
e-mail: richard.marsland6@hmcts.gsi.gov.uk

TCC Judges
His Honour Judge Mark Raeside QC (Judge in Charge of TCC in North East Region)
His Honour Judge John Behrens
His Honour Judge Roger Kaye QC
His Honour Judge Andrew Saffman

Liverpool District Registry: Liverpool Combined Court Centre
Liverpool Civil & Family Courts
35 Vernon Street
Liverpool L2 2BX

TCC listing officer: Jackie Jones
Tel: 0151 296 2444
Fax: 0151 295 2201

TCC Judges
His Honour Judge Wood QC

Appendix D – Contact details for Technology and Construction Court

Manchester District Registry

Manchester Civil Justice Centre
1 Bridge Street West
Manchester M60 9DJ

TCC clerk: Isobel Rich
Tel: 0161 240 5305
Fax: 0161 240 5399
e-mail: manchester.tcc@hmcts.gsi.gov.uk

TCC Judges
His Honour Judge Philip Raynor QC (full time TCC judge)
His Honour Judge Stephen Davies (full time TCC judge)

The following judges at Manchester are nominated to deal with TCC business:
HHJ David Waksman QC
HHJ Mark Pelling QC
HHJ David Hodge QC
HHJ Nigel Bird
HHJ Graham Platts
HHJ Allan Gore QC

Mold County Court

Law Courts
Civic Centre
Mold
Flintshire
Wales CH7 1AE TCC

Listing officer: Selina Wilkes
Tel: 01352 707405
Fax: 01352 753874

TCC Judges
Will attend from Cardiff when required

Newcastle upon Tyne Combined Court Centre

The Law Courts
The Quayside
Newcastle upon Tyne NE1 3LA

Tel: 0191 201 2029

Listing Officer: Mrs Carol Gallagher
Email: carol.gallagher@hmcts.gsi.gov.uk
Tel: 0191 201 2047
Fax: 0191 201 2001

TCC Judges
His Honour Judge Christopher Walton
District Judge Atherton

Nottingham District Registry: Nottingham County Court
60 Canal Street
Nottingham NG1 7EJ

Tel 0115 910 3500
Fax: 0115 910 3510

TCC Judges
His Honour Judge Richard Inglis
His Honour Judge Nigel Godsmark QC

Sheffield Combined Court Centre
The Law Courts
50 West Bar
Sheffield S3 8PH

Tel: 0114 281 2419
Fax: 0114 281 2585

TCC Judge
His Honour Judge John Bullimore

Winchester Combined Court Centre
The Law Courts
Winchester
Hampshire SO23 9EL

Switchboard: 01962 814 100
Fax: 01962 814 260
Diary Manager: Mr Wayne Hacking
Email: wayne.hacking@hmcts.gsi.gov.uk
Tel: 023 8021 3254
Civil Listing Officer: Mrs Karen Hart
Email: karen.hart@hmcts.gsi.gov.uk
Tel: 01962 814 113

TCC Judge
His Honour Judge Iain Hughes QC

Appendix E – Draft ADR Order

1. By [date/time] the parties shall exchange lists of three neutral individuals who have indicated their availability to conduct a mediation or ENE or other form of ADR in this case prior to [date].

2. By [date/time] the parties shall agree an individual from the exchanged lists to conduct the mediation or ENE or other form of ADR by [date]. If the parties are unable to agree on the neutral individual, they will apply to the Court in writing by [date/time] and the Court will choose one of the listed individuals to conduct the mediation or ENE or other form of ADR.

3. There will be a stay of the proceedings until [date/time] to allow the mediation or ENE or other form of ADR to take place. On or before that date, the Court shall be informed as to whether or not the case has been finally settled. If it has not been finally settled, the parties will:

    a) comply with all outstanding directions made by the Court;

    b) attend for a review CMC on [date/time].

DATED this   day of   201

Appendix F – Draft directions order in adjudication enforcement proceedings

BEFORE the Hon Mr Justice [   ] sitting in the High Court of Justice, Queen's Bench Division, Technology and Construction Court

UPON reading the application notice dated [   ], and the witness statement of [   ] dated [   ],

IT IS HEREBY ORDERED THAT:

1) The Claimant shall as soon as practicable after receipt of this Order serve this application upon the Defendant together with:
   a) The Claim Form, Response Pack and any statement relied upon
   b) This Order.

2) The time for the Defendant to file its Acknowledgement of Service is abridged to [four] working days. The Defendant is advised that failure to comply with the requirement to file this Acknowledgment can lead to judgment in default being entered against it. The Claimant is reminded that if there is such failure, serious consideration should be given to entering judgment in default as a cheaper option than taking the matter through to a hearing.

3) Any further evidence shall be served and filed:
   a) By the Defendant, on or by [about 14 days after order]
   b) By the Claimant, in response to that of the Defendant, on or by [7 days later];
   and in either case no later than 4.00 pm that day.

4) The Claimant has permission to issue an application for summary judgment prior to service by the Defendant of either Acknowledgement of Service or a Defence, pursuant to CPR Rule 24.4. The period of notice to be given to the Defendant is abridged to [four] working days.

5) There shall be an oral hearing on [   ] at [   ] with a time estimate of [   ] for the hearing of the Claimant's summary judgment application (this time may be varied at short notice to accommodate the listing requirements of the court).

6) The Claimant shall serve and file a paginated bundle comprising all relevant documents, statements, pleadings and otherwise by 1.00 pm on [   ].

7) Any skeleton arguments and any authorities to be relied upon (an agreed bundle, if possible) shall be served and filed by 1.00 pm on [   ].

8) The costs of and incidental to these directions are reserved.

9) The parties have permission to apply to set aside or vary these directions on [two] working days' written notice to the other.

Dated this   day of   201

Appendix G – Draft Court Settlement Order

Court Settlement

1. The Court Settlement Process under this Order is a confidential, voluntary and non-binding dispute resolution process in which the Settlement Judge assists the Parties in reaching an amicable settlement at a Court Settlement Conference.

2. This Order provides for the process by which the Court assists in the resolution of the disputes in the Proceedings. This Order is made by consent of the Parties with a view to achieving the amicable settlement of such disputes. It is agreed that the Settlement Judge may vary this Order at any time as he thinks appropriate or in accordance with the agreement of the Parties.

3. The following definitions shall apply:
   (1) The Parties shall be [names]
   (2) The Proceedings are [identify]
   (3) The Settlement Judge is [name]

The Court Settlement Process

4. The Settlement Judge may conduct the Court Settlement Process in such manner, as the Judge considers appropriate, taking into account the circumstances of the case, the wishes of the Parties and the overriding objective in Part 1 of the Civil Procedure Rules. A Preliminary Court Settlement Conference shall be held, either in person or in some other convenient manner, at which the Parties and the Settlement Judge shall determine, in general terms, the procedure to be adopted for the Court Settlement Process, the venue of the Court Settlement Conference, the estimated duration of the Court Settlement Conference and the material which will be read by the Settlement Judge in advance of the Court Settlement Conference.

5. Unless the Parties otherwise agree, during the Court Settlement Conference the Settlement Judge may communicate with the Parties together or with any Party separately, including private meetings at which the Settlement Judge may express views on the disputes. Each Party shall cooperate with the Settlement Judge. A Party may request a private meeting with the Settlement Judge at any time during the Court Settlement Conference. The Parties shall give full assistance to enable the Court Settlement Conference to proceed and be concluded within the time stipulated by the Settlement Judge.

6. In advance of the Court Settlement Conference, each Party shall notify the Settlement Judge and the other Party or Parties of the names and the role of all persons involved in the Court Settlement Conference. Each Party shall nominate a person having full authority to settle the disputes.

7. No offers or promises or agreements shall have any legal effect unless and until they are included in a written agreement signed by representatives of all Parties (the "Settlement Agreement").

8. If the Court Settlement Conference does not lead to a Settlement Agreement, the Settlement Judge may, if requested by the Parties, send the Parties such assessment setting out his views on such matters as the Parties shall request, which may include, for instance, his views on the disputes, his views on prospects of success on individual issues, the likely outcome of the case and what would be an appropriate settlement. Such assessment shall be confidential to the parties and may not be used or referred to in any subsequent proceedings.

Appendix G – Draft Court Settlement Order

Termination of the Settlement Process

9. The Court Settlement Process shall come to end upon the signing of a Settlement Agreement by the Parties in respect of the disputes or when the Settlement Judge so directs or upon written notification by any Party at any time to the Settlement Judge and the other Party or Parties that the Court Settlement Process is terminated.

Confidentiality

10. The Court Settlement Process is private and confidential. Every document, communication or other form of information disclosed, made or produced by any Party specifically for the purpose of the Court Settlement Process shall be treated as being disclosed on a privileged and without prejudice basis and no privilege or confidentiality shall be waived by such disclosure.

11. Nothing said or done during the course of the Court Settlement Process is intended to or shall in any way affect the rights or prejudice the position of the Parties to the dispute in the Proceedings or any subsequent arbitration, adjudication or litigation. If the Settlement Judge is told by a Party that information is being provided to the Settlement Judge in confidence, the Settlement Judge will not disclose that information to any other Party in the course of the Court Settlement Process or to any other person at any time.

Costs

12. Unless otherwise agreed, each Party shall bear its own costs and shall share equally the Court costs of the Court Settlement Process.

Settlement Judge's Role in Subsequent Proceedings

13. The Settlement Judge shall from the date of this Order not take any further part in the Proceedings nor in any subsequent proceedings arising out of the Court Settlement Process and no party shall be entitled to call the Settlement Judge as a witness in any subsequent adjudication, arbitration or judicial proceedings arising out of or connected with the Court Settlement Process.

Exclusion of Liability

14. For the avoidance of doubt, the Parties agree that the Settlement Judge shall have the same immunity from suit in relation to a Court Settlement Process as the Settlement Judge would have if acting otherwise as a Judge in the Proceedings.

Particular Directions

15. A Court Settlement Conference shall take place on [date] at [place] commencing at [time].

16. If by [date] the Parties have not concluded a settlement agreement, the matter shall be listed on the first available date before an appropriate judge who shall be allocated for the future management and trial of the Proceedings.

17. The Court Settlement Process shall proceed on the basis of such documents as might be determined at the Preliminary Court Settlement Conference and which may include the documents filed in the court proceedings and further documents critical to the understanding of the issues in the dispute and the positions of the Parties.

Dated this   day of   201

Appendix 2

Pre-Action Protocol for Construction and Engineering Disputes, 2nd edition

Pre-Action Protocol for Construction and Engineering Disputes 2nd edition

1 Introduction

1.1 This Pre-Action Protocol applies to all construction and engineering disputes (including professional negligence claims against architects, engineers and quantity surveyors).

2 Exceptions

2.1 A Claimant shall not be required to comply with this Protocol before commencing proceedings to the extent that the proposed proceedings (i) are for the enforcement of the decision of an adjudicator to whom a dispute has been referred pursuant to section 108 of the Housing Grants, Construction and Regeneration Act 1996 ("the 1996 Act"), (ii) include a claim for interim injunctive relief, (iii) will be the subject of a claim for summary judgment pursuant to Part 24 of the Civil Procedure Rules, or (iv) relate to the same or substantially the same issues as have been the subject of recent adjudication under the 1996 Act, or some other formal alternative dispute resolution procedure.

2.2 A Claimant shall not be required to comply with this Protocol before commencing proceedings if all the parties to the proposed proceedings expressly so agree in writing.

3 Objectives

3.1 The objectives of this Protocol are:

3.1.1 to exchange sufficient information about the proposed proceedings broadly to allow the parties to understand each other's position and make informed decisions about settlement and how to proceed;

3.1.2 to make appropriate attempts to resolve the matter without starting proceedings and, in particular, to consider the use of an appropriate form of ADR in order to do so.

4 Compliance

4.1 If proceedings are commenced, the Court will be able to treat the standards set in this Protocol as the normal reasonable and proportionate approach to pre-action conduct. It is likely to be only in exceptional circumstances, such as a flagrant or very significant disregard for the terms of this Protocol, that the Court will impose cost consequences on a party for non-compliance with this Protocol.

5 Proportionality

5.1 The overriding objective (CPR rule 1.1) applies to the pre-action period. The Protocol must not be used as a tactical device to secure advantage for one party or to generate unnecessary costs. In many cases, including those of modest value, the letter of claim and the response can be simple and the costs of both sides should be kept to a modest level. In all cases, the costs incurred at the Protocol stage should be proportionate to the complexity of the case and the amount of money which is at stake. The Protocol is not intended to impose a requirement on the parties to marshal and disclose all the supporting details and evidence that may ultimately be required if the case proceeds to litigation.

6 Overview of the Protocol

General aim

6.1 The general aim of this Protocol is to ensure that before Court proceedings commence:

6.1.1 the Claimant and the Defendant have provided sufficient information for each party to know the outline nature of the other's case;

6.1.2 each party has had an opportunity to consider the outline of the other's case, and to accept or reject all or any part of the outline case made against him at the earliest possible stage;

6.1.3 there is more pre-action contact between the parties;

6.1.4 better and earlier exchange of information occurs;

6.1.5 there is better pre-action investigation by the parties;

6.1.6 the parties have usually met formally on at least one occasion; and

6.1.7 the parties are in a position where they may be able to settle cases early, fairly and inexpensively without recourse to litigation; and

6.1.8 proceedings will be conducted efficiently if litigation does become necessary.

7 The Letter of Claim

7.1 Prior to commencing proceedings, the Claimant or his solicitor shall send to each proposed Defendant (if appropriate to his registered address) a copy of a letter of claim which shall contain the following information:

7.1.1 the Claimant's full name and address;

7.1.2 the full name and address of each proposed Defendant;

7.1.3 a brief summary of the claim or claims including (a) a list of principal contractual or statutory provisions relied on (b) a summary of the relief claimed including, where applicable, the monetary value of any claim or claims with a proportionate level of breakdown. The extent of the brief summary should be proportionate to the claim. Generally, it is not expected or required that expert reports should be provided but, in cases where they are succinct and central to the claim, they can form a helpful way of explaining the Claimant's position;

7.1.4 the names of any experts already instructed by the Claimant on whose evidence he intends to rely identifying the issues to which that evidence will be directed; and

7.1.5 the Claimant's confirmation as to whether or not it wishes the Protocol Referee Procedure to apply as provided at paragraph 11 below.

8 The Defendant's Response

The Defendant's acknowledgment

8.1 Within 14 calendar days of receipt of the letter of claim, the Defendant should acknowledge its receipt in writing and may give the name and address of his insurer (if any) and shall also confirm whether or not it wishes the Protocol Referee Procedure as provided at paragraph 11 below to apply. If there has been no acknowledgment by or on behalf of the Defendant within 14 days, the Claimant will be entitled to commence proceedings without further compliance with this Protocol.

Objections to the Court's jurisdiction or the named Defendant

8.2 If the Defendant intends to take any objection to all or any part of the Claimant's claim on the grounds that (i) the Court lacks jurisdiction, (ii) the matter should be referred to arbitration, or (iii) the Defendant named in the letter of claim is the wrong Defendant, that objection should be raised by the Defendant within 28 days after receipt of the Letter of Claim. The letter of objection shall specify the parts of the claim to which the objection relates, setting out the grounds relied on, and, where appropriate, shall identify the correct Defendant (if known). Any failure to take such objection shall not prejudice the Defendant's rights to do so in any subsequent proceedings, but the Court may take such failure into account when considering the question of costs.

8.3 Where such notice of objection is given, the Defendant is not required to send a letter of response in accordance with paragraph 8.5 in relation to the claim or those parts of it to which the objection relates (as the case may be).

8.4 If at any stage before the Claimant commences proceedings, the Defendant withdraws his objection, then paragraph 8.5 and the remaining part of this Protocol will apply to the claim or those parts of it to which the objection related as if the letter of claim had been received on the date on which notice of withdrawal of the objection had been given.

The Defendant's Response

8.5 Within 28 days from the date of receipt of the letter of claim, the Defendant shall send a letter of response to the Claimant which shall contain the following information:

8.5.1 A brief and proportionate summary of the Defendant's response to the claim or claims and, if the Defendant intends to make a Counterclaim, a brief summary of the Counterclaim containing the matters set out in paragraph 7.1.3 above;

8.5.2 the names of any experts already instructed on whose evidence it is intended to rely, identifying the issues to which that evidence will be directed;

8.5.3 the names of any third parties the Defendant intends to/is considering submitting to a Pre-action Protocol process.

8.6 If no response is received by the Claimant within the period of 28 days, the Claimant shall be entitled to commence proceedings without further compliance with this Protocol.

Claimant's Response to Counterclaim

8.7 The Claimant shall provide a Response to any Counterclaim within 21 days of the Defendant's Letter of Response. The Response shall contain a brief and proportionate summary of the Claimant's Response to the Counterclaim.

9 Pre-Action Meeting

9.1 Within 21 days after receipt by the Claimant of the Defendant's letter of response, or (if the Claimant intends to respond to the Counterclaim) after receipt by the Defendant of the Claimant's letter of response to the Counterclaim, the parties should normally meet.

9.2 It is not intended by this Protocol to prescribe in detail the manner in which the meeting should be conducted. However, the Court will normally expect that those attending will include:

9.2.1 where the party is an individual, that individual, and where the party is a corporate body, a representative of that body who has authority to settle or recommend settlement of the dispute;

9.2.2 a legal representative of each party (if one has been instructed);

9.2.3 where the involvement of insurers has been disclosed, a representative of the insurer (who may be its legal representative); and

9.2.4 where a claim is made or defended on behalf of some other party (such as, for example, a claim made by a main contractor pursuant to a contractual obligation to pass on subcontractor claims), the party on whose behalf the claim is made or defended and/or his legal representatives.

9.3 Generally, the aim of the meeting is for the parties to agree what are the main issues in the case, to identify the root cause of disagreement, and to consider (i) whether, and if so how, the case might be resolved without recourse to litigation, and (ii) if litigation is unavoidable, what steps should be taken to ensure that it is conducted in accordance with the overriding objective as defined in rule 1.1 of the Civil Procedure Rules. Alternatively, the meeting can itself take the form of an ADR process such as mediation.

9.4 If the parties are unable to agree on a means of resolving the dispute other than by litigation they should seek to agree:

9.4.1 if there is any area where expert evidence is likely to be required, how expert evidence is to be dealt with including whether a joint expert might be appointed, and if so, who that should be; and (so far as is practicable);

9.4.2 the extent of disclosure of documents with a view to saving costs and to the use of the e-disclosure protocol; and

9.4.3 the conduct of the litigation with the aim of minimising cost and delay.

9.5 Any party who attended any pre-action meeting shall be at liberty and may be required to disclose to the Court:

9.5.1 that the meeting took place, when and who attended;

9.5.2 the identity of any party who refused to attend, and the grounds for such refusal;

9.5.3 if the meeting did not take place, why not;

9.5.4 any agreements concluded between the parties; and

9.5.5 the fact of whether alternative means of resolving the dispute were considered or agreed.

9.6 Except as provided in paragraph 9.5, everything said at a pre-action meeting shall be treated as "without prejudice".

10 Other Matters

10.1 The parties may agree longer periods of time for compliance with any of the steps described above save that no extension in respect of any step shall exceed 28 days in the aggregate.

10.2 The Protocol process will be concluded at the completion of the pre-action meeting or, if no meeting takes place, 14 days after the expiry of the period in which the meeting should otherwise have taken place.

11 Protocol Referee Procedure

11.1 For the purposes of assisting the parties in participating in and complying with the Protocol, the parties may agree to engage in the current version of the Protocol Referee Procedure.

11.2 The Protocol Referee Procedure shall be published from time to time jointly by TeCSA and TECBAR on their respective websites.

12 Limitation of Action

12.1 If by reason of complying with any part of this protocol a Claimant's claim may be time-barred under any provision of the Limitation Act 1980, or any other legislation which imposes a time limit for bringing an action, the Claimant may commence proceedings without complying with this Protocol. In such circumstances, a Claimant who commences proceedings without complying with all, or any part, of this Protocol must apply to the Court on notice for directions as to the timetable and form of procedure to be adopted, at the same time as he requests the Court to issue proceedings. The Court will consider whether to order a stay of the whole or part of the proceedings pending compliance with this Protocol.

Updated: Friday, 17 February 2017

Appendix 3

TCC Guidance Note on Procedures for Public Procurement Cases

TCC GUIDANCE NOTE ON PROCEDURES FOR PUBLIC PROCUREMENT CASES

(Appendix H to the TCC Guide)

Introduction

1. This protocol provides guidance on the management of public procurement claims. This is a rapidly developing area of law; while this guide should assist, practitioners must ensure that they are aware of the most recent relevant case law.

2. Public procurement cases, particularly those involving claims which seek to set aside the decision to award the contract in question, raise singular procedural issues and difficulties. The claimant commonly feels that it has insufficient evidence or documentation fully to particularise its case or otherwise prepare for trial, while the short limitation and mandatory standstill periods mean that proceedings are necessarily issued hastily. The provision of pleadings and documentation on disclosure often gives rise to serious difficulties in connection with confidentiality, particularly where there is a real risk that there will have to be a re-tendering process. Confidentiality rings will often need to be set up by agreement or order.

3. The issue and notice of proceedings challenging a contract award decision before the contract has been entered into, results in automatic suspension of the conclusion of the contract with the successful tenderer. The latter has a particular interest in the protection of the confidential information in its documents, many of which will be in the possession of the contracting authority[1], and may wish to make representations in relation to confidentiality and other matters. It is therefore not unusual for the successful tenderer to make an application to be joined in the proceedings or to have its interests protected by some other means.

---

[1] This protocol refers to contracting authorities, but the same issues arise in relation to utilities under the relevant Utilities Contracts Regulations.

Pre-Action Process and ADR

4. Given the short limitation period, the time for any pre-action process is limited. As the mandatory standstill period is only 10 days, a potential claimant may need to commence proceedings without delay to obtain automatic suspension of the award of the contract. Whilst a claimant is not bound to comply with the Protocol, it aims to enable parties to settle the issues between them without the need to start proceedings, by encouraging the parties to exchange information about the claim, and to consider using Alternative Dispute Resolution (ADR) to resolve cases before or during proceedings. Litigation should always be a last resort. Therefore, to the extent that this is practical and does not make it unreasonably difficult to issue and serve proceedings within the limitation period, the parties are encouraged to use a pre-action process.

5. The pre-action process which is recommended is as follows:

    (1) The potential claimant will send a letter before claim to the contracting authority. This should identify the procurement process to which the claim relates; the grounds then known for the claim (both factual and legal); any information sought from the authority; the remedy required, and any request for an extension of the standstill period and/or a request not to enter into the contract for a specific period of time and/or not to do so without a specified period of notice to the potential claimant. The letter should propose an appropriate, short, time limit for a response.

    (2) The authority should promptly acknowledge receipt of the letter before claim, notify its solicitors' details and (if requested) indicate whether the standstill period will be extended and if so, by how long. The authority should then provide any information to which the claimant may be entitled as soon as possible, and send a substantive response within the timescale proposed by the claimant, or as soon as practical thereafter.

    (3) Having exchanged correspondence and information, the parties should continue to make appropriate and proportionate efforts to resolve the dispute without the need to commence proceedings.

6. The parties should act co-operatively and reasonably in dealing with all aspects of the litigation, including requests for extensions of time, taking into account the expiry of the

standstill period and/or any limitation periods. The parties should also act co-operatively and reasonably in dealing with all aspects of the litigation, including amendments following further disclosure.

7. The parties should also act reasonably and proportionately in providing one another with information, taking into account any genuine concerns with regard to confidentiality, whether their own, or those of third parties. The parties should consider the use of confidentiality rings and undertakings to support resolution of the dispute prior to the issue of proceedings (as to confidentiality rings and undertakings see below). The aim should be to avoid the need to issue proceedings simply to obtain early specific disclosure. The authority is strongly encouraged to disclose the key decision materials at an early stage where relevant to the complaint made[2].

8. ADR processes are encouraged, both before and during proceedings. The Court may order a stay of proceedings, direct a window in the timetable leading up to trial to enable mediation or other ADR to take place, or make an ADR order in the terms of **Appendix E** (see **paragraph 7.3.2**) particularly if (due to the claim being or becoming limited to damages) there is less urgency in fixing an early trial date.

Institution of Proceedings

Service of the Claim Form

9. The Claim Form must be served on the Defendant within 7 days after the date of issue, the first day of the 7 being the day following the day on which the Court seals the Claim Form: accordingly, a claim form issued on Wednesday must be served no later than the following Wednesday. "Service" for the purposes of the regulations requires the claimant to complete the step constituting service under CPR 7.5(1) within 7 days of issuing the Claim Form[3].

Service of the Particulars of Claim

10. Parties should be aware of the provisions of CPR 7.4 (1) and (2). CPR 7.4(2) requires that the Particulars of Claim be served no later than the latest time for serving the Claim Form.

---

[2] *Roche Diagnostics Limited v the Mid Yorkshire Hospitals NHS Trust* [2013] EWHC 933
[3] *Heron Bros. Ltd. V Central Bedfordshire Borough Council* [2015] EWHC 604 (TCC)

11. If the Particulars of Claim (or other pleadings) contain confidential information, the party serving the pleading should lodge with the Court (a) a non-confidential version of the pleading redacted so as to preserve confidential information and (b) an unredacted version marked as confidential and sealed in an envelope also marked as confidential and seek an order by letter, copied to the other party and any relevant third parties, that the access to the Court file be restricted. Wherever possible, confidential information should be contained in a self-contained schedule or annex. Where a pleading is served electronically, the party serving it should ensure that redaction is effective and should give consideration to methods of protecting confidentiality, such as password protection. The continued arrangements to protect confidentiality should be addressed at the first CMC pursuant to paragraph 22 below.

Judicial Review

12. Sometimes claimants find it necessary to bring proceedings for Judicial Review in the Administrative Court as well as issuing a claim under the Regulations in the TCC. This usually happens where the claimant's right to bring a claim under the Regulations is or may be disputed, but there may be other reasons.

13. Where this happens the claim for Judicial Review will, unless otherwise ordered by the Judge in Charge of either the Administrative Court or the TCC, be heard and case managed together with the related claim in the TCC before a TCC judge who is also a designated judge of the Administrative Court.

14. In this situation claimants are to take the following steps:

    (1) At the time of issuing the claim form in the Administrative Court the claimant's solicitors are to write to the Administrative Court Office, with a copy to the Judges in Charge of both the Administrative Court and the TCC, to request that the claim be heard alongside the related claim in the TCC.

    (2) The letter is to be clearly marked

    "URGENT REQUEST FOR THE HEARING OF A PUBLIC PROCUREMENT CLAIM BY A JUDGE OF THE TCC WHO IS A DESIGNATED JUDGE OF THE ADMINISTRATIVE COURT"

    (3) If they are not notified within 3 days of the issue of the claim form that the papers will be transferred to the TCC, the claimant's solicitors should contact the Administrative Court Office and thereafter keep the TCC informed of the position.

15. This procedure is to apply only when claim forms are issued by the same claimant against the same defendant in both the Administrative Court and the TCC almost simultaneously (in other words, within 48 hours of each other, excluding non-working days).

16. When the papers are transferred to the TCC by the Administrative Court Office the Judge in Charge of the TCC will review the papers immediately to ensure that it is appropriate for the two claims to be case managed and/or heard together by a judge of the Administrative Court who is also a judge of the TCC.

17. The Judge in Charge of the TCC will then notify the claimants and the Administrative Court Office whether or not both claims should proceed in the TCC. If it appears that the claim for Judicial Review should not be heard by a judge of the TCC, the Judge in Charge of the TCC will, after consultation with the Judge in Charge of the Administrative Court, transfer the case back to the Administrative Court and give his/her reasons for doing so.

18. If it is directed that the claim for Judicial Review should be heard by a judge of the TCC, the Judge in Charge of the TCC will ensure that the application for permission to apply for Judicial Review is determined at the earliest opportunity by a judge of the TCC who is also a designated judge of the Administrative Court.

19. If permission is granted, the claim will be case managed and heard by a TCC judge who is a designated judge of the Administrative Court, save that routine directions may, if it is appropriate and expedient to do so, be given by a judge of the TCC who is not a designated charge of the Administrative Court.

20. At all stages of the proceedings the titles of all documents filed in the JR proceedings are to bear the Administrative Court title and case number and are to state that the claim is being heard and managed together with TCC Case No HT-[ ]-[ ].

CMC

21. An early CMC may be appropriate, so that the Court may assess the urgency and fix appropriate dates for trial, specific anticipated applications (such as applications for lifting the statutory suspension, or applications for specific disclosure or expedited trial) and other stages of trial or other matters such as disclosure, witness statements and expert reports (the deployment of expert evidence will require clear justification). Either party may request the Court to fix the first CMC and the Court will endeavour to accommodate such requests.

22. The parties should be aware of the pilot scheme for Shorter and Flexible Trial Procedures and Practice Direction 51N and to address their minds to the question of whether either scheme might be appropriate for their case. These issues should be addressed at the first CMC.

Cost budgeting

23. The provisions in the CPR about preparation of costs budgets (CPR Part 3.13 and Practice Direction 3E) and electronic disclosure (Practice Direction 31B) apply. However, if there is uncertainty as to the course the proceedings may take so that it is not possible to prepare a realistic costs budget, or if the speed at which proceedings are being pursued is such that there is insufficient time for the parties to prepare and file sensible costs budgets or to take the steps required in connection with electronic disclosure in time for the CMC fixed by the Court, it is recommended that the claimant apply to the Court in writing, either before or at the same time as applying to fix the CMC, for an urgent order that the parties do not have to serve costs budgets 7 days before the CMC or dis-applying the provisions of 31BPD.4 in relation to disclosure of electronic documents. Unless one party objects, the Court will deal with such applications on paper.

Specific and Early Disclosure

24. Early disclosure may be justified to enable the claimant to plead its case properly or to secure finalised pleadings if and when expedited trials are ordered.

25. Contracting authorities are encouraged to provide their key decision making materials at a very early stage of proceedings or during any pre-action correspondence. This may include the documentation referred to in Regulation 84 of the Public Contracts Regulations 2015 ("the 2015 Regulations").

26. The question of disclosure will be considered at the first CMC. Applications which are likely to be contested should be brought on promptly; early hearings can be fixed if required. The parties' attention is drawn to the general provisions on disclosure in this **Guide** at **Section 11** and to the protocol for e-disclosure prepared by TeCSA of 9 January 2015.

Confidentiality generally

27. Public procurement claims frequently involve the disclosure of, and reliance upon, confidential information. Confidentiality is not a bar to disclosure.[4] However, the need to protect confidential information needs to be balanced by the basic principle of open justice. Managing the use of confidential information in the proceedings tends to increase both the cost and complexity of the litigation. The Court will seek to manage the proceedings so that confidentiality is protected where genuinely necessary but ensuring that the issue of confidentiality does not give rise to unnecessary cost or complexity. Assertions of confidentiality should only be made where properly warranted.

28. Once a case has been allocated to a particular TCC judge, papers and communications, particularly those which are to be treated as confidential, should generally be passed through the relevant Judge's Clerk to limit the risk of inadvertent disclosure.

29. Papers delivered to and communications with the Court and the Judge's Clerk should be marked as "Confidential" if they are confidential.

30. It is recommended that documents containing confidential material are provided on coloured paper so that their confidential status is immediately apparent (practitioners are asked to take care that the print remains legible when printed on a coloured background). Where relevant, the level of confidentiality should be identified either by a stamp or mark (e.g. "Confidential 1st Tier"[5]) or by a particular colour of paper.

31. Where necessary to protect confidential information the Court may, if requested, make an order restricting inspection of the Court files. Requests to restrict inspection should only be made where necessary. Any member of the public may seek an order from the Court varying any such restrictions. Consideration should be given to providing appropriately redacted pleadings for the Court file so as to permit public access to them. As to the management of confidential information in pleadings generally, see paragraph 11 above.

---

[4] *Science Research Council v Nasse* [1980] AC 1028.
[5] As to the use of tiers in confidentiality rings see paragraphs 41 and 42

Redactions

32. Redaction of disclosed documents, statements or pleadings can be justified on the grounds that the redactions cover privileged and/or confidential material. In the latter case, redactions may be justified to enable documents to be more widely disclosable to people outside any confidentiality rings. In such cases, a schedule should be prepared which explains the justification for the redactions. The schedule should list the information in respect of which confidential treatment is claimed and the reasons for the claim for confidentiality. The schedule should contain two columns: the first giving the relevant page and paragraph reference (a line number should be added if there are a number of pieces of confidential information in one paragraph in the document concerned); and the second setting out the reasons for asserting confidentiality. For example:

Document Title	
Location in Document	**Reason for assertion of confidentiality**
Page 15, paragraph 4.2	The deleted material relates to ABC Limited's confidential costs and prices
	The information is in the nature of a business secret

33. Save in exceptional circumstances or where redacted material is irrelevant, the Court should, at the appropriate stage, be provided with the redacted documents also in unredacted form with the redactions highlighted in a prominent colour which does not obscure the information beneath it, together with the schedule of redactions. This can be important on specific disclosure applications as well as at trial. Each page of the document must include the header "CONTAINS CONFIDENTIAL INFORMATION".

Confidentiality Rings and Undertakings

34. Confidentiality rings may be established where necessary to facilitate the disclosure of confidential information. A confidentiality ring comprises persons to whom documents containing confidential information may be disclosed on the basis of their undertakings to preserve confidentiality.

35. It is highly desirable that any confidentiality ring is established as early as feasible. Agreements or proposals for confidentiality rings, their scope and limitations should be put before the Court at the first CMC or application for specific disclosure, whichever is earlier, with explanations as to why they are justified. The Court may make orders implementing, approving or amending the parties' agreements or proposals.

36. The terms of any confidentiality ring will depend on the circumstances of the particular case, including the matters in dispute and the nature of the material to be disclosed. Generally, however, it will be necessary to determine (1) who should be admitted to the ring and (2) the terms of the undertakings which any members of the ring may be required to give.

37. As to personnel, a party's external legal advisors (solicitors and counsel) will need to be admitted to any ring that is established.

38. Parties, and in particular the claimant, may also wish to include certain of their own employees in the ring, who may be in house lawyers or other personnel. This will usually be for the purpose of understanding material disclosed into the ring and/or for giving instructions to external lawyers.

39. Where a party proposes to admit an employee representative, and the ring contains material which is confidential to a commercial competitor of that party, relevant factors are likely to include that party's right to pursue its claim, the principle of open justice, the confidential nature of the document and the need to avoid distortions of competition and/or the creation of unfair advantages in the market (including any retender) as a result of disclosure.

40. In considering whether a particular person should be admitted to the ring, the Court will take account of his/her role and responsibilities within the organisation; the extent of the risk that competition will be distorted as a result of disclosure to them; the extent to which that risk can be avoided or controlled by restrictions on the terms of disclosure; and the impact that any proposed restrictions would have on that individual (for example by prohibiting them from participating in a re-tender or future tenders for a period of time).

41. In order to manage these risks employee representatives may be admitted to a confidentiality ring on different terms from external representatives. Employee representatives may also have access to some but not all of the material disclosed into the ring (for example, technical material but not pricing information). This is sometimes referred to as a "two tier" ring.

42. Under an alternative form of two tier ring, the external representatives of a party in the first tier may apply for an employee representative in the second tier to have access to a particular document or documents, whether in open form or partly redacted. One way of dealing with this is for notice to be given to any person affected by the proposed disclosure, identifying the document, the form in which its disclosure to members of the second tier is sought, and the reasons why disclosure to the second tier is sought, and for the person affected to consent or object within a fixed time. The person or persons affected may be the contracting authority and/or the owner of the confidential information. In cases subject to expedition the period for response may be short and, in appropriate cases, less than a working day. Two tier rings necessarily introduce additional cost and complexity and will need to be justified in the circumstances.

43. Other specialist advisors (such as accountants or those with other expertise) may also be admitted to the ring if that is demonstrated to be necessary, either in lieu of or in addition to employee representatives.[6]

44. As to the terms of disclosure, the Court will order that confidential documents, information or pleadings are only to be provided to members of the ring if undertakings are given to the Court. Such undertakings will preclude the use of the relevant material other than for the purposes of the proceedings and prevent disclosure outside the ring. They will also contain provisions controlling the terms on which confidential information must be stored and the making of copies, and requiring the receiving person to either return or destroy the documents in question, or render them practically inaccessible, at the conclusion of the proceedings.

45. Additional undertakings may be required, particularly where there are concerns that disclosure could have an impact on competition and/or any subsequent procurement. These may include terms:

---

[6] The provision of such advice is to be distinguished from acting as an expert witness.

(1) Preventing employee representatives from holding copies of documents at their place of work and requiring them to inspect the material at a defined location (such as the offices of their external lawyers);

(2) Limiting the involvement of a recipient of a document in any re-procurement of the contract which is the subject of the litigation;

(3) Limiting the role which a recipient can play in competitions for other similar contracts for a fixed period of time in a defined geographic area; and/or

(4) Preventing the recipient from advising on or having any involvement in certain matters, again for a fixed period of time.

46. Whilst the Court will give weight to the need to protect competition in the market, the more onerous the proposed restriction is, the more clearly it will need to be justified. Further, the terms of the ring will need to be workable taking account of the timetable for the litigation, including any order for expedition.

47. Confidentiality rings will also contain provisions which establish how confidential information is to be identified as such, and how claims to confidentiality may be challenged.

48. Where documents are disclosed into the ring in confidential form, further non-confidential versions of those documents should also be disclosed with necessary redactions.

Suspension lifting applications

49. The Court can lift the statutory suspension that prevents the contracting authority from entering into the contract in question. The timing of the application is a matter for the applicant but, if urgency in placing the contract is to form part of any balance of convenience test, the application needs to be brought on expeditiously. However, enough time needs to be provided for the respondent to submit evidence and for there to be any evidence in reply before any hearing.

50. If the Court orders that the suspension is to be lifted a stay of such an order will only be granted when it is appropriate to do so. The Court, if it considers that a stay is appropriate, and particularly when it has refused permission to appeal, will give consideration to a short

stay of 1-2 working days to enable the applicant to seek expedited permission and to enable the Court of Appeal to set a timetable; such a stay will often be accompanied by a requirement that any application for permission or for an extended stay should be on notice to the other party, to enable it to make representations to the Court of Appeal.

Interested Parties

51. Procurement claims frequently engage the interests of parties other than the claimant and the contracting authority ("interested parties"; in this protocol the term "interested party" is given a wider meaning than in CPR Part 54).

52. In particular, the successful bidder may be affected by the relief sought in a procurement claim, which typically claims an order setting aside the award decision in his favour. The successful bidder may also be affected by the disclosure of confidential information contained in his bid, as may other unsuccessful bidders.

53. Whilst an interested party may apply to become a full party to the proceedings, its interests can usually be considered and addressed by the Court without that being necessary.

54. The claimant and the defendant should take steps to ensure that an interested party is on notice of matters which affect its interests. It will often be appropriate for the defendant to ensure that other bidding parties are given such notice. However, particularly where applications are made as a matter of urgency, it may be appropriate for the claimant to ensure that the interested party has been given appropriate notice.

55. In order to allow an interested party to consider its position, it may be necessary to provide it with copies of any pleadings, redacted if necessary, any relevant application, supporting evidence and/or other relevant documentation.

56. An interested party needs to apply to be represented (if it so wishes) as soon as practicable. A written application, which may take the form of a letter to the Court, should be sent to the Court and served on all litigation parties (and any other interested parties). The application should clearly indicate the scope of the interested party's proposed involvement. If the

interested party's involvement is agreed with the litigation parties, then that should be made clear in the application. In general, the Court will expect to hear from interested parties who are affected by an application or claim.

57. The Court may direct that an interested party is to be treated as a respondent to an application (CPR 23.1) but a direction to this effect is not essential, particularly in cases of urgency. The Court may order that an interested party is permitted or entitled to participate in particular applications, hearings or issues and/or may order that the involvement of the interested party is to be limited in defined respects.

58. If expedition so demands, the application for the interested party to be represented may be heard immediately before the relevant substantive application. However, earlier resolution is preferable to allow orderly preparation for hearings and the preparation of relevant evidence or submissions.

59. Attention is drawn to the requirement under Regulation 47F(3) of the Public Contracts Regulations (As Amended) 2006 and Regulation 94(3) of the Public Contracts Regulations 2015 to the requirement to give notice to the party to whom the contract was awarded in relation to claims for ineffectiveness.

60. Other interested parties who may express interest in procurement claims include sector regulators, competition authorities and/or sub-contractors, and the Court will give directions in relation to their involvement as appropriate.

61. An interested party can recover or be required to pay costs[7].

Expedition

62. Article 1 of Directive 89/665/EC (as amended by Article 1 of Directive 2007/66/EC) requires member states to ensure that decisions taken by contracting authorities may be reviewed "as rapidly as possible". Particularly in cases where the automatic suspension has been maintained, and subject to the principles set out in paragraph 1.1.4 of this Guide, the TCC is

---

[7] See e.g. Section 51(3) of the Senior Courts Act 1981 and *Bolton Metropolitan District Council v The Secretary of State for the Environment* [1995] 1 WLR 1176.

likely to support (and in appropriate cases may impose) rapid progress to a trial as early as is practicable. An expedited trial may in particular be appropriate where it will enable the contracting authority to enter into the contract without undue disruption to its timetable, or where the automatic suspension is maintained following an application for its termination.

63. In considering whether the trial should be expedited, it will be necessary to consider how the required procedural steps will be accomplished within the abbreviated timetable. In particular, adequate time will be required for disclosure and for the hearing of any interim applications which are expected. The Court may use its powers to control and define the scope of disclosure in cases where expedition is ordered.

64. The party applying for an expedited trial should do so on notice and at as early a stage as is practicable. The party applying should set out the reasons why expedited trial is appropriate and the party's proposals for the management of procedural steps. The Court should be provided with details of any third parties affected and third parties (in particular the successful tenderer) should be put on notice of the application. Where appropriate it will be part of the agenda for the first CMC.

Trial

65. Consideration needs to be given to confidentiality in terms of what may be reported, whether there should be restricted access to the Court recording of the proceedings and who can be present in the courtroom. The Court will as a matter of generality require as much of the trial as possible to be open to all who wish to attend and limit restrictions to those which are legitimate, fair and proportionate.

Judgments

66. Judgments in procurement cases will be handed down as open documents, save in the most exceptional circumstances (for instance in cases involving Official Secrets). Any confidential information will usually be contained in a separate schedule to the judgment (or such other form as appropriate) which will not be available more widely than the membership of any confidentiality ring (if applicable) without an order of the Court. Counsel should co-operate through the Judge's Clerk to agree what may be made publicly available.

INDEX

absence of evidence 3.22
acceleration claims 5.46–5.53
achieving milestones 4.51
Acknowledgement of Service 2.10
addition of other parties 2.16
adjournment 10.12–10.16
adjudication 1.5, 9.1–9.26; after the adjudication 9.10–9.18; before the adjudication 9.2–9.4; dispute resolution 1.5; during the adjudication 9.5–9.9; introduction 9.1; stays of execution 9.19–9.26
administrative matters 3.77–3.78
ADR *see* alternative dispute resolution
after the adjudication 9.10–9.18
Akenhead J 4.73, 4.124, 5.26, 10.20
alternative dispute resolution 2.16, 10.1–10.32; cost sanctions 10.25–10.29; early neutral evaluation 10.30–10.31; enforcement of contractual schemes 10.5–10.11; and general case management 10.22–10.24; introduction 10.1–10.2; jurisdiction, adjournment, stay? 10.12–10.16; mediation 10.32; and Pre-action Protocol 10.17–10.21; what ADR is 10.3–10.4
ambush 9.8
apparent bias 11.17
appeal 2.51–2.52, 11.20–11.25
appeal bundles 3.76
applications 3.64–3.66; to lift automatic suspension 7.7–7.18
appointing experts 6.34–6.37
approach to consideration of costs budgets 8.19–8.23
Arbitral Tribunal 11.7, 11.14, 11.16
arbitration 11.1–11.25; appeal 11.20–11.25; extension of time limits 11.10–11.12; introduction 11.1–11.2; jurisdiction of arbitrator 11.8–11.9; powers in relation to procedure 11.13–11.19; stay of proceedings 10.3–10.7
arbitration v litigation 1.6–1.11
as-built programme 2.34, 4.65–4.66

as-planned critical path 4.115–4.116; relevance 4.115–4.116
as-planned programme 4.55–4.57
authorities in pleading requirements 4.21–4.23
automatic injunction 7.2, 7.10, 7.17–7.18

'balance of interests' test 7.12
bankruptcy 9.22
Barry, David 4.150
baseline programme 2.34, 4.55–4.57
before the adjudication 9.2–9.4
best practice 3.78
Beware the Dark Arts 4.150
bilateral nature of arbitration 1.10
black box delay analysis 4.154
breach 2.7, 2.12, 6.8, 6.25
Brexit referendum 7.5
Briggs LJ 10.28
bringing a challenge 7.21
Brooke LJ 3.9
burden of proof 4.24–4.25
Business and Property Courts 1.1, 1.4, 3.3
'but for' test 4.2

calling witnesses 3.24–3.25
Case Management Conference 2.15–2.17, 3.61–3.63
Case Management Information Sheet 2.16
causation 2.12, 3.31, 4.128
Centre for Dispute Resolution 10.6
challenging presentation of defects claims 6.24–6.33
changing baseline 4.63–4.64
'chess-clock' arrangement 2.46
choosing an expert 3.33–3.35; *see also* appointing experts
Civil Procedure Rules 2.8, 2.14, 4.19–4.20, 8.15–8.16, 9.21; Part 16.4 4.19; Part 25.1 6.40; Part 35.10(3) 3.36, 3.42; Part 35.12 6.19; Part 35.9 6.40; Part 62 11.24; Rule 44.2(8) 8.24

INDEX

Claim Form 2.6–2.10, 3.61, 8.28, 9.11–9.12, 10.19, 11.24
claim overview *see* overview of a claim
CMC *see* Case Management Conference
coaching of witnesses 2.47
Colman J. 4.7
commencement of proceedings 2.8–2.10
completing delay claim process 4.106–4.109
completion date 4.17, 4.96–4.99; constraints on 4.96–4.99
completion of proceedings 2.16
complex critical path 4.111–4.114
complexities of defending a claim 4.110–4.116; complex/multiple critical paths 4.111–4.114; relevance of critical path at particular points 4.115–4.116
compliance 2.10, 3.42–3.47, 7.13
conciliation 10.4
concurrent delay 4.112
confidential information 7.36–7.55
constraints 4.96–4.99
construction delays 4.1–4.2
contractor critical delay-related claims 5.11–5.31; increased costs due to inflation 5.31; introduction 5.11–5.13; loss of profit claims 5.30; overheads claims 5.23–5.29; preliminaries/prolongation cost claims 5.14–5.22
contractor delay-related claims under contract 5.2–5.10; different tests for time and money 5.3; introduction 5.2; notice 5.10; relevance of contractual provisions 5.4–5.7; relevance of tender pricing 5.8–5.9
contractor preference 4.102
contractor-risk event 4.18, 4.112
contractual ADR schemes 10.5–10.11
contractual notice provisions 4.126–4.127
contractual provisions re valuation 5.4–5.7
contractual requirements for prospective approach 4.37–4.46
controlling presentation of defects claims 6.24–6.33
cost of arbitration 1.8
cost sanctions 10.25–10.29
costs budgeting 2.16, 8.1–8.29; approach to consideration of 8.19–8.23; and interim payments 8.23–8.26; introduction 8.1–8.8; practical considerations 8.27–8.29; presentation 8.9–8.14; timing 8.15–8.18
costs of inflation 5.31
Coulson J 3.16, 9.10, 9.13–9.16, 9.18, 9.26, 10.15, 10.23–10.24
Coulson on Construction Adjudication 9.10, 9.23
Court Settlement Process 10.32

CPR *see* Civil Procedure Rules
critical delay 4.4
critical path 4.71–4.87
critical path analysis 4.87
cross-examination 2.33, 3.6, 3.18–3.19, 3.21–3.22, 3.28, 3.31, 3.35, 3.58, 3.74, 5.28
crystallisation 9.2
custodians 2.22

DB *see* Dispute Adjudication Board
date of trial 2.164.102
de-duplication 2.22, 2.24, 3.70, 3.73
'death by a thousand cuts' 4.28
declaratory relief 7.6
defects claims 6.1–6.44; controlling presentation 6.24–6.33; defending the case 6.10–6.23; general nature of defect claim 6.1–6.6; instructing appropriate expertise 6.34–6.44; prosecution a defects claim 6.7–6.9
Defence to Counterclaim 2.16
defending defects claims 6.10–6.23; liability defences 6.10–6.14; limitation 6.21–6.23; quantum defences 6.15–6.20
defending a delay claim 4.26–4.109; concluding the process 4.106–4.109; identifying critical path 4.71–4.87; identifying delay events 4.67–4.70; identifying how delay was caused 4, 88–4.105; identifying period of delay 4.50–4.66; introduction 4.26–4.33; prospective or retrospective 4.34–4.49
defining critical path 4.71–4.72
defining disruption 5.32–5.33
delay analysis using baseline programme 4.58–4.62
delay claims 4.1–4.159; difficulties and complexities 4.110–4.116; frequent mistakes made 4.117–4.159; introduction 4.1–4.2; legal requirements 4.3–4.18; making/defending in practice 4.26–4.109; pleading requirements 4.19–4.25
delay and disruption money claims 5.1–5.55; acceleration claims 5.46–5.53; contractor's critical delay-related claims 5.11–5.31; contractor's delay-related claims under contract 5.2–5.10; disruption claims 5.32–5.43; employer claims 5.54–5.55; introduction 5.1; subcontractor claims 5.44–5.45
delay events 4.67–4.70
delay statement 3.14
delayed critical path activity 4.92
deployment of evidence 3.1–3.3
detriment 9.5
different tests for time and money 5.3

INDEX

disclosure 2.16, 2.18–2.24, 7.19–7.35; early disclosure in procurement litigation 7.22–7.27; introductory matters 7.19–7.21; tactical considerations 7.28–7.35
Disclosure of Electronic Documents 2.21
discretionary stay 2.10
dismissal 11.25
disproportionate budgets 8.20
Dispute Adjudication Board 10.4
dispute resolution 1.5
Dispute Resolution Board 10.4
disruption claims 5.32–5.43; authorities 5.34–5.37; introduction 5.32–5.33; practicalities 5.38–5.41; 'thickening' costs 5.42–5.43
disruption statement 3.14
documentary evidence 3.58–3.78; administrative matters 3.77–3.78; appeal bundles 3.76; applications 3.64–3.66; Case Management Conference 3.61–3.63; electronic trial bundles 3.72–3.75; trial 3.67–3.71
domestic arbitration 1.6, 1.11
DRB *see* Dispute Resolution Board
during the adjudication 9.5–9.9
Dyson LJ 2.38

e-disclosure 2.21–2.22
early disclosure in procurement 7.22–7.27
early neutral evaluation 10.4, 10.30–10.31, 11.1
Edwards-Stuart J 2.38, 9.5–9.7, 9.22
effect of constraint on successor activities 4.103–4.105
efficacy of ADR 10.22
electronic programme-based analysis 4.144–4.159; logic links 4.145–4.148; methods 4.149–4.150; reliability of 4.151–4.159
electronic trial bundles 3.72–3.75
Emden formula 5.25–5.26
employer claims for delay 5.54–5.55
employer-risk event 4.18, 4.112, 5.40, 5.48
Employer's Requirements 6.8, 6.23
encouragement to settle disputes 10.1–10.2
ENE *see* early neutral evaluation
enforcement of contractual ADR schemes 10.5–10.11
EOT *see* extension of time clauses
equitable discretion 11.3
establishing how event caused delay 4.88–4.105; contractor preference 4.102; constraints between follow-on activities 4.96–4.99; effect of constraints 4.103–4.105; introduction 4.88–4.95; physical constraints 4.100; resource constraints 4.101
establishing liability 4.118–4.120
EU Court of Justice 7.27

European Commission 7.9
evidence 3.1–3.78; documentary evidence 3.58–3.78; expert reports and joint statements 3.26–3.57; introduction 3.1–3.3; witness statements 3.4–3.25
evidence at trial 3.54–3.57, 4.128–4.129
expert determination 1.5
expert evidence 2.31–2.39, 4.143, 6.41–6.44
'expert' factual witnesses 3.8–3.12
expert meetings 3.48–3.53
expert reports 2.3, 2.16, 3.26–3.57; choosing an expert 3.33–3.35; compliance 3.42–3.47; evidence at trial 3.54–3.57; joint statements/ expert meetings 3.48–3.53; need for independent expert 3.26–3.32; preparing an expert 3.36–3.41; reports 3.42–3.47
'expert shopping' 2.38–2.39
extension of time clauses 4.4–4.18, 4.138
extension of time limits for referral 11.10–11.12

factual causation of defect 4.32, 6.8
factual witness evidence 2.16, 4.130–4.142
fast track projects 4.60
FIDIC 5.2
finish-to-finish link 4.145
finish-to-start link 4.145
first Case Management Conference 2.15–2.17
fitness for purpose obligations 6.8
flagrant breach 10.12
float 4.17–4.18
focus on immediately affected activity only 4.121–4.122
focus on last event to delay completion 4.123–4.125
focus on liability only 4.118–4.120
follow-on activity constraints 4.96–4.99
frequent mistakes in practice 4.117–4.159; electronic programme-based analysis 4.144–4.159; evidence at trial 4.128–4.129; expert evidence 4.143; factual witness evidence 4.130–4.142; focus on immediately affected activity 4.121–4.122; focus on last delaying event 4.123–4.125; focus on liability only 4.118–4.120; ignoring contractual notice provisions 4.126–4.127; introduction 4.117
friendly discussion 10.10

general case management 10.22–10.24
general nature of defects claims 6.1–6.6
global claims 5.34–5.38
good faith negotiation 10.6, 10.10
Government Procurement Agreement 7.5
gross approach 4.124
group actions 1.3
Guidance Note for Public Procurement Cases 7.3

INDEX

Hamblen J. 4.11–4.12, 4.15
handling confidential information 7.36–7.55
Haroun and the Sea of Stories 4.155
head of cost 5.11–5.13
HHJ Toulmin CMG, QC 4.156
HHJ Wilcox 9.5–9.6
'hired gun' 3.38
HM Courts and Tribunals Service 1.12
hot-tubbing 2.48, 3.56–3.57
Hudson formula 5.25–5.26
Hughes LJ 2.38
hybrid applications 7.22, 9.18

ICE contracts 1.6, 1.11
identifying critical path 4.71–4.87; definition 4.71–4.72; importance in delay claims 4.73–4.80; in practice 4.81–4.87
identifying defects 6.8
identifying delay events 4.67–4.70
identifying period of delay in delay claim 4.50–4.66; as-built programme 4.65–4.66; as-planned or baseline programme 4.55–4.57; changing baseline 4.63–4.64; realism of baseline programme 4.58–4.62
ignoring contractual notice provisions 4.126–4.127
importance of critical path 4.73–4.80
incidental costs 2.5
increased costs from inflation 5.31
independence of experts 3.38, 6.41–6.44
ineffectiveness 7.4
inflation costs 5.31
ineffectiveness 7.4
insolvency 9.22
instructing appropriate expertise 6.34–6.44; appointment of experts 6.34–6.37; independence and quality of expert evidence 6.41–6.44; investigations 6.38–6.40
interim payments 8.24–8.26
interlocutory applications 7.1, 7.3
international cases 1.3
introduction to litigation 1–1–1.12; arbitration v litigation 1.6–1.11; dispute resolution 1.5; TCC guide 1.12; what the TCC is 1.1–1.4
introductory disclosure 7.19–7.21
investigations 6.38–6.40
Irish law 11.12
irregularity 11.21

Jackson ADR Handbook 10.27, 10.29
Jackson reforms 8.1–8.8
JCT contracts 1.6, 4.4, 4.38–4.39, 4.124, 5.3–5.4, 5.10, 5.22, 5.36
joint statements 3.26–3.57; *see also* expert reports

judgment 2.50
jurisdiction 10.12–10.16
jurisdiction of arbitrator 11.8–11.9
'jurisdictional' argument 9.5
knock-on effect of delay 4.88–4.95

lack of credibility 4.48
landscape of construction dispute resolution 9.1
law of interpretative presumption 10.9
legal causation of defect 6.8
legal requirements in delay claims 4.3–4.18; extension of time clauses 4.4–4.18; float 4.17–4.18; prevention principle 4.13–4.16
Leggatt J 10.7
length of trial 2.16
liability defences 6.10–6.14
lifting automatic suspension 7.7–7.18
limitation 6.8, 6.21–6.23
liquidated damages 4.5, 4.24, 4.30, 4.138
logic links 4.145–4.148
Lord Denning 4.14, 10.11
Lord Drummond Young 4.157
Lord Hope 9.22
Lord Oliver 4.21–4.22, 4.88
loss 6.8
loss of profit claims 5.30

main programme obligations 2.12
making a delay claim 4.26–4.109; concluding the process 4.106–4.109; identifying critical path 4.71–4.87; identifying delay events 4.67–4.70; identifying how delay was caused 4.88–4.105; identifying period of delay 4.50–4.66; introduction 4.26–4.33; prospective or retrospective 4.34–4.49
material change 7.4, 7.17
mediation 2.4, 10.4, 10.32
methods of programme-based analysis 4.149–4.150
mitigation 4.32, 4.102, 5.49, 6.15
mock trial 2.47
Mr Justice Jackson 3.10
Mr Recorder Furst QC 10.26
multi-party disputes 1.10
multiple critical paths 4.111–4.114
Mustill & Boyd 11.5

narrative of performance 6.8
narrative statement 2.12
near-critical path 4.115–4.116
NEC contracts 1.11, 4.39, 5.4; NEC 3 4.39
need for independent expert 3.26–3.32
negligence 10.19
nexus 4.23, 4.68
non-binding recommendation 10.4

INDEX

notice 5.10
number of witnesses 3.4–3.7

O&M manuals 4.145
obligations 6.8
OCR *see* Optical Character Recognition
O'Farrell J 9.8
Office of the Government Commerce Response 7.12
Official Referees 1.1–1.2
OHP *see* overheads and profit percentage
one stop contractor 1.10
'opinion' evidence 4.141
Optical Character Recognition 3.74
outlier budgets 8.12
overhead claims 5.23–5.29
overheads and profit percentage 5.24
overview of a claim 2.1–2.52; appeal 2.51–2.52; commencement of proceedings 2.8–2.10; disclosure 2.18–2.24; expert evidence 2.31–2.39; first Case Management Conference 2.15–2.17; introduction 2.1; judgment 2.50; pleadings 2.11–2.14; pre-action phase 2.2–2.7; Pre-Trial Review 2.40; trial 2.41–2.49; witness statements 2.25–2.30

Part 18 Request for Further Information 2.16
Particulars of Claim 2.9, 2.12
parties 6.8
party autonomy 11.11
personal confidentiality 1.9, 7.36–7.55
personal injury 1.3
physical constraints 4.100
platform providers 2.21
pleading requirements in delay claims 4.19–4.25; authorities as to 4.21–4.23; burden of proof 4.24–4.25; Civil Procedure Rules 4.19–4.20
pleadings 2.11–2.14
policing presentation of defects claims 6.24–6.33
practical considerations of costs budgets 8.27–8.29
practicalities 5.38–5.41
Practice Direction 31B 2.21
Practice Direction 52 3.76
practice of identifying critical path 4.81–4.87
pre-action phase of litigation 2.2–2.7
Pre-Action Protocol for Construction and Engineering Disputes 2.2, 2.7, 10.17–10.21
pre-emptive declaration 9.13
Pre-Trial Review 2.17, 2.40
Precedent H schedules 8.4
preliminaries 5.14–5.22
preliminary issues 2.16

preparing an expert 3.36–3.41
presentation of costs budgets 8.9–8.14
prevention principle 4.13–4.16
Primavera 4.57, 4.143
principle of futility 10.7
principle of law of interpretative presumption 10.9
Privy Council 4.21–4.22
problems with prospective analysis 4.41–4.49
procedural aspects of arbitration 11.13–11.19
process of litigation 1.7
procurement litigation *see* public procurement litigation
Professional Negligence Pre-Action Protocol 2.2
Professional Standards Committee of the Bar Council 2.47
programme-based analysis 4.144–4.159; logic links 4.145–4.148; methods 4.149–4.150; reliability of 4.151–4.159
prolixity 6.9
prolongation cost claims 5.14–5.22
prosecuting defects claims 6.7–6.9
prospective analysis 4.34–4.49; contractual requirements 4.37–4.40; problems with 4.41–4.49; or retrospective analysis? 4.36
PTR *see* Pre-Trial Review
Public Contracts Regulations 7.4, 7.7
public nuisance 1.3
public procurement litigation 7.1–7.55; applications to lift automatic suspension 7.7–7.18; disclosure 7.19–7.35; handling confidential information 7.36–7.55; introduction 7.1–7.6

QS *see* quantity surveying
quality of expert evidence 6.41–6.44
quantification of loss 2.12
quantity surveying 6.37
quantum defences 6.15–6.20
quantum evidence 2.16
quantum experts 2.16, 2.31

'race to contract' 7.9
Ramsey J 2.23–2.24, 4.94, 9.25, 10.8, 10.10, 10.29
realism of baseline programme 4.58–4.62
reasonable endeavours clause 10.9
recourse to arbitration 11.19
recoverable costs 10.14
regional centres of the TCC 1.4
relevance of as-planned critical path 4.115–4.116
relevance of contractual provisions to valuation 5.4–5.7

INDEX

relevance of critical path in delay claims 4.73–4.80
relevance of tender pricing 5.8–5.9
Relevant Matter 5.3
reliability of programme-based analysis 4.151–4.159
remedial schemes 2.34
remediation 6.7, 6.15–6.17
Remedies Directive 7.7, 7.9, 7.12, 7.14
remit of the TCC 1.2–1.3
report compliance 3.42–3.47
Request for Further Information 2.14, 2.16, 3.67, 3.78, 6.28
resource constraints 4.101
results from retrospective v prospective analysis 4.36
retrospective analysis 4.34–4.49; of prospective analysis? 4.36
RFI *see* Request for Further Information
Richard Fernyhough QC 4.89
Rules of Supreme Court Order 47 9.21
Rushdie, Salman 4.155

sanctions of cost 10.25–10.29
SCL Delay and Disruption Protocol 4.150
Scott Schedule 2.13
Second Public Consultation 7.12
sequence of calling witnesses 3.24–3.25
shape of litigation 2.1
Shipbuilder's Association of Japan form 4.4
'smash and grab' adjudication 9.17
snagging 4.124
Society for Computers and Law 2.21
split trial 2.16
standard disclosure 1.8, 2.18–2.20
Standard Form of Contract 4.4, 4.38–4.39, 4.124, 5.3–5.4, 5.10, 5.22, 5.36
start-to-start link 4.145
starting with money 5.1
statement of case 6.7–6.9
stay of proceedings 10.12–10.16, 11.3–11.7
stays of execution 9.19–9.26
strike out judgment 7.2
structure of statement of case 6.7–6.9
structuring witness statements 3.13–3.23
Stuart Smith J 8.20
subcontractor claims 5.44–5.45
submissions 3.58
substantive appeal 11.25
substantive breach 2.7
summary judgment 7.2
supporting arbitral process 11.1–11.2

tactical considerations in procurement 7.28–7.35
tactical silence 3.22
taking witness statements 3.13–3.23
Teare J. 10.10–10.11
TECBAR 2.21
technical breach 2.7
technical causation of defect 6.8
Technology and Construction Court guide 1.3, 1.12, 2.3–2.4, 2.13, 2.16, 2.18–2.21, 2.26, 2.32, 2.43–2.46, 3.56, 7.55; 5.1.6 6.30; 5.5.5 6.30; 5.6.1 6.31; 5.6.2 6.31; 5.6.3 6.31; 7.2.2 10.13; 8.4.1 2.16; 9.4.3 9.13; 11.1.1 2.19; 13.3.4 6.40; 13.3.5 6.40; 13.8.2 3.56; 15.2.2 3.78; 15.2.3 3.67, 3.70; Appendix E 10.16; Appendix G 10.32; Appendix H 7.32, 7.35, 7.49, 7.53, 7.55; Section 7.5 10.30; Section 8 2.16, 10.18
TeCSA 2.21
template for defence 4.26–4.33
tender pricing 5.8–5.9; relevance 5.8–5.9
tests for money 5.3
'thickening' costs 5.42–5.43
third-party action 2.12
time clauses 4.4–4.18
time limit of public procurement litigation 7.1–7.6
time limits for referral 11.10–11.12
timing of costs budgets 8.15–8.18
tort 6.8
Toulson J 11.11
trial 2.41–2.49, 3.67–3.71

unfair terms 11.6
unreasonable conduct 10.28

vergens ad inopiam 9.22

Waller LJ 11.11
what ADR is 10.3–10.4
what the TCC is 1.1–1.4
White Book 3.3
'windows' 2.12
without prejudice meeting 2.4, 2.36, 10.19
witness statements 2.16, 2.25–2.30, 3.4–3.25; 'expert' factual witnesses 3.8–3.12; number of witnesses 3.4–3.7; sequence of calling witnesses 3.24–3.25; taking/structuring witness statements 3.13–3.23
World Trade Organization 7.5
WP offer 10.29